BUILDING HIGH PERFORMANCE

TOOLS AND TECHNIQUES
FOR TRAINING AND LEARNING

Edited by

KAREN VANDER LINDE
and
ELAINE BIECH

For more information, please contact PricewaterhouseCoopers Publishing, 12902 Federal Park Drive, Fairfax, VA 22033-4412, phone 703-633-4000.

Karen Vander Linde and Elaine Biech, Editors
Building High Performance: Tools and Techniques for Training and Learning

ISBN 0-944533-25-6

Library of Congress Catalog No. 98-067403

Portions of this book were previously published in *Training & Development* and are used with permission of the American Society for Training and Development, 1640 King Street, PO Box 1443, Alexandria, VA 22313, phone 703-683-8100.

"Performance Assessment: Taking Your Team's Pulse," by Richard P. Kropp and Kristen Ciolkosz, is reprinted from *Best Practices for Teams Volume 2*, edited by Glenn M. Parker, copyright 1998, where it appears under the title of "Taking the Team's Pulse." Reprinted by permission of the publisher, HRD Press, Inc., 22 Amherst Road, Amgerst, MA 01002, 1-800-822-2801, (413) 253-3488, fax (413) 253-3490.

"Survey of Innovation Capability," by David Francis, is reprinted from *The 1998 Pfeiffer Annual, Volume 2: Consulting*, copyright 1998, where it appears under the title "Innovation Capability Audit." Reprinted by permission of Jossey-Bass/Pfeiffer, 350 Sansome Street, 5th Floor, San Francisco, CA 94104-1342, phone (800) 274-4434, (415) 433-1740, Internet www.pfeiffer.com.

Bulk quantities of this book may be obtained at a discount from:

> Bookmasters, Inc.
> Distribution Center
> 1444 State Rt. 42
> RD 11
> Mansfield, Ohio 44903
> Telephone: 1-800-247-6553
> Fax: (419) 281-6883

PricewaterhouseCoopers Publications

PricewaterhouseCoopers takes pride in presenting leading-edge information that our clients and potential clients use for operations improvements. Following is a list of our recent books on management and government.

Public Dollars, Common Sense: New Roles for Financial Managers, by William R. Phillips, Bonnie L. Brown, and Andrew C. West. *The Government Accountants Journal* calls this "...the government financial manager's Bible... an indispensable guide to the new financial reforms..." Washington, DC: Coopers & Lybrand Publishing. 342 pages, 1997. ISBN 0-944533-24-8.

Postal Performance: The Transformation of a Global Industry, by John M. Downson, Edward E. Horgan, and T. Wood Parker. Throughout the world, postal administrations are responding to the challenges of a dramatically changing business environment. This book describes the transformation of the postal industry, focusing on the best practices postal services must adopt to be competitive. Washington, DC: Coopers & Lybrand Publishing. 247 pages, 1997. ISBN 0-944533-23-X.

Activity-Based Management in Government, by Joseph Kehoe, William Dodson, Robert Reeve, and Gustav Plato. An extensive review of how public sector organizations can and do apply activity-based costing and management to create more cost-conscious, cost-effective governance. Washington, DC: Coopers & Lybrand Publishing. 296 pages, 1995. ISBN 0-944533-10-8.

Best Practices in Reengineering: What Works and What Doesn't in the Reengineering Process, by David K. Carr and Henry Johansson. Based on a major survey of organizations that practice reengineering, this book explains how to select strategic processes, get the highest return on improvement investment, and ensure continuous improvement in redesigned processes. New York:McGraw-Hill. 235 pages, 1995. ISBN 0-07-011224-X.

Forthcoming in 1998

Transforming Government Services: A Global Perspective, by Lynton Barker, David K. Carr, Joseph G. Kehoe, and Ian D. Littman. This new book discusses trends and lessons learned in the world-wide effort to align government service delivery with a global economy and society. It includes best practices in key areas of managing government institutions. Washington, DC: PricewaterhouseCoopers.189 pages, 1998 ISBN 0-944533-26-4.

Information Leadership: A Government Executive's Guide. Based on interviews with dozens of federal, state, and local government information and technology executives in the United States and overseas, this new book describes the emerging roles of chief information officers and their staffs.

Acknowledgments

Producing *Building High Performance: Tools and Techniques for Training and Learning* was a team effort—and what a team! First and foremost, we appreciate the contributions of the book's many authors, who found time in crowded schedules to set down on paper their innovative ideas and practical tips. Our readers who also are writers will appreciate the hard work involved. All learning professionals know how to prepare lectures, presentations, courseware, exercises, and other training material. Also, we all can deliver that material in training and learning settings. It is an entirely different matter to transform both material and experience into written documents that must stand alone, without someone there to explain them. Technically, this takes special talent. Personally, it means deciding to go the extra mile to share valuable knowledge with colleagues. Usually, that extra mile is traveled after hours and on weekends, mostly for the satisfaction of advancing not so much one's own career, but one's profession. So, while we acknowledge the authors' excellent written contributions, we applaud their dedication.

Next, we recognize the many team members who worked behind the scenes to help us move the book from concept to finished product. At PwC, Partner Ian Littman helped assemble the resources for the book; Debra Eshelman and Diane DeBerry reviewed and commented on early drafts; and Joan Berkson and Jill Foley helped rework several articles. We appreciate the support of Nancy Olson, Vice President of Publications, and Kathie St. Clair, publications assistant, both of the American Society for Training and Development, for their assistance in every step of the process.

Finally, this book would not have been possible without the superb work of our editorial and production team members. We especially want to thank Nancy Letsinger, project manager at PwC, who was the real driver behind this effort. Also at PwC, we thank technical editor Joy Mara, consulting editor/advisor Steve Clyburn, production manager Mike Clover, word processor Ana Fano, and graphic artist Patrick Scroggins. At ebb associates inc, Beth Drake handled the many tasks involved in contacting authors and coordinating operations at her end. Grammarians, Inc., team members include pre-production manager Mellen Candage, layout designer Steve Hall, copy editor Richard Mason, and proofreader Thea Clarke. Ellen Burns of Carter Cosgrove designed the book cover.

To all of you, our sincere thanks.

About the Editors

Listing the subjects for which **Elaine Biech** and **Karen M. Vander Linde** provide training and development services is another way of defining high-performance learning. A sample includes strategic planning, change management, knowledge management, information systems and technology, total quality management, reengineering, time management, mentoring and coaching, teamwork, group facilitation, fostering creativity, and customer service. They have much in common, starting with more than 20 years each of experience in the training and learning professions, ranging from needs assessments and training systems development to computer-based training and knowledge management. Ms. Vander Linde currently is on the Board of Directors of the American Society for Training and Development (ASTD), and Ms. Biech is a former Board member and secretary of the Society. As consultants, their clients include Fortune 500 companies, government agencies, non-profits, and associations. Long-time colleagues, business associates, and friends, *Building High Performance* is a natural collaboration for these two trendsetters in training and learning.

Karen M. Vander Linde is a Partner in PricewaterhouseCoopers (PwC) and works in Fairfax, Virginia. PwC (www.pwcglobal.com), the world's largest professional services organization helps its clients build value, manage risk, and improve their performance. Ms. Vander Linde leads PwC's Center of Excellence for Performance and Learning. Her clients include organizations in Asia, Europe, Latin America, and the United States, and she works with international corporations on leadership development, knowledge management, and introducing new management concepts and methods. As well, she planned and directed the reengineering of the entire corporate training and development function of an organization with more than 800,000 employees. Ms. Vander Linde is a doctoral candidate in human resource development and business management at The George Washington University, holds a MA in English and communications from the University of Illinois-Champaign/ Urbana, and a BA in English and history from Kalamazoo College. She can be reached at PricewaterhouseCoopers, 12902 Federal Systems Park Drive, Fairfax, VA 22033-4412, phone 703-633-4000, e-mail karen.vander.linde@pwcglobal.com.

Elaine Biech is president of ebb associates inc, a management consulting firm with offices in Portage, Wisconsin and Norfolk, Virginia. Her company specializes in custom designed training programs and consulting services for executives, managers, employees, and consulting and training professionals. Known as a "trainer's trainer," she received the national ASTD's Torch Award in 1992, and serves on the National Nominating Committee and formerly with the HRD Consulting Network Board. Ms. Biech is the consulting editor to the prestigious *Annual* series for human resource professionals published by Jossey-Bass/Pfeiffer and has co-authored two dozen books and articles on training and development, business management, and communications. Recent titles include *The Business of Consulting* (1998, Jossey-Bass/Pfeiffer), *Interpersonal Skills: Understanding Your Impact on Others* (1996, Kendall/Hunt), and *The ASTD Sourcebook: Creativity and Innovation—Widen Your Spectrum* (1996, McGraw-Hill/ASTD). In 1995, Ms. Biech was selected for the Wisconsin Women Entrepreneur's Mentor Award. She holds a MS in human resource development and a BS in business education and consulting from the University of Wisconsin-Superior. She can be reached at ebb associates inc, Box 657, Portage, WI 53901, phone 608-742-5005, e-mail ebbiech@aol.com.

List of Contributors

Donna Abernathy *is associate editor of Training & Development.*

Michele A. Armitage *is a consultant with PricewaterhouseCoopers in Fairfax, Virginia. Her most recent work involves planning and delivering change management approaches, communications plans, and learning programs for a large-scale change initiative for the Government of Puerto Rico.*

Kristin Arnold *maintains a private consulting practice specializing in facilitation services and training, with an emphasis on strategic planning, strategic partnerships, collaborative problem solving, and team building. Ms. Arnold has extensive experience as both an internal and external consultant to a wide variety of manufacturing and service industries as well as the government sector.*

Mary Ashton *is a consultant with PricewaterhouseCoopers in Fairfax, Virginia. She assists organizations and communities in developing and implementing strategic change initiatives, and provides consulting services in the areas of change management, organizational effectiveness, training and learning system design, and leadership development and coaching.*

Marcy Abelson Bandick *is a human resource manager at a major pharmaceuticals company*

Robert C. Bartolo, Jr., *is a consultant with PricewaterhouseCoopers in Fairfax, Virginia. His skills include facilitation, training, and training development, as well as strategic planning, benchmarking, and process redesign. He has experience with both private and public sector clients of all levels.*

Joan Berkson *is a consultant with PricewaterhouseCoopers in Fairfax, Virginia. Her specialties include organization development, project management, training, and communications. She has analyzed and developed organizational systems, and designed and implemented*

change management and business process reengineering activities.

Wendy Boiles *is a consultant with PricewaterhouseCoopers in Fairfax, Virginia. She consults in the areas of change management, strategic planning, leadership development and coaching, process reengineering, organizational and team effectiveness, training design and delivery, and activity-based management.*

Susan K. Boyle *is a senior human resources specialist at Douglas Aircraft Company in Long Beach, California.*

Lisa A. Burke *is a visiting assistant professor in the department of management at the University of Dayton, in Ohio.*

W. Warner Burke *is president of W. Warner Burke Associates. He is a thought leader and internationally known expert in change management.*

Sarah E. Burley *is a consultant with PricewaterhouseCoopers in Fairfax, Virginia. Ms. Burley has experience in the areas of training and development, change management, corporate communications, process redesign, and strategic planning. She has been a consultant to a variety of private and public sector clients.*

Gianluigi Caldiera *is with PricewaterhouseCoopers's government practice. In his 20 years of professional and academic experience, he has worked with government and industry in Europe and the United States. His research and professional activities are in software engineering and distributed tools and techniques for training, learning, and cooperative work.*

Gene Calvert *is a partner at the Learning Advantage and an adjunct professor of management at the University of Maryland and Johns Hopkins University.*

Pat Case, *a partner in MetaSkills Consulting Group, Inc., specializes in large-scale organizational transformation projects. She has been involved in several successful turnaround efforts. Ms. Case is* currently engaged in research on organizational innovation and individual creativity.

Kristen Ciolkosz has four years of experience in training and organizational development work for The Kropp Group, Inc. Her client involvement focuses on instructional design, material development, needs assessment, and program evaluation. She has designed and developed performance management and team building programs for various clients in the chemical, healthcare, and telecommunication industries.

Steve Cohen is president of The Learning Design Group, a custom training company in Minneapolis, Minnesota.

Chandler Cox is a consultant with PricewaterhouseCoopers in Fairfax, Virginia. He focuses on organizational development, process reengineering, change management, and strategic planning. He has worked with commercial and government executive teams to develop strategic plans and to plan and execute corporate transformations.

Adrian B. Durelli is a consultant with PricewaterhouseCoopers in Fairfax, Virginia. He is experienced in strategic planning, facilitation, organizational analysis, and process redesign supporting change management in public and private organizations.

Debra Eshelman is a consultant with PricewaterhouseCoopers in Fairfax, Virginia. She has extensive experience in training design, development, delivery, and administration. She has assisted public and private sector clients in the implementation of a variety of training initiatives.

Jill K. Foley is a consultant with PricewaterhouseCoopers in Fairfax, Virginia. She focuses on training, organizational development, and human resources. She has developed and delivered training, designed performance management systems, conducted job analyses, and performed competency assessments for public and private sector clients.

David Francis is leader of the Innovation Consulting Group at the Centre for Research in Innovation Management based at the University of Brighton in the United Kingdom. He is a behavioral scientist specializing in developing productive innovation in organizations. He has written or co-authored 23 books, including Improving Work Groups and Step-by-Step Competitive Strategy.

John Gasiewski is an independent consultant, formerly with Coopers & Lybrand Consulting and Andersen Consulting. His work includes curriculum and course design and development, interactive multimedia simulations on project management, and an accreditation program for assessing and training professional staff in a global organization.

Sheridan Gates is a consultant with PricewaterhouseCoopers in Fairfax, Virginia. She has more than 12 years of experience in training, including design, development, platform delivery, and facilitation. Her areas of concentration include management development, project management, change management, and facilitator training. Ms.Gates also has an extensive background in marketing and finance.

Adrianne H. Geiger-DuMond is an organizational development consultant with the DuMond Somers Group in Westminster, California.

Jane Green is a consultant with PricewaterhouseCoopers in Fairfax, Virginia. She is experienced in strategic planning, group facilitation, training design and delivery, and competency development. She offers organization development, human resources, and health care management experience to client services.

Candice Harp is a consultant based in Atlanta, Georgia.

Nicholas F. Horney is Vice-President for Consulting at ODR Inc., in Atlanta, Georgia. Formerly with Coopers & Lybrand Consulting, he has worked extensively in change management and organizational development with public and private sector clients.

Bruce Hunt is a consultant with PricewaterhouseCoopers in Chicago. He has considerable experience consulting with organizations on diversity strategies and facilitating diversity educational programs. He specializes in design and delivery of a range of management development activities, including individual and team coaching.

Marianne Hunt *is a consultant with PricewaterhouseCoopers in Fairfax, Virginia. Co-author of* The Creativity Jogger, *a handbook introducing tools and techniques to enhance individual creative problem-solving skills, Ms. Hunt specializes in process improvement and redesign.*

Ed Jones *is vice president of human resources for TGC Stores. He authored* You Developed It! Can Your Training Programs Survive the Reality Test? *which describes research and practical solutions to skill transfer problems. He is a partner at Leading Edge, an HR and training consulting company. He has managed several HRD and HR functions, and has spoken at national conferences.*

Joan Jurkovic *is vice president of The Learning Design Group, a custom training company in Minneapolis, Minnesota.*

Margaret Kaeter *is co-author of* BusinessSpeak *and* Pursuing Total Quality.

Karin Kolodziejski, *a partner in MetaSkills Consulting Group, Inc., specializes in executive and management development. She has developed numerous executive and management development programs for both large and small companies. Ms. Kolodziejski also has a one-on-one executive assessment and coaching practice.*

Richard Koonce *is a career-planning consultant and the author of* Career Power! 12 Winning Habits to Get You From Where You Are to Where You Want to Be.

Richard P. Kropp, Jr., *has more than 20 years of experience as an HRD consultant and manager, with clients including NYNEX and PictureTel Corporation. He is a professor at Boston University, active in ASTD, co-author of* 50 Activities for Team Building, *and a contributor to* The Handbook of Best Practices for Teams.

Nancy Letsinger *is a consultant with PricewaterhouseCoopers in Fairfax, Virginia. She has provided consulting services to government, corporate, and multinational clients in organizational development, change management, and training. She has conducted organizational assessments, developed competency models, and designed and delivered curricula.*

Sue Lodgen *is a principal in PricewaterhouseCoopers's Human Resource Advisory group in Chicago. She consults with human resource functions of medium and large companies to shape HR strategy, and she designs, develops, and presents management development programs on finance, strategy, role, and culture change.*

Lisa Marshall *is a senior associate at the Learning Advantage.*

Bryan Mattimore *is president of the Mattimore Group in Stamford, Connecticut.*

G. Douglas Mayo *is a psychologist who has specialized in training and education for more than 25 years. He headed a group that developed the U.S. Navy Computer Managed Instruction System and, subsequent to that, a group whose purpose was to improve instruction throughout a university. He is the author of some 40 articles and books, including* The Complete Book of Training.

Lynda McDermott *is president of EquiPro International. She is author of* Caught in the Middle: How To Survive and Thrive in Today's Management Squeeze.

Michael Michalko *is a creativity expert and author of* Thinkertoys: A Handbook of Business Creativity for the 1990s.

John F. Middlebrook *is a principal and managing director of Kepner-Tregoe.*

Sandra Mobley *is a partner at the Learning Advantage and an organizational development consultant for firms including General Electric, DuPont, EDS, Mitre, and the U.S. Department of Agriculture.*

Kenneth M. Nowack *is president of Organizational Performance Dimensions in Santa Monica, California.*

Sylvia Odenwald *is president of the Odenwald Connection in Dallas, Texas.*

Scott B. Parry *is chairman of Training House in Princeton, New Jersey.*

Craig Petrun *is a consultant with PricewaterhouseCoopers in Fairfax, Virginia. He has consulted with public and private organizations to enhance the quality of software and hardware solutions through the use of computer-supported cooperative workgroup tools and methodologies (groupware). Most recently, he used electronic meeting support tools to facilitate organizational reengineering and change management meetings for various departments within the U.S. Government.*

Allison Rossett *is a professor of educational technology at San Diego State University, California.*

John Sample *is a principal in the consulting firm of Sample & Associates. The firm, located in Tallahassee, Florida, specializes in the management, development, and training of human resources. He is a previous contributor to* The HR Handbook *and has published more than 50 articles and book chapters.*

John Satzinger *is on the faculty of the Computer Information Systems department at Southwest Missouri State University in Springfield, Missouri.*

Sandra Taylor *is an assistant professor at the University of Wisconsin-Green Bay in Wisconsin.*

Bill Trahant *is a partner and the director of the National Center of Excellence for Change Management at PricewaterhouseCoopers in Fairfax, Virginia. He is responsible for developing and refining C&L's change management methods, and is an international consultant in that field and in continuous improvement, total quality management, organizational analysis and assessment, program planning, team building, group dynamics, and activity-based management.*

Karen Vander Linde *is a partner at PricewaterhouseCoopers in Fairfax, Virginia. She is director of the Performance and Learning Center of Excellence, and provides consulting services to organizations in the areas of learning systems strategy, management, assessment, design, development, delivery, and measurement. She also serves as a senior facilitator for executive teams, and is a member of the board of directors for ASTD.*

Kevin Walker *is a consultant with PricewaterhouseCoopers in Fairfax, Virginia, and manages the firm's National Survey Center, providing a broad range of survey research services to the firm's clients internationally. In addition, he has worked on a broad range of organizational change initiatives, including survey research, business process reengineering, process improvement, systems implementation, and organization development.*

Sue Walther *is a former consultant with Coopers & Lybrand Consulting in Washington, DC. Her experience includes training development, group facilitation, marketing, creativity, innovation, and the development of multimedia training materials. She is co-author of* The Side Ways Thinker, *a desk-top tool to help individuals and teams unleash their creativity. Ms. Walther is currently leading the marketing web team at MicroStrategy.*

Luan B. Watkins *is vice president of quality for Tenneco Automotive, headquartered in Deerfield, Illinois.*

Bernard P. Willis *is a consultant with PricewaterhouseCoopers in Fairfax, Virginia. He has provided consulting services to projects in both the public and private sectors in reengineering, total quality management, process management, activity-based costing, and large system implementations.*

Scott Wimer *is a principal of Wimer Associates in Santa Monica, California.*

Robert A. Younglove *is a performance coach and training consultant specializing in goal setting and turning good intentions into results. His mission is to help people change their behavior and lifestyle to become healthier, happier, and more successful in their career. He has authored books and articles on career transition, and is a frequent speaker on strategies for wellness and the prevention of stress.*

Table of Contents

INTRODUCTION
Focusing on High Performance:
New Goals, Roles for Learning Professionals

Training Departments aren't what they used to be. Like the businesses they support, training departments are changing their priorities and processes, focusing on core competencies and developing new knowledge and skills to enhance their performance. Moving away from providing traditional training and development services, today's learning professionals increasingly focus on linking learning with job performance and business results to create competitive advantage for companies. They also are helping businesses become learning organizations and address other challenges of today's global, high-performance-seeking enterprises.

The High-performance Phenomenon

As a result of global competition, yesterday's standards of performance no longer produce successful business outcomes in many industries. In the past decade, organizations have sought breakthrough gains in productivity, customer service, cost reduction, and new product development to stay ahead of or keep pace with competitors. To maximize performance in every sector, they need to adopt new ways of working, new ways of organizing themselves, and new ways of thinking about the role of training and learning.

Business analysts have coined the term "high performance" to describe companies that keep the focus on results in every aspect of their operations. The Malcolm Baldrige National Quality Award, which annually honors businesses that exemplify high-quality work practices, defines high performance as "work approaches used to systematically pursue ever higher levels of overall company and human performance, including quality, productivity, and time performance." These approaches include:

- cooperation between workforce and management, often involving teams;

- employee input to planning; individual and organizational skill-building and learning;

- learning from other organizations; flexibility in job design and work assignments; and

- effective use of performance measures, including comparisons.

Some high-performance companies use monetary incentives for employees or teams, based on factors such as corporate performance and individual or team contributions and skill-building. In addition, "high-performance work approaches usually seek to align the design of organizations, work, jobs, employee development, and incentives."

Besides adopting these approaches, high-performance-seeking organizations have made other changes to support the new ways of doing business. Because change is a constant, managing change has become a high-performance fundamental. Because many breakthrough gains have come from technology, the ability to harness it to maximum advantage also has become a major competitive edge.

Not surprisingly, achieving this focus takes time and effort, and most interested companies are moving incrementally toward implementation of high-performance systems. A 1995 study for the American Society for Training & Development (ASTD) found that, while less than 10 percent of responding companies had completed the transformation, the majority had established some of the features associated with the high-performance phenomenon. This trend is expected to accelerate in coming years. For example, a recent Conference Board report noted that 98 percent of companies responding to a survey said they need to gain more productivity and higher performance from their workforces.

Implications for Learning Professionals

Changes in the organizations they serve mean changes for training departments and people who may have long thought of themselves as training professionals. Most fundamentally, that means reflecting the performance focus in the department's internal activities and in the ways that departments and individual professionals align their services with company goals and collaborate with other departments to add value. In a survey of training professionals at ASTD's 1996 International Conference, 89 percent strongly agreed or agreed that the shift from training to performance is a top trend. Some organizations have reflected this shift by renaming the Training Department the "Performance and Learning" Department.

These changes have already begun to occur, and for those in leading edge companies, they have become a way of life. One indication of the implications for "training departments" in improvement/results-driven companies comes from a recent survey conducted for Coopers & Lybrand, L.L.P. (C&L). Responding organizations emphasized the integrative role and strategic value of training for employees, customers, and suppli-

ers—and spent more money on learning than companies without a high-performance push. In these companies, training professionals work as partners with business units rather than in isolation, and they serve as advisors to management on learning and performance, as well as continuing to design and present learning programs and facilitate groups. In a related benchmarking study, C&L learned that companies in this category were:

- Aligning training to support performance expectations and business goals and strategies. For learning professionals, this means working closely with leadership and management, both to tie organizational training to their needs and vision and to give them support and learning experiences that improve the leadership function.

- Operating closer to the customer (such as having HR staff work with business units instead of in a centralized training department) and creating learning experiences driven by customer needs.

- Assessing their own performance and the extent to which training/learning has an impact on performance.

- Focusing learning experiences on people's

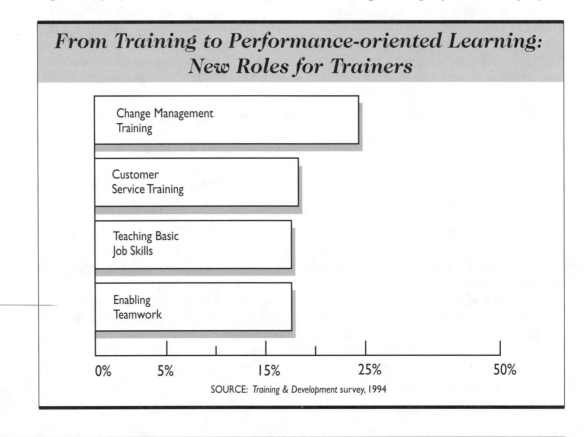

From Training to Performance-oriented Learning: New Roles for Trainers

Change Management Training

Customer Service Training

Teaching Basic Job Skills

Enabling Teamwork

0%   5%   15%   25%   50%

SOURCE: *Training & Development survey, 1994*

jobs, both in skill-building and in ensuring a good fit between employees and their work.

- Embedding learning in jobs.
- Supporting innovation and creativity in business units and HR functions.
- Focusing on key corporate measures of results, such as shortening cycle times, reducing costs, and improving quality.

According to a recent Training & Development survey, trainers themselves report becoming increasingly involved in high-performance-related training. For example, 22 percent more people are doing change management training; 17 percent are teaching basic job skills; 18 percent are doing customer service training; and 17 percent more are enabling teamwork. As performance learning becomes everyone's job, learning professionals will continue to shift away from a "training-in-a-box" approach to helping their companies reap a competitive advantage from learning that improves performance.

How This Book Can Help

This book is designed to help learning professionals make this transition from traditional training to a performance focus in organizations that are, or may become, high-performance organizations. Its six sections offer short articles and proven tools, techniques, and exercises on learning issues of importance for high-performance-seeking organizations, performance and learning managers and consultants, and learning program designers/presenters. It is designed to provide both substantive topic updates and a related "toolbox" of exercises and worksheets in one package.

The section that opens the book, "New Trends in Training and Learning," has diverse materials to enable self-study and group or one-to-one learning experiences for learning professionals. To help you meet today's key challenges in high-performing organizations, topics include performance-directed learning, distance learning, enhancing training/learning presentation skills, outsourcing of training tasks, and measuring training performance and return on investment.

The next five sections address topics relevant to training learning professionals in today's results-oriented organizations. These include managing change, coaching/on-the-job training, leadership/strategic planning, teamwork, and promoting innovation and creativity. A collaborative effort of the American Society for Training & Development, ebb associates, and Coopers & Lybrand Consulting, each section contains a collection of materials developed by a diverse group of experts. Authors include HR professionals, performance and learning consultants, management/business specialists, and contributors to *Training & Development,* the journal of the American Society for Training & Development.

Each entry in the collection is action-oriented, designed for you to use and pass on, not just to read. Most feature either instructions for presenting or adapting the information in a training session; outlines of group exercises; or other facilitative tools, such as survey instruments, assessment tools, checklists, or models. Some background articles are included both to update you on topics of interest to business and to provide resources that can be used as self-study tools, background for developing a learning session, training prework, or training handouts for organization personnel and management.

For ease of use, each section opens with a chart that offers a visual overview of its contents. For example, the chart in the section, "Enabling Teamwork," could help you quickly locate a small group exercise for team self-assessment and tools to help the team complete it; a self-study tool for learning professionals on creating and managing global teams; or a set of tools to help teams reach decisions or consensus. Charts in all sections also show for whom the materials are most appropriate:

- *Learning Professionals.* This group includes those who may currently think of themselves as training and development professionals, human resource professionals with learning-related functions, and those with knowledge management responsibilities. Of course, at the broadest level, all of the pieces in the book are for learning professionals. However, when a chart indicates that you are an audience for a piece, it means the piece is designed to enhance your own knowledge or skills, instead of or in addition to using it with other audiences.

- *Staff and Supervisors.* Those on the front lines—who direct and perform the basic work processes of an organization—fall into this category. Most of the pieces directed at this group are training exercises.

- *Teams.* Materials throughout this book, not just in the teamwork chapter, can be relevant for teams. They are intended for any type of team that has a charter and meets formally and regularly, including management teams, change teams, issue management/planning teams, unit work teams, improvement teams, and self-managed teams. The role of the learning professional may differ, however, depending on the type of team. For example, you may facilitate an exercise or workshop for a management team while providing an exercise (and some one-on-one coaching) to the team leader or standing facilitator of a self-directed or improvement team.

- *Management.* This category on the charts includes both top management and middle managers. In practice and in different organization structures, however, some pieces may be more relevant to leaders versus managers in your company. You will need to make this determination based on your situation.

In addition, each piece opens with a chart listing its audiences, purpose, and suggestions for use.

As you enhance your performance focus, each of these sections is designed to help you fill in the gaps and apply your own creative adaptations. The ideas have been used effectively by professionals in the field, but each will work best if it is appropriate for and adapted to your organization's unique situation.

References

Bassi, L., and Van Buren, M. Sustaining High Performance in Bad Times. *Training & Development.* June 1997, pp. 32–41.

Bassi, L., Cheny, S., and Van Buren, M. Training Industry Trends 1997. *Training & Development.* November 1997, pp. 46–59.

Benson, F. Research Update. *Training & Development.* May 1997, pp. 93–94.

FaxForum Results. *Training & Development.* April 1995, p. 20.

Galagan, P. Reinventing the Profession. *Training & Development.* December 1994, pp. 20–27.

U.S. Department of Commerce. National Institute of Standards and Technology. Malcolm Baldrige National Quality Award 1998 Criteria for Performance.

Vander Linde, K., Horney, N., and Koonce, R. Seven Ways to Make Your Training Department One of the Best. *Training & Development.* August 1997, pp. 20–28.

SECTION 1:
NEW TRENDS IN TRAINING AND LEARNING

Section 1 at a Glance

MATERIAL

	Page	Learning Professionals	Staff and Supervisors	Teams	Management	Self-study/Resource for Training	Group Exercise	Tool
The Learning Organization	*Page*							
Grasping the Learning Organization	1-7	●			●	●		
Seven Ways to Make Your Training Department One of the Best	1-12	●				●		
Creating a Business Strategy for the Training and Development Function	1-21	●				●		●
How to Create a Training and Development Needs Assessment Survey	1-33	●				●		●
Developing Competency-based Curricula	1-40	●				●		●
That Was a Great Class, But . . .	1-47	●				●		●
Measuring Training's ROI	1-56	●				●		
Technology and Learning	*Page*							
Many Paths to Learning Software	1-62	●				●		●
A Start-up Guide to Distance Learning	1-68	●				●		●
Planning and Implementing a Distributed Learning Program	1-77	●				●		●
Outsourcing	*Page*							
An Outsourcing Primer	1-85	●			●	●		
How to Select a Consultant	1-92	●			●	●		

Introduction:
Tools and Techniques to Meet Learning Professionals' Own Performance Improvement Needs

Learning plays a central role in high-performing organizations. In fact, recent experience suggests that a company's ability to promote learning and manage knowledge can improve business results and lead to competitive advantage. This section includes materials designed to assist training and development professionals in assuming learning management roles in companies that are or may become high-performing learning organizations.

Learning Professionals in a Learning Organization

Terms like "learning organization," "intellectual capital," and "knowledge management" are all variations on a new way of looking at learning, which includes the following concepts.

- Creating, capturing, and using knowledge to enhance organizational performance.

- Formally recognizing the strategic importance of knowledge-related assets, often by putting a senior manager in charge of them. These assets include intellectual property; know-how; patents and trademarks; employee knowledge, competencies, and motivation; technologies; and learning systems and processes.

- Making continuous learning, which may occur formally or informally as a part of work, everyone's responsibility.

- Increasing opportunities for self-directed learning.

- Integrating learning into key performance-driven activities, such as redesigning the structure of a company, transforming business processes, working in teams, and pursuing customer-defined quality in products and services.

- Using group training to create knowledge, enhance teamwork, or focus on shared goals rather than simply to transfer information or teach skills.

- Offering learning on a "just-in-time" basis and in the context of a job or task.

- Promoting dialogue, sharing best practices, and encouraging collaboration and team learning.

- Creating systems and processes that capture knowledge (e.g., about customers and suppliers or about how to do a task) and pass it on to appropriate users.

- Rewarding employees who show a capacity and a propensity to learn.

- Developing systems to measure the value produced by investments in human capital, such as training.

In a 1997 ASTD National HRD Executive Survey, responses underlined the growing prevalence of these new approaches to learning. For example, 75 percent said their companies were working to become a learning organization. Almost 100 percent said that organizational learning was an integral part of their companies, and 40 percent had someone overseeing it. In addition, 98 percent said that HR professionals have a role in developing intellectual capital, which respondents associated with factors such as knowledge, learning, sharing best practices, and capacity to learn.

As companies embrace new perspectives on learning and knowledge, the roles of learning professionals are changing. Training becomes only one tool to achieve performance-oriented learning, and learning managers become learning brokers. This means they facilitate and exploit informal learning and integrate it with formal training efforts and knowledge systems (which they may need to create). They also become key players in identifying results-oriented competencies, setting learning priorities that match and

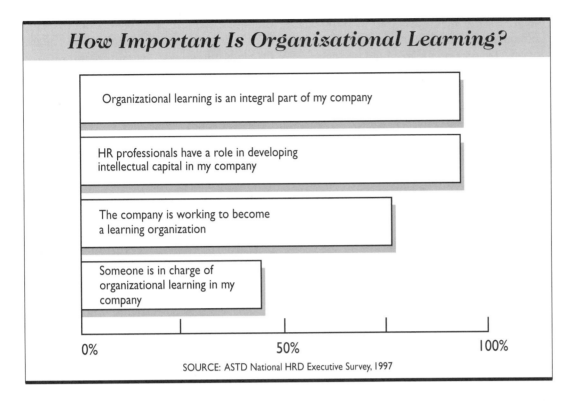

How Important Is Organizational Learning?

Organizational learning is an integral part of my company

HR professionals have a role in developing intellectual capital in my company

The company is working to become a learning organization

Someone is in charge of organizational learning in my company

0%   50%   100%

SOURCE: ASTD National HRD Executive Survey, 1997

support business goals, coordinating learning experiences companywide, and creating opportunities for people to share knowledge and best practices. In addition, learning professionals help align performance appraisal and rewards with new learning approaches and goals.

How This Section Can Help

New roles create a need for new skills and new knowledge, including mastering new learning theories, facilitation, performance analysis, needs assessment, and business operations. The first set of articles in this section contains materials that can help fa-

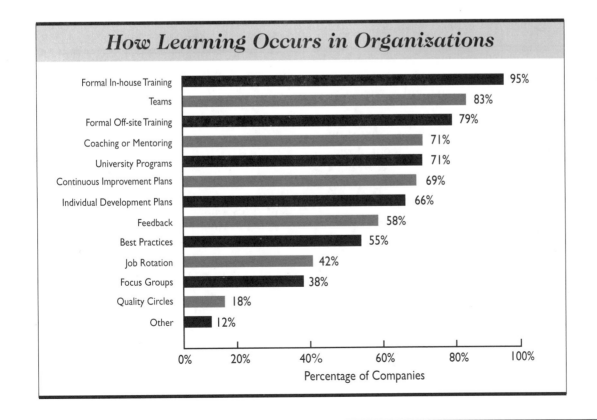

How Learning Occurs in Organizations

Formal In-house Training	95%
Teams	83%
Formal Off-site Training	79%
Coaching or Mentoring	71%
University Programs	71%
Continuous Improvement Plans	69%
Individual Development Plans	66%
Feedback	58%
Best Practices	55%
Job Rotation	42%
Focus Groups	38%
Quality Circles	18%
Other	12%

0%   20%   40%   60%   80%   100%

Percentage of Companies

miliarize learning professionals with the new demands and possibilities learning organizations present and tools to help you assume new responsibilities.

The environment for workplace learning is also changing. The pieces in this section present materials to help you learn about, teach about, and respond to some of today's key trends: Using technology for learning and knowledge management systems and outsourcing aspects of performance-oriented learning.

Technology and Learning

Learning professionals have two potential roles related to technology and learning. First, high-performing businesses increasingly rely on technology to improve processes and business results. As a result, teaching employees how to use new computer software and related tools is an important need that learning professionals are helping companies to meet. In fact, ASTD's 1997 National HRD Executive Survey found that the year's top trend was computer skills training.

Second, technologies such as digital electronics, optical data storage, portable computers, and distributed computing have changed the way information is stored and used. They allow information-sharing and exchange that expand learning opportunities and can radically redefine the training experience. Learning professionals have the opportunity to be the experts that guide corporate decisions about and applications of these technologies.

According to the executive survey cited above, the use of learning technologies is substantial and growing each year. For example, about 55 percent of respondents reported using computer-distributed learning via disk or hard drive in 1996, with 63.5 percent expecting to use it in 1997. Video and computer teleconferencing, CD-ROM, interactive television/video, and use of Intranets (a computer network within an organization that uses the Internet) show similar trends. Executives predicted that the number one electronic learning technology by the year 2000 would be Intranets, although only 13.5 percent were using them in 1996. In addition, 81 percent of the companies

that are members of ASTD's Benchmarking Forum expect to increase their use of the Internet for internal training—and one estimate suggests that the on-line training market will be greater than $1 billion by 2000.

The potential benefits of using these technologies explain their growing popularity. The National Workforce Collaborative cited greater cost-effectiveness; increased quality of instruction; ability to provide self-paced, individualized, decentralized convenient learning; reduced resource requirements (e.g., classrooms, trainers); and tireless delivery as major pluses.

As a result of these trends, technoliteracy is becoming a critical competency for learning professionals. As learning managers, you play a key role in assessing whether technology is appropriate to varied learning needs, and, if so, which learning technologies should be used and what it will take to support a system after it is installed. Additional roles may include assessing the effectiveness of the new technologies and determining potential applications that can justify their initial expense. The rapid rate of change in all of today's technologies increases the challenge. Materials in this section present an overview of currently available learning technologies and their best uses (and pitfalls to avoid). Authors also provide tools for assessing which technologies or learning approaches are best for the job (and most suitable for meeting particular trainee needs), and for planning and implementing new programs using electronic learning technologies.

Outsourcing

In a recent survey conducted by ASTD's *Training & Development* journal, 33 percent of respondents said outsourcing had increased in their training departments over the past year. This mirrors an overall business trend in which growing numbers of companies have decided to contract out for services outside their core competencies or services that can be delivered at lower cost by outside vendors.

This trend is significant because training and other HR functions often are not considered core competencies and thus become

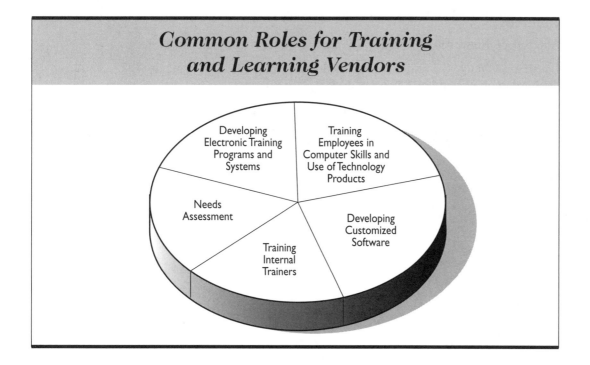

Common Roles for Training and Learning Vendors

- Developing Electronic Training Programs and Systems
- Training Employees in Computer Skills and Use of Technology Products
- Needs Assessment
- Developing Customized Software
- Training Internal Trainers

potential candidates for outsourcing. According to a survey conducted in 1996 by the Manufacturers Alliance, only 3 percent of companies reported outsourcing all aspects of training delivery—but only 13 percent kept it completely in-house. The rest outsourced some elements of the function.

For example, vendors that develop electronic training programs and systems have grown in recent years as companies have sought outside experts to enable rapid adoption of new learning technologies. External suppliers also are often used to train employees in computer skills and in using technology products. Other common roles for outside vendors are developing customized courseware, training internal trainers, and conducting needs assessment. Some companies have chosen to rely on contractors for specific skills training while keeping strategic learning functions in-house.

Who is providing these external services? One major source of interest to high-performance-seeking organizations is performance consultants, who may help departments develop new competencies in today's results-

oriented environment. For example, if training is the appropriate intervention, they may assist in-house professionals in linking training to results, linking learning to innovation, and developing systems to promote continuous learning. Professional and trade associations and local four-year and community colleges and technical institutes also are important providers for many companies. Some associations set standards, develop courseware for employers, offer certification programs, and provide distance learning opportunities. Colleges and institutes offer a wide range of classroom training that usually focuses on job skills and may be taught by practicing professionals in the field.

In this environment, key challenges for performance and learning departments are deciding whether outsourcing could add value to their organization's performance, what aspects of their responsibilities could be better handled by contractors, and how to select, manage, and evaluate vendors for best results. The materials in this section address each of these needs.

References

Allerton, H. News You Can Use. *Training & Development,* June 1997, p. 9.

Bassi, L., Cheny, S., and Van Buren, M. Training Industry Trends 1997. *Training & Development,* November 1997, pp. 46–55.

Benson, G. Battle of the Buzzwords. *Training & Development,* July 1997, p. 51.

Galagan, P. Reinventing the Profession. *Training & Development,* December 1994, pp. 20–26.

FaxForum Results. *Training & Development,* April 1995, p. 20.

Grasping the Learning Organization

By Gene Calvert, Sandra Mobley, and Lisa Marshall

Audience	Learning Professionals, Managers
Purpose	—Understand the concept of the learning organization —Understand how learning organizations have been developed —Appreciate the evolving nature of this phenomenon
Suggested Uses	Self-study/handout in related sessions Resource for training presentation

Right now—explain what a "learning organization" is and does. Can you answer completely? Perhaps you'd prefer to turn the tables—if you could grill other practitioners about learning organizations, what would you ask them?

In a recent series of focus groups, HRD professionals and frontline managers had the chance to take turns as explainers and interrogators, sharing what they already knew about learning organizations and telling what they would like to know.

Nearly 50 practitioners representing most regions of the United States participated in the focus groups. Participants included senior trainers, HRD managers, line managers, and internal and external OD consultants. They represented private industry, universities, and government agencies, including Apple Computers, Amdahl, ASTD, Cable & Wireless Communications, General Electric, George Washington University, Hewlett-Packard, Levi-Strauss, Martin Marietta, Marriott Corporation, Pacific Gas & Electric, U.S. Defense Information Systems Agency, U.S. Office of Personnel Management, and Westinghouse.

We designed the five sessions to elicit different ideas and perspectives about learning organizations. Using David Bohm's concept of "dialogue," we asked the dozen or so participants at each one-day session to view each other as inquiring colleagues, suspend their assumptions, and explore possibilities, rather than advocate their points of view. We asked them to explore freely their beliefs, expectations, and questions about learning organizations.

We restricted our roles to clarifying their discussion agendas, keeping the conversation on track, managing time, relating topics and themes when needed, and handling other basic facilitation tasks.

Among other things, participants addressed such questions as the following:

* What definitions of a learning organization make sense?
* What distinguishes organizational learning from individual learning?
* What does a learning organization look like and how can it be measured?
* Would training and development specialists play different roles inside a learning organization?

Reprinted with permission from *Training & Development,* published by the American Society for Training & Development.

Grasping the Elephant

Like the blind characters examining an elephant in the ancient fable, participants' answers depended on what parts of the concept they grasped. Each person started with some preconceptions. No one could articulate precisely why and how some organizations learn better than others.

Participants weighed the merits of nearly 20 definitions of a learning organization, debating which one explained the concept most lucidly and usefully. They also discussed how the definition of organizational learning differs from the definition of a learning organization.

Participants preferred definitions they considered concrete and nonacademic. Many tried to amend and combine definitions to produce a complete and precise one; these efforts proved difficult and perplexing.

Ultimately, the definition of a learning organization offered by Peter Senge in *The Fifth Discipline* most consistently captured the hearts and minds of participants: "Where people continually expand their capacity to create results they truly desire, where new and expansive patterns of thinking are nurtured, where collective aspiration is set free, and where people are continually learning how to learn together."

Most participants preferred the definition of organizational learning offered by Nancy Dixon of George Washington University: "The intentional action of an organization to continuously transform itself through both adaptive and innovative learning."

According to the focus groups, "the learning organization" describes an organization that excels at advanced, systematic, collective learning. "Organizational learning" refers to methods of collective learning. This distinction in meaning suggests three useful, if debatable, conclusions:

- All organizations learn. (In other words, they use organizational learning methods.)
- All organizations learn at different levels of proficiency and at different paces.
- To become a "learning organization," an organization must find ways to make learning more intentional and more systemic.

Silence and a Blank Flipchart

Given that all organizations learn, for good or ill, how do learning organizations differ from other organizations? If you take away from us our security-blanket copies of *The Fifth Discipline* or any book by Chris Argyris, what do we actually know about learning organizations and organizational learning?

Faced with silence and a blank flipchart, participants gave off-the-top-of-their-heads responses to this question that showed they know a lot about learning-organization theory but far less about how to apply it, which they readily admitted. Learning organizations are works in progress, both conceptually and practically.

What Does a Learning Organization Learn?

What do learning organizations learn that other organizations do not? Learning organizations learn:

- ▶ to use learning to reach their goals
- ▶ to help people value the effects of their learning on their organizations
- ▶ to avoid making the same mistakes again (and again)
- ▶ to share information in ways that prompt appropriate action
- ▶ to link individual performance with organizational performance
- ▶ to tie rewards to key measures of performance
- ▶ to take in a lot of environmental information at all times
- ▶ to create structures and procedures that support the learning process
- ▶ to foster ongoing and orderly dialogues
- ▶ to make it safe for people to share openly and take risks

---

What Does a Learning Organization Look Like?

A learning organization:

▶ learns collaboratively, openly, and across boundaries

▶ values how it learns as well as what it learns

▶ invests in staying ahead of the learning curve in its industry

▶ gains a competitive edge by learning faster and smarter than competitors

▶ turns data into useful knowledge quickly and at the right time and place

▶ enables every employee to feel that every experience provides him or her a chance to learn something potentially useful, even if only for leveraging future learning

▶ exhibits little fear and defensiveness; rewards and learns from what goes wrong ("failure" learning) and right ("success" learning)

▶ takes risks but avoids jeopardizing the basic security of the organization

▶ invests in experimental and seemingly tangential learning

▶ supports people and teams who want to pursue action-learning projects

▶ depoliticizes learning by not penalizing individuals or groups for sharing information and conclusions

Participants agreed on many criteria for learning organizations. Learning organizations, they said, employ a distinctive set of learning strategies and tactics. Their learning differs from that of other organizations, for example, in its effectiveness, productivity, adaptiveness, and link to achieving goals.

But participants also decided that descriptions of learning organizations sometimes muddle understanding. Some organizations meet certain criteria yet learn ineffectively or inefficiently. Other organizations fail to meet criteria, yet learn productively.

The answer, participants suggested, can be found in key characteristics of learning organizations, which are difficult to articulate—the characteristics that create the conditions for learning. Collectively, these catalysts might be described as an organization's spirit, or its character.

Avoid the Magic Bullet

The allure and the elusiveness of the learning organization make it tempting for organizations to seize the notion in order to fulfill any number of needs, from a quick fix to a boost for a sagging Total Quality Management (TQM) initiative.

Participants warned of the potential for organizations to latch onto the concept of the learning organization as a magic bullet. They cautioned each other against moving too quickly to label any organization as a learning organization. Trendy phrases used to excess can generate a backlash—the TQM movement offers an example.

Participants agreed that organizational learning, like quality, happens in small steps taken with strong commitment and clear intention throughout the organization. "Breakthrough" experiences are few and far between.

As focus group discussions unfolded, examples of learning organizations in-the-making emerged. For example:

- Martin Marietta gathers all of its engineers at the completion of a project to capture lessons learned and to share this information with other teams.

- Cable and Wireless Communications provides training budgets to self-managed teams to enable them to take responsibility for their own learning. This forces the training department to be unusually flexible and expert in offering just-in-time support.

- AT&T eliminated most corporate vice presidents. Instead, operating managers meet with the CEO once a month for two days so they can update each other, work more synergistically, and learn more collaboratively.

How Does a Learning Organization Evolve?

What are the first steps to becoming a learning organization? A budding learning organization can begin by:

▶ questioning current assumptions about learning

▶ getting an outside perspective

▶ tying the goal of becoming a learning organization to its organizational vision

▶ finding or creating a champion in top management

▶ looking for the "pain" in the organization—the place where more effective

learning could help

▶ articulating learning-organization ideas plainly

▶ rewarding group as well as individual learning successes and failures

▶ finding an external enemy to spur greater cooperative learning

▶ finding ways to collaborate internally in and unhampered by boundaries

---

From these and other real-world examples emerged some of the ways HRD professionals and line managers can advance or slow down the process of intentionally developing a learning organization.

Strategies that seem to encourage organizational learning include talking about learning with the learner's vocabulary, making learning tangible, and addressing the learner's work priorities. Conversely, actions that diminish organizational learning include using professional jargon, being "the expert," and solving hypothetical problems.

Examples suggest that HRD specialists and managers can use case studies of organizational learning to develop broad strategies for fostering more effective learning in their own organizations.

The Moose on the Table

Although we asked participants what learning organizations learn, what they look like, and how to start building one, we did not ask an important question: "What *should* learning organizations learn?"

Based on the dialogue that took place, we speculate that in response to this query, participants would have cited such knowledge as environmental scanning and rigorous verification—and truth-telling.

Within a true learning organization, learners will know how to talk honestly with each other about what is really happening, both inside and outside the organization. Within a true learning organization, people learn to say the unsayable—to point out, as representatives from Westinghouse put it, that there is a sick moose on the table, and to ask for help in diagnosing and curing it.

Clear organizational learning goals must be rooted in honest assessments of the current learning environment. Truth-telling short-circuits what Chris Argyris calls "skilled incompetence"—defensive routines born of fear, which perpetuate inaccurate and unreal perceptions and prevent organizational learning from happening. Organizations that learn the best engage in double-loop learning—they look at the beliefs and values they hold and notice how these affect their behavior and, in turn, the solutions they create.

Senge calls this kind of learning "personal mastery": The ability of individuals and their organizations to examine their mental models, the behaviors that arise from those models, and the effect both mental models and behavior have on their organizations' systems.

Just visualizing what a learning organization would look like poses an enormous task. Creating or sustaining one is even more daunting. Senge himself notes that the concept called the learning organization has yet to be "reduced to practice," as engineers describe the process of turning ideas into working prototypes.

Participating in the focus groups enabled participants to examine their own and others' mental models. Pooling their perceptions brought the organizational elephant called a learning organization into sharper focus.

But many participants urged their colleagues to risk staying confused or curious for a while about the nature and implementation of the learning organization. Instead of devising instant and unproven answers, they suggested that the role of HRD professionals may be to ask fresh and constructive questions—to act as master learners who use the art of not knowing to strengthen the learning process, as well as the results.

Better Learning and the Bottom Line

What connections do trainers, line managers, and consultants see between organizational learning and organizational profitability?

When organizational learning directly addresses operations—for example, as with training for TQM—people are less likely to question the positive connection between organizational learning and profitability. The same could be said of any training initiative targeted at improving organizational productivity and performance.

Focus groups addressed the connection between organizational learning and profits by contrasting the positive effects learning has on profits with the negative effects that occur when no learning takes place.

Consider, for example, the effect on the bottom line of unsolved customer problems or missed new-market opportunities. Compare those scenarios with the bottom-line gains that would be realized if a company learned to solve customer problems or exploit new markets.

Participants suggested ways that organizational learning can increase profits. Organizations can use learning to better their bottom lines by:

▶ Using action learning to solve business problems or seize business opportunities

▶ Reflecting on learning experiences, such as asking what prevented or permitted seeing better solutions

▶ Improving processes by learning from more knowledgeable people

▶ Developing awareness of the gains that can be squeezed from mistakes and successes

▶ Shortening competitive cycles, as in developing new products more quickly

▶ Helping management to recognize learning as a factor that affects the bottom line

▶ Increasing individual and group accountability for learning

▶ Leveraging key learning points, such as learning to acquire the most critical data, not all data

Seven Ways to Make Your Training Department One of the Best

By Karen Vander Linde, Nicholas Horney, and Richard Koonce

Audience ➤	Learning Professionals
Purpose ➤	—Understand the key success factors for creating a high-performance organization —Learn best practices from highly successful organizations
Suggested Uses ➤	Self-study Resource for training presentation Benchmarking input to strategic planning for training department

We may be tired of the words downsizing, restructuring, and reengineering, but they aren't going to go away. U.S. organizations will continue to undergo those changes in the years ahead. So, what role should training and HRD functions play in helping to guide such efforts?

On a more operational level, how will you create the necessary links within your organization to ensure that training objectives and programs achieve maximum return?— whether it's to boost productivity and profitability, reinforce new business strategies, assist in the redesign of key work processes, or give employees from executives to frontline supervisors and workers the skills they need to be successful.

Organizations are beginning to recognize that the key to being a future market leader requires different things from them and their people than in the past: Many are recognizing that training is critical in helping close the gap between employees' current competencies and the competencies needed in high-performance organizations.

Because organizational change is a continuous, complex phenomenon with potentially devastating consequences if not done correctly, there is a new appreciation for training as a way to move a company to new levels of productivity and effectiveness, especially after downsizing or restructuring.

A company's training function appears well-positioned to enable organizational success. But in many cases, companies don't know how to create high-performance training functions to help them meet evolving needs. And in too many cases, training professionals haven't become full partners with senior executives and line managers in business development and strategic planning. In such situations, training continues to play a reactive role in organizational life instead of an integrative and transformational role in decision making, strategic development, policy formulation, and business management.

Emerging Management Practices

The emergence of high-performance organizations in the private and public sectors is prompting a redesign of the traditional training department. But how can you create a new, high-performance training organization? What does such an organization look like? How do you align it to support companywide business goals and plans? And what are the requirements of the training professionals in high-performance companies?

To answer those questions, Coopers & Lybrand—with the American Society of Quality Control, Rutgers University Center for Public Productivity, and National Institute of Canada—conducted a survey of 300 "improvement-driven" organizations to understand the implications for training departments. The 1994 survey documented the management practices used by those organizations to improve quality, customer satisfaction, and financial performance. The survey aimed to identify the best practices of each organization in these areas:

- Leadership
- Customer focus
- Employee involvement
- Innovation
- Process improvement
- Improvement measurement
- Change management

The survey was designed to identify the critical inter-relationships between practices in different organizational areas that can be critical predictors of effectiveness and financial success.

Not surprisingly, the high-performance organizations in the survey emphasized the integrative role of training. They recognized the strategic value in training for employees, customers, and suppliers. And they tended to invest more money in training than other companies.

In the high-performance organizations, there was also a tight link between training and organizational strategy. In such organizations, training had a strong partnership with business units or operational groups, instead of operating as an isolated staff function. And the training professionals were involved in activities at senior-executive and line levels. They played such roles as senior business advisor, learning system specialist, and performance consultant—in addition to instructor, facilitator, and instructional designer.

The survey suggests that in high-performance organizations, training is viewed as a function that operates laterally across the company and that plays an integrative and even transformational role.

Coopers & Lybrand also conducted a benchmarking study subsequent to the 1994 survey. The new study included these companies:

- A computer-parts maker
- An auto manufacturer
- A telecommunications firm
- Two international postal organizations
- A major retail chain
- A computer-systems firm

Each exhibited traits of the improvement-driven companies on the prior survey; each was aligning training to support performance expectations and business goals, as well a long-term organizational objective and strategies.

Here are the principal findings of the benchmarking study in the critical areas identified by the 1994 survey.

Customer focus. High-performance organizations collect customer-satisfaction data systematically and regularly. They understand their customers' needs and desires better than low-performing organizations, and customer feedback is used to improve work processes.

In traditional organizations, training often operates as a staff function separate from line operations and without performance metrics to assess quantitatively whether the training produces results in terms of organizational goals and plans. Typically, training in such organizations has a limited customer focus (for example, a classroom of participants). Satisfaction measurements tend to be event based (for example, course evaluation forms) rather than continuous and organizational.

Training that is closer to customers. In high-performance organizations, the training function is closer to customers than in low-performing organizations. Training is "driven" by customers' needs, developed and designed in conjunction with customers, and evaluated continuously.

For example, the auto manufacturer in the benchmarking study has in-house training and development leaders at all of its plants. Those leaders operate as business partners with plant managers, helping to create and customize training programs that are specific to the needs of the plants and the company as a whole. The computer-parts maker and telecommunications firm have internal training organizations that report directly to their business units.

In fact, the computer-parts maker has more than 60 training organizations aligned with different customer bases, and most of the training dollars are distributed in individual business units. To ensure that training is relevant and reexamined regularly, each course has a "functional owner" and a "course owner." Functional owners are training managers for specific business units and are responsible for all courses. Course owners (who are also trainers) ensure the overall quality of courses, which they monitor and revise as needed. If a course doesn't have both a functional owner and a course owner, it's eliminated from the curriculum.

In the telecommunications firm, most of the business units have their own training organizations that provide the product training unique to each unit. Typically, new training needs are identified through discussions with line and department managers, through the company's annual employee-culture climate survey, or through other input. Designing and developing new courses take one to three months. But when an unexpected need for customized training arises, the training organizations can act quickly, turning in new courses or training modules in as little as a week.

Leadership. The 1994 survey of improvement-driven organizations showed that a critical predictor of success in achieving measurable improvement is strong, hands-on leadership by the CEO. But it isn't a silver bullet. It must be backed by the hands-on involvement of supervisors helping employees perform their jobs more effectively.

What does the emphasis on strong execu-tive communication suggest about the training efforts of high-performance organizations? Traditionally, training has been more reactive than proactive in communicating an organization's values and business priorities. Most training hasn't been tied to business initiatives, but has consisted mainly of static courses and off-the-shelf packages that weren't updated routinely or customized to meet evolving job requirements and core competencies. In high-performance organizations, however, close and specific links exist between what senior managers think is important to the business and the kind of training employees receive.

The emergence of corporate universities in three of the companies in the benchmarking study signals an awareness that their training functions are becoming integral to helping guide their overall business goals and strategies.

At the auto manufacturer, there isn't an articulated training mission. Instead, the training staff shares a vision for the company's business with other employees. Says one senior training manager, "We're not in the training business; we are in the automotive business." The training staff works in tandem with line managers at all levels. When developing training goals and programs, staff members ask themselves these questions:

- What is the company supposed to be doing?
- What do people need to achieve to be a success?
- How do we measure success?
- What is the gap between what people need and what they have?
- How do we close that gap in the best, fastest way possible?

One of the postal organizations in the study aligns the activities of all employees in support of organizational goals, to which end training's role is to eliminate deficiencies and to give employees tools they need to make the postal business succeed.

At the retail chain, training is used at multiple levels to create a strong "guest culture" for customers—a goal that is articulated frequently by the company's top leaders as critical to the chain's success.

In all of the benchmarked companies, training is aligned clearly with senior management priorities and used to communicate and reinforce key organizational and business goals, articulated regularly and consistently by top management.

Employee involvement. The survey of improvement-driven organizations determined that in high-performance organizations, employees understand the link between their work and company strategies more clearly than do employees in low-performing organizations. Employees in high-performance organizations work continuously to improve work processes and to ensure that products and services meet customers' needs. And quality improvement is an important factor in employees' performance evaluations.

Those findings suggest that in high-performance organizations, it's likely that there is a tight fit between training programs and people's jobs. There also seems to be a stronger link between training and HRD systems (such as performance evaluation) than typically found in low-performing organizations. Employees in high-performance organizations also tend to have more ownership of their job performance and employability.

Of the high-performance organizations in the benchmarking study, three have development curricula linked to people's jobs. One has an automated assessment instrument employees use to determine whether particular courses are appropriate; another views employee development as part of a larger process that includes selection, training, and job rotation; and another (the retail chain) requires at least one employee at each store to participate in Disney's customer-service training to ensure that employees learn customer service from an industry leader.

At the computer-parts maker, the training philosophy is that each employee is responsible for his or her employability. Though there aren't any specific training requirements, employees are expected to work closely with their managers on development plans that ensure that the employees develop the necessary skills for high-tech, precision-oriented jobs.

The company views training not just as a way to equip people to do their jobs, but also as a way to ensure a good fit between workers and their jobs. Top executives are compensated, in part, on the degree to which training helps assimilate employees into the company successfully.

At several companies in the benchmarking study (especially at the telecommunications firm), employees are expected to take much of the responsibility for their own development, though the companies provide training and evaluation systems with which to assess, monitor, and improve employees' performance.

Innovation. The survey of improvement-driven organizations showed that they provide a more favorable climate for developing and implementing new ideas than do low-performing companies. In high-performance organizations, ideas for new products and services originate at many levels, and employees' innovative ideas are accepted readily by management.

Those findings suggest that high-performance organizations emphasize learning and innovation. In fact, innovation is seen frequently in such areas as course design, development, delivery, and evaluation.

The telecommunications firm uses a game format (jeopardy, tic-tac-toe, and so forth) to create pre- and post-tests that can be delivered, administered, and scored via e-mail. That test system, developed by an outside contractor, enables the firm to vary the content of evaluations and fosters learning even before participants attend a course.

To deliver its training, the computer-parts maker uses a mix of sophisticated CBT and multimedia.

Other companies not in the study, such as Federal Express, use embedded desktop learning to enhance the professionalism of their front-line service people. Some firms, such as Motorola, are implementing robotics and virtual reality as part of their training delivery. (See the box, The Motorola Story: An Interview.)

Many high-performance organizations use groupware and other software to facilitate senior-level meetings, group learning sessions, and team brainstorming. (See "Meetings Go High-Tech" by Jim Clark and Richard Koonce, *Training & Development,* November 1995.) Groupware enables users to collect and organize participants' input instantly and verbatim. Groupware can also speed the evaluation, rejection, and adoption of new ideas. And it can help people develop new business approaches and gain consensus because it lets them contribute opinions anonymously. That privacy facilitates creative discussion and learning among people who are uncomfortable being on record before they know how others stand.

Process improvement. How do high-performance organizations treat the issue of process improvement? Although many companies claim to improve work and business processes continuously, top-performing organizations actually do. For example, most respondents of the 1994 survey said they "strongly agreed" that customer satisfaction data are used to drive process improvements. Respondents from low-performing organizations generally disagreed.

High-performance organizations in the benchmarking study have several mechanisms for ensuring the continuous improvement of training approaches and content. For example, to reduce cycle time, the training organizations of the telecommunications firm operate fluidly when programs need developing or updating, sort of like SWAT teams to bring in as many people as needed. Subject matter experts (SMEs) or contractors design and develop courses to eliminate the "hand-off and wait time" that usually occurs when SMEs aren't involved in design and development. To ensure continuous improvement in training programs, training staff operate as internal consultants actively engaged with clients in brainstorming problems and developing customized programs.

That approach is also used by the computer-systems firm and the auto manufacturer. The computer-systems firm has three distinct training groups: delivery, development, and marketing and needs assessment. Members of the latter group serve as performance consultants and help determine appropriate training interventions.

Training staff at the auto manufacturer have been repositioned as performance improvement specialists. Their needs analyses are seen as the front door to potential solutions to business problems, of which training may be only one.

Says a senior training manager, "Training isn't always the only answer to performance issues here. Sometimes it's not even the preferred way. We might suggest job aids, self-paced learning, or a job redesign." Performance interventions are customized to fit individual employees or a group.

Improvement measurement. Closely linked with process improvement is improvement measurement. High-performance organizations in the 1994 survey paid more attention to improvement measurement than low-performing organizations. High-performance organizations recognize the importance of using multiple measurements such as quality, cost, and time to assess organizational performance. Top-performing companies also recognize that a single measure (for example, quality) is an insufficient benchmark for gauging business performance.

We found, in general, that HRD professionals in high-performance organizations focus more attention on such issues as shortening cycle times; reducing costs; and improving quality in products, services, and training than their counterparts in lesser-performing organizations. HRD professionals in high-performance organizations are knowledgeable about such topics as supply chain management and the reduction of product defect rates. In fact, their work often involves conducting interventions and measuring improvements in such areas.

The auto manufacturer has a detailed system for evaluating training impact at multiple levels, including how well employees assimilate new learning, how that affects productivity and behavioral change at the work level, and how those affect return on investment. Evaluation criteria are interdependent and linked with specific courses.

The computer-parts maker routinely conducts cost-benefit analyses on training in an attempt to ascertain nearly 80 percent of the time what value and impact training has (by program) across the company. Focus groups determine the questions to ask training participants, sending them and their supervisors on-line evaluation surveys on a random basis.

Though high-performance organizations pay more attention to improvement measurement in the area of training than low-performing organizations, they don't always collect hard data to determine training ROI Many still rely on evaluation tools and historical experience for feedback and as a basis for evaluating training effectiveness and improvement.

Change management. Conventional thinking suggests that the management of organizational change is, at best, undisciplined and isn't easy to track, monitor, or assess.

Yet, the benchmarked high-performance organizations have strong links between change management activities and other business activities, including training. For instance, the auto manufacturer uses training to accelerate job redesign, as it continues to restructure and reposition to compete more effectively.

In one of the postal organizations, training is a principal driver of large-scale change. The training helps eliminate bureaucracy, improve efficiency, and make the company more market-driven and customer-friendly. The retail chain uses training to create a culture of customer-friendly stores.

Several high-performance organizations in the benchmarking study use training as the basis for continuous process improvement which is, in fact, the way to operationalize a culture change at the transactional level where the work is done.

All of the organizations in the study have communicated to employees a compelling need for change as the reason jobs are being redesigned, processes are being reengineered, and people are being asked to work in new and different ways. Training serves as the vehicle for operationalizing and sustaining the changes.

All of the organizations also focus on such variables as empowering front-line workers

through new management approaches and on appropriate links between HRD systems and training goals.

A Change Engine

Clearly, training's new role in high-performance organizations is far from the traditional, stove piped function that it used to be and still is in many companies.

In high-performance organizations, training is emerging to play a critical, integrative role as a driver of cultural change, process alignment, job redesign, and continuous improvement. In a very real sense, it is serving as a change engine to help generate an organization's resilience and core competencies. Those are the success traits an organization needs to compete effectively in a constantly changing, often turbulent business environment.

So, what do those changes spell for us as HR professionals? Whether or not we work in a high-performance organization, we must step out of our traditional roles as trainers, course presenters, and instructional designers to play more active and substantive roles as change agents, internal consultants, and business partners with such people as executives and line managers. We must be able to operate effectively at a high level in our organizations to help them develop and implement new business visions and strategies. We also have to operate at the day-to-day work level to help line managers and reengineering teams redesign key work processes. Then, we can help ensure that our organizations achieve and sustain effectiveness and vitality into the next century.

It's time to step up to the plate. We must be adaptable, resourceful, and resilient if we are to work with executives, line managers, process owners, and teams. They are our colleagues and our customers.

The Motorola Story: An Interview

Training and a strong learning ethic are embedded parts of Motorola's culture. The company has learned that a few dollars spent on training translates to process improvement and empowered workers. Those are key ingredients of business success in an industry in which rapid response and the accelerated application of new learning in areas from manufacturing to billing make the difference between lackluster performance and marketplace dominance.

In this interview, coauthor Richard Koonce talks with Vince Serritella, director of planning, quality, and communications at Motorola University. Serritella discusses the company's training philosophy and how, from a structural and organizational point of view, it strives to align training with the continuously evolving needs of the business.

Koonce: *Talk a little about the philosophy of Motorola University. What role does it play in helping organizational and individual learning?*

Serritella: It acts as a change agent within Motorola. It's the role of Motorola University to understand, design, and develop learning interventions to drive critical business issues. We balance being responsive to what our customers are asking for with the need to think about long term learning interventions and initiatives that may be needed to deal successfully with market pressures 10 or 15 years down the road.

So, you strive to balance "here and now" training needs with strategic planning for training throughout the company?

That's right. We're the strategic training organization of the company, but we still do a lot of tactical training development and delivery because our customers request it.

How do you achieve that balance?

First, you have to be an organization that prizes integrated thinking. We're at an advantage because Motorola University has strong competencies in research and instructional design. That enables us to envision the company's future requirements for training and education. For example, we have a high-end instructional design team that works with Motorola's high-end technologists to develop technology road maps. But the balancing core competency is training delivery through each of our 14 delivery centers. The centers sit, live, and breathe with our customers on a global basis.

You also have training operations in each of Motorola's business units. How do the delivery centers relate to those?

They are networked into the HRD training organizations in all of the units. That is one of the ways that we maintain our training balance. Our high-end instructional systems designers run an empirically based, technology-based, and road map-based instructional systems design process that builds great training programs. On the other hand, that process is balanced with the people in the business unit, who are being hit every day with customer needs and business realities.

Do Motorola University's training endeavors overlap with or intersect with what's happening in the business units?

We have an integrated business training planning process between Motorola University and the business units. In addition, our lead managers from the design centers and delivery centers are involved directly in identifying the business units' critical business issues, because they work closely with the units' key managers.

Then, is it fair to say that, organizationally speaking, Motorola is more disciplined and structured than most companies for ensuring that training is aligned with business needs?

The Motorola Story (continued)

Compared to the companies that come here to benchmark us, especially across an entire industrial university like ours, Motorola is more disciplined than a lot of them. But we're not nearly as disciplined as we want to be. That's our challenge.

Where do you feel your performance gap is? What still needs to happen?

We need an even tighter linkage between business planning and strategic quality planning. At the moment, they run parallel, and they need to intersect. They do intersect, but not often enough or systematically enough. That's one challenge.

Another challenge is to make sure our overall business training planning is more integrated with the training planning that goes on in each of the business units.

Motorola is doing some innovative things with training delivery. Can you talk about that?

We've integrated an "emerging technologies" team into each of our design centers. We now say to all of our design, development, and distribution people, "You have to think about alternative delivery every step of the way as you design and develop programs." And we're moving ahead with alternative delivery systems. About 25 percent of our training courses are ready to go on the Web or our Intranet via satellite delivery, CBT, or e-mail and CD ROM. We also have advanced teaching-manufacturing laboratories and a virtual reality lab.

When and how did you make the move to using virtual reality?

In one instance, our premier advanced manufacturing lab replicated a line of pagers. However, it was so costly that we knew we couldn't build a bunch of labs like that and ship them around the world. Moreover, the labs aren't something you can loan, put in a box, and send for six months to Motorola's operation in Tianjin, China, for example. So, our Technology Education Center said, "Virtual reality is the next logical approach." Now, we have three VR courses, all pieces of the advanced manufacturing lab. In addition, we have a lab in robotics.

Besides the savings, what makes the labs a powerful learning tool?

For one thing, the technology is so user friendly that everyone from manufacturing associates to lead engineers can use it. Fifth graders have worked in some parts of the VR lab when they have visited Motorola University and our Museum of Electronics.

Talk about why Motorola decided that it had to integrate training into line functions and operations.

There are many reasons. Almost half of Motorola's employees are outside the United States, so globalization is one factor that forced us to coordinate and integrate training across the company. (Another factor) is technological complexity. We recognize that no one training organization in Motorola can do it all. The training organizations in our business units play a critical role in training and developing people in the units. But those organizations recognize that training is always a make-buy decision. So, a partnership approach among our training organizations is critical if we are to succeed and cover everything.

But perhaps most importantly, Motorola recognizes that training no matter how and where it's delivered is a key competitive advantage. There's more awareness of that than ever. Motorola is doing a good job of building systems solutions for its customers. As a result, we have to be integrated and matrixed if we're going to support those kinds of efforts. If you're not integrated and matrixed, you're not going to get there.

The Motorola Story *(continued)*

Does Motorola's integrated, strategic approach to training relate to technical training only? Or does it also relate to soft skills training?

It's used for everything we develop and deliver. That's because our training has cross-functional impact. Our manufacturing processes, for example, have embedded knowledge that exists in many other parts of the company, areas such as billing and order entry. Because our business processes are interdependent, the way we work in one area of the company has to be mirrored elsewhere.

That's why a big part of the curriculum has to do with administrative cycle time. Cycle time is as critical in administrative services as it is in manufacturing.

More than many companies, Motorola values training for its own sake. Why?

That's true. We have what one consultant humorously called, "a cosmic appreciation of training." That's due in large part to the strategic vision of Bob Galvin, son of Motorola's founder. He continues to be a strong proponent of learning and is very active in the company, still pushing everyone: "What are you learning? Are you learning the right things?" Another variable is that when we began our renaissance in quality in the late 1970s, under Bob's leadership, we developed a strong appreciation for the fact that you can't empower people and drive decision making down to the individual level unless you give people the tools. It's great to say, "You're empowered to stop the line." But you have to teach people when and why to stop the line. Every time we put a dollar against training to drive one of our quality initiatives, we get enormous benefits.

Can you give an example?

We run an "I recommend" program that is a sort of a bottoms up suggestion program on how everyone in the company can reduce waste in cycle time, administrative processes, or manufacturing. We found that as we put people through training in decision making, teamwork, how to run effective meetings, and how to design cycle time for manufacturability, the quality of suggestions increased enormously. It didn't take a rocket scientist to figure out that training works.

We've been religious about measuring quality, cycle time, and customer satisfaction. We've kept the discipline and rigor of training, not just in Motorola University but also across the company. And that has helped build a companywide appreciation for how critical training and education are to this company's success.

Creating a Business Strategy for the Training and Development Function

By Sue Lodgen

Audience ➤	Learning Professionals, Training Departments, HR Professionals
Purpose ➤	—Learn a process for creating a T&D business strategy —Understand how to use the process in different business contexts
Suggested Uses ➤	Self-study Tools for workgroup developing strategy

Why Strategy, Why Now?

Developing business strategy has not necessarily been a core competence of Training and Development professionals. Some have done it well. But all need to do it now to build a strong, aligned, value-creating, and valued Learning/Training and Development function.

- Performance improvement requires it. The old Training and Development (T&D) function is moving, or has already moved, toward performance improvement. Now learning professionals find themselves clearly expected to drive toward the same return on investment standard as the rest of the people in the business. Performance and learning professionals must understand business performance goals. Inevitably they have to know the business strategies, and define the training strategies to support these.

- The intensification of global competition requires it. It has been a while since companies made money just by being there. Companies see that if they do not carefully coordinate their resources they will water down their efforts, waste resources, pay out more cash than they take in, and eventually lose in a competitive market-

place. Companies that are not finely coordinated actually destroy value and cause the company to decline over time. Companies have rethought their business processes to ensure this coordination. Now many companies insist that *every* core and support process be organized to serve the customer and produce value. They have developed a fine eye for the unnecessary. Task forces will emerge to redesign processes that appear redundant, inefficient, or not targeted to the business purposes and customer. In this very valid context, training cannot afford to do things that are "valuable" only in some looser sense. It must clearly support the overall business strategy.

- Reengineering requires it. T&D functions themselves are in many places just now going through the process of reengineering that has made its way through much of the rest of the organization. Redesign of T&D processes must be built on absolute clarity about the learning/training strategy to support the business directions. If not, the T&D function is likely to be arbitrarily diminished, poorly redesigned, or outsourced.

- The shift to seeing HR and learning professionals as business partners requires it. HR functions in the past often focused primarily on administrative, personal, and developmental support of the company's people. Often HR was an employee advocate. Increasingly, now HR is being asked to focus instead on the success of the business. HR is driving to create value, take accountability for results, and communicate to the business in the language of business about results it achieves for the business. The move to performance improvement in T&D is a part of this same rethinking. The participant-pleasing activities and favorable smile sheet ratings of yesterday that marked a successful training event are today certainly seen as nice but secondary. The real business of learning in companies is creating value. Like other HR people, learning professionals will need to be, and be perceived as, business partners. Building a business-focused training strategy is one means of becoming a business partner.

- The growing importance of human capital as a competitive advantage requires it. Finally, companies are increasingly aware that in a global marketplace, one of the few durable advantages they can have is people. Strategic learning processes take on a new urgency.

So lining up T&D with the organization strategies and priorities is critical to performance improvement, creating value—and being valued. Below is a simple process for accomplishing this alignment, a process of defining the training strategies that will support the business priorities.

What's Hard About This Process

Here's what's hard about doing a business strategy for T&D:

- We may not be "business people" ourselves in the sense of having the habit of mind that primarily focuses on creating shareholder value. Thinking this way requires learning new habits.
- We may not be placed in the organization in a way that gives us insight into the business directions. That's a real handicap, not just to this process, but to our credibility and employment. But we can use this process to better position ourselves.

- The HR function within which we sit may not have a business strategy. That's okay. We can work within that context and maybe catalyze strategic activity in the larger HR function.
- We don't have a process. The intent of this article is to provide a simple, feasible process that a training manager, perhaps with some appropriate support, can use with dramatic outcomes.

The Basic Business Strategy Steps

The basic T&D business strategy process—its input and output, and the process of working through to the output—is fundamentally the same across many situations.

1. **Determine the business requirements** and how to support them. Secure, understand, and lay out the business's strategy, initiatives, and value drivers. These constitute the requirements that you must support.

2. **Line up the HR business strategy** to address the critical business value drivers. The T&D strategy, in ideal circumstances, is part of the HR strategy to respond to the business requirements.

3. **Frame the broad T&D business strategy** within this context: Define what training must do to support these business and HR requirements.

4. **Develop a detailed T&D strategy.** Within each "arena" of training activity, identify the implications of the training strategy.

5. **Complete T&D planning and implementation.** Use the strategy framework provided to drive and shape specific training initiatives and plans.

Each of the steps will be described in detail below. Even with the detail, it's not easy to "just do" the steps. The steps must be accomplished in the context of different organizational structures and politics. Organizations are different in structure; business strategies are developed to different extents in these organizations; HR strategies are developed to different extents in the organizations; and T&D people are positioned differently in these organizations. Because of these contextual issues, we have presented each step of the strategy process descriptions below into two parts: dealing with the context, and carrying out the steps.

Step 1: Determine the Business Requirements and How to Support Them

Dealing with the Context

Several situations, and combinations of these, can affect the way in which the training function goes about developing the training business strategy.

- The business has well-defined goals, strategy, initiatives, and priorities. This is the easiest situation. Request a print copy of these to use in formulating T&D business strategy. Proceed to process step 1A below.
- The business has little strategy, but a plan with many current initiatives. It is unlikely that you will be able to inspire the leadership team to develop a strategy only in order to meet your needs. Probably you can work with the plan and initiatives. Proceed to process step 1D below.
- The business has no defined strategy, goals, etc. This is a tough one. You have three choices: (1) draft what you think the strategy is, based on evidence of action, and proceed to step 1D; (2) if the unit's actions show no evidence of strategy or direction, decide what you think the main business directions should be, and draft a training strategy based on that, starting with step 1C; or (3) send out your resume.
- The T&D function is not seen as a business partner, and/or does not participate in the business's strategy process, and/or has weak connections with senior management. This is common. Because this strategic process can help position you

---

Critical Success Factors for the T&D Strategy

Doing this process successfully requires that certain elements be in place.

▶ *Clarity that creating value is the goal for Human Resources.* Human Resources must agree that creating value means creating shareholder value. It does not mean doing those many things that Human Resources people or people in general may find "worthwhile" or "valuable."

▶ *Company and/or line of business articulation of its strategy.* Human Resources must ensure that the business unit has defined its strategy before undertaking the HR plan. On the other hand, often the HR strategy process can be used to facilitate clarification of the company strategy.

▶ *Focus.* Human Resources must define which among the many possible "valuable" pursuits of Human Resources it will undertake to achieve value for the business.

▶ *Agreement.* The HR and T&D strategy must be agreed to by the business leaders.

▶ *Buy-in to T&D Roles, Processes, Skills.* The new strategy often requires new HR and T&D roles, processes, and sometimes structures, as well as function skills. These must be identified as one outcome of the process. The next, planning step, will determine how to achieve these.

▶ *Starting from business unit needs versus starting from current HR/T&D.* At many companies, there has been an inclination to "justify" Human Resources and T&D plans by loosely verbalizing some form of connection between what Human Resources has already been doing or intending to do, and the initiatives identified by the business for the plan year. This is what we call "starting from current HR." In fact, the current Human Resources/T&D directions may not be the services of highest priority to achieving business unit results. It is important that business unit Human Resources/T&D be willing to "start from business unit needs" rather than from those things already in progress.

---

better, we suggest moving forward with step 1A. Determine who in the organization is the owner of the written strategy, and ask for a copy, communicating your interest in better understanding the organization's future so that you can be sure training will be positioned to respond to it. Subsequent steps will reinforce your reputation as someone who cares about the organization.

- The Human Resources function is not seen as a business partner, and/or does not participate in the business's strategy process, and/or has weak connections with senior management. You will be tarred with the same brush unless you take actions, as above, to differentiate yourself. But this may also be an opportunity to do all of the above work in collaboration with the VP of HR. Here you can contribute to building the whole department. Work in a team with a small group of HR people, with the VP's blessing, to undertake the tasks starting at step 1A below.

Carrying Out the Steps

1A. Get strategy and/or plan document. Review it. Underline it. Work to understand it. Be sure you understand what the unit perceives as the major challenges and opportunities in the business environment, since these will shape its strategies. *They may be, for example, an increasingly competitive environment for the company's main product, higher cost structure than competitors, or changes in environmental regulation affecting the company.*

1B. Identify the major goals of the unit. Summarize these, including measures where available. *For example, a goal may be to achieve a 20 percent return on equity by doubling total U.S. market share and controlling costs at today's level.* (Although two of those goals are means to the larger end, and therefore, in a sense, strategies, they do not really tell you how the unit will approach achieving the goals. An approach is really a strategy.)

1C. Summarize in outline form the important strategies to achieve these goals.

This involves articulating what the business has decided to do to succeed. *For example, is it expanding export markets? Moving facilities overseas? Developing a new higher margin business? An important strategy to double market share may be to offer new lines of products targeted to ethnic communities.*

1D. Identify the major initiatives to achieve these strategies and lay them into your outline. Strategies are good, but initiatives drive action. Generally, the executives will have articulated the major thrusts they will use to achieve a particular strategy. *Initiatives related to the ethnic market strategy might include market research to define the ethnic communities that are the most promising targets, and redesigning the product and distribution system to effectively approach these markets.*

1E. Get from the business unit manager or an equivalent "owner" of the plans the most important unit priorities among the large list of strategies and initiatives. Companies have hundreds of initiatives, and you probably do not have the resources to support them all. It will help you to understand which priorities they rank as most critical to the achievement of unit goals over the next 1–2 years. You will want confirmation that consensus on the priorities exists— or you risk being blindsided. We recommend a "run it up the flagpole" process here, in which you sit with the "owners" of the plans with the request for (1) review/validation of your summary of goals, strategies, and initiatives to be sure it is current and correct, and (2) prioritization of the initiatives. This process builds the relationship and the perception of you as a business partner. Priorities require consensus of top management.

Prioritization is best accomplished by getting two ratings on each initiative: (1) criticality to the business's targeted results and financial performance, and (2) magnitude of gap between the current situation and the effective implementation of this initiative. We usually use a 5-point scale for each. As a result of this effort, you should be able to lay the strategies out on a matrix like the one below.

Step 2: Line up the HR Business Strategy

Dealing with the Context

In an ideal world, the HR vision and strategy will have already been completed by the time you initiate your T&D strategy, and the process of having developed it will roughly fit the description below. Most importantly, it will focus on support of the business value drivers, and will have agreement from the leaders of the business. However, in the real world, probably less than half of HR departments have completed a business strategy. You must work with the HR function's situation as it is, without simply acquiescing

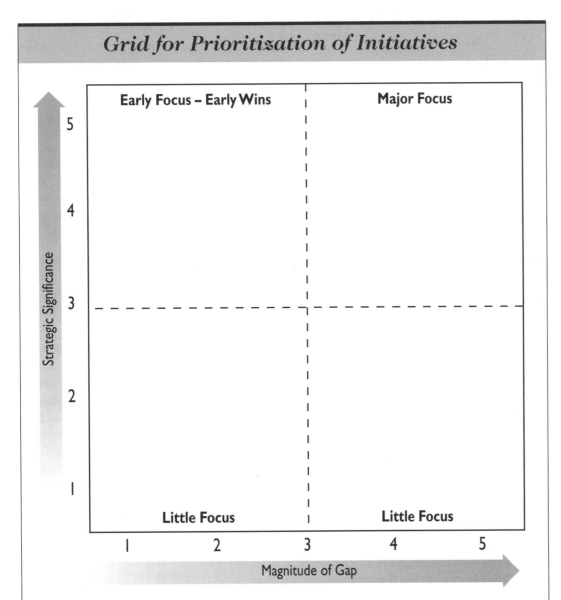

Grid for Prioritization of Initiatives

Early Focus – Early Wins · Major Focus

Strategic Significance

Little Focus · Little Focus

Magnitude of Gap

Laying out this matrix using these criteria helps focus on the real "value drivers" of the unit, i.e., those directions that are absolutely essential to the unit's achieving success. The value drivers are the directions that HR and T&D must certainly support. By the end of this step, you will have a more solid understanding of the business, a better relationship with business management, and a strong sense of the business's priorities, which constitute a framework for your strategy.

to a strategy that is not in support of the business. Likely situations include the following:

- The HR function has completed a strategy that fits the description below, and perhaps has tasked you with developing the next level, i.e., your own T&D strategy. Go for it. Use the HR strategy and business strategy as guidance, and move on to step 2C below.

- The HR function has not completed a strategy but is interested in doing so. Offer yourself as a part of the team, and work through all the steps below.

- The HR function has completed a strategy that is not a business strategy but believes it is well done. Very often, you will be able to build on this base, focusing on T&D, and firmly linking the T&D strategy to the business strategy. By doing so, you may be able to infuse the HR strategy process with business input by a process of influence or osmosis. Here you will start with the business strategy steps, 1A–1E above, and proceed to step 2A below. If, however, this is clearly impolitic, you again have the resume option.

- The HR function has not completed a strategy, and you view it as unlikely that they will want to. Go through the steps 1A-E and 2A-F yourself for the purpose of building your training strategy only, and run the draft results up the flagpole to the VP of HR before moving on to the training strategy. Success in this process requires an HR function that will accept your intent as aligning training with the business and not perceive you as presumptuous for this effort.

Carrying Out the Steps

2A. Using the business goals, strategies, and initiatives as guidance, define HR goals for the next several years. For example, HR must support the drive to:

   —*Rapid revenue growth through the ethnic market initiative.*

   —*Cost reduction in all noncritical areas to contribute to price competitiveness in the marketplace.*

   —*An effective transition to an Enterprise Resource Information System to ensure best-in-class coordination*

of all efforts in service of the customer.

This task is generally done by the HR directors and the VP of HR, based on the previous work in understanding the business strategy. In some situations, these business requirements are simply the value drivers of the business, as identified in the business strategy above. But some of those may be irrelevant to HR, and these may be eliminated from the business requirements that HR tasks itself to meet. *For example, possible restructuring of the company's financing is critical to the business, but it may have little need for HR support.* It is important to summarize, and to limit, these business requirements and to get agreement from the business leaders that priorities chosen in fact shape HR's mandate. The agreement with the business leaders constitutes a step in HR's partnership with the business. We generally go to the business leadership—the senior HR team with the senior business team—with the list of proposed requirements, have an hour's discussion with them, make some modifications, and let them know we will be coming back to them with a proposed HR strategy, also for their concurrence.

2B. Define the HR requirements/strategies to support the business requirements. Human Resources now undertakes a process of identifying HR requirements for each HR area through which the function supports the business value drivers. Use the HR support processes or major arenas of work to shape the brainstorming about what will be required of HR:

- Leadership effectiveness

- Organization, team, and job design

- Development of individual and team capabilities

- Staffing; selection

- HR management processes

- HR systems

- Rewards and recognition, including compensation and benefit

- Work culture

You may find that you want to break out the HR arenas in a different way, but we recommend that you break them out with at least this level of detail.

Then a matrix like the one below guides the brainstorming work effort.

— Deal with each business requirement broadly first. Brainstorm what the requirement will demand of people, leadership, and the organization that

thinking about the implications for each arena of HR. Summarize your broad conclusions about the HR implications of each business requirement.

— Now discuss the content of "the boxes." Go across each business requirement row, brainstorming about the implications of this requirement and its demands on people, the organization, and leadership, for each HR

Brainstorming Matrix

Business Requirements	Leadership Effectiveness	Organization, Team, and Job Design	Individual and Team Capabilities	HR Management Processes	HR Systems	Rewards and Recognition	Work Culture
Growth Through Ethnic Marketing							

may not currently be in place. *For example, if the company intends to pursue ethnic markets, it may be very clear that it lacks representation of ethnic groups in the marketing function, lacks understanding of the buying decisions and values of the target populations, and has historically had a very slow process of bringing new products to market.* Brainstorming here will frame your

arena. This takes time. It works best when the people in charge of or involved in each arena draft up possibilities before a senior-level HR meeting, giving the meeting more substance to work with. You will need at least an hour per business requirement, and very likely more. A notetaker should record the conclusions, and lay key words for the conclusions in the matrix. The completed matrix will very likely be illuminating about the future directions required of the function.

2C. Set priorities. After completion of each business requirement, participants stand back and summarize the implications of that requirement for HR. Which of the efforts are absolutely critical to success? Which represent the biggest HR gaps versus the current situation? The conclusions about importance and gaps are arrayed on a matrix such as that used for the business "value drivers." The matrix now defines the HR value drivers, the most critical arenas for HR work.

2D. Ensure leadership concurrence with the HR directions. The senior HR leadership agrees on coordinated priorities and directions, and organizes these by business initiative (not by HR function,

yet). They present these to the business leaders, modify as needed, and agree on the HR priorities to support the business directions. There are subsequent steps: HR priorities are not yet initiatives with measurable outcomes, for example. But that is for a subsequent stage of planning.

2E. Organize by HR arena. Finally, with the business's concurrence to the HR directions, lay these directions out by HR arena or function. You may find that there is no current HR function responsible for some critical HR directions. That kind of major discovery is the value of this bigger-picture HR thinking.

2F. Develop strategies to achieve the directions. Now the HR functions or arenas have their broad marching orders, and can begin to think through what

Brainstorming Matrix

Business Requirements	Leadership Effectiveness	Organization, Team, and Job Design	Individual and Team Capabilities	HR Management Processes	HR Systems	Rewards and Recognition	Work Culture
Growth Through Ethnic Marketing	Senior leadership that "looks like" America, and articulates these values	Teams across marketing, R&D, production, sales	Managing in diverse teams New product to market process skills	Fair performance management, unbiased by majority assumptions		Rewards for effective speed to market	A culture of valuing differences and change

the business requirements/HR directions mean for them. And they can do so with the confidence that the HR elements will be aligned in support of the business direction. Research is very strong in showing that only the system of HR practices creates value, i.e., economic validation of what you have long known in training: It must be a process, not an event.

By the end of the HR strategic process, T&D has a clear understanding of its direction, certainty that its directions will be coordinated with the directions of other HR functions, and confidence that these directions support the organization and have buy-in from the leadership. The business partnership has become stronger.

Steps 3 and 4: Define the T&D Strategy, First Broadly, Then in Detail

Dealing with the Context

The head of T&D cannot work alone on the T&D strategy. Now is the time to bring in the other senior T&D leadership of the unit. Their involvement at this point ensures that they will understand the business requirements, the HR direction, and the implications for T&D. They will all be marching to the same drummer. The strategy process is a significant builder of leadership in T&D.

Carrying Out the Steps

3/4A. Brief the T&D leadership team on the business requirements, HR directions, and directions given to date to T&D. Review all the elements in columns on the HR matrix that bear on training/learning/development. Review the specific functional summary of elements that relate to training.

3/4B. Get input on what this means specifically for T&D. Input, of course, makes the strategy stronger and builds understanding and commitment. You are looking here for broad conclusions; *for example, the training function must represent the targeted ethnic mix; we must work in partnership with R&D and marketing to develop a new product to market process, train in it, and implement it.*

Step 5: T&D Planning and Implementation

Now you are on to the part that is recognizably the training strategy. You have built an understanding of the business unit's directions, strengthened the support of those directions by the HR function, and developed the partnership of HR with the business. You have also built the understanding that you need to make a business strategy for the training function. At this point, depending on how the process has gone, probably all of the units reporting to HR have developed the general framework for their strategies, and are ready to detail that framework for their individual functions.

Dealing with the Context

The best process here involves developing the business strategy for training with a small core of training people in the business, and then getting validation for that strategy by reviewing and refining it with the senior business people. Ideally, the end point is a "contract," real or implied, about the nature of training support you will provide to the business. There are several context variants:

- **You are a solo training person for the business.** This is a hard job to do as a solo. We suggest that you work the process described below with a partner in a similar role in another HR function, raising issues for discussion as you go. This will continue to build your understanding of the business and the implications of business issues for training, and will ensure that you have wider perspective and alternatives. We estimate a full day for this work.

- **You have a group of direct reports, trainers, designers, or administrators.** They are not experienced in thinking strategically. You may not be certain of their developmental potential in this area. You have two choices. You and your colleague can work the training strategy as above, and bring it to your direct reports for review and refinement. This contributes to their development and to their commitment to the business strategy, and it eliminates the difficulty of actually doing the creating together in a group with little experience. On the other hand, this is a real "teachable moment." If you can make yourself comfortable enough with the process to facilitate it with your group, the shared struggle to create the training business strategy will strengthen and coalesce your group. If you need assistance on the facilitation, you may seek it from someone who has done this before, or who was on the HR team that developed the strategy.

- **The business unit expects Training and Development to ask how high when requested to jump, and not to have a strategy.** This is, in part, the business unit's contribution to Training not being a business partner. This is the line perspective that produces a laundry list of training "needs" such as "communication skills, supervision, motivation, management," and then results in cutting the training department as inessential when business is tough. If you explain to them your process of lining up against their strategy, they will understand that you can be both a business partner and also responsive to more short-term needs. Make the process of review of T&D strategy educational for them; show clearly the link from business strategy to change to core understanding and competencies, to training. Get them to prioritize the key training "value drivers." The result will be a training organization more tightly linked with the business.

Carrying Out the Steps

Now you will be working to detail the implications for training of the business and HR requirements outlined previously. Again, this involves working in a matrix-like fashion, where the left side of the matrix will be the prioritized requirements for the human resources function in support of the business requirements. Or, if the HR function did not define a strategy, it lists the key business requirements or "value drivers" themselves.

In looking at the training function, you must consider where training support will be required. Lay out the following categories across the top of the matrix, and work through the implications of each business/HR requirement for each of these arenas. (You may find you want to use the matrix just to tick off each area you have considered, while recording the actual thinking work separately.)

5A. **Training support required by each strategic area/reasons.** List here the kinds of training support required for each strategic area, and the reasons for this. *For example, the critical value driver of increasing globalization of sales may require training in global business strategy, global marketing, global sales force management, and perhaps managing across diverse cultures. Reasons might include the fact that the company has never before undertaken any cross-geography marketing.*

5B. **Changes requiring training support.** Because training is one support available for organization change, it is useful to summarize the changes that will be required. This helps T&D ensure that it plays the right roles in change and that other aspects of managing the change are in place. *For example, executives must change from being domestically focused to globally focused; the entire marketing and production process must change from assuming that the U.S. way is the only way, to recognizing that the United States is one market, and driving toward efficient production and marketing across markets.* Considering these changes may help identify additional training support required. *For example, now you know that training may be required in producing for world markets.*

5C. **Messages to be incorporated in training.** If the company must change to drive its new strategy, there will be some messages that must be incorporated across all training, not just in designated training programs. This ensures that training helps support the entire change process. The entire "face" of training to the organization must change. Here you list the key messages that will be driven into the organization over the strategic period. Here you formulate these, get revisions as needed and, by so doing, both link training to the business and help the company formulate its key messages. *For example, The world is our world.*

All management is global management. Every business must be number 1 or 2 globally, or it will not be a part of our strategic future.

5D. Competencies; skills, knowledge/understanding, attitude/focus; requirements for competency definition. At this point, you do not know what competencies will be required by the new strategy, but there will be some clear areas in which new configurations of competencies will be essential for success. Here you identify the probable level or job role areas requiring competency definition and probably assessment as vehicles for defining hiring, promotion, and T&D processes. Doing these competency definitions becomes part of your strategic plan. By incorporating this into the training strategy and getting buy-in from the executives, you shape their expectations for this process. *For example, at least four roles will change to drive the new globalization strategy: global executives, global managers, global marketing and selling managers and professionals, and global manufacturing and distribution professionals and managers.*

5E. Leadership linkages. Above and beyond the new competencies required for executives, there may be roles that leadership will need to take in driving the training. These should be flagged here, up front, in the training strategy, to shape executive expectations of their roles. *For example, presumably senior executives would want to kick off the training in global marketing, strategy, etc., and if that training is action learning focused on the company's own critical initiatives, it would want to define the work initiatives in which managers participate.*

5F. Communication linkages. Because in some ways training is the small group medium for communication, and there are many other media, you will want to achieve good timing linkages with the communication function, and with the executives, as they roll their messages out to the organization. Each training class or process becomes an opportunity for them to give a broader message. *For example, you may flag here that the company global marketing initiatives undertaken by each successive class will also be the occasion for articles in each company newsletter.*

5G. Organizational levels and locations requiring training. This gives you a chance to consider the entire organization, current and future. Which levels and geographies will need training and/or development to achieve the new strategy? *For example, hiring the new Far East sales force will require a competency definition for the role, then a targeted selection process for the interviewers, and then the sales force will need product training immediately upon hiring. This tells you something about timing as well as about the need for resources in the Far East.*

5H. Implications for training media. Now you can draw some conclusions about the appropriate media for training. *For example, because the global marketing and sales management training involves a major cultural change, you may propose that this requires getting cross-geography groups together in action-learning sessions. On the other hand, the targeted selection training, which must be accomplished simultaneously, globally, and is an individual skill, may be provided on CD-ROM with some certification through the company's Intranet.*

5I. Implications for staff/resources. Similarly, now you can draw some conclusions about staff and resources required. For shorter-term needs, you will want to partner with outside firms with specific expertise. For longer-term needs, you may need hires with specific capabilities located in specific geographical regions. *For example, it may have become clear that you will need a training expert in global manufacturing strategy and processes to provide service to the unit's several dozen plants over several years. You may see that you need to line up resources for competency definition and assessment, with Internet capabilities.*

5J. **Probable investment requirements.** At this point, you will only be able to come up with a rough estimate of training costs. We suggest that you do so by major element of the identified strategy. You are helping the executives frame their judgment of priorities, establishing a "ballpark" in their minds, and saving yourself from disabling individual item haggling. *For example, you conclude that the total package of T&D associated with the globalization strategy is $3 million out of pocket over three years, and you break it into major items.*

5K. **Summarize.** Finally, you pull all this together in an orderly layout, generally by business/HR requirement. You will appear very impressive: clear-headed, focused, businesslike! Now run this by your direct manager, make necessary changes, and move to the final step in business partnership.

5L. **Validate the outcomes with the executive group of the unit. Your goal is to:**

- Elicit their overall priorities, using the matrix provided earlier, importance to the strategy, and gaps versus current state.

- Get their agreement on which of the training strategies you must drive during the coming year.

- Get their agreement on approximate resource implications.

Conclusion

This is a continuing process. It can earn you a seat at the table when the business people are discussing strategy. It can enable you to understand changes that may occur in the business in the context of your own needs for action. You can make appropriate changes and get agreement on them more rapidly. You are a business partner. You are probably still employed.

How to Create a Training and Development Needs Assessment Survey

By John Gasiewski and Karen Vander Linde

Audience	HR Professionals
Purpose	—Learn a process for developing a learning needs assessment —Learn tips and techniques to maximize survey effectiveness
Suggested Uses	Self-study Model for action Adapt questionnaire sample for use in your organization

Introduction

In the spring of 1996 an effort began to improve Coopers & Lybrand Consulting's (CLC's) training and development programs for professional staff. This effort was motivated by a number of factors, including the need for CLC to create competitive advantage in an environment of increased training budgets and significant spending on training and development ($3,000 to $8,000 per professional per year is typical for consulting firms). Improved learning opportunities are also seen as key to recruiting and retaining top-level professionals in CLC. Part of this effort has been to design and conduct a Training and Development Needs Assessment Survey administered over the firm's Lotus Notes network. This document describes the objectives, audience, approach, survey creation process, survey delivery medium (Lotus Notes), and results. Other organizations can adapt this process to develop needs assessments for their high-performance-seeking organizations. Sample sections of the CLC questionnaire follow the how-to presentation.

Objectives of the Needs Assessment

- To identify priority topics within a curriculum drafted by CLC's Learning Advisory Committee, based on performance needs of consultants at different levels and lengths of service in the organization.

- To determine the preferred learning delivery methods of consultants and test the feasibility of using alternative delivery methods.

- To communicate to consulting professionals as a whole that action is being taken to improve the training and development program at CLC.

Audience

This survey was distributed to all CLC professionals who have access to Lotus Notes, which the company uses to link worldwide offices electronically (approximately 86 percent of the entire consulting population). Provisions also were made to distribute the survey via other methods to consultants who did not have access to Lotus Notes.

Approach

The primary focus of the survey was to find out from respondents which topics from the planned curriculum they believed were important to their job performance. Since the Learning Advisory Committee created a curriculum that links to the strategic goals of CLC, topics such as proprietary methodologies, project management, and communication skills feature prominently. Selected topics would form the basis of courses within the curriculum that addressed needs among different staff levels (associate to partner) and length of service (new hires versus non-new hires).

CLC further prioritized topics through a "Gap" analysis. Respondents were asked what they felt their current skill level was for each topic. Those topics that were considered as (extremely) important to job performance and in which the participants had an inadequate current skill level—e.g., those topics with the largest "gap" between importance and current skill level—became development priorities for the new curriculum.

In case respondents felt that their specific performance needs warranted topics not included in the survey, they could submit their own topics in spaces provided. An open-ended item in the survey allowed respondents to comment on the knowledge/skills related to topics they considered important to job performance. The item appears in italics below:

Review the survey topics above and make any comments to help us better understand your needs on the job. Describe briefly (but with enough context to be understandable):

- *in specific terms why a topic(s) is (are) important to improving work that you perform, and*
- *what you need to know and/or do about the topic(s) to improve your performance.*

This feature allowed respondents to add definition to topics that were necessarily at a high level because of the broad scope of the survey.

In the next part of the survey, respondents rated learning delivery methods (i.e., classroom, multimedia, videoconferencing, etc.) on a scale from least to most valuable. Although respondents might have been asked to rate delivery methods according to the priority topics they identified (i.e., high importance to job and inadequate current skill level), the final survey did not incorporate this idea. We determined that this requirement would have made an already lengthy survey more time-consuming and complex.

Finally, an "additional comments," open-ended question allowed respondents to make any additional points they wanted to express. Sample questions from the survey appear on page 1-37.

In addition to the survey, CLC conducted structured interviews of two types at all staff levels and within various Business Units to provide another qualitative source of information on learning needs. The interviews focused either on interactive exploration of topics featured in the survey or, if the interviewee had not taken the survey, they followed a critical incident interview format.

Process and Roles

The table on page 1-35 summarizes the process and roles for developing and distributing the survey instrument

Lotus Notes as the Survey Delivery Method

Using Notes to distribute the survey had some decided advantages over mailing paper copies of the survey. First, respondents could submit the survey on-line as soon as they were finished completing it; no mailing effort was required. The project team could count responses immediately to give up-to-the-minute status. In addition, data from respondents existed within a Notes database and could be put into a statistical software package (such as SPSS) without any manual data entry.

Despite these advantages, some words of caution are in order when using Notes for this kind of application. First, with over 13 percent of CLC professionals not on Notes, systematic exclusion of an entire group (for example, the Utilities consulting group out of Chicago) was possible. Thus, we provided a paper-based version as a backup and conducted research to ensure that a major group (e.g., Business Unit) was not overlooked. Second, taking the survey in Notes differs from filling out the paper-based version in that the format for questions must be very clearly laid out to prevent making the user scroll back and forth from directions to survey items. Scrolling in this manner can take considerable time if respondents are connected to Notes remotely, and this could cause the respondent to exit from the survey without completing it.

We took several precautions to avoid these problems. On the communications side, a key sponsor issued a memo to Business Unit leaders announcing the survey and enlisting their support in publicizing it and the availability of a paper-based alternative. Another precaution was to establish a 24-hour 800 number hotline where respondents could call in with technical/content problems and receive responses within 24 hours. This allowed for the few minor technical problems encountered to be investigated and for paper-based versions of the survey to be distributed for those not on Notes. The final precaution was to test and retest the survey thoroughly for any potential problems, such as inconsistently formatted or confusing directions. Testing occurred both in a limited pilot of the survey to about 30 people and with the survey designer/developer and Lotus Notes technical developer.

Results

Overall, more than 25 percent of the CLC population surveyed responded, with 86 percent of the CLC population accessible through Lotus Notes. The response rate probably suffered from conducting the survey in the middle of a popular month for vacationing and also from the short, 11-day time window in which CLC professionals could respond, yet the response rate was more than adequate for the target population. Furthermore, the responses represented a balanced profile of business units and levels in the organization.

Although specific results cannot be shared for proprietary reasons, the gap analysis revealed some surprises and confirmed some expected results. For instance, it was no surprise that topics related to people development (giving performance feedback, mentoring, etc.) emerged as priorities for the higher levels in the organization. However, we had not anticipated that all levels in CLC

\multicolumn{3}{c}{*Implementing a Training and Development Needs Assessment Survey*}		
Stage	*What happened*	*Who did it*
1	Development of workplan and budget	Project Manager, project team
2	Exploratory interviews with sponsors (Learning Advisory Committee and Subject Matter "Champions")	Designer/developer
3	Design of Survey Questions	Designer/developer, National Survey Center, reviewers
4	Lotus Notes programming and piloting	Designer/developer, Notes Tech. Advisor, piloters
5	Distribution	Notes Tech. Advisor, survey audience
6	Structured interviews	Designer/developer
7	Analysis and report	Designer/developer, National Survey Center, Project Manager

would express a consistent need for knowledge of products and services within the organization, which turned out to be the case.

Once results had identified these and other priority topics for new hires and associates through partners, CLC modified the existing curriculum. Course development followed.

Open-ended responses also helped identify a number of important issues that are central to job performance and learning but would not have been captured in the list of topics in the survey. One issue that came up re-peatedly was a need to know how to use the firm's vast knowledge and human resources more effectively on engagements. Other factors mentioned frequently pointed to the need for a comprehensive "learning system" within CLC in which course offerings, learning paths through the curriculum, training policies (e.g., on attending external courses), and a yearly training process, among other areas, are presented in a consistent manner to the entire organization. This learning system is now under development.

Sample Questions from the C&L Survey

Demographic Information

Please answer the following questions:

I. What is your staff class?

( ) Partner   ( ) Senior Associate   ( ) Research Analyst

( ) Managing Associate   ( ) Associate   ( ) _____

II. How many years have you been with CLC?

( ) <1   ( ) 2-3   ( ) 4+

( ) 1-2   ( ) 3-4

III. Total years of business experience?

( ) <1   ( ) 1-10   ( ) 10+

Part I

For each item below, indicate which topics are key to performing on the job by selecting a number from one to five for each topic in the scale labeled "Importance to Your Job Performance."

Then in the second column, labeled "Current Skill Level," indicate your current skill level for each topic.

Firm Knowledge

1. Background and History, Culture and Values, Professional Standards

   Importance to Your Job
   ( ) 1 Not at all important
   ( ) 2
   ( ) 3
   ( ) 4
   ( ) 5 Very important

   Current Skill Level
   ( ) 1 Completely inadequate
   ( ) 2
   ( ) 3
   ( ) 4
   ( ) 5 Completely adequate

2. Organizational Structure, Administrative Procedures

   Importance to Your Job
   ( ) 1 Not at all important
   ( ) 2
   ( ) 3
   ( ) 4
   ( ) 5 Very important

   Current Skill Level
   ( ) 1 Completely inadequate
   ( ) 2
   ( ) 3
   ( ) 4
   ( ) 5 Completely adequate

Consulting Analysis and Problem Solving

11. Understanding business issues, identifying applicable theories, developing hypotheses, interviewing & other data gathering techniques, analysis, drawing conclusions, making recommendations

    Importance to Your Job
    ( ) 1 Not at all important
    ( ) 2
    ( ) 3
    ( ) 4
    ( ) 5 Very important

    Current Skill Level
    ( ) 1 Completely inadequate
    ( ) 2
    ( ) 3
    ( ) 4
    ( ) 5 Completely adequate

Verbal and Written Communication Skills

12. Verbal: presenting, facilitating, teambuilding	*Importance to Your Job*	*Current Skill Level*
	( ) 1 Not at all important	( ) 1 Completely inadequate
	( ) 2	( ) 2
	( ) 3	( ) 3
	( ) 4	( ) 4
	( ) 5 Very important	( ) 5 Completely adequate

Computer Skills

14. PC, networking (e.g., Lotus Notes)	*Importance to Your Job*	*Current Skill Level*
	( ) 1 Not at all important	( ) 1 Completely inadequate
	( ) 2	( ) 2
	( ) 3	( ) 3
	( ) 4	( ) 4
	( ) 5 Very important	( ) 5 Completely adequate

19. People development (mentoring, coaching, giving performance feedback)	*Importance to Your Job*	*Current Skill Level*
	( ) 1 Not at all important	( ) 1 Completely inadequate
	( ) 2	( ) 2
	( ) 3	( ) 3
	( ) 4	( ) 4
	( ) 5 Very important	( ) 5 Completely adequate

Creativity

25. Specific techniques (e.g., de Bono's "Lateral Thinking")	*Importance to Your Job*	*Current Skill Level*
	( ) 1 Not at all important	( ) 1 Completely inadequate
	( ) 2	( ) 2
	( ) 3	( ) 3
	( ) 4	( ) 4

Industry

26. Industry Overview	*Importance to Your Job*	*Current Skill Level*
	( ) 1 Not at all important	( ) 1 Completely inadequate
	( ) 2	( ) 2
	( ) 3	( ) 3
	( ) 4	( ) 4
	( ) 5 Very important	( ) 5 Completely adequate

Rank each type of training and development experience from 1–5 based on how valuable you find it.

35. Self-study courses (paper-based)

( ) 1 not at all valuable
( ) 2
( ) 3
( ) 4
( ) 5 extremely valuable
( ) _____

36. Other primarily text-based materials (including professional or industry publications, CLC publications, methodologies, etc.)

( ) 1 not at all valuable
( ) 2
( ) 3
( ) 4
( ) 5 extremely valuable
( ) _____

37. Computer-based training (including simulations)

( ) 1 not at all valuable
( ) 2
( ) 3
( ) 4
( ) 5 extremely valuable

38. Classroom experiences

( ) 1 not at all valuable
( ) 2
( ) 3
( ) 4
( ) 5 extremely valuable
( ) _____

39. Distance Learning (videoconferencing—e.g., PictureTel)

( ) 1 not at all valuable
( ) 2
( ) 3
( ) 4
( ) 5 extremely valuable
( ) _____

40. Distance Learning (e.g., Lotus Notes, Internet)

( ) 1 not at all valuable
( ) 2
( ) 3
( ) 4
( ) 5 extremely valuable
( ) _____

Developing Competency-based Curricula

By Nancy Letsinger

Audience	HR Professionals
Purpose	—Learn how to determine training priorities based on a competency assessment —Be able to interview subject matter experts to determine competencies required for a position, a department, or an organization
Suggested Uses	Self-study Model process Adapt sample protocol tool for use in your organization

Many training functions struggle with how to provide training that has real impact and will lead to improved job and organizational performance. It can be a challenge to determine what training employees really need and how to deliver it so that learning is transferred and applied on the job. The process of identifying and assessing staff on competencies provides a systematic approach to training needs analysis. Competencies are defined as the knowledge, skills, abilities, and behaviors that are required for success in a job. By using competencies as the foundation for curricula, you can develop learning opportunities that are targeted to the business, focused on performance and results, and geared to employees' skill levels and needs.

You can use the following competency-based approach to develop curricula for a single staff position, a department with multiple staff positions, or an entire organization. The methodology outlined below will help you to:

- Align training and learning activities with the business needs.
- Gain the input and support of key stakeholders.
- Identify the knowledge, skills, and abilities that employees need to perform successfully in their positions.
- Assess current staff skill levels in these competency areas.
- Determine whether or not training is needed in these competency areas and what the relative priorities are.
- Develop a comprehensive training plan/curriculum.

Step 1: Conduct Stakeholder Interviews

As the first step in developing a competency-based curriculum, conduct one-on-one interviews with key stakeholders to gain their perspective on: the current work being performed by the target audience, the needs for improvement, the future direction of the organization and the industry, and how this direction might change the work performed and/or the skills needed for effectiveness. Important stakeholders might include managers of the target audience, customers, and leaders of the organization. Conducting these stakeholder interviews helps to ensure that training will be customer-focused and future-oriented. Meeting with key stakeholders can also build buy-in and support for the curricula initiative.

Step 2: Inventory Past and Current Learning Opportunities

Gather information about what learning opportunities have been offered and are currently available for the target audience. (Consider both formal training and non-training interventions.) This information will provide a context for the next phase of interviews and can help direct some of your questioning. In collecting this information, note the following:

- Whether the learning opportunity is currently available or when it was last provided
- Provider (external vendor or internal providers?)
- Description of the learning opportunity (if a training course, summary of course content)
- Program duration
- Delivery mechanisms (classroom training, coaching, CBT, etc.)
- Participation
- Evaluation ratings and comments

As you prepare for the next round of interviewing, use this information to develop questions around learning opportunities. Look for trends and aspects that you'd like to further probe. If possible, collect feedback from the instructors of past training programs to learn what, from their perspective, was effective or ineffective about the training and what would help to better meet the needs of the target audience.

In addition to guiding the next phase of interviewing, the information that you collect about past and current learning opportunities will also provide input to the later step of curricula development (Step 6). You can refer back to this information about learning opportunities that have or are being offered to consider how well programs already developed are aligned with the competencies. Through this analysis, you can determine whether existing programs will meet the needs of the target audience, whether these programs need to be modified, and/or what new programs need to be developed. The information that you collect at this stage can also provide design ideas and considerations for future course development.

Step 3: Identify Competencies

To conduct the next data-gathering phase, *identify competencies,* identify high performers in each staff position who will be included in the curriculum to serve as subject matter experts (SMEs). Identify your SMEs based on the input of managers and business leaders who have worked with the target audience. Agree on a set of criteria to determine high performers (e.g. prior reviews, results, client feedback, sought out by peers, etc.). In choosing SMEs to interview, you may need to consider demographic issues

---

Example of Competency and Behavioral Indicators

Competency:

▶ Oral communication/listening skills: Demonstrates the ability to effectively transfer thoughts and express ideas, using speech in individual or group situations.

Behavioral Indicators:

▶ Uses effective questioning techniques to determine issues.

▶ Presents oneself clearly and articulately when speaking with an individual or before a group.

▶ Adapts speech, presentation, or conversation to the understanding of the audience to facilitate clear communication

▶ Utilizes active listening techniques (e.g. paraphrasing, open-ended questions, summarizing, etc.) to check the understanding and clarity of communications between parties.

---

such as geographic location to ensure an appropriate cross-representation of staff.

Conduct one-on-one SME interviews or focus groups to identify the competencies (knowledge, skills, abilities, and behaviors) critical for success in the represented staff position. Competencies should be observable and measurable. Using an interview protocol, identify general competencies (such as teamwork, initiative, oral communication, etc.) as well as technical competencies (such as cost-benefit analysis, database management, econometric modeling, etc.) for the position. A sample SME protocol appears on pages 1-45 and 1-46. Determine which competencies are *threshold competencies* (necessary to achieve a standard level of performance in the position) and which competencies are *distinguishing competencies* (differentiating superior performance from average performance in the position). To fully define the competencies, document the most critical 3–5 *behavioral indicators* for each—how a competency would be manifested in a work situation or how someone who was applying the competency would behave. Be sure that the

competencies take into account the future state as determined in Step 1.

For the final portion of the SME interview, discuss learning opportunities surrounding the competencies. Ask the SME how he/she learned each of the competencies and what learning opportunities exist for others to learn the competencies. Be sure to probe for opportunities other than formal training or academic classes (i.e. coaching, membership in professional associations, etc.). Determine what training in these areas has been effective or ineffective and why. What could be effective if available?

Step 4: Develop and Validate Competency Models

Based on the SME interviews, develop a competency model for each staff position that is part of your target audience for the curriculum. Summarize overlapping competency items and descriptions from the various SME interviews and rectify any opposing statements. The model will typically begin with a definition of the competency and include 3–5 key behavioral indicators that define the competency.

Sample Rating Scales

Importance:
- 1 = "Not Important" to my position and its activities
- 2 = "Somewhat Important" to my position and its activities
- 3 = "Important" to my position and its activities
- 4 = "Very Important" to my position and its activities
- 5 = "Extremely Important" to my position and its activities

Level of Performance Needed:
- 1 = Conceptual knowledge, no working experience
- 2 = Working knowledge, ability to apply with some guidance
- 3 = Proficiency, ability to apply with self-sufficiency
- 4 = Some expertise, ability to guide others
- 5 = Mastery, recognized as authority in knowledge and ability to apply

Frequency (how often the SME exhibits the competency):
- 1 = "Yearly" (usually once per year)
- 2 = "Monthly" (usually once per month)
- 3 = "Weekly" (usually once per week)
- 4 = "Daily" (usually once per day)
- 5 = "Several" (several times each day)

After building the initial competency models, the next step is to establish which competencies are most critical for the respective positions. Develop an instrument that will allow the SMEs to rate each competency in terms of: Importance, Level of Performance Needed, and Frequency of Application.

In the box on page 1-42 are sample rating scales for each of these areas.

These ratings will allow you to determine the relative weight, or importance, of each competency for the positions under consideration. If some competencies are rated as significantly less important than the others, you should eliminate them from the model or downplay their importance.

After developing draft competency models, validate the models with one or more of the following groups by asking them to consider what's missing, what's part of the model that doesn't belong, and what needs to be reworded or clarified. You may choose to validate the models with:

- A set of SMEs who did not participate in the initial SME interviews.

- Managers of the target group.

- A focus group of the original SMEs so that they can hear each other's comments, argue their positions, and gain agreement as a group.

Step 5: Conduct a Training Needs Assessment of Staff

Using the competency models as a basis, the next step in the process is to design an assessment instrument to measure current staff skill levels for each competency and the urgency of training needs in each area. This step will enable you to quantify and conduct more thorough analysis of the training needs.

Develop the training needs assessment based on either the competencies or behavioral indicators (or a combination of both), depending upon the level of detail you will need to identify and develop learning opportunities. For example, with the Oral Communication/Listening Skills competency already shown, an assessment at the behavioral indicator level could drive the development of several different learning opportunities (i.e., Customer Interviewing and Contracting, Presentation Skills, Communicating Technical Material to a non-Technical Audience, etc.). Depending upon the number of staff in the target audience and the resources available, you may want to conduct the survey with either the entire target audience or a representative sample.

Listed in the box below are sample scales to assess competency skill levels and the urgency of training needs.

Step 6: Develop Curricula

Having identified the competencies required for each position, begin to evaluate the extent to which existing learning opportunities are targeted to these competencies. Drawing on the information gathered in Step 2, determine whether there are existing learning opportunities that meet the newly defined needs as the programs currently exist and whether there are learning opportunities that would meet the newly defined needs if the programs were modified. Refer back to your initial inventory of learning opportunities

---

Sample Scales for Assessing Competency and Urgency of Training Needs

Effectiveness Displaying Competency Skill Levels:

1 = Low
2 =
3 = Medium
4 =
5 = High

Urgency of Training Needs:

1 = None, have the skills needed for effectiveness
2 = 9+ months
3 = 5–9 months
4 = 1–4 months
5 = Immediately

---

and also consider what you heard during the competency interviews and your discussions with SMEs around learning opportunities. Through this process, you should also identify those competencies that are not covered by existing learning opportunities and for which entirely new programs need to be developed.

To begin framing the curricula, translate all of the staff needs into learning objectives, and bundle the learning objectives by content and level. Determine curricula tracks and courses for each position. Look at the courses that overlap positions and determine in which instances a single course is appropriate for different staff positions and in which cases there will need to be different versions of the course. Also identify appropriate non-training interventions to support competency development.

To develop learning opportunities for the curricula, follow an instructional design model based around the following high-level steps:

Analyze

- Articulate target audience and learning objectives.
- Consider results of the Competency and Training Needs Assessment:
  — Determine target performance levels, current performance levels, and the performance gap.
  — Determine the perceived urgency for training.
- Assess existing or related course material.

Design

- Create a high-level program design.
- Determine instructional methods and media.
- Develop a detailed program design.
- Determine implementation and evaluation strategies.

Develop

- Prepare the program content (draft materials, exercises, etc.).
- Pilot the learning experience and assess effectiveness.
- Finalize the learning experience.

Implement & Evaluate

- Finalize the implementation strategy.
- Deliver programs.
- Evaluate programs.

With this six-step approach to developing competency-based curricula, you can develop curricula that are targeted to the business, focused on performance and results, and geared to employees' specific skill levels and needs. This curricula approach will help the workforce and the business by aligning learning opportunities with real, on-the-job needs and by preparing staff to meet the future challenges of the business and marketplace. By creating and implementing competency-based curricula, you can improve business results and the return on investment from training and learning initiatives. This, in turn, can help you demonstrate the benefit and value of the training function to your organization.

Sample Subject Matter Expert (SME) Protocol

Interviewee: _____ Date_____

Position: _____ Interviewer: _____

Introduction to Interview (10 minutes):
- Introduce the initiative and answer any initial questions
  —What you're doing
  —How the process will be used, etc.
- Explain why you asked to speak with them in particular
  —Identified as someone knowledgeable in the particular subject matter
  —Able to articulate the competencies needed for effective performance in the position
  —Have a strategic, futuristic outlook; can see how the competency demands (e.g., skills needed, importance of certain skills, etc.) will change in the next 3–5 years
  —Can talk about different opportunities available for someone to develop the necessary skills
- Cover the agenda for the time period (2 hours)
  —Position responsibilities
  —Activities and tasks
  —Competencies needed for effective performance
  —Learning opportunities for the position
- Answer any additional questions

Protocol (1 hour and 45 minutes):

Position Responsibilities:

- In 2–3 sentences, what are the main responsibilities of your position within the organization?
- What are the primary tasks and/or outcomes of your job?

Activities and Tasks:

- What are the key tasks or activities you must complete to achieve the primary outcome(s)?
- What tools do you need to perform these tasks effectively? What tools will you need in the future?

Sample Subject Matter Expert (SME) Protocol

Competencies (choose from the following):

- What skills and knowledge are most critical to success in this job?
- How are the competencies demonstrated on the job (e.g., what behaviors)?
- If you were to hire someone into this position, what would you screen him or her on?
- Describe a high performer in this job. What does he/she do? Know?
- What sets a high performer apart from an average performer? What behaviors?
- How will this job change in the future? What knowledge, skills, and abilities will become more important? Less important?

Learning Opportunities:

- How did you learn these particular competencies (e.g., college coursework, on-the-job training, work experience, etc.)?
- What courses have you taken in an effort to improve your skills in these areas?
  —Were they effective/ineffective? Why?
  —Which competencies did they focus on?
- What are other ways for people to improve in these competency areas (traditional training courses and other non-training options)? What would be the most effective approaches and why?
- If you were to design a course to teach these particular competencies, what areas/topics would you focus on?

Closing (5 minutes):

Points to include:

1. Describe next steps in project (how competency models will be developed, validated, etc.).
2. Answer any questions they may have.
3. Leave name and number for further questions/contact.
4. Thank them for their time.

That Was a Great Class, But...

By Allison Rossett

Audience ⟶	Learning Professionals
Purpose ⟶	—Understand the difference between the training and performance-focused learning perspectives —Learn techniques for reducing the barriers to application of training on the job —Understand the importance of focusing on the outcome of training from the outset
Suggested Uses ⟶	Self-study Resource for developing a presentation on this topic Tools for prequalifying training participants and their managers could be used prior to any learning experience

The aftermath of a training course can be wonderful. Participants ask questions, discuss the topic, practice what they learned, do well on tests, promise to keep in touch with each other, and so forth. Sometimes, they even applaud.

But a few years ago, I had a sobering experience. While waiting for an elevator after having just conducted a course, I overheard something that silenced the applause still ringing in my ears. One participant said to another, "That was a great class, but I won't get to use it." The other participant nodded in agreement, "Yeah, great. But there's no time for it where I work."

Two aberrations? I don't think so. Since then, I have kept an eye peeled for post-class dismay. In fact, I have discussed that phenomenon with hundreds of training professionals in the United States, Canada, and Europe. I found that it's important to read between the lines of evaluations and to query participants about the likely outcome of the training.

The phrase, "Great class, but..." could become a mantra for our business.

But What?

Why do many participants leave a training course and shrug?

One likely reason is that they think they are returning to an obstructionist manager who either doesn't understand or favor the training. A painful example that I have some responsibility for involves a professional development program for course developers. For a little more than a year in the 1980s, 24 developers traveled to attend workshops in

From Training to Performance

Training	Performance
▶ Learning outcomes	▶ Learning and performance outcomes
▶ A focus on individuals	▶ A focus on individuals and the organization
▶ Measured by how many butts in the seats	▶ Measured by business results
▶ Events	▶ Systems
▶ Classes	▶ Solution-type systems that involve training and such related interventions as job redesign and incentives
▶ Habit- and pocket-driven	▶ Driven by needs assessment and a customer focus
▶ Training edifice, classrooms	▶ Support is available everywhere, including in classrooms and from human and automated coaching

instructional design and technologies. Never, ever, did their direct supervisors choose to attend—even when beseeched by me and the other trainer. The results shouldn't have surprised anyone. In the best cases, returning participants were ignored. And in one instance, some were greeted by a manager who smirked and said, "Get back to the real work."

The Trainer's Lament

Sue Reynolds, from California Housing Partnership, expresses the typical trainer's lament. She trains project managers of affordable rental housing in a variety of skills, including scheduling their complex project tasks. Some of the participants never implement the systems they learn because when they return to their community agencies, they report to executives who have other priorities and aren't convinced of the value of the systems.

But it doesn't have to be that dismal. Recently, a group of training professionals from

Harris Bank in Chicago were delighted because their manager and her manager joined the group to take a two-day needs assessment class.

Motorola Worldwide Learning Services has demonstrated that same type of commitment to alignment, but a little differently. At the close of a two-day class for Motorola, I asked participants what obstacles they anticipated and how their managers could move them forward in the areas covered in the training. Their comments served as grist for a subsequent meeting of the managers.

A Mighty Training Class

Through incentive policies and actions, an organization tells its people what it cares about. For example, a company that evaluates call-center employees by the number of calls answered per hour will have a difficult time convincing them that customer satisfaction is a top priority.

Sears's experience in its auto-parts division

is a classic example. Sears trained employees on ethics and customer service, but it also tacked financial incentives to parts sales. Not surprisingly, Sears got what it put its money behind—and unfavorable press coverage. Determined to correct the situation, Sears altered the incentives, thereby sending a consistent message.

A few years back, I was involved with a company that successfully shifted its sales employees to a quality movement via executive sponsorship, training, and incentives. Later, the company wanted to use similar quality processes in its manufacturing settings and asked for my help. But when I presented the opportunity to pair incentives with quality outcomes, the company's leaders balked. They were unwilling to link performance and pay, even for valued outcomes. That had never been done before in manufacturing. What they wanted was a mighty training class.

Another problem is a flawed work environment. Nothing causes more agitation among computer training and support professionals than a discussion on how screwed-up tools and conditions hinder technical training. They tell tales of training software installed on machines with insufficient memory, software with great features that goes buggy, and training on software that people are "going to love when they get it."

A colleague in sales training describes her experience beating her head against a wall during a course on a new high-technology product. During the class, she dazzled salespeople with the features, comparative benefits, and compatibility with the existing product line. For a while, they were enthusiastic. But that soon faded. They said, "We like it, but when will the sales offices get demonstrators? Last time, it took months. Even when they were available, we didn't have the budget to get our hands on them."

Another example of the effect of a flawed work environment involves a county office of education. Hundreds of teachers attended classes on the Internet. The training was chock full of uses and practices applicable for public school teachers. Unfortunately, most of them walked out of the training saying, "The Internet is wonderful, and the class was great. But I can't use any of this." Why?

Several of the teachers didn't have computers. Some didn't have modems. And nearly all of them didn't have telephone connections in their classrooms.

Beads on a String

Another common comment among training participants is, "It was a great class, but I don't see how it fits with that other class." Or, "I liked that class, but it's just like the one we had on market-focused-strategic-seamless selling." The lesson: Learning must be part of a consistent, clear message. Often, it isn't.

A colleague at a computer company describes its sales and marketing training as "beads on a string." The beads are the individual classes; the string is the curriculum associated with a job position or product line. As new courses are created, they're snapped onto the end of the string. The relationship between the beads and the string is negligible. Breaking that pattern of distinct offerings is a hefty challenge.

Universities provide another example. Typically, professors "own" their courses, focusing on them rather than on the relationship between them. Most times, different departments don't integrate courses and programs. That's also true in corporate and government training.

The way some jobs are perceived can also be a barrier to training transfer. In such cases, participants may say, "A lot of good ideas in the class, but that's not my job." I've heard that from people who train bank tellers, managers, and many others.

With tellers, the problem is a dichotomy between service and sales. Financial institutions have a long history of selecting tellers for their ability to provide direct, able, and responsive customer service. But cataclysmic changes are occurring in banking. More customer service and support are handled electronically and via telephone. In California, bank branches are vanishing. Tellers that remain in retail banking are increasingly expected to deal directly with customers, but with an emphasis on sales.

Managers in all kinds of businesses are also experiencing changing roles, as leadership paradigms shift from a command-and-control approach to nurturing and coaching knowledge workers. There are thousands of courses for managers about empowering employees, working in teams, and so forth, but production and appraisal expectations haven't caught up. Managers sit in such classes, but during their breaks, they pick up their e-mails and voice mails exhorting them to achieve production targets.

Hell-o?

Here's a typical scenario, in which an executive from a large company calls a training consultant for help in shifting training and HRD professionals toward new roles and directions.

Consultant: "Glad you called. What do you have in mind?"

Caller: "It's our annual educators' conference, and our theme is Performance in the 21st Century. I heard you speak in Atlanta last year and thought you could rally our troops. It would be a 90-minute slot."

Consultant: "Can you give me a sense of what direction you're trying to rally them?"

Caller: "Sure. A new strategy to link more closely with business results. That means shifting from training to performance, getting our people involved with needs assessment and evaluation, and focusing on what's involved in helping employees perform better. No doubt you know where I'm heading."

Consultant: "I do, and I agree. Can you tell me what else you're doing to accomplish that change, besides my presentation? Are there things already in place that reflect the new priorities?"

Caller: "Not yet. Maybe I'll put together a committee to work on that. I think a great place to start is your presentation and then maybe a workshop on needs assessment. What's your fax number so that we can get this squared away?"

For that mission, the caller (and his or her organization) needs a strategy that uses a solution-type system in which effective training is a pivotal, but not solitary, element and in which presentations and training are preceded by new incentives, recognition programs, job descriptions, and work processes.

The irony is the caller's attempt to move forward with an isolated training event to motivate professionals to stop doing isolated training events.

There are many costs associated with tossing training at people without regard to the larger contexts in which they work. Some obvious ones are the failure to influence business results and frittered-away opportunities and resources. When even the federal government is measuring and demanding financial results, does training dare to lag behind?

What is unaligned training causing in people? The answer: cynicism. Because most participants try to connect what they're taught with what they have experienced and expect to experience at work, many of them become cynical. In such cases, they scoff, in covert and overt ways, at training as nothing more than a public display—without the organizational commitment that should be manifested in supervisory support, incentives, tools, and job design. They give credit for a great class, a fine event, and a good show. But when given time to stew, they become annoyed.

Participants' cynicism has three targets: the topic, the organization, and the training. Cynicism about the topic sounds like this: "Flavor of the month." I recall a friend in government who described a numbing array of mandated classes on hazardous materials, teamwork, and so forth. I nodded sympathetically as he poked fun at the topics. But consider the topics. Should we skip safety training? He dismissed the topic because the training wasn't reinforced.

Cynicism about the wisdom of organizations is rampant. A training specialist for a large computer company says, "Every spring, it's the same thing. Some new initiative. Market-driven quality. Teams. Empowerment. Virtual officing. Whatever. We're told to prepare a course, a really potent course. And that's it. Like a course is going to change the company's culture. Are they living in a dream world at headquarters?"

A training coordinator told a gathering of her training peers about being called into the plant manager's office. He asked, "When can you get a diversity class scheduled? I want something on the books right away." When she pressed for his reasons for wanting the class and what he would do to support it, he directed her attention to finding a supplier, and fast. What amazed me wasn't the tale, but her willingness to share it, considering that many people in the room knew her manager. She said that her experience wasn't remarkable. She and her associates expected the company and its leaders to behave for public consumption, not performance. Their cynicism fueled hers.

Training departments are also the recipients of cynicism. People deride training because, as their memory of classes fades, they recall only that they were a waste of time. When training is superfluous, a quick fix, or an afterthought, participants will tell others. Their perceptions are contagious.

Years of unsupported training have caused a new spin on our profession. A friend of mine works at a company with hundreds of training professionals associated with many business units. The current growth industry in her training community is marketing. Training marketers are trying to fight years of accumulated cynicism and resistance with

electronic ad campaigns, lotteries, and giveaways. "Come to class and get a free T-shirt," they say. "What about a free daily organizer?" Still not enough response? "Well, how about an *electronic* organizer?"

What to Do

What's a training professional to do? Marketing or mandating courses may keep up enrollment, but they also tend to keep up the cynicism and the need for ever-escalating lures. It's better to use an approach that aims to strengthen the link between training and the contexts in which people work—and between training and performance. Here are some ways to link those elements.

Screening. Ask participants and their managers to screen their work environments and themselves prior to training. Managers should be aware of any obstacles, including their own understanding of the training, before sending people to class. Ask managers to reflect on employees' readiness and predispositions, and whether they have been prepared for the training.

A negative response to any statement in

Unearthing the Barriers

Here's a needs assessment with questions designed to identify potential barriers to training transfer and improved performance.

- Do the participants and their managers know what the training will contribute?

- Did participants and managers help define the direction of the training?

- Do participants want to take the training?

- Do managers want to send their people to the training?

- Are there already changed expectations about work that will press participants to use what they will learn in the training?

- Have those expectations been communicated to participants?

- Do managers know enough about the training to discuss it with participants? To coach afterwards?

- Are the appropriate support tools and technologies available at participants' work sites?

- Have similar courses in the past been supported by the organization?

- Have senior-level managers done anything to show that they support the training and its desired outcomes?

- Does the organization's culture encourage participants to use what they learn in training? If not, what might get in the way?

Table 1. Prequalifying Managers and Supervisors for Training

A negative response to any of these statements raises a red flag that the respondent might not understand or favor the training.

Check the appropriate box.

I have a good sense of what the class is about...	☐ Agree	☐ Disagree
I know how the training matches what I need for employees to do..	☐ Agree	☐ Disagree
There are tangible ways that the training will help employees	☐ Agree	☐ Disagree
There are tangible ways that the training will help our unit..	☐ Agree	☐ Disagree
I can see why the organization is interested in providing the training..............................	☐ Agree	☐ Disagree
In performance appraisals, I can evaluate employees on what they learn in the class............	☐ Agree	☐ Disagree
I know enough about the training to support employees when they return to work......................	☐ Agree	☐ Disagree
We have the tools and technologies that will be discussed in class..	☐ Agree	☐ Disagree
I'm glad employees are attending the class..	☐ Agree	☐ Disagree
I've discussed the topic and the class with the employees who will participate........................	☐ Agree	☐ Disagree
They know that I care about what will be taught in the class..	☐ Agree	☐ Disagree

Table 1 on this page suggests that the respondent doesn't understand or favor the training.

Participants should also reflect on how primed they and their organizations are for the training. A negative response to any statement in Table 2 (see page 1-53) suggests that the respondent may not be sufficiently prepared for the training.

You can also conduct a needs assessment with questions designed to identify potential barriers to training transfer and improved performance. The box, Unearthing the Barriers, suggests some questions to which negative responses would raise red flags. The purpose is to get beyond a blanket statement about "problems in the organization" to a finer understanding and disaggregation of the reasons for a possible lack of support for training.

Ann Leon of IBM Skills Planning describes some barriers for its salespeople. Though many factors contribute to critical goals—such as sharing knowledge and leveraging capabilities—salespeople often point to the absence of team incentives and automated databases as obstacles. Leon and her associates are acknowledging those barriers and augmenting training with support tools and

Table 2. Prequalifying Participants for Training

A negative response to any of these statements raises a red flag that the respondent (or the organization) might not be sufficiently prepared for the training.

Check the appropriate box.

Statement	Agree	Disagree
I have a pretty good sense of what the class is about..	☐ Agree	☐ Disagree
I can see how I might use what I'll learn in the class..	☐ Agree	☐ Disagree
There are ways that the training could help me perform my job better	☐ Agree	☐ Disagree
There are ways that the training could help my unit..	☐ Agree	☐ Disagree
What I learn in class is likely to count on my performance appraisals..	☐ Agree	☐ Disagree
My manager knows about the training topic...	☐ Agree	☐ Disagree
The class appears to focus on problems and opportunities that matter to me...............................	☐ Agree	☐ Disagree
I'm glad to have the chance to learn more about the training topic...	☐ Agree	☐ Disagree
My manager seems to care about my acquiring some skills and knowledge in the area covered by the training..	☐ Agree	☐ Disagree
When I return to work, I'll have the tools I need to use what I learned in the class......................	☐ Agree	☐ Disagree

other interventions. Unearthing barriers enables training professionals to use targeted solutions. That's not easy to sell in an organization, but it can and does happen, as the IBM initiative illustrates.

Even more challenging is when companies with far-flung customers and suppliers enter unknown situations in which they can't assess or address the barriers. The people who show up for training may come from everywhere, with vastly different barriers and support. Generally, external trainers feel less able than internal ones to overcome a company's obstacles. Though any trainer might be able to deal with diverse skill levels and interests, no one's arms are long enough to reach into all of the units and organizations to which participants may return.

The statements in Tables 1 and 2 serve as a way to prequalify participants and help them get the most from training.

Establishing collaborative relationships. It's important to partner with management developers, human resource and organizational development professionals, and internal and external trainers to get different entities in an organization to coordinate with nontraining collaborators. How can empowerment, diversity appreciation, or virtual ways of working succeed without the cooperation of human resources, organiza-

---

tional effectiveness, and information technology?—just to name a few likely partners. People who manage the allocation of technology resources, job definition and selection, management development, or recognition and incentive programs know some of what is needed to align training with organizational goals.

Efforts to facilitate that type of collaboration are under way in many organizations. The United States Coast Guard, for example, has established a performance technology unit. Its purpose is to assess barriers and ensure that a cross-functional approach produces results. Amoco's Organizational Capability Group is another example. At Amoco, education and training make up one of the units, or capabilities, that collaborate to serve line outcomes.

During training, it's important to include some discussion of barriers and training transfer. Too often, training professionals don't prepare participants for the real world in which they will attempt to use what they learned in class. Trainers should work on performance barriers in the domain they can control, their classrooms. They can share data from the needs assessment on unearthing barriers and offer ways to overcome them.

Trainers can also discuss with participants their managers' or coworkers' possible objections. The participants can practice their responses. In other words, trainers can inoculate participants against the thoughts, words, and deeds of resistance. They can share suggestions from participants who were able to transfer what they learned in training and who came up with successful approaches to get more computer resources, supervisory support, and so forth.

I have used an audiotape of a fictional scenario with hundreds of training professionals to show what should *not* be done. It goes as follows:

An executive calls a training manager into his office. The executive has just returned from a conference and is eager to roll out a new idea to 175 managers and supervisors. He is certain that his idea, herbal leadership, has much to offer his people. He'd like to "cycle his folks" through an herbal leadership class during the next few months and wants "something powerful that will take advantage of adult learning exercises in which they can get involved with the concepts." The trainer asks when he'd like to start the training and notes that because a recent diversity class pulled people off work, the executive might encounter some resistance. He is willing to postpone briefly, but urges the trainer to schedule the class. She agrees.

People tend to chuckle while listening to the tape. They say that the trainer is motivated to set up the herbal leadership class without asking enough questions. They also note that she isn't doing the right thing, saying that the perfunctory scheduling of training is more likely to annoy managers and supervisors than make them adopt a more participatory style. They say that the herbal leadership class, in and of itself, can't bring about a culture change of that magnitude.

But what stuns me is that no one has ever said that the example is unrealistic. They usually say, "That's typical. We don't push back. We don't sell the importance of solution-type systems or convey the costs of ignoring organizational barriers. She should admit that a class won't get it done." When I ask whether she should refuse to offer the class if the executive opposes a needs assessment and an integrated solution system, they say, "She should, but she won't."

In this article, I have argued for permeable class boundaries, for a larger role for trainers, for the prequalification of participants and their managers, and for the extension of our ken beyond classroom walls to anticipating and removing obstacles to performance. I have also pressed for in-class approaches to help participants deal with the obstructions they may confront after training is completed.

You can probably remember other people or even yourself thinking, "That was a great class, but...." Does a course that evokes only that sentiment deserve to be called great? Is it ethical to be satisfied with delivering "great" workshops and courses or to be immune to organizational realities that affect performance? Will technology bust classroom boundaries and obliterate our comfort in conventional roles within four walls?

As I was writing this article, the telephone rang. A friend in the local training community told me about a recent conversation with a manager at a utility company. The manager agonized over the jolt of deregulation on the employees. She wanted my friend to conduct a class to improve their morale.

My friend was skeptical, but she was going to try.

Instead of just raising my eyebrows, I sent my friend a draft of this article, and I'm awaiting her reaction. Perhaps I have also become cynical, but I sort of expect her to call and say, "Great article, but...."

Measuring Training's ROI

By Scott B. Parry

Audience ➡	Learning Professionals
Purpose ➡	—Understand the importance of measuring training return on investment —Learn four measurement methods
Suggested Uses ➡	Self-study/handout Resource for training presentation Use cost-benefit worksheet provided to facilitate calculations

"Training doesn't cost...it pays! HRD is an investment, not an expense."

Rare is the trainer who doesn't believe this. Far more common is the trainer who doesn't believe that a return on the training investment can (or even should) be calculated.

Should all training programs be required to show a return on investment (ROI)? Not at all. However, courses of three days or more that are offered many times to reach a large number of trainees (say 100 or more) represent a significant expense. The professional trainer should justify this expense by calculating the ROI.

We're talking about Level Four: Results on Donald Kirkpatrick's evaluation model, and it's the most difficult to measure. Level One: Reaction, and Level Two: Learning can be measured with relative ease in class, using paper-and-pencil instruments and simulations. Level Three: Application at work is more difficult, because it means measuring performances on the job where many variables are affecting the performance of our graduates. Level Four: Results are usually shown as a return on investment—the dollar value of the benefits of training over and above the cost of the training itself.

And there's the rub. Many factors make this level of measurement the most difficult by far. Here are some of the more common difficulties that are cited as reasons for not doing a Level Four evaluation:

- The costs of training are known and expressed in dollars, but the benefits are often soft, subjective, and difficult to quantify and convert to dollars.

- We have enough trouble getting managers to send people to training without imposing additional requirements to collect data to document the impact.

- Costs are known up front, before training, but benefits may accrue slowly over time. At what point after training do you attempt to measure impact?

- As trainers, we lack the time and the accounting skills to do a cost-benefit analysis. Besides, our requests for data disrupt productivity.

- We probably will continue to run most of our popular training programs even if costs exceed benefits. So why bother?

Reprinted with permission from *Training & Development*, published by the American Society for Training & Development

We're not a profit center.

- The outcomes could be damaging to the HRD staff and to budget support from top management. We may be better off not knowing.
- People at work perform the way they do for many reasons, only one of which relates to training. How can we take credit or blame for their performance?
- The very act of collecting data on the dollar value of performance will tend to bias the information we get, making it hard for us to present a true picture.

If you've been looking for some reasons for not evaluating the ROI of your training efforts, read no further. This list should enable you to persuade the most insistent believer that any attempt to prove that training pays for itself is sheer folly! Let sleeping dogs lie— what we don't know can't hurt us. Right?

Wrong! Lest we be accused of favoritism, let's give equal time to a list of reasons why we should take the time and effort to calculate the costs and the benefits of our major training programs. Here are some supporting reasons:

- HRD budgets can be justified and even expanded when training can contribute to profit and is not seen as an act of faith or a cost of doing business.
- Course objectives and content will become more lean, relevant, and behavioral with focus on monetary results rather than on the acquisition of information.
- Better commitment of trainees and their managers who become responsible for follow-up and ROI, and not just for filling seats.
- Action plans, individual development plans, and managers' briefings will be taken seriously, thus strengthening the trainee-manager partnership.
- Better performance by HRD staff in containing costs and maximizing benefits. They become performance managers and not just instructors.
- HRD staff has solid data about where training is effective and where it is weak, so that courses can be revised and fine-tuned to produce the best returns.
- The curriculum of courses offered can be determined on a financial basis and not

just on popularity, rank of the manager requesting it, and so forth.

- Course enrollments will be serious, with trainees aware of the expectations that follow graduation. We'll get the right faces in the right places at the right times.
- By calculating ROI on the courses where it is possible, we are more apt to be trusted on the ones we can't evaluate at Level Four.

Four Ways to Measure ROI on Training

Now that we've examined the pros and cons of calculating the ROI of a training program, let's look at four ways of doing so. The nature of the training and the course objectives will determine which method is most appropriate.

1. **When hard data exist.** Performance data are routinely collected on many jobs for which we provide training. Examples include driver safety (monetary value of reduced accidents, lower insurance); machine maintenance (fewer repairs, less downtime); sales training (increased volume, fewer returns); and bank tellers (fewer "overs and shorts," more services and customers handled per hour).

Many technical training programs have data on existing performance before the course is launched. By comparing the costs of inadequate performance prior to training with the reduced costs of better performance after training, we can see the return on investment.

Even courses that teach "soft skills" can have a "hard data" side to performance. Examples include writing skills (time saved via shorter letters, understood without subsequent clarification); meeting leadership (shorter meetings, better follow-up); and EEO and diversity (fewer grievances and lawsuits).

Notice that our examples focus on the quantitative aspects of performance—things that can be counted in minutes, dollars saved or gained, and so forth. To be sure, these courses also have qualitative aspects. But these are more difficult to measure (such as courteous driving, more professional selling, clearer writing, more participative meeting leadership). Hard data probably don't exist to evaluate these qualities, so we have no way of comparing pre-training and post-training performance.

Conclusion: If we want to take credit for the impact of training on workplace performance, we must establish a "bench level" of what the performance was before we launched the training program.

2. **Estimates by trainees and their managers.** This method is the easiest way to estimate ROI, but also the most subjective. Several months after completing each cycle of a training program, send a memo to each graduate and manager (sponsor). State the actual cost to the organization of the trainee's participation in the course. Ask the two to get together, discuss the actual improved performance that has taken place since the course, agree on a dollar value of this improvement, and project the total value over the coming year (or whatever period is appropriate to the application of the concepts and skills that were learned).

The two then send this projected dollar value in, along with a one- to two-paragraph explanation of how the estimate was made. By comparing the costs of those who responded with their dollar estimates of value added to workplace performance, we can arrive at a crude estimate of the cost-benefit ratio.

In situations where bench levels were not established before the course was launched, this method of estimating ROI has appeal. What it lacks in accuracy it makes up for in getting trainees and their managers to recognize that the responsibility for making training effective is primarily theirs and not the trainer's.

3. **Action plans, managers' briefing.** During a training program, each participant prepares an action plan that spells out how the concepts and skills learned will be applied back at work. If the course involves teaching the entire job to a new employee, then the action plan will resemble a job description. If the course is for present employees (such as supervisors, team leaders, project managers), then the action plan spells out those actions the participant will take back to the job, which will differ from other participants whose needs are different.

After the training program, participants share their action plans with their managers and anyone else who is a stakeholder in their growth and development. This helps to build the participants' managers into their development—as coaches, mentors, and overseers of the implementations of the action plan. (A pre-training meeting with the participants' managers is important: to cover course objectives, how the action plans work, and how managers can help their enrollees in the post-training follow-through.)

Several months after the training, participants and their managers come together for a two- to three-hour meeting at which each participant reports on the results since implementing the action plan, along with the cost of doing so and the value of the benefits. Managers work with their participants prior to this meeting to arrive at the dollar value of the costs and the benefits. By tallying the numbers reported by the participants and adding the cost of the course, the return on investment is obtained.

4. **Cost-benefit analysis via accounting.** This method is the most demanding way to calculate ROI, but also the most accurate. Costs can be listed under seven categories, as noted below:

- Course development (time) or purchase (price, license fees).
- Instructional materials: per participant (expendables) and instructor (durables).
- Equipment and hardware: projectors, computers, video ("fair share" use).
- Facilities: rental of conference center and "fair share" use of classroom overhead.
- Travel, lodging, meals, breaks, shipping of materials, and so forth.
- Salary of instructor and support staff (prorated), consultants' fees, and so forth.
- Lost productivity (if applicable) or cost of temporary replacements for participants.

These costs are of three types: one-time (such as needs analysis and design), cost per offering (such as facility rental, instructor's salary), and cost per participant (such as meals, notebooks, coffee breaks). Costs must therefore be calculated over the life of the training program.

Benefits fall into four major categories as shown below:

- Time savings (less time needed to reach proficiency, less supervision needed, and so forth).
- Better quantity (faster work rate, less downtime, no waiting for help, and so forth).
- Better quality (fewer rejects, lost sales, reduced accidents, lower legal costs, and so forth).
- Personnel data (less absenteeism, fewer medical claims, reduced grievances, and so forth).

Benefits accrue long after training and can be projected over the life of the trainees in the job for which they were trained (typically one to five years). While costs can be calculated by HRD managers, the benefits should be calculated by the trainees and their managers after they have had enough experience in the workplace to collect enough data to project the benefits over the payback period. A comparison of the total costs to the total benefits yields our ROI.

Eight Observations on Conducting a Cost-Benefit Analysis

- Some courses should be offered without expectation of a measurable return on the investment (such as orientation of new employees and retirement planning). Because the benefits of conducting such programs are difficult if not impossible to measure, and because organizations offer them without expectation of any tangible return on the investment, it is foolish to attempt a cost-benefit analysis.
- Training programs for employees whose jobs have well-defined and quantified expectations (standards, goals, quotas) are the most appropriate ones for measuring return on the training investment because performance measurement systems already exist.
- By contrast, training for supervisors, managers, technical experts, project coordinators, and others for whom performance measurement systems do not exist are much more difficult to evaluate via Level

Four (cost-benefit analysis). The responsibility rests with each participant to generate pre-training data and post-training data on performance, and to assign dollar values to these two sets of data.

- Most cost-benefit analyses are comparative studies that show how the performance levels obtained by installing a new training program compare with the performance levels obtained by no training (such as safety, drugs, stress reduction) or by some alternative form of training (such as on-the-job training versus classroom, individualized versus group, centralized versus regional, and so forth). As in the third item, pre-training data on performance prior to installation of the new program may not have been collected. This must be done prior to carrying out a cost-benefit analysis.
- When training is conducted to accompany the installation of new equipment (procedures, products, policies, technology) and no prior training of a similar nature existed, a cost-benefit analysis is inappropriate for two reasons: There are no prior performance measures with which to compare the results of the new training, and the impact of installing the new changes makes it impossible to separate "performance attributable to training" from "performance attributable to innovation." (Examples include moving from manual to PC operations and learning to use e-mail.)
- The costs of training are known up front and should be calculated by HRD managers and others whose budgets are funding the program. The major unknown is based on the shelf life of the course—how many times (cycles) it will be run before it is no longer needed (such as when all eligible trainees have received it or when changes in technology have rendered it obsolete). Costs should be calculated over the shelf life of the program.
- Similarly, the benefits of training should extend well beyond the final offering (cycle) of the program. Different behaviors that were "shaped" by training have different life-cycles. The payback period on skills that are practiced regularly (such as time management) might be projected

Cost-Benefit Worksheet	One-Time Costs	Cost Per Offering	Cost Per Participant
COSTS			
1. **Course development (time) or selection (price, fees)**		N/A	N/A
▶ Needs analysis and research		N/A	N/A
▶ Design and creation of blueprint		N/A	N/A
▶ Writing, validating, and revising		N/A	N/A
▶ Producing (typesetting, illustrating, reproducing)		N/A	N/A
2. **Instructional materials**			
▶ Per participant (expendables: notebooks, handouts, tests, and so forth)	N/A	N/A	
▶ Per instructor (durables: videotape, film, software, overheads)			N/A
3. **Equipment (hardware)**			
▶ Projectors, VHS, computers, flipcharts, training aids			N/A
4. **Facilities**			
▶ Rental or allocated "fair share" use of classrooms, and so forth	N/A		N/A
5. **Off-site expenses (if applicable)**			
▶ Travel, hotel accommodations, meals, breaks	N/A	N/A	
▶ Shipping of materials, rental of A/V equipment, and so forth	N/A		N/A
6. **Salary**			
▶ Participants (number of instruction hours × average hourly rate)	N/A	N/A	
▶ Instructor, course administrator, program manager, and so forth			N/A
▶ Fees to consultants or outside instructors			N/A
▶ Support staff (audiovisual, administrative, and so forth)	N/A		N/A
7. **Lost productivity (if applicable)**			
▶ Production rate losses or material losses	N/A	N/A	
A. Total of all one-time "up front" costs		N/A	N/A
B. Total of all costs incurred each time course is offered	N/A		N/A
C. This sum (box B) × number of times course is run (_____)	N/A		N/A
D. Total of all costs incurred for each participant	N/A	N/A	
E. This sum (box D) × number of participants (_____) over life of course	N/A	N/A	
F. Total costs (sum of boxes A, C, and E)			
BENEFITS			
1. **Time savings**			
▶ Shorter lead time to reach proficiency (hours saved × $)	N/A		N/A
▶ Less time required to perform an operation (hours saved × $)	N/A	N/A	
▶ Less supervision needed (supervisory hours saved × supervisory $)	N/A		
▶ Better time management (hours freed up × $)	N/A	N/A	
2. **Better productivity (quantity)**			
▶ Faster work rate ($ value of additional units, sales, and so forth)	N/A	N/A	N/A
▶ Time saved by not having to wait for help (hours saved × $)	N/A	N/A	
▶ Less down time ($ value of reduced nonproductive time)	N/A	N/A	
3. **Improved quality of output**			
▶ Fewer rejects (to scrap, lost sales, returns, and so forth—$ value)	N/A	N/A	
▶ Value added to output (bigger sales, smoother castings—$)	N/A	N/A	
▶ Reduced accidents ($ value of savings on claims, lost work)		N/A	
▶ Reduced legal costs (EEO, OSHA, WC settlements—$)		N/A	
▶ Improved competitiveness (change in market share—$)		N/A	N/A
4. **Better personnel performance**			
▶ Less absenteeism/tardiness (self or subordinates—$ saved)	N/A	N/A	
▶ Improved health ($ saved on medical and lost time)		N/A	
▶ Reduced grievances, claims, job actions ($ saved)		N/A	
▶ Same output with fewer employees ($ on jobs eliminated)		N/A	N/A
A. Total of all one-time benefits		N/A	N/A
B. Total of all benefits occurring once per participant	N/A		N/A
C. Total value of all improvements per participant per month	N/A	N/A	
D. Length of payback period in months	N/A	N/A	
E. Number of employees affected during this period (D)	N/A		N/A
F. Total of B × E	N/A		N/A
G. Total of C × D × E	N/A	N/A	
H. Total benefits (sum of A + F + G)			

over the employment life of the trainee, whereas skills that are called on less frequently (such as selection interviewing in a downsized economy) may have a much shorter payback period.

- Although training costs are best calculated by HRD managers, the benefits should be identified, quantified, and converted to dollar values by management (the trainees' supervisors, department heads, and so forth). There are two reasons for this: They are in the best position to observe changes in performance attributable to training, and their data are more objective and less suspect than if HRD specialists attempted to collect them.

Four Examples of Applications of Cost-Benefit Analysis

- A rapidly growing fast-food chain had a three-week apprentice training program that prepared employees for promotion as assistant managers. The corporate HRD manager felt that training time could be reduced to one week with a formal training program at headquarters. The one-week formal program required travel and hotel costs not associated with the three-week local apprentice training program. However, the company's ability to place assistant managers in outlets two weeks earlier resulted in savings that more than offset the cost of developing the program and bringing the trainees to a central location. It also ensured uniform quality of instruction that was lacking in the decentralized apprentice training that had taken place in each outlet.

- A major corporation had relied on two professors from the state university to conduct a supervisory training program, using their own handouts, visuals, and hands-on exercises. Some 93 supervisors went through the five-day program in classes of 15 to 16 participants each. Three years later when the company offered supervisory training again, it purchased a packaged course with videos,

workbooks, and instructor guidelines for its own internal instructors. Although the package cost $27,000, the company ended up saving $16,000 (the professors had charged $36,000 for labor and $7,000 for materials). Moreover, post-workshop evaluations showed that transfer of training from workshop to workplace had improved results significantly.

- A government agency ran a three-day workshop on project management with six offerings for 20 participants each. During the year following each workshop, the trainers surveyed the graduates to see how their post-training performance on projects compared with their pre-training behavior (as assessed during the needs analysis prior to training). Factors evaluated included percentage of projects completed on time and within budget, level of client satisfaction, and estimate of time/money saved as a result of improved project management. The agency concluded that a $95,000 training investment had saved an estimated $670,000. This figure did not include one reported savings of $2 million projected over five years.

- An automotive manufacturer installed a management development program as part of the company's TQM/empowerment efforts and put 220 managers at an assembly plant through the program. The average length was six days. After the first day of assessment, each manager attended only those workshops that dealt with the competencies and skills that received lower scores. Six months after the training, participants were assessed again. Benefits were evaluated on three factors: the degree to which each manager's individual development plan had been implemented, the change in productivity of the manager's work group, and the improvement in scores (percentiles against nationwide norms) by each manager on the two assessments. All three measures showed that the benefits far outweighed the costs.

Many Paths to Learning Software

By Candice Harp, John Satzinger, and Sandra Taylor

Audience	Learning Professionals
Purpose	—Learn about alternative methods for teaching employees to use new computer software —Learn how to survey prospective software trainees about their learning preferences
Suggested Uses	Self-study Questionnaire included could be adapted for use in other organizations

Organizations spend billions of dollars on software training, including materials, classroom time, and time employees spend reading manuals and experimenting with software. Though learning also occurs outside of the classroom, especially between coworkers, many organizations think instructor-led training is the only way to teach employees how to use new software. In fact, there are other useful and inexpensive approaches.

A study at the University of Georgia examined different ways people learn software, based on their learning styles and preferences, type of work, and experience. The findings can help companies create learning support systems for diverse software users.

Inexpensive, Readily Available

Participants were drawn randomly from a large database of licensed software users. They received a letter introducing the study and took part in structured, 15-minute telephone interviews in which they described the way they learn how to use new software.

Participants were asked to rank 30 activities associated with learning software, including attending courses, referring to the manual, and using trial and error. They rated each activity on a scale of 1 (least useful) to 5 (most useful). The overall response rate was

Participant Profile

Average age:	42
Gender:	69% male 31% female
Average education:	2 years of college

Average experience:
- 11.5 years of computer experience
- 11.8 different applications

Type of work:
- 14% clerical workers
- 48% knowledge workers
- 34% managers

Table 1. Preferred Learning Activities

LEARNING ACTIVITY	Rank	Avg. Score 1 = low 5 = high
▶ Experimenting with the software (for example, trial and error)	1	4.37
▶ Relying on consistent features in the software...........	2	4.23
▶ Asking coworkers for help	3	3.95
▶ Searching menus........................	4	3.94
▶ Reading prompts and messages	5	3.90
▶ Thinking about how similar programs work...............	6	3.87
▶ Asking an instructor a follow-up question..................	7	3.87
▶ Working one-on-one with a consultant......................	8	3.83
▶ Referring to the manual........................	9	3.79
▶ Asking a friend for help	10	3.79
▶ Thinking about how the software worked in an earlier version........................	11	3.77
▶ Calling supplier support	12	3.72
▶ Reading a third-party book........................	13	
▶ Using the on-line help feature........................	14	3.60
▶ Remembering how someone used the software to accomplish a task	15	3.57
▶ Reading magazines about the software	16	3.47
▶ Looking at on-line examples and sample files before using the software........................	17	3.43
▶ Following on-line tutorials........................	18	3.40
▶ Attending university courses........................	19	3.29
▶ Thinking about how dissimilar programs work...........	20	3.26
▶ Visualizing how someone used the software step-by-step to accomplish a task	21	3.21
▶ Calling the in-house help desk	22	3.18
▶ Attending formal training........................	23	3.17
▶ Using reference cards and keyboard templates...........	24	3.15
▶ Taking computer-based training produced by an outside party........................	25	3.14
▶ Accessing bulletin board services........................	26	3.12
▶ Attending user support groups	27	3.10
▶ Referring to training materials from class..................	28	3.06
▶ Watching videotaped lectures or demonstrations	29	2.63
▶ Attending professional trade meetings not in the computer industry........................	30	2.52

89 percent. (See Table 1 for a list of the activities in order of respondents' preference.)

Respondents rated experimenting with the software as the single most useful learning activity. Yet, some network administrators don't let people access new software until they've attended formal training. That may minimize the support staff's workload, but it overlooks an effective learning approach.

Another highly rated activity was searching through a software program's menus and reading the screen prompts. Because that approach is available to almost all users, support staff should promote it. For example, telephone support staff can ask users to review onscreen messages while they work through a problem. The support person can say, "Choose 'format make it fit expert' from the menu bar. Now, tell me what the message on your screen says." But in the study many respondents said that support staff solved problems without explaining how.

An instructor can also encourage participants to read screen messages and menus. For example, suppose trainees ask, "Can the program convert lower-case letters to mixed-case letters?" The instructor says, "Yes, choose 'edit convert case' from the menu bar." To encourage participants further to use the menus, the instructor can say, "Let's search through the menu bar and see if we can locate a feature like that."

Another inexpensive, readily available learning resource is coworkers. It's usually efficient for an inexperienced user to ask a knowledgeable one for help. In some organizations, a lead user from the administrative staff is assigned to each software package, and employees are encouraged to ask the designated lead for help before calling the help desk.

In one company in the study, the professional development department uses an "art gallery" to encourage coworkers to share their learning by posting samples from various software packages near the training room. One caption says, "Created with PowerPoint by importing scanned images of beverage cans and using those images as replacement symbols for charting. The scanned images are available from Jane Doe, ext. 999." The caption also tells who can answer questions about PowerPoint.

The study shows that the least useful learning activities include watching videos, attending user support groups, and referring to training manuals. Yet, many organizations still evaluate prospective suppliers by reviewing their training manuals.

Videos consistently ranked low on the study for usefulness for learning software. Despite that, companies with geographically dispersed employees tend to rely on videos as a primary training tool. Training courses also ranked low, 23 out of 30. One reason may be that training is usually evaluated at the end of a class, before participants have tested their new skills. The most common complaint respondents made about courses was that they already knew the material and resented spending hours in training.

An Important Question

Respondents' different opinions about which activities were useful led to an important question: Do some types of users find some learning activities more useful than others? To answer that question, the study classified participants by experience, work type, and learner type.

Experience. The study classified participants according to experience, determined by the number of software packages they had used and what types, including word processing, database, graphics, and spreadsheets. Users equal to or below the group median were classified as "less experienced"; those above the median were classified as "more experienced." Table 2 presents the preferred learning activities of more experienced and less experienced users.

More experienced users said that they were often asked for help, but rarely received help from more knowledgeable users. Less experienced users found it more useful to ask instructors follow-up questions. The study indicates that experienced users often draw from prior experience using similar software, and they refer to the manual. Respondents commented that it wasn't particularly helpful to keep just one copy at a LAN administrator's desk or in a learning center.

Work type. When participants were classified according to work type, the ranking of useful teaming activities changed. For the purpose of the study, knowledge workers

Overall		LEARNING ACTIVITY	Less Experienced n = 141		More Experienced n = 122	
Rank	Score		Rank	Score	Rank	Score
1	4.37	Experimenting with the software (for example, trial and error)	1	4.29	1	4.47
2	4.23	Relying on consistent features in the software	2	4.19	2	4.28
3	3.95	Asking coworkers for help	3	4.17	7	3.75
4	3.94	Searching menus	8	3.90	4	3.99
5	3.90	Reading prompts and messages	7	3.90	5	3.89
6	3.87	Thinking about how similar programs work	12	3.69	3	4.06
7	3.87	Asking an instructor a follow-up question	4	4.09	11	3.65
8	3.83	Working one-on-one with a consultant	5	4.00	12	3.64
9	3.79	Referring to the manual	11	3.71	6	3.88
10	3.79	Asking a friend for help	6	3.93	13	3.62

Table 2. Preferences Based on Software Experience

were defined as staff-level professionals (scientists, analysts, writers, and accountants) who were not clerical workers or managers.

Clerical workers rated one-on-one interaction with instructors and consultants more useful than did knowledge workers and managers. Clerical workers also rated courses useful. And they rated supplier support (ranked 40) more useful than did knowledge workers (ranked 13) (see Table 3).

Knowledge workers and managers pointed to consistent program features as useful for learning new software. They also found coworkers' help more useful than did clerical workers. More than clerical workers, knowledge workers and managers relied on their knowledge of similar programs, and they found it useful to search menus. Several of the clerical workers said that it never occurred to them to search menus.

Learner type. When participants were classified according to learning styles, the ranking of activities changed again. Learner type classification was based on responses to six questions about a user's willingness and ability to learn software autonomously. Of 263 users, 49 (19 percent) were classified as "dependent learners," 185 (70 percent) were classified as "self-directed learners," and 29 (11 percent) were undetermined, so they were omitted from the results (see Table 4).

The study indicates that dependent learners generally prefer a directed approach; self-directed learners generally prefer an autonomous approach. Self-directed learners like more control over what, when, and how to learn. Dependent learners prefer one-on-one discussions with trainers and consultants. Self-directed learners find it more useful to experiment with the software and search menus.

Considering that only 19 percent of respondents were classified as dependent learners, it's surprising that many organizations rely almost exclusively on formal training to teach software use.

Developing a Support System

A first step in implementing new software is to recognize that different types of users ben-

Table 3. Preferences Based on Work Type

Overall		LEARNING ACTIVITY	Clerical Workers n = 36		Knowledge Workers and Managers n = 217	
Rank	Score		Rank	Score	Rank	Score
1	4.37	Experimenting with the software (for example, trial and error)	1	4.44	1	4.34
2	4.23	Relying on consistent features in the software	6	4.03	2	4.26
3	3.95	Asking coworkers for help	8	4.00	3	3.94
4	3.94	Searching menus	9	3.97	4	3.93
5	3.90	Reading prompts and messages	7	4.03	6	3.87
6	3.87	Thinking about how similar programs work	15	3.64	5	3.90
7	3.87	Asking an instructor a follow-up question	2	4.17	8	3.79
8	3.83	Working one-on-one with a consultant	3	4.17	10	3.76
9	3.79	Referring to the manual	16	3.61	9	3.79
10	3.79	Asking a friend for help	5	4.09	11	3.73

Table 4. Preferences Based on Learner Type

Overall		LEARNING ACTIVITY	Dependent Learners n = 49		Self-Directed Learners n = 185	
Rank	Score		Rank	Score	Rank	Score
1	4.37	Experimenting with the software (for example, trial and error)	9	3.80	1	4.53
2	4.23	Relying on consistent features in the software	3	4.15	2	4.21
3	3.95	Asking coworkers for help	4	4.11	5	3.89
4	3.94	Searching menus	14	3.63	3	4.03
5	3.90	Reading prompts and messages	5	4.02	6	3.85
6	3.87	Thinking about how similar programs work	15	3.61	4	3.99
7	3.87	Asking an instructor a follow-up question	2	4.32	9	3.77
8	3.83	Working one-on-one with a consultant	1	4.40	13	3.61
9	3.79	Referring to the manual	13	3.67	7	3.85
10	3.79	Asking a friend for help	8	3.80	10	3.75

efit from different types of learning activities. Here are some effective ways to support software learning.

- Enable employees to experiment with new software before or instead of formal training.
- Reward knowledgeable employees who serve as resident experts. If necessary, include their support as a measurable goal on their performance appraisals.
- Make a variety of learning activities convenient and available to employees, including manuals, "third-party" books (books about the software written by people other than the supplier or internal technology support staff), supplier support numbers and guidelines, and current training programs redesigned to explain how to use the new software's help feature and menus.
- Provide a two-hour jump-start session with an overview of the software.

- Offer full-day classes for people who prefer structured training.
- Provide half-day, quick-paced classes for self-directed learners and experienced users.
- Provide half-day or full-day open computer labs where users can work on problems and projects. Advertise in advance and encourage attendance from all levels.
- Encourage users to drop by a class in progress. They may learn something by just observing.
- Implement an art gallery in a common area to showcase users' work with the software, with their names and phone numbers. You can block out sensitive data.

The study indicates a need to support diverse learners. We need to rethink and redesign training so that we embed learning support. And we need to transform training departments into learning support centers.

A Start-up Guide to Distance Learning

By Donna Abernathy

Audience ➡	Learning Professionals
Purpose ➡	—Learn about the various distance learning technologies —Be able to use a decision-making tool for selecting technologies appropriate to the learning purpose —Learn success factors for developing programs using these technologies —Have resources for finding more information
Suggested Uses ➡	Self-study/handout Resource for developing training presentation on this topic

Nicholas Negroponte, *Wired* columnist and author of *Being Digital,* tells us: "Distance is irrelevant: New York to London is only five miles farther than New York to Newark via satellite." What a concept.

Distance learning is clearly changing the way we do business. Plain and simple: Workplace technology affects training delivery. Organizations still rely heavily on such traditional means as lecture and videotapes to deliver training, but there's growing, widespread interest in using such tools as the Internet, videoconferencing, and corporate networks.

One factor in this shift to technology-based training is cost. Distance learning enables companies to reach more employees at a lower cost. Another factor is the more competitive business environment. Using technologies to deliver training at a distance can help organizations to:

- Cut training expenses
- Improve productivity
- Reduce trainee backlogs without increasing resources significantly
- Increase access to subject matter experts
- Make training more flexible
- Access alternative instructional resources

Here's what you need to know to get started.

The Trends and Tools

Ford Motor, AT&T, Oracle, and Unisys are just some companies that have documented proof that distance learning is effective. Such organizations are using distance learning to enhance training, marketing, and communications.

Workers are using distance learning to reinforce their skills. They're asking: What do I want to learn and need to learn? What skills will help me now or later? They're controlling their careers with courses and tools in self-directed learning on the job, at home, or on the road. That means they use computers, video, audio, and other technologies to learn. Classroom training is becoming an option rather than the rule.

Training departments are designing and delivering courses on technical skills and critical thinking. The "new" trainers help workers learn on or off the job—by assessing training needs, by providing subject content and resources, and by challenging and guiding trainees, before, during, and after a course has been delivered by distance learning.

Distance learning is adaptable to almost all traditional training approaches, including lecture, videotapes, and role play. Distance learning can also incorporate any technology, as long as a structured two-way communication is created for learner-trainer interaction.

Technologies can be categorized as interactive or noninteractive. Interactive technologies have a two-way communication channel built in. Noninteractive technologies have one-way communication capabilities. By combining any of the noninteractive technologies with a phone, fax, or interactive technology, you can create a distance learning environment. (See the box, Distance Learning Technologies, below.)

Coaching trainees through the repair of a complex machine may require two-way video capability plus whiteboard sketches. A training meeting may work with just two-way audio and a single camera for slides.

You can use a technology checklist to weigh your goals against tool availability, appropriateness, and cost restraints. Whatever the application, distance learning doesn't force you into a narrow presentation format. (See Checklist: Which Technology?, page 1-70 and 1-71.) The bottom line: Will it work for you?

How to Develop a Program

It's vital to build interactivity into each distance learning course. The rule of thumb is to add creative and engaging interactive activities every five to seven minutes. The Interactivity Guide Pyramid can help you develop and deliver a well-balanced program. (See the figure on page 1-72.)

The Interactivity Guide Pyramid works like a food guide pyramid. For example, choose from the following groupings:

- 3 to 5 servings of activities from the Personalize Group
- 3 to 4 servings of activities from the Participate Group

Distance Learning Technologies

Here are some different types of distance learning technologies:

Interactive	Noninteractive*
▶ Audioconference	▶ One-way satellite/microwave
▶ Audiographics	▶ Radio
▶ Videoconferencing	▶ Printed materials
▶ Computer conference (Internet, e-mail)	▶ Audiotape
▶ Two-way satellite/microwave	▶ Computer disk/CD-ROM/laser disc
▶ Desktop videoconference	▶ Videotape
▶ One-way satellite with keypad	▶ Cable/broadcast television
▶ Voicemail	
▶ Virtual reality	

Requires phone, fax, or one of the interactive technologies to create a two-way communication channel for distance learning.

Source: adapted from *Info-line: Effective Distance Learning,* edited by Mary O'Neill (ASTD, July 1996).

Checklist: Which Technology?

	Pros	Cons	Will it Work for You?
Audioconference. Training through telephone connection. Audio only; no visual. Send prework via mail, e-mail, or fax in advance. Discuss as a group in an audioconference with multiple sites.	Inexpensive and relatively easy to set up	No visual cues	☐
Audiographics. Computer and phone linkage. Participants listen and respond to the trainer via speaker phone, while observing computer screen training. They respond with a writing whiteboard linked to their computer screens. All sites linked "live" at same time. All linkage via phone lines.	Includes visual and auditory components; very interactive	Requires purchase of software and whiteboard; need expert to set up	☐
Videoconferencing. Television screens at all sites with camera and microphones to transmit visual images and audio. Trainer and participants can see and hear each other at multiple sites. Data and graphics can also be transmitted.	Two-way video, audio, and data; very interactive	Cost to purchase equipment can be high; consider renting	☐
Desktop Videoconference. Same as group videoconference, but participants sit at a computer with camera and microphone attached. Can see trainer, other participants, and data on computer screen, and hear/participate in all conversations.	Participants can take part at their own desks; very interactive	New technology; not readily available but low cost	☐
Computer Conference (Internet, e-mail). Training via e-mail or the Internet. Training material sent to participants on-line; they read and respond via on-line discussions (one-way: copy each other on responses or two-way: use a "live chat" function and "talk" at same time on-line).	Easy to design and implement; very effective for small classes	Must have e-mail or Internet access; need accountability for participation	☐
One-Way Satellite/Microwave. Training program delivered via satellite or microwave link. Participants watch, then respond via phone, fax, or e-mail. (Microwave links are becoming outdated, due to cost and distance limitations.)	Good for short, informational-type courses with wide audiences	Can be boring if not designed correctly; old method	☐
Two-Way Satellite/Microwave. Same as above but with television cameras at participants' end so there is two-way video and audio. Similar to videoconferencing but with different equipment.	Two-way video and audio; very interactive	Incredibly expensive; rarely done	☐
One-Way Satellite with Keypad. Same as one-way satellite above, but with an electronic keypad as a response tool for participants. They respond to the trainer by selecting their choice on the keypad. Answers are displayed on a TV screen at all sites.	More interactive than one-way; participants prefer it	Cost goes up with keypads; installation issues	☐

Checklist: Which Technology?

	Pros	Cons	Will it Work for You?
Voicemail. Trainer sends out material in advance, then asks participants to leave responses on voicemail. Trainer responds to each via voicemail. Can also set up so all participants hear each others' responses and have discussion.	Easy to implement; low cost; good for short classes	Need good course design; must install voicemail	☐
Cable/Broadcast Television. Same as one-way satellite/microwave, but with cable television. Instructor teaches from a TV station. Materials sent in advance; participants respond via phone, fax, or e-mail. Used by many universities for home study.	Good for short, informational-type courses with wide audiences	Can be boring if not designed correctly; old method	☐
Printed Materials. The oldest distance learning technology; send printed materials with course lesson. Participants mail responses back. Trainer provides feedback via mail or phone. This is the model used in correspondence courses.	Simple to implement; inexpensive	Need good course design; participants must be motivated to finish	☐
Videotape. Mail out videotape with course. Participants respond to trainer via phone, fax, or e-mail. Older method of distance learning.	Same as above	Same as above	☐
Audiotape. Mail out audiotape with course. Participants respond to trainer via phone, fax, or e-mail, or they make own audiotape response. Old method.	Same as above	Same as above	☐
Computer Disk/CD-ROM/Laser Disc. Mail out with course. Participants respond to trainer via phone, fax, e-mail, or computer disk.	Same as above	Same as above	☐
Radio. Old method. Course was broadcast via radio waves. Participants responded via mail or phone. Used in Australia to teach students in the outback.	Can reach many people across vast distances	Outdated method; new alternatives have replaced it	☐
Virtual Reality. Participants placed in a realistic situation to learn a new skill where they must respond verbally, visually, and kinesthetically. Involves computer simulation of some type. A flight simulator is a good example. Other equipment includes virtual reality technology.	Taps into all senses and learning styles; exciting experience	Technology very new; costs very high; not yet readily available	☐

Source: adapted from *Info-line: Effective Distance Learning,* edited by Mary O'Neill (ASTD, July 1996).

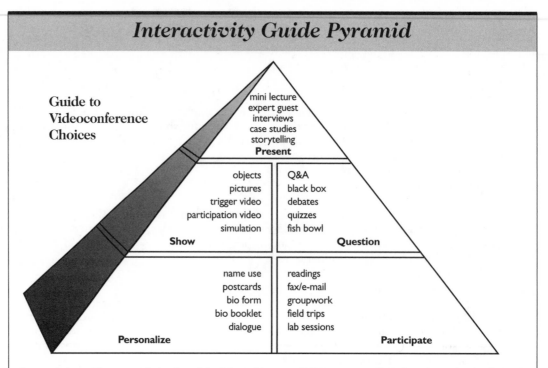

Interactivity Guide Pyramid

Guide to Videoconference Choices

mini lecture
expert guest
interviews
case studies
storytelling
Present

objects
pictures
trigger video
participation video
simulation
Show

Q&A
black box
debates
quizzes
fish bowl
Question

name use
postcards
bio form
bio booklet
dialogue
Personalize

readings
fax/e-mail
groupwork
field trips
lab sessions
Participate

Interactivity guide pyramid developed by Mavis Mortson, UW-Extension, 1995, based on the Food Guide Pyramid (U.S. Department of Agriculture and Department of Health and Human Services, 1993); appears in Lehman, Rosemary (1996) The Essential Compressed Video Guide: 7 Keys to Success, Instructional Communications Systems, UW-Extension, Madison, Wisconsin (p. 23), Interactivity Spectrum developed by Rosemary Lehman, UW-Extension, 1995, appears in Lehman, Rosemary (1996), The Essential Compressed Video Guide: 7 Keys to Success, Instructional Commmunications Systems, UW-Extension, Madison, Wisconsin (p. 19) Permission to reprint these copyrighted materials is given by Instructional Communications Systems.

- 2 to 3 servings of activities from the Show Group

- 3 to 5 servings from the Question Group

- Sparingly from the Presentation Group (if a one-way presentation) or generously (if mixed with activities from the other groups)

A compressed-video environment leads logically to an emphasis on interaction. Interactivity can involve participants at remote sites, and off-site for communication and individual or group projects. The activities should be short, intense, well-planned, meaningful, enjoyable, and involving. They should also match objectives. Interactivity spans the spectrum from simple to complex. It includes ways to present, personalize, show, participate, and question.

A course development team consists of an instructional designer and instructional developer, a technology support person, a trainer or an instructor, distant-site facilitators, a materials supporter and facilities supporter, and a management sponsor. That team develops new courses or revises existing courses to be used with a selected technology in distance learning. Adaptation may include breaking a course into small modules, turning overheads into computer graphics, or designing new interactive exercises to fit the technology.

Let's say that you've decided to adapt a supervisory course, Constructive Feedback, to a distance learning format, videoconferencing. The classroom version is four hours long, with short lectures with overheads, a videotape, and role play.

To adapt the course to videoconferencing, you divide it into two two-hour sections and develop a prework package for trainees explaining the distance learning format, with prereading on constructive feedback. Participants also complete a short preassessment, which they fax or e-mail back. You convert the overheads to a colorful videographics presentation to be shown on a videoconferencing computer. You can show the videotape as is. For the role play, the trainer or instructor explains the exercise. He or she mutes distant-site microphones as trainees practice. The site facilitators observe the practice and provide feedback. The instructor observes the skill practice via a camera. The participants regroup to debrief.

No More Talking Heads

Lorne Parker, president of the Teletraining Institute in Stillwater, Oklahoma, emphasizes that teaching via teletraining can and should be as lively and interesting as a face-to-face presentation. (See the box, Tips for Smoother Teletraining.) He offers the following guidelines for blending one's personal style with teletraining techniques.

- **Incorporate "humanizing" into your planning.** Humanizing means focusing on the importance of each individual and generating group rapport. It lets participants know that, although separated from the trainer by distance, their needs are important. Many may be alone at their locations, may not have used teleconferencing systems before, and may expect

something quite different from the actual teletraining experience. The first minutes of a session are critical. That's when participants get acquainted with the instructor, other trainees, equipment, and ground rules.

Effective humanizing techniques include opening a session with a five-minute icebreaker, explaining the mechanics of the particular setup, and suggesting protocol for trainees and sites to take turns, such as alphabetical order.

- **Actively promote participation.** Spontaneous interaction among trainees can be even more important in distance education than in traditional settings. It keeps up people's interest and commitment. But participation doesn't just happen; you have to plan for it.

Because people have different comfort levels, it's useful to provide different ways for them to get involved. For instance, the instructor can ask trainees to think about

---

Tips For Smoother Teletraining

Here are some tips for teletraining instructors:

Improve roll calls

▶ Have trainees introduce themselves one at a time and share their expectations.

▶ At large sites, have on-the-job facilitators take roll call ahead of time and fax it to you.

▶ Try these icebreakers for new courses: Have each trainee give a safety tip or tell what kind of automobile best describes his or her personality.

Remember names

▶ Draw a map to show the locations and names of participants. Place a check after each name when that person makes a comment.

▶ Ask for a photo of each trainee and create a chart with names. Keep it handy during each session.

▶ Use file cards to record trainees' names. As the course progresses, jot down notes to help you remember their interests and backgrounds.

Use pacing and vocal techniques

▶ Vary your inflection. Circle an occasional line of text in your notes to remind you.

▶ Pause to draw attention to an important topic. Allow trainees time to reflect and ask questions.

Summarize key points frequently.

Lecture in 10-minute chunks.

Source: *Teletechniques: Skills for Distance Education Instructors and Course Developers*, by Lorne Parker, Teletraining Institute, 1993.

---

an issue before a discussion begins. Fixed time slots will ensure that everyone gets a turn. The instructor also should let trainees know that even "wrong" answers are legitimate. He or she should provide feedback that shows participants have been heard and understood.

- **Adjust the message style.** Get rid of the talking heads. Take into consideration such adult learning concepts as learner retention, short-segment planning, and media-rich approaches. In teletraining, you must create a relationship between the audio and visual aspects by using various media. For instance, you may need to silence the audio at certain points to give trainees time to "record" a visual message. A color slide or video roll-in can enhance the audio presentation. Print backups reinforce what trainees hear, and they serve as permanent records for review.

- **Seek constant feedback.** Feedback can help you become a better communicator because it answers these questions: Is what I am saying interesting or boring? Does everyone understand what I am saying or showing? Did I leave out any important details? Feedback becomes a stimulus to help you decide your next action.

The easiest way to incorporate feedback into teletraining is to, at each natural division in the material, ask such questions as, "Was the message too fast or too complex?" Just as important, give trainees feedback, such as, "Your group did that well."

- **Use several instructional approaches.** No single format works in all situations. You get the best results by mixing several styles. Teletraining lends itself to creative formats, such as team teaching, brainstorming, and role play. The number of trainees and sites, equipment, and make-up of the group are just some factors to consider. You may have to adapt on the fly.

Delivery Tips

Here are some tips for effective distance learning:

▶ **Conduct** a pilot of the first session.

▶ **Train** the trainer or instructor on how to facilitate via the technology. That may require new skills and new ways to promote interaction.

▶ **Rehearse,** even before the pilot, so that the trainer or instructor can become familiar and comfortable with the new platform. Some training professionals have described distance learning as "training in the dark" because of the lack of visual—and sometimes auditory—cues. It takes a new set of skills to train effectively using the various technologies.

▶ **Provide** communication protocols. The trainer will need to give clear instructions in advance on how the interaction and activities will take place via distance learning—in other words, who will talk when. For example, in an on-line chat session, the trainer will type in a question. To answer, a trainee must type an exclamation point (!) to show that he or she wants to respond. Participants must also signal when they're finished. The trainer may need to call on people by name to ensure that everyone participates.

▶ **Promote** interaction between participants through various exercises, discussion, and work between sessions. For example, as homework, participants at each site can prepare a presentation for the other sites and deliver it through voicemail, e-mail, a videoconference, or as overheads faxed to the trainer to present via satellite or cable television.

▶ **Ensure** that the trainer knows the names of the site facilitators and introduces them at the beginning of a course.

▶ **Have** a course roster and introductions. The trainer should have a list of all of the participants at each site and make sure that everyone gets a chance to introduce themselves.

Source: adapted from *Info-line: Effective Distance Learning,* edited by Mary O'Neill (ASTD, July 1996).

Rapid advances in communications technology have given distance learning a high profile. The *Wall Street Journal* pronounced it "a rapidly growing and flexible alternative to traditional learning." Companies have to become more productive to compete with others in a fast-paced market. Distance learning enables them to provide more effective learning to more people—when and where it's needed—while reducing travel and downtime costs, and encouraging a global perspective.

Know the Lingo!

Here's a glossary of distance learning terms:

Audiographics. The transmission of images and graphics over standard telephone lines to enhance audio interaction.

Bandwidth. The range of frequencies that can be carried by a telecommunications medium without undue distortion.

Bridge. A hardware device or software product that interconnects three or more telephone lines; used to link multiple locations.

Broadband. A telecommunications medium that carries high-frequency signals, such as television frequencies.

Compressed video. Images that have been compressed to eliminate redundant information and reduce bandwidth required to transmit them.

Downlink. To beam signals from a satellite to Earth stations. Also, an antenna that receives satellite signals.

H.320/H.323/H.324. Standards set by the International Telecommunications Union to guarantee that video-conferencing systems made by different suppliers will work together over data networks, local area networks, the Internet, and ordinary telephone networks.

ISDN. Integrated Services Digital Network—digital telecommunications standards that allow for an integrated transmission of voice, video, and data.

Multiplexing. The technique of sending multiple information streams on a single carrier at the same time.

Multipoint Conference Unit (MCU). The bridge linking three or more videoconferencing locations.

Narrowband. A telecommunications medium that carries low-frequency signals, such as telephone voice signals.

T.120. An interoperability standard set by the ITU that describes how computers communicate during a data conference.

TCP/IP. Transmission Control Protocol/Internet Protocol—the basic program or suite of protocols used to handle Internet data.

VSAT. Very Small Aperture Terminal—a small Earth station (signal receptor) used for satellite communications.

Videoconferencing. Conferencing in which participants see and hear each other via two-way or multipoint connections.

Additional Resources

Here are some resources for information on distance learning:

Organizations

**American Center for the
Study of Distance Education**
Pennsylvania State University
110 Rackley Building
University Park, PA 16802-3202
Phone 814.863.3764
http://www.cde.psu.edu/acsde

Center for Distance Learning Research
Texas A&M University
College Station, TX 77843-1588
Phone 409.862.7574
http://www.cdir.tamu.edu

**Distance Education and
Training Council**
1601 18th Street NW
Washington, DC 20009-2529
Phone 202.234.5100
http://www.detc.org

**Distance Learning
Resource Network
WestEd**
730 Harrison Street
San Francisco, CA 94107-1214
Phone 800.662.4160

**International Centre for
Distance Learning**
The Open University, Walton Hall
Milton Keynes
MK7 6AA
United Kingdom
Phone +44.1980.653537
http://www-icdl.open.ac.uk

**International Society for
Technology in Education**
1787 Agate Street
Eugene, OR 97403-1923
Phone 541.346.4414
http://www.iste.org

International Teleconferencing Association
100 Four Falls Corporate Center, #105
Route 23 and Woodmount Road
West Conchohocken, PA 19424
Phone 610.941.2020
http://www.itca.org

Office of Learning Technologies
15 Eddy Street
Hull, Quebec, Canada K1A 0C9
Phone 819.953.0300
http://olt-bta.hrdc-drhc.gc.ca

**Society for Applied
Learning Technologies**
50 Culpepper Street
Warrenton, VA 20186
Phone 540.347.0055
http://www.salt.org

**United States Distance
Learning Association**
USDLA
P.O. Box 5129
Sam Ramon, CA 94583
Phone 510.606.5160
http://www.usdla.org

Books

Creating the Virtual Classroom: Distance Learning with the Internet, by Lynnette R. Porter (John Wiley & Sons, 1997)

Distance Learning: A Step-by-Step Guide for Trainers, by Karen Mantyla and J. Richard Gividen (ASTD, 1997)

Planning and Implementing a Distributed Learning Program

By Gianluigi Caldiera and Sarah E. Burley

Audience ⟶	Learning Professionals
Purpose ⟶	—Understand the major issues and steps involved in distance learning program planning —Have a tool they can use to guide the planning process
Suggested Uses ⟶	Self-study to review what is entailed Tool for developing plan

Introduction

The American Council on Education defines distributed learning as a system and a process that connects learners with distributed learning resources, characterized by:

- Separation of place and time between instructor and learners
- Interaction between learners and instructors conducted through media

In simpler words this means that lessons are provided through a "virtual classroom" accessible in many cases through a computer. The learning experience can include live lectures in which an instructor presents course contents to a group of learners, and individual interactive lessons in which each learner studies the class materials on his or her own.

A large number of educational organizations, government agencies, and corporations are considering distributed learning as the solution to the training problems that they are encountering. Even though many recognize that a better trained workforce is necessary for meeting the challenges of a global market, time and resources for training are not as available as they should be. Distributed learning offers organizations the opportunity to provide high-quality training at low cost and without disrupting the routine of the workforce.

In this paper we propose an innovative approach to distributed learning, based on Internet technology. First, we briefly discuss the issues that the proposed approach aims to address. Then, we outline the proposed solution and discuss a feasible path to its implementation.

Today's Training Environment: New Challenges

The changing needs of businesses and the behavior of employees have created a new, more challenging environment for training and learning. Mergers and acquisitions have increased the size and geographic expanse of organizations, and the expansion/globalization demanded of competitive businesses has contributed to the sprawl of the employee base. Employees in certain functional areas, such as business development or training, find themselves "on travel" more often than they find themselves working at headquarters. More flexible work arrangements, including job-sharing and telecommuting, have also had an impact on the way employees function within their organizations.

The traditional workplace, where every employee has a desk and sits in that same desk every day, is no longer. Judging from the trends in corporate America, the virtual office, where employees interact and conduct business using various technological tools, may be here to stay.

These new working conditions give added importance to the training and skill development function. Remote and mobile employees are less likely to interact with colleagues and mentors, and are therefore less apt to accumulate new skills in an informal way, through their coworkers, or more experienced managers. In addition, employees' work experiences become divergent, and they do not necessarily transfer their learning experiences in ways that benefit others. These factors not only increase the criticality of a thorough and consistent training program, but they also simultaneously pose new challenges to those involved in training development. Those challenges include:

- Ensuring that consistent messages are shared across the workforce.

- Providing current information/training to an increasingly remote workforce engaged in telecommuting and other unconventional work practices.

- Facilitating communications between experts and novices.

- Ensuring that workforce knowledge is current and competitive, in an age where rapidly changing technology and evolving management techniques make certain skills obsolete almost immediately.

- Growing in-house experts and mentors from the existing employee base.

- Providing necessary training without disrupting the ongoing activities/daily routine of workforce.

- Reducing the cost of providing training and shortening training cycle time.

Granted, these challenges also may be daunting to institutions dealing with a stable, centrally located workforce. However, their level of criticality and their significance escalates when one considers the new working conditions influencing many of today's organizations.

Any organization facing these challenges should consider adopting distributed learning technology, designed with the right features to suit its business and employee base.

Concept of the Distributed Learning Environment

Today's computer and communication technology provides a simple and flexible solution to meet some of the challenges outlined in the previous section. New solutions allow users to transcend the limits of the traditional physical classroom, where instructor and learners must meet in the same place at the same time in order to transmit, use, and create knowledge. Instead, learning takes place in a "virtual" classroom where the same activities occur over a digital computer network.

A Distributed Learning Environment* (DLE) is a computer-based system in which several different media (e.g., sound, graphics, text, and video) and computer capabilities are embedded into a telecommunications network. This network mediates the flow of information between an instructor and class participants (i.e., the students).

The main goal of a DLE is to provide hands-on instruction to participants where it is not cost effective or feasible to bring all participants together in the same place at the same time. It is not, however, merely a forum for "dispensing" information to learners in remote locations. As educational consultant Daniel E. Kinnaman notes, "distance education is not dispensing information; it's about a collaboration between teachers and technology to help students learn."

Figure 1 highlights some of the differences between a traditional (i.e., classroom-based) learning environment and a distributed one.

From the participants' perspective, a DLE offers a virtual classroom where lessons are available in a variety of media. Class participants can attend courses through a remote computer connection via desktop computer. Through this connection, they can attend class lectures, send and receive class assignments, examine supporting class material, and interact with both the class in-

---

*More commonly referred to as "Distance Learning Environment." We prefer to emphasize the 'distribution' concept over the "distance" one, which often has a negative connotation.

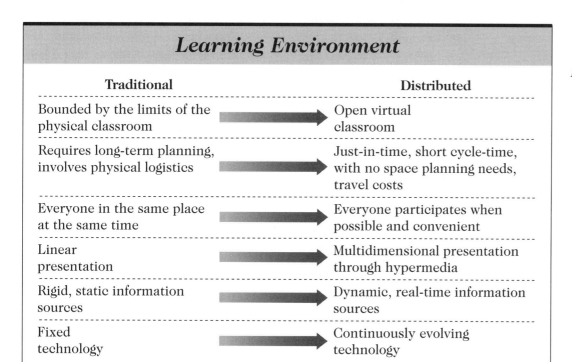

Figure 1

structor and fellow participants. Those who cannot connect with the virtual classroom at the designated times can download the record of the session at any convenient time. The DLE gives participants a measurement of their progress and maintains their personal profile. The nature of the class lectures enables the participant to see the lectures again, allowing review of difficult material.

From the instructor's perspective, a DLE provides the tools necessary to prepare course materials via an "authoring" system and a mechanism for the instructor to interact with participants (via the instructor's desktop computer). The instructor can post class assignments in an assignment bin or may e-mail the participants directly. Similarly, the participants may post completed assignments in personal, confidential folders or may e-mail the instructor directly. In support of class lectures and assignments, the instructor may create a virtual library of related materials.

To give the participants and instructor an opportunity to interact, chat rooms may be created. These chat rooms may be structured (e.g., the "instructor's room" offers direct interaction with the instructor at predetermined times) or unstructured (e.g., instructors may create special topic chat rooms to provoke further thought on the part of the participants). The variety of tools that facilitate interaction are conducive to a rich learning environment. Such an environment is characterized by what sociologist A. A. Moles describes as "opulence communicationnelle" (communication wealth).

Internet technology (Figure 2) provides a seamless integration of voice, video, and data connections among learners, instructors, organizations, virtual libraries, subject matter experts, and educational content providers.

Three factors make Internet technology ideal for distributed learning:

1. Internet architecture sees the "world" as a collection of clients that need services and servers who can provide those services on demand. This allows DLE designers to construct learning environments suited to the needs of a specific class. For instance, if live voice or video interaction would contribute to a particular class, it can be arranged for the participants and instructor to have access to this feature.

2. Internet communication protocols provide a "dial tone" understood by almost every computer. This means that the vir-

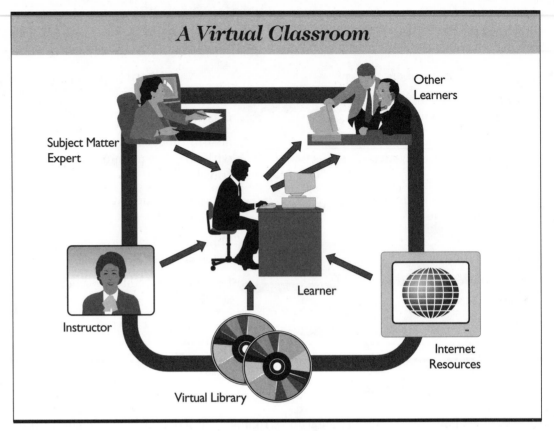

A Virtual Classroom

Subject Matter Expert

Other Learners

Instructor

Learner

Virtual Library

Internet Resources

Figure 2

tual classroom has potentially no limits and can encompass a continuously growing community of learners.

3. A large population already uses and understands the Internet. There is often little or no need to teach the instructors or the participants how to use the technology.

Distributed learning appears to be a potentially universal tool to transmit, use, and create knowledge, and indeed it can be integrated into the educational or training programs of almost every organization. Like all tools, however, there are limitations to its applicability.

Some limitations are purely technical. The limited bandwidth of the Internet does limit the amount of multimedia contents (especially video) that can be shared. When servers and communication links become overloaded, it significantly slows down the activities of the virtual classroom. In addition, the open environment allows for intrusion and manipulation of information by unauthorized parties. These technical limi-

tations eventually will be removed by developments in computer and communication technology.

Other limitations are intrinsic to the media involved. The virtual classroom does not provide for the human relationships that develop in the physical classroom. Team building and role definition evolve more slowly over a computer network. Therefore, organizations relying on training sessions to nurture cooperative working environments and team-playing should introduce appropriate instruments (such as nonmoderated group chat rooms) to achieve those goals.

DLE Success Factors

In order to deliver the desired benefits, a Distributed Learning Environment must have certain features. This section will briefly discuss the characteristics that we perceive to be most critical.

Modular Architecture

To accommodate the needs of different kinds of classes, DLE architecture should be highly modular. It should allow course designers to select the group of tools most appropriate for presenting and manipulating any given course material. Examples of tools appropriate for different contexts are text browsers, buttons to navigate text, buttons to ask questions, "whiteboards" shared across several computers, video and audio players, performance evaluation tools, moderated and unmoderated discussion mechanisms, chat rooms, and related controls. The architecture of the environment must also allow class designers to add or remove capabilities and tools from specific desktops. This allows for a technical framework that may evolve as the needs of the users change or as the designer's understanding of the tools increases.

Asynchronous Learning Tools

The second set of essential DLE features provides support for individual learning. Sometimes learners can better absorb the contents of a specific class module through individual work at the computer. For instance, if one were designing a class on a technical topic, such as a programming language, independent learning and practice would play a major role. In other cases, one might want to support learners with limited time for participation by giving them access to previously held live classes. Individual learning tools satisfy all these needs. Asynchronous, or individual, learning tools can include hypertext browsers like the ones included in every Web browser, content visiting tools that allow the user to choose the level of detail in the information presented, interactive testing mechanisms, and mentoring tools that guide the learner through practical examples and exercises.

Synchronous Learning Tools

The third set of essential features directly supports live teaching by presenting the instructor with a control panel, which allows him or her to show class materials to participants, to highlight contents, to improvise contents through a "whiteboard" visible to everybody, to talk and listen, and to see and be seen. Another tool allows an instructor to answer questions and moderate a discussion. One mechanism allows participants to "raise a hand" when they want to say something.

Administrative Tools

The last set of features is meant to support not the individual class or course but the training program as a whole. Courses are related to each other either by sharing contents or by fulfilling prerequisites. The DLE must support these relationships and help the organization manage them. Course participants are registered and their performance in the different classes is monitored and recorded in order to control their access to additional classes.

How to Implement the DLE: A Recommended Approach

This section presents an overview of a recommended approach to the development of a DLE. A key point to remember is that a DLE is a distributed computer system that must be designed like any other computer system, starting with an "information needs" analysis that defines the scope and the purpose of the desired environment. This information is then used to design the distributed learning environment efficiently and to implement its features. Prototyping, of the system and of the course presentation, is therefore essential to tailor the system to the needs and the culture of the organization for which it is designed. As in any other educational context, the one-size-fits-all approach is ineffective; only an approach customized for the audience and culture can lead to success.

Figure 3 illustrates the four phases of the recommended implementation approach.

Phase I: Planning

The purpose of this phase is to identify the training needs of the organization and to translate them into a strategic plan for distributed learning.

An inventory of an organization's training needs includes data on both the population that must be trained (e.g., number of people, education, proficiency with the computer, availability of computer resources, normal work schedule) and the topics that need to be covered (e.g., technical training on specific tools or techniques, management techniques, quality assurance techniques, financial management techniques). Other, less concrete, information to be gathered in the

The Four Phases of the Recommended Implementation Approach

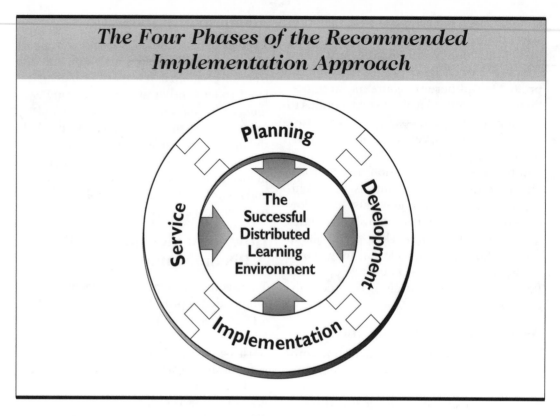

Figure 3

Planning phase includes an understanding of the organization's culture, its priorities, people's preferences for information presentation, the level of discipline, and the relationships between organizational units. This information facilitates implementation of a distributed learning program with high potential for success.

The strategic plan should contain a description of the desired environment, of the procedures for its use and administration, and of the subject areas the training will cover. It should also contain a description of implementation phases and intermediate products, and an estimate of the resources needed. Important elements of the strategic plan are:

- The technical requirements for the DLE.

- Recommendations for adaptation and enhancement of the existing technology.

- Desired product features to suit the organization's environment.

- An approach for integrating DLE into the organization's overall training and personnel development strategy.

Phase II: Development

The purpose of this phase is to design the initial technical environment and to introduce a pilot project.

Based on the requirements described in the strategic plan, technical personnel design and install an initial technical environment to serve as the development laboratory for the desired features and an experimental class. The initial environment must be scaleable (i.e., expandable to the environment that will eventually support the whole organization) and highly flexible. The development approach should be based on a system development methodology, possibly following the object-oriented paradigm and an evolutionary model.

The success of the program depends on the developers' understanding the best instruction delivery mode for a specific group of learners. This can be achieved by using a prototyping approach, including developing an experimental class, presenting it to selected participants, and collecting their impressions and feedback. This phase may be performed using a standard focus group approach and methodology.

Phase III: Implementation

The goal of this phase is to transfer the technical environment from its initial version, in the laboratory setting, to its full-scale version, and to produce and deliver all classes needed by the organization.

The technical transfer, if planned in advance, should not present any major challenges. If any of the parameters (e.g., number of users, characteristics of sites) initially considered by the DLE engineers has changed, some redesign may be needed. Therefore, it is important in this phase to confirm parameters with the users.

In some cases, the feedback from the experimental class focus groups may result in changes to the software used to distribute and manage the classes. These changes should be promptly applied in order to demonstrate, especially to the most skeptical personnel, that responsiveness and flexibility are characteristics and advantages of a distributed learning program.

A training plan, developed in this phase, should control the production and delivery of classes. The plan should cover:

- The set of skills needed and when they are needed.
- The skills that will be obtained through the distributed learning environment.
- The training that is required, for whom it is required, and when it is required.
- The classes that will be developed, the versions that will be offered, and to whom they will be offered.
- The classes that will be purchased off the shelf.
- Class development work plan and targeted delivery dates.
- Incentives and control mechanisms for the organization personnel.

An on-line version of the class calendar should be managed by the DLE and its administrators.

Phase IV: Performance Measurement

The purpose of this phase is to evaluate the performance and quality of the DLE as a training tool, so as to make improvements to enhance its usefulness. Administrators of the program create measures to evaluate current features and determine necessary adjustments. A typical set of measures is composed of the following:

- User satisfaction measures (such as the feedback provided by users after each course).
- Institutional usage and performance measures (such as the percentage of people who take one or several classes, or instructional performance records).
- Technical measures (such as system throughput and response time).

Based on all the information collected, the administrators should make adjustments and enhancements to the distributed learning environment. It is critical to the success of the program that the system demonstrate the highest level of performance and responsiveness.

DLE Program Staffing Needs

To develop an effective DLE program, an organization must allocate the proper resources to its design and maintenance. Following is a list of staffing roles essential to the development of a successful distributed learning environment.

- *Strategic Planner/Training Manager:* Develops the distributed learning strategic plan and training plan.
- *System Architect and Engineering* Staff: Translates the requirements contained in the strategic plan into a feasible technical environment, implementing and supporting this environment, and altering it as required.
- *System Administrator:* Manages the DLE program, determines need for additional support, and acquires additional technical support when needed.
- *Subject Matter Experts, Instructional Designers, and Graphic Designers:* Develop classes and instructor guides.
- *Instructors:* Deliver the classes and assist the class participants.
- *Focus Groups:* Evaluate the technical environment, content, and presentation of specific classes, providing input regarding enhancements to be made.

Conclusion

Numerous organizations have found the distributed, or distance learning, model to be beneficial in handling the logistical challenges of training and in increasing the effectiveness of their training. Educational institutions have been especially quick to embrace the concept of distributed learning. Surveys show that 758 colleges and universities in the United States and Canada now offer more than 1,000 degree programs and 240 certificates through distance learning. Approximately 60 areas of study for bachelor's degrees and 44 certificates are available with no traditional on-campus requirements.

Training departments of many large corporations, such as Motorola and J.C. Penney, as well as government entities such as the U.S. Department of Energy, have also begun to reap the benefits of distance learning. Figure 4 represents the welcome page for Coopers & Lybrand's "virtual campus."

Distributed learning is becoming an essential tool for many public and private organizations dedicated to providing up-to-the-minute, customized training for members of their community. It is hoped that in using the approach outlined here, other institutions will be able to gauge this tool's suitability for their own training environments.

References

Kinnaman, D. The Future of Distance Education. *Technology and Learning,* January 1995, p. 58.

Peraya, D. Distance Education and the WWW. http://tecfa.unige.ch/edu-comp/edu-ws94/contrib/peraya.fm.html, p. 3.

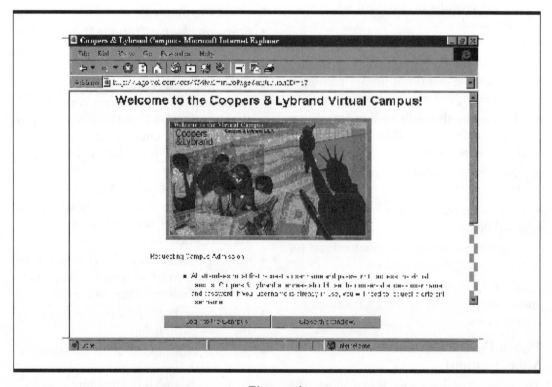

Figure 4

An Outsourcing Primer

By Margaret Kaeter

Audience ➡	Learning Professionals, HR Department Managers
Purpose ➡	—Learn the right questions to ask in deciding whether to outsource aspects of training —Learn the right questions to ask potential vendors —Be able to develop a plan for working constructively with an outsourcing partner
Suggested Uses ➡	Self-study Resource for developing a presentation on this topic

Many training managers now find themselves in situations they never dreamed possible. The value of their efforts is being scrutinized more than ever before. And they're being asked how those efforts fit with corporate goals.

It's an exciting time. Training is becoming a key competitive strategy as companies recognize that employees are a strategic resource. It's also a time of change. If training programs aren't relevant to a company's overall business goals, the training department will be turned inside-out and upside-down.

That's what happened at Conoco—a Houston-based oil-and-gas company. Senior staff training associate Lee Anna Washington says, "A few years ago, our training was 98 percent internal. But from a standpoint of added value, the complaint was that we weren't providing quality. We were too generalized; we were trying to please everyone."

Executives at Conoco quickly came up with a solution: They downsized the training function from 12 employees to one. Washington now helps workers and supervisors learn to manage their own development needs. When a nontechnical course needs updating, Washington either creates a new course or purchases a customized one. External consultants deliver all of the company's training.

"The bottom line is that we are in the business of producing oil and gas, not training our employees," says Washington. "Our whole focus has shifted to increasing employees' competency. We get the resources as they're needed."

Enter the world of outsourcing.

Variations on a Theme

Many organizations have bought training videos, sent employees to external workshops, or hired consultants to develop or deliver training programs. But outsourcing has taken on new meaning. More companies are

---

Reprinted with permission from *Training & Development*, published by the American Society for Training & Development.

beginning to view their external training suppliers as strategic partners, not just vendors.

For example, Andersen Consulting looks to "gainsharing" with its clients. "It's interesting how productive the relationship can be, when the goal isn't just to complete a project or contract but to increase competitiveness," says Reinhard Ziegler, partner in charge of change development at Andersen's office in Dallas, Texas.

Another much-talked-about partnership is the one between DuPont in Wilmington, Delaware, and the Forum Corporation, a Boston-based consulting firm. Except for a few technical-training efforts, DuPont has disbanded its training department and brought in Forum to oversee the internal training function.

"We felt that the whole would be greater than the sum of the parts," says Ed Trolley, manager of training and education at DuPont. "We could concentrate on what we're good at, running our business, while Forum would bring all the training skills. Forum would be charged with meeting our needs in any way necessary, including finding other consultants to provide training in areas in which it couldn't."

But tight-knit, exclusive partnerships are only one way of outsourcing. Many organizations have found other kinds of arrangements that meet their needs. For example, Conoco lets employees pick their own training courses; a clearinghouse tells them what courses are available.

"It works well for the technical training our people need and for things like presentation training," says Washington. "But it's not perfect. One disadvantage is that there's no opportunity for follow-up. Another problem is that people were used to getting training in-house. When they see the high price tags of some outside training, they sometimes opt for lesser quality courses."

In another example, Westinghouse trimmed its training staff from 21 people to five. The company continues to develop training internally, turning to external suppliers to deliver programs. Emily Schultheiss—lead consultant with HR Worksource, Westinghouse's internal training function—says, "Our char-ter is to focus on training development, not on delivery."

Bill Germino—manager of information-systems training for Babson College in Wellesley, Massachusetts—used to turn to internal experts to provide staff with training in computer software. Now, 80 percent of such training is done by an external supplier. Germino still customizes training activities and other materials.

"In the past, I had up to 16 internal part-time training instructors. Getting them to learn the product and give a polished delivery was draining our resources. Now, the external instructors get higher evaluations than the internal instructors did."

Other companies hold to the tried-and-true model of outsourcing: a course here and a development project there. "There's not a single model people should move to," says Ziegler. "You have to look at the strengths and weaknesses of your company. Can you get a competitive workforce by choosing a good consultant and pointing him or her in the right direction?"

Asking the Right Questions

Even minimal outsourcing can have advantages. But even outsourcing enthusiasts agree that it's not right for every company in every situation.

"When we think we might outsource, we spend a lot of time examining the issues," says Katherine Vanover, training and OD manager at Jergens. "Sometimes, we find that even though outsourcing looks right, we really need to keep certain training inside."

In deciding to outsource a particular program or to develop a strategic partnership with a supplier, it's important to ask several questions.

Is there a time crunch? If the training is needed immediately and can't be done internally, going outside may be the only choice.

"We had one client who needed to train 20,000 employees within six months," says Alice Pescuric, vice president of training and development technologies at Development Dimensions International, a consulting firm based in the Pittsburgh, Pennsylvania, area. "Very few internal training departments could handle that."

Is there a resource constraint? "I believe in life-cycle costing," says Larry Tagrin, a training and development professional with 15 years' experience. "Look at the five-year projected cost to develop, deliver, and maintain the program—compared with buying a course. Every course has a breakpoint."

Pescuric recommends looking also at the "opportunity" costs of the trainers and developers. "Many organizations used to look at training only in terms of expense. But now they focus on training as a major element to future success. In that context, training professionals are too important to do instructional design. They should be working on the important issues that only they can address."

But Pescuric also says, "When you look at a company's long-term need, you may find that you have to develop one or more internal experts."

Is there an expertise constraint? Not every company can afford to maintain internal experts in every area, especially considering how fast technology changes. That's why outsourcing is most common in technical subjects.

"When we needed a Taguchi expert to teach a course in designing experiments, we went to the local college," says Vanover. "That made more sense than trying to bring an inside trainer up to speed," she adds.

Technical changes are so fast and frequent that it's difficult to keep internal trainers current and certified, according to Kris DeWolf, director of sales and marketing at Connect Educational Services in Eden Prairie, Minnesota. "Technical classrooms and labs are capital-intensive. If you're going to give employees the best training, you may have to send them outside."

Clearly, the training's subject matter can drive outsourcing decisions. But so can training technology. If a company wants to create a multimedia program but doesn't have an expert in that area on staff, it makes sense to go to an external provider.

Would an outsider have more credibility? "If an external trainer—no matter how expert—doesn't understand the company's business operations, he or she is likely to fail in some areas, such as consultative selling," says Marilyn Carlstedt, regional training manager at Amoco, based in Chicago, Illinois. "You have to know your audience and what it will tolerate. You have to know the culture of the company."

"We found that when we hired dealers from other gas companies to train Amoco dealers, the external trainers had greater credibility with our people."

"An external voice can be a bit like benchmarking," says Dave Erdman, president and CEO of Learning International, a training and consulting firm based in Stamford, Connecticut.

"If there's a strategic change in the organization, you might want to look for voices that can help deliver the message with more perspective. People listen differently to someone outside of the company."

Is the training part of the core business? Examine how the company views its competitive niche, recommends Ziegler. He recommends keeping training in those core areas internal. At DuPont, product training, safety training, and training for operators and mechanics are kept inside because they're critical to the company.

"I don't think quality training should ever be outsourced," says Carlstedt. "It doesn't matter who you're working with. In every class, an enormous amount of company-specific information comes out. If an internal person facilitates the training, the company can grow and learn from it. Outside people defeat the purpose of quality training. They walk out the door with valuable information."

How generic is the training? Even in core competencies, there are generic areas in which any expert can do the training.

"We have three training courses on hazardous materials," says Tagrin. "Two are universal and must be federally certified. Anyone with the proper license can teach them."

How frequent is the course; how big is the audience? The more frequently the course is delivered and the smaller the audience, the more sense it makes to have an external provider involved.

"We wanted to offer an advanced computer-programming course to four employees out of 5,000 in the company. It would have taken three years for us to develop the course," says Tagrin. "There was no question that we had to outsource it."

Can the outsourcing be managed effectively? Outsourcing isn't an end to all worries. In fact, it can create a multitude of new ones.

"I think the most important question is whether you have the expertise to manage and measure the success of outsourcing," says Pescuric. She also recommends ensuring that the systems for selecting, communicating with, and paying suppliers are in place before launching an outsourcing effort.

More Questions

There's no shortage of consultants in the world. But there are few perfect matches.

To find the best fit—for either a one-time supplier or an outsourcing partner—you should ask yourself and potential suppliers some crucial questions.

The first question to ask is whether the supplier's values match the values of the company. "For example," advises Pescuric, "if a company values employee empowerment, it's important that the external consultant be willing to seek employees' input. The consultant can't just say that he or she has the same values; he or she has to live by them."

Does the relationship feel right? "Communication with the potential supplier or partner should be open and honest," says Erdman. "There should be a strong sense of trust that the external provider will do the job."

Does the supplier understand the company's business? A common way to find an outsourcing partner is to expand an existing relationship.

"We like to build relationships with suppliers over time," says Tamara Scott, dean of the

---

Ask Before You Leap

Once you've decided to outsource—whether it's a single program or an entire function—you'll want to hire the supplier who can best meet your needs. To find an outsourcing partner who is a perfect fit, be sure to ask the following questions as you screen candidates:

- ▶ Do the supplier's values match the company's?
- ▶ Does the relationship feel right?
- ▶ Does the supplier understand the company's business?
- ▶ What does the network say?
- ▶ Does the supplier meet the company's geographic needs?
- ▶ What is the budget?
- ▶ Does the supplier meet needs regarding time and volume?
- ▶ What is the supplier's expertise?
- ▶ Does the supplier really listen?

- ▶ Does the supplier "walk the talk"?
- ▶ Does the supplier understand organizational change?
- ▶ Can the supplier meet the company's long-term needs?
- ▶ Is the supplier a strategic orchestrator?
- ▶ Does the supplier work well with other suppliers?
- ▶ What is the training content?
- ▶ Do the materials fit the company's culture?
- ▶ Is the supplier flexible about delivery?

---

training university at Van Kampen American Capital. "That way, we can learn their capabilities slowly—and they can learn our organization in-depth—before taking on too much."

The Coca-Cola Company takes this a step further: It hires former employees as consultants. "To do a good job, you have to understand and appreciate Coca-Cola's culture," says Chris Gilliam, a principal of the Gilliam Group in Baltimore, Maryland, and one of Coca-Cola's training consultants.

"You have to understand the business, product and services, strategies, and subcultures. You have to know the key players in order to gear training to their strengths and weaknesses."

But Millar Farewell—assistant manager of the motorcycle service education department at American Honda in Torrance, California—says that consultants hired for their technical expertise shouldn't necessarily have to understand a company's business.

"I choose our external providers for their expertise in course structure and sequencing. I can't expect them to know about motorcycle repair, too. If this is a team effort, I expect us to contribute our part."

Next, go to your network of colleagues and counterparts at other firms. What do those associates say about the suppliers you're considering? Farewell says that he asks other companies what happened after the training. "Did trainees remember it? Were they able to apply it on the job? Did the company see a better bottom line? I want to know that it worked."

Does the supplier meet the company's geographic needs? If the company is planning an international effort, it is likely to want a supplier with an international presence. That can save travel time and ensure that the trainers are fluent in the language and habits of the target cultures. In addition, the trainers should be able to "culturize" any course quickly.

The budget is always an important consideration. "If it's a light budget, I won't be flying people out of California," says Amoco's Carlstedt, who is based in Chicago. "If the supplier wants the business, it can find a way to get someone to us."

Does the supplier meet the company's needs regarding time and volume? Sometimes a training manager will ignore this question, opting instead to use a favorite supplier. That supplier may fit all of the other criteria. But if it can't deliver what the company needs when it needs it, the training manager should look elsewhere.

What is the supplier's area of expertise? "Consultants specializing in compensation may say that they can train. But if training isn't their core skill, that could defeat the purpose of going outside," explains Pescuric. "If you're looking to outsource training because it isn't the company's core competence, make sure it's the supplier's core competence."

And don't forget to make sure the supplier is licensed, when applicable. "I've had several suppliers say that they were licensed to deliver a particular program," says Carlstedt. "But when I checked, they weren't."

Does the supplier really listen? Erdman suggests asking a potential supplier to reiterate the company's needs.

"I worked with a supplier that was highly recommended to train in presentation skills. But before the session, no one called to see what trainees' current skill levels were," says Carlstedt. "The program was so basic that it insulted participants."

Does the supplier "walk the talk"? "If a supplier doesn't embody what it sells, it's in big trouble," says Scott. "I would expect a supplier that sells negotiation-skills training to try to negotiate the contract with us. I'd expect a supplier that sells telephone-skills training to have perfect receptionists."

Does the supplier understand organizational change? "Training can raise organizational issues," says DeWolf. "Suppliers must provide holistic trainers who understand change, team skills, and negotiation skills. That's almost more important than the technical skills."

Can the supplier meet the company's long-term needs? "With training being strategic, the supplier or partner should be flexible enough to grow in the many directions the

---

company might go in the future," says Erdman.

Is the supplier a strategic orchestrator? Will the supplier help resolve issues that come up between itself and the company? Will the supplier look to other sources to solve problems it can't handle?

"The supplier or partner should pull out all its resources for you," says Erdman. "That's what adds value to the relationship."

Says Carlstedt, "The account executives are critical. They're the ones who will run interference. They can make or break the relationship."

Does the supplier work well with other suppliers? A good supplier will admit when it can't provide something. And it will help find a solution, or understand when the company goes elsewhere. "I'm not concerned when a client uses two consultants on a project," says DDI's Pescuric. "We work with a client that has one supplier do the hype while we do the nuts and bolts. It makes sense to me to use the best in each area."

What is the content of the training program? "If a supplier is going to be training my trainers, I want a detailed account of the certification program," says Carlstedt. "Some consultants don't have skill practice. They just watch videos."

Do the materials fit the company's culture? In the 1980s, we had an employee-involvement program in which the videos were geared toward clerical and manufacturing people," says Carlstedt. "The tapes didn't fit our engineering culture. Once we reshot them, the program had good acceptance."

Is the supplier flexible about delivery? "I want the option to deliver externally or internally," says Carlstedt. "In 1989, we did a targeted employee-selection program. I wanted to train 1,000 people in four weeks; I knew I couldn't do that internally. But once the program was up and running, we took over with internal sessions for new people."

Now What?

Once a company has decided to outsource and has selected the supplier, it's ready to move. Right? Wrong. First, there are some key steps to take.

Put it in writing. Be clear up front what the arrangement is, advises Gilliam. That includes managing finances and outlining who does what at each step of the training process.

Pescuric recommends defining a win-win relationship. "In one case, we agreed to turn over the technology we developed. In return, the supplier let us use its locations as field-test sites and to get marketing feedback."

Teach the supplier about the organization. "Share the company's business plan," says Scott. "I want my training suppliers to understand the company's goals and objectives as well as I do. You can't expect a supplier to perform well if it doesn't know everything about the company, good and bad."

Set up a plan to handle conflict. "The supplier/partner relationship should be like a marriage," says Erdman. "It won't always be perfect. But you'll likely benefit from the supplier's different perspective, if it's well presented. I think a form of 'premarital counseling' should outline how the parties will proceed when conflict occurs. If the parties aren't satisfying each other's needs, they should say so. Any relationship can improve, even the best."

Request follow-up. "When working with outside consultants, follow-up is often missing," says Washington. "Many of them just want to do the training and leave. They may do a cursory evaluation. But they won't sit down with you to discuss what was good and what needs improvement. If you plan to make the relationship a long-term one, you need follow-up."

Make adjustments. When Ken Tumas—director of corporate training and safety for Neles-Janesbury in Wooster, Massachusetts—saw his suppliers' instructors in action, he requested that some of them not teach again. "It's not that employees didn't learn. But something was missing in the relationship between some instructors and the trainees. You can't predict which people will be effective, until you see them with your employees."

Remain flexible. "We thought we'd start at corporate headquarters and slowly expand," says Trolley. "But we're already working internationally."

Trolley recommends going slowly regarding the breadth of topics covered by outside suppliers. But he says, "Use what you've developed to the fullest."

Point/Counterpoint

Many organizations are recognizing the value of outsourcing. But controversy still rages over how much outsourcing to do.

Here are some opposing views from two training and development practitioners:

- -

Larry Tagrin: "It's stupid to outsource completely. That's like taking the heart and soul of a company, and letting someone else run it.

"You also lose control over the training function. You have to train the supplier's people, but it can move them at any time. Who gets the superstars?

"If the supplier isn't in tune with your culture, the training might not be applicable—even if you're housing the external trainers at your offices or hiring former employees to do the training.

"Security is a problem. The supplier has to know a lot of information about the company. If a supplier is working with Ford Motor Company, it probably also has Toyota and General Motors as prospects, if not clients. No confidentiality clause can keep all of the information inside your company.

"Outsourcing can send the message that training your most competitive asset, your workforce, isn't important enough to keep inside. Employees pick up on that."

Edward Trolley: "At DuPont, we realized that to reach our vision of becoming global, employee development was critical.

"We had a lot of training and development people, and a catalog with thousands of courses. We had to transform that, to add value and link training to business. At first, DuPont sought to rebuild the training department into a world-class training organization. But we ruled that out. The training function as it was didn't meet the necessary requirements for transformation. And our fixed costs would remain too high.

"A new outsourcing relationship with the Forum Corporation completely changed the face of training at DuPont. Now, two-thirds of the training is business-linked. We offer workshops in such areas as profitable growth, customer retainment, and market assessment. It doesn't look like traditional training.

"Our vendors also have a relationship with Forum. We don't have to worry about contracts and administrative details. If the work doesn't add value, we shouldn't do it."

- -

How to Select a Consultant

By Lisa A. Burke and Marcy Abelson Bandick

Audience ➤	Learning Professionals, HR Managers
Purpose ➤	—Learn a process for finding and selecting appropriate consultants —Understand the characteristics to look for in a consultant and how to set priorities among them
Suggested Uses ➤	Self-study

In a meeting with top management, the chief financial officer asks you to implement a technical skills training curriculum for new financial analysts. On reflection, you realize how big that project really is—you need to conduct a formal needs assessment, design a technical skills curriculum, develop materials, and implement and evaluate a final product. Whew!

Your organization occasionally uses outside consultants, but you have no idea where to begin to identify and select the best consultant for your project.

A first step is to identify the project areas that you can handle yourself and which need the expertise of an outside consultant. For example, you may be experienced in conducting a needs analysis to identify the scope of the potential training solution, but you need an outside consultant to develop the training materials. By clearly delineating parts of the project that demand outside expertise, you'll have a clearer view of the consulting skills you're in the market for.

Next, create a list of people who can provide the services you're seeking. Explore the following sources:

- Management development resources in your firm

- Coworkers who have used consultants for a similar purpose

- Consultants who have worked for your company before

- Other companies (specifically, your counterpart in another firm)

- Advertisements in industry publications

Such leads will help you generate a pool of consultants to choose from. Next, gather information from each consultant, using a request for information (RFI). An RFI solicits information about a consultant's abilities and potential fees. The RFI should contain a checklist of needed information, a confidentiality statement, and a deadline for the information. Information returned by the consultants will help you eliminate some candidates.

To continue the narrowing down process, submit a request for proposal (RFP) to the most qualified consultants. The purpose of an RFP is to solicit consultants' proposals for your project, based on evaluation criteria that are important to you. In an RFP, identify your specific needs for the project; provide a detailed list of the criteria you'll use to evaluate the proposals and select the final consultant; and explain any constraints you face, such as time. Ask consultants to describe the

Reprinted with permission from *Training & Development*, published by the American Society for Training & Development.

exact service they'll provide and the cost of their services. Also request a summary of their experience and a list of references.

How to Evaluate the Candidates

You'll evaluate each consultant's proposal, and you also may want to meet each one. Set up an interview, request a presentation, or schedule an "audition" (especially if a consultant will conduct training). In any event, identify the specific evaluation criteria to be used when selecting the consultant who will best meet your needs. Here are some criteria to consider.

Credentials and expertise. Know a consultant's relevant experience, qualifications, and knowledge base. Investigate the credentials of anyone who may work on your project because the lead consultant will often employ less experienced associates. All outside staff should be knowledgeable about the most recent technology in HRD and creative instruction approaches.

We recommend that a consultant have at least 10 years' experience in instructional design and a list of current clientele you can contact as references. Another sign of expertise is a consultant's active involvement in professional associations. If a consultant is familiar with your area of business or industry, he or she may be able to make important connections between your specific requirements and a changing business climate.

How to Select a Consultant

▶ **Credentials and expertise.** Know who you'll be working with.

▶ **Compatibility and communication skills.** Find someone that you can work with closely.

▶ **Commitment and results-orientation.** Gauge how your project fits into a consultant's schedule.

▶ **Stability and location.** Check turnover rates, backup staff, and geographic location. It all adds up.

Bottom line: It's critical that you know who you'll be working with.

Compatibility and communication skills. In addition to the technical expertise of a consultant (and his or her staff), you must feel comfortable in one-on-one communications. Pay close attention to how a consultant interacts with you and others in your firm. Notice how a consultant also interacts with his or her own staff. Your project may last a long time, so you have to feel that you can work closely with the people you hire.

Specifically, a consultant should have strong oral and written communication skills, should be able to manage conflict constructively, and should be objective. A consultant's job is not to tell you what you want to hear. In fact, you should be cautious of a consultant who is too cooperative and agreeable. You're seeking an outsider's perspective; make sure you're going to get it.

Commitment and results-orientation. Because a consultant will be responsible for providing a specific product or service for you, he or she needs to demonstrate a firm commitment and clear results-orientation. To gauge those intentions, ask a consultant's present and past clients whether he or she meets deadlines, sets realistic goals, and produces superior results. Ask a consultant about his or her current workload and obligations, judge how your project will fit into that workload, and determine what resources the consultant can bring to your project.

Gauge a consultant's commitment by how responsive he or she is during the information-gathering phase. A consultant should be quickly accessible via telephone, voicemail, fax, and e-mail.

Stability and location. Become familiar with the economic stability and long-term viability of a consultant's business. Ask about the frequency of staff turnover. Ideally, a consultant will have highly qualified people as backups in case changes are necessary during the project.

In addition, be conscious of how a consultant's geographic location will affect the progress and cost of your project. Clearly, the closer he or she is to your organization, the less travel expenses and total cost. If a consultant is long distance, you'll need to estimate the number of trips and travel expenses. Most importantly, look into viable ways to communicate and share information electronically.

Project Priorities

While evaluating the candidates, you should clarify the priorities that drive your project. Those priorities will play a major role in the final selection.

For example, how important is cost, the quality of work, and the timing? All of those variables may be interrelated, but it's crucial to identify your top priority and the tradeoffs. For example, if your top priority is quality, be prepared to pay for it. However, compare quality and cost to make sure that you're maximizing your investment. Define specifically what quality means to you—for example, format versus training content. If you're concerned primarily about cost, you may have to concede on quality. Consequently, your familiarity with a consultant's work is imperative. If possible, ask to see some of his or her materials for similar projects, or ask to observe a consultant instructing a class. Because consultants can calculate fees using different pricing structures, it's important to know a consultant's particular method for pricing and how it compares with others.

Here are some examples of ways consultants determine their fees.

Time and materials. With this method, a consultant bills you as tasks are completed.

Typically, the invoice is itemized by labor and materials. There may also be parameters regarding how much you'll pay for labor, materials, and travel expenses.

Fixed bid. In a fixed bid, a consultant provides a set fee for the project, including labor, materials, travel expenses, and so forth.

Per diem. In this pricing method, a consultant charges a daily rate that generally includes his or her services and meals, but not travel.

Phased approach. With a phased approach, a consultant makes separate bids on different parts of the overall project, such as the needs analysis. After that is completed, the consultant may provide a second bid for developing materials.

Clearly, you'll need to compare those pricing structures carefully if cost is a driving priority. Even if cost isn't your primary priority, you have to know how a consultant will bill you for services. You don't want any surprises.

Identifying and selecting the right consultant can make or break your project. In addition to using the evaluation criteria and identifying your priorities, you should trust your intuition. If your gut feeling is that someone is misrepresenting his or her abilities or knowledge, or misleading you about what his or her firm can contribute to your project, don't ignore that. Trust your instincts, because you and your company deserve and need to get the most value for your consulting dollar.

SECTION 2: SUPPORTING PERFORMANCE-FOCUSED LEADERSHIP

Section 2 at a Glance

MATERIAL

Material	Page	Learning Professionals	Staff and Supervisors	Teams	Management	Self-study/Resource for Training	Group Exercise	Tool
		AUDIENCES				**FORMATS**		
How to Manage Individual Performance	2-4	●			●	●		●
Program Checklist for Planning and Managing Large-scale or Global Programs	2-9				●	●		●
The Opportunity Grid: A Strategic Planning Tool	2-14				●	●	●	●
Workshop: Implementing a Strategic Plan at the Operational Level	2-18	●			●		●	●
Exercise for Managers: Setting Individual Goals That Support Organizational Strategy	2-31				●		●	

Introduction:
Helping Leadership and Management
Improve Performance

While a variety of practices characterize high-performing organizations, one feature is constant: strong leadership and management. For example, a 1994 Coopers & Lybrand (C&L) survey of improvement-driven organizations found that strong, involved leadership by the CEO is a critical predictor of success in achieving measurable improvement. However, the hands-on involvement of other managers in helping employees perform their jobs more effectively is another key success factor. A 1997 C&L study of best practices for accelerating organizational change also underlined the importance of strong top managers who are involved from the outset in identifying, shaping, articulating, and implementing performance improvement and change management strategies.

Management specialist John Kotter says that producing change is the primary function of leadership. Like the 1994 C&L survey, he and others distinguish between leadership and management. Good managers plan deductively and produce orderly results, while leaders set direction and develop vision and strategies. Managers organize staff activities and help employees achieve higher performance, while leaders align people and departments with the high-performing vision by communicating goals and empowering action.

C&L research and analysis regarding the world's most successful companies point to three ways companies can support effective leadership and management:

- Developing leaders at all levels.
- Nurturing a constant source of new leaders and managers.
- Encouraging leaders and managers to teach others.

Learning professionals are already playing a significant role in helping companies develop and support leadership and management for today's business challenges. When asked what their organizations were doing to become more effective, nearly three out of four respondents to a recent ASTD survey cited management/leadership development. In addition to developing capabilities and skills, however, learning professionals can also support leadership and management processes, such as strategic planning, visioning, and aligning goals.

How This Section Can Help

This section contains tools, exercises, and materials that learning professionals can use to help their organizations build leadership and management that can energize and enable high performance. The first four pieces help you support effective leadership processes in developing large-scale global performance improvement initiatives, assessing an organization's performance management capability, and strategic planning and operationalizing organizational goals company-wide. The last entry addresses individual leadership and management skills: helping managers develop and enhance leadership qualities.

References

Benson, G. Research Update. *Training & Development.* July 1997, p. 52.

Coopers & Lybrand. Building Transformational Leaders. Coopers & Lybrand, 1997.

Kotter, J. A Force for Change: How Leadership Differs From Management. New York: The Free Press, 1990.

Smith, R. Leaders Accelerating Change. Knowledge Knowhow. June–July, 1997.

Vander Linde, K., Horney, N., and Koonce, R. Seven Ways to Make Your Training Department One of the Best. *Training & Development.* August 1997, pp. 20–28.

How to Manage Individual Performance

By John F. Middlebrook

Audience ➡	Learning Professionals, Managers, Supervisors
Purpose ➡	—Understand what they can do to help individual employees improve performance and contribute to meeting business goals —Learn a performance model they can use to assess individual needs —Be able to use an assessment tool to rate their organization's management performance
Suggested Uses ➡	Self-study/handout Resource for developing a presentation on this topic Assessment tool could be used by management teams or by a group of managers/supervisors in a work unit

Organizations have been putting people last.

As an HRD professional, you might agree with that statement. You know that investments in state-of-the-art technology, equipment, and information systems are money wasted unless organizations also invest in the people who make such systems work. You know that employees play a pivotal role in organizational success. So, why are people often ignored when companies look for ways to sharpen their competitive edge?

Kepner-Tregoe is one company that asked the same question. To find an answer, it conducted a survey of 4,000 workers and managers in a range of organizations, with 1,516 responding. Overall, the survey shows that cost-cutting, restructuring, and reengineering have focused on the nonhuman elements of business. These efforts have glossed over the importance of human resources and made workers feel alienated, unappreciated, and vulnerable. The results have been widespread worker dissatisfaction and increasingly poor job performance.

The survey also reveals several dichotomies:

- Less than half of the workers who responded to the survey perceive that their coworkers are glad to be employed by their companies; two-thirds of the managers believe the workers are happy at their jobs.

- More than 40 percent of the workers said that they don't feel valued by their companies; half of the managers said the companies value their employees.

- Only one-third of the workers believe that their supervisors know what motivates them; more than half of the managers agree.

Reprinted with permission from *Training & Development*, published by the American Society for Training & Development.

- Less than half of the workers said that they receive recognition from their supervisors for jobs well done; half of the supervisors corroborate.
- Most of the workers rely on their own knowledge of their jobs to determine whether they've done a task well; less than half of the managers give workers immediate feedback when they've performed well.

Such findings aren't indicative of high-performance workplaces. But other survey responses show that the situation isn't hopeless. Most workers take pride in a job well done. They want to improve their work performance and contribute to their companies' success. Time and again, they said that they could do a better job if only they received the support they need.

In another survey, conducted in 1995 by Yankelovich Partners for the firm of William M. Mercer, 1,200 workers said that, on average, they could improve their daily output by at least 26 percent—if only they weren't hindered by the lack of direction, support, training, and equipment. One in four said that they could raise productivity by 50 percent.

What can management do to get workers to turn in their best performance? How can you help?

A Prescription for Performance

First and foremost, organizations must change the way they think about performance. Many managers look at only one part of the overall performance system, employees. If performance levels are off, managers tend to focus on specific employees or work teams, usually to assign blame and administer reprimands. But such actions don't correct the underlying problems or have a lasting impact on employees' behavior.

To raise the level of work performance and maintain it, managers must look beyond individual or team performance to a larger field of play: the performance system. That means taking a hard look at the following interconnected elements:

- Situation
- Performer

A Five-part Performance Model

Situation

▶ How clear are the performance expectations?

▶ How well are they understood by employees?

▶ Does the work environment support performance expectations?

Performer

▶ How capable are employees (performers) to meet the organization's performance expectations?

Response

▶ What is the observed performance?

▶ How does that compare with expectations?

Consequences

▶ How well do the consequences of meeting (or not meeting) expectations encourage the expected performance?

Feedback

▶ How appropriate is feedback?

▶ Is it used effectively to influence performance?

- Response
- Consequences
- Feedback

A Case in Point

The $525 million-a-year long-products division of BHP Steel, the largest private corporation in Australia, is an excellent example of incorporating the interconnected elements—situation, performer, response, consequences, and feedback—into a company's performance system.

When George Edgar took over as general manager, the division was in deep trouble. Competition was fierce, manufacturing costs had skyrocketed, and the workforce was overpopulated. Edgar moved rapidly, but cautiously, to cut operating costs. He knew that a lot of employees had to go, but he wanted to preserve the commitment and contributions of those who remained. Edgar didn't just pay lip service to the idea that people were the organization's most valuable asset. To prove it, he reconfigured the performance system.

In the past, workers had received little feedback. So, Edgar set about providing it. He walked the aisles of the plant, talked to workers, asked questions, and made suggestions. He also saw to it that formal measures were developed to track employee performance and provide direct feedback.

Edgar insisted that employees be provided with all of the information they needed to do their jobs and with the training that would enable them to use the information. He had the division's cost-reporting system overhauled so that work teams would have quick access to financial and production figures. Now the plant provides extensive training in analytic problem solving, decision making, statistical process control, true-cost performance, and similar skills.

The division is also developing a formal reward-and-recognition system. In the meantime, Edgar and his management team are using a variety of informal incentives to let employees know that their efforts don't go unnoticed.

Within three years of these changes, plant productivity increased from 250 to 575 tons per worker. Fully absorbed cost per ton declined by 30 percent. And plant yield rose by 11 percent.

A Herculean Task

Several years ago, Hewlett-Packard—one of the largest U.S. manufacturers of heavy equipment—started a new product line, developing a new structure and process to go along with it. The HR department faced a Herculean task in developing a comprehensive training plan to prepare employees for their new jobs.

Working hand-in-hand with line managers, the HR people examined each new position to identify new job profiles and standards. Then, they compared employees' skills with the skills needed in their new jobs. The HR department created a plan to close skill gaps and develop a well-trained, capable workforce that could easily make the transition to the new product line. It also made sure that frequent feedback went to employees soon after start-up and continued—and that the feedback was based on the measurement of actual performance against clear standards.

At a time when such industry giants as IBM and Digital Equipment were foundering, Hewlett-Packard was turning in record profits, without massive layoffs. It is no coincidence that for many years Hewlett-Packard has had a formal performance system. The company carefully and deliberately created a work environment with many opportunities for workers to show initiative, helping to retain talented employees. In effect, Hewlett-Packard developed a self-reliant workforce. Thanks to the performance system, employees know that if they apply their energies and talents to the company's performance objectives, everyone will come out a winner.

Adapting the Model

Managing the key elements of the five-part performance model as an integrated whole can improve performance at every level of an organization.

For example, by focusing on the "situation" element, HR professionals can ensure that the "what" and "why" of performance are clear and that the expectations of the departments and the organization are aligned. When such alignment exists, developing job standards becomes less ad hoc and more an opportunity to identify core competencies that are vital to success. HR people can compare needed skills with current skills to identify the appropriate training for meeting an organization's strategic goals.

A common complaint of the workers who responded to the Kepner-Tregoe survey was that supervisors "played favorites." Such favoritism can be overcome by examining each job, focusing on the five elements: situation, performer, response, consequences, and feedback. Then, ask these questions: What standards and outputs does this element suggest? Are they consistent with overall business strategy?

The result is likely to be a consistent, results-based appraisal system that will help eliminate favoritism as a factor in poor job performance.

Knowing the five key elements of the performance model can also prove helpful in troubleshooting specific performance problems. The model serves as a template to identify the root causes of problems, without the usual finger-pointing.

For example, what at first glance may appear to be a "people" or "performer" problem may, on closer examination, prove to be a deviation in another element of the model. Remember: Training and rah-rah motivational efforts directed at employees won't improve performance when the real culprit is unclear expectations or inadequate feedback.

So, how's your organization doing?

To gauge whether your organization has a work environment for optimal employee performance, take the quiz shown on page 2-8. You can even pass the quiz along to others in your organization. You may discover that there is much you can do right now to start your company—and its employees—on the road to higher performance.

To rate your organization in 10 areas, use the following scale:

- **10—excellent;** little room for improvement
- **5—adequate;** needs major improvement
- **1—poor;** needs to make fundamental changes

1. Commitment

Do employees react positively to change? Is the turnover rate among high achievers low? Can the organization live and thrive with the current level of absenteeism?

❏ excellent (10)   ❏ adequate (5)   ❏ poor (1)

2. Rewards and Recognition

Do senior managers recognize outstanding achievement throughout the organization? Are there monetary rewards? Is there ongoing recognition for excellence? Does the company promote from within?

❏ excellent (10)   ❏ adequate (5)   ❏ poor (1)

3. Information

Can employees explain the organization's business strategies? Do they know the general financial picture? Do they know the specifics of their own units' performances?

❏ excellent (10)   ❏ adequate (5)   ❏ poor (1)

4. Feedback

Is employee feedback regular, specific, and timely? Does the feedback promote desired behavior? Is feedback communicated in a positive, nonthreatening manner? Does the organization view feedback as a learning opportunity?

❏ excellent (10)   ❏ adequate (5)   ❏ poor (1)

5. Performance Standards

Do employees know when they've done a good job? Are the performance standards against which they're judged clear and well-communicated? Are the standards understood by employees? Are they achieved?

❏ excellent (10)   ❏ adequate (5)   ❏ poor (1)

6. Empowerment

Are employee recommendations regularly sought, listened to, and implemented? Are employees responsible for correcting problems, making decisions, and recommending improvements in their units? Do they have the information and skills they need for those responsibilities?

❏ excellent (10)   ❏ adequate (5)   ❏ poor (1)

7. Teams

Do employee teams participate in decision making? Do they address serious business issues rather than trivial matters? Are team roles and responsibilities clear? Do teams receive rewards and recognition for their efforts?

❏ excellent (10)   ❏ adequate (5)   ❏ poor (1)

8. Employee Readiness

Do employees have the necessary knowledge and skills to accomplish their tasks? If not, are they given the time and resources to acquire them? Does the organization provide an environment in which learning is viewed as continuous and integral to employees' jobs?

❏ excellent (10)   ❏ adequate (5)   ❏ poor (1)

9. Systematic Performance Management

The last time that the organization began a change initiative, did you and other employees ask the following questions?:

- Why must we change?
- Who is responsible for getting the job done?
- What skills are needed?
- In what other areas must changes be made as a result of the change initiative—including individual and team behavior, as well as systems, structures, and processes?
- What are the consequences—such as reward and punishment systems—that encourage making the required changes?
- How will we know that we are meeting goals?

❏ excellent (10)   ❏ adequate (5)   ❏ poor (1)

10. Motivation

What do managers believe are the key motivators of human performance? Do they recognize that motivation involves external, workplace factors and employees' "inner persons"?

❏ excellent (10)   ❏ adequate (5)   ❏ poor (1)

Interpreting Your Score

To determine the total score, add the points in all 10 areas.

85–100. If your organization is in this range, it has top-flight people managers.

50–84. If your organization is in this range, it is just muddling through. It needs to identify problem areas and create plans for addressing those areas.

10–49. If your organization is in this range, it needs to take decisive and radical action to improve employee performance.

Program Checklist for Planning and Managing Large-scale or Global Programs

By Karin Kolodziejski and Pat Case

Audience	Top Management, Other Managers Responsible for Planning and Managing Large-scale Strategic Projects (e.g., reengineering, reorganization, TQM)
Purpose	—Learn a process for planning large-scale programs
Suggested Uses	Tool for management steering teams creating a large-scale project plan Handout for strategic planning workshop Resource for presentation on global program planning how-to

Introduction

An effective planning process for any program is multifaceted and is accomplished incrementally over time. Planning for large-scale global programs is particularly complex. Because effective planning involves those who will be affected by change, a large number of people may be involved in a full planning process. The checklist that follows can help organizations develop a complete, capable process; monitor the process and ensure steps are not overlooked; and help everyone involved in the process follow a consistent approach.

Program Checklist: Planning and Managing Large-scale or Global Programs

1. **Assess the Business Drivers**
- Understand the current global business strategy and vision for the future:
  - ✔ Read company publications.
  - ✔ Review market and financial analyst reports.
  - ✔ Get inputs from a variety of knowledgeable sources (internal and external).
  - ✔ Ask senior leaders to describe the strategy from their perspective.
- Identify the general implications of the global business strategy and vision for the project:
  - ✔ Question senior leaders about their perspectives.
  - ✔ Conduct exploratory benchmarking visits.
  - ✔ Create preliminary development assumptions.

2. **Implement a Steering Process**
- Establish a steering team to:
  - ✔ Manage the process.
  - ✔ Interface with top management.
  - ✔ Provide access to information and content experts throughout the organization.
  - ✔ Review recommendations.
  - ✔ Make key decisions.
- Ensure the steering team has:
  - ✔ Power and/or decision-making capability.

✔ Key stakeholders as part of its membership.
✔ A big picture perspective.
✔ Diversity and breadth of perspective.
✔ People who understand the business issues.
✔ People who have experience working in a variety of cultural settings.

- Set up periodic reviews throughout the program development process:

  ✔ Plan meetings well in advance.
  ✔ Review meeting content with primary sponsor(s) prior to distributing to other members of the steering team.
  ✔ Send meeting content to members of the steering team prior to the meeting; collect and consolidate feedback.
  ✔ Be prepared to facilitate effective voice and video conferencing.
  ✔ Document meeting discussions, agreed-upon revisions, and key decisions.
  ✔ Distribute meeting notes promptly.

3. **Conduct a Needs Assessment**

- Create a needs assessment strategy:

  ✔ Determine rationale for needs assessment.
  ✔ Define the boundaries of the process, i.e., the kind of information needed.
  ✔ Review previous assessment strategies and data related to the topic.
  ✔ Determine the appropriate needs assessment methodology (focus groups, tabulated surveys, individual interviews) based on an analysis of:
  —The organizational culture
  —The organization's capacity to participate
  —Timing; conflicting initiatives
  —The type of information needed
  ✔ Determine the target audience and specific participants within it.
  ✔ Determine necessary demographic categories to be analyzed:
  —Geographic breakouts
  —Other
  ✔ Identify who needs to be involved in orchestrating, implementing, and managing the assessment process.
  ✔ Identify other types of information needed, which can be acquired through means other than interviews and/or surveys, i.e., information on:

—Existing organizational or training and development programs
—Relevant strategic issues, product and service offerings, etc.
✔ Develop a schedule.
✔ Review the proposed strategy with members of the steering team.

- Develop the assessment protocol (questionnaire survey format):

  ✔ Create a draft list of questions.
  ✔ Circulate draft to key members of the steering team for review.
  ✔ Update the draft.
  ✔ Pilot protocol with small group of target audience participants.
  ✔ Update the protocol.

- Implement the needs assessment:

  ✔ Schedule interviews as appropriate.
  ✔ Be prepared to conduct interviews across global time zones.
  ✔ Produce participant surveys as appropriate.
  ✔ Investigate the need for language translations.
  ✔ Mail surveys and/or conduct interviews/focus groups.

- Gather data on existing training and/or organizational interventions that relate to the issues being addressed.

- Analyze results:

  ✔ Tabulate any numerical data.
  ✔ Analyze content statements.
  ✔ Identify recurring themes, issues, polarities, etc.
  ✔ Analyze demographic differences.
  ✔ Geographic.
  ✔ Other.
  ✔ Analyze results in light of previous survey results and/or information pertaining to related development efforts.
  ✔ Develop conclusions and implications.
  ✔ Check out your conclusions, i.e., report and test conclusions and implications with the steering team prior to developing and reporting recommendations.

4. **Develop and Communicate Recommendations**

- Develop recommendations:

  ✔ Determine recommendation criteria,

i.e., what conditions/situations, etc., must the recommendations satisfy, for example, they must be:

— Implementable worldwide

— Fully integrated with existing development efforts

✔ Connect classroom learning with on-the-job experience.

✔ Determine the degree to which existing information/interventions, etc., can be used and/or modified to support the development needs of global leaders.

✔ Generate creative options to address the conclusions and implications.

✔ Consider both training and development interventions and related infrastructure interventions as appropriate.

✔ Involve steering team members as appropriate.

✔ Assess options against recommendation criteria.

✔ Estimate costs associated with recommendations.

✔ Select best options.

• Present the findings:

✔ Prepare a draft presentation.

✔ Review the draft presentation with prime sponsor(s).

✔ Update the presentation accordingly.

✔ Schedule a review meeting with the steering team.

✔ Distribute presentation to steering team members in advance of the review meeting.

✔ Collect and incorporate feedback from steering team members as appropriate.

✔ Present the consolidated recommendations.

✔ Get input on next steps.

• Revise recommendations based on input from the meeting:

✔ Document the revisions.

✔ Communicate revisions and obtain agreement.

✔ Reestimate costs.

• Determine next steps:

✔ Develop a detailed project plan, including key milestones and review dates.

✔ Review project plan with the prime sponsor.

• Review project plan with the steering committee.

5. **Determine the Scope of the Effort**

• Assess the kinds of interventions required:

✔ To what extent are the requirements systemic, i.e., to what extent would the requirements dictate changes to the reward system, the reporting structure of the organization, organizational processes, etc.?

✔ To what extent are the requirements oriented toward a training and development solution?

• Identify the number of projects and their interdependencies.

• Determine the best way to manage interdependencies between projects.

• Determine resource requirements:

✔ Who will need to participate internally?

✔ Will external consultants be required?

• Develop detailed cost estimates associated with each component of the project.

• Review scoping requirements with steering team.

• Update scope of project based on feedback from the steering team.

6. **Establish the Design Team**

• Finalize who will participate on the design team (for the most part these would be the key players, as previously determined):

✔ Be sure to reconsider the kind of expertise required for each aspect of the program to be designed. Do we have the right people involved on the design team?

• Determine if there will need to be separate subdesign teams for the primary categories of intervention:

✔ Who, other than the core design team, will need to be involved?

✔ What will their relationship be to the design team?

✔ How will accountabilities be established?

• Determine how often the design team will need to meet. (Ideally, the design team should meet as a single, large group when the design phase begins and at key milestone dates thereafter.)

- Determine specific roles and responsibilities for design team members:
  ✔ Who will be responsible for which element of the project?
  ✔ Who will provide content expertise and input?
    ✔ How will decisions get made?
- Determine when the steering team will need to review the design (as the design is evolving or at the completion of the design phase).

7. **Design and Develop**

Design Change Management Process

- Be sure that the recommended changes and related strategies align with the company strategy and vision.
- Determine key stakeholders, i.e., people who will be affected by the changes.
- Ensure buy-in by the leadership team.
- Obtain input about the proposed change, as follows:
  ✔ Communicate proposed infrastructure changes, including the rationale and implications to key stakeholders and people who will be affected.
  ✔ Gather reactions and input regarding barriers and benefits.
  ✔ Alter the design based on inputs received.
  ✔ Design a process for ongoing communication.
  ✔ Design a process for dealing with resistance.
- Assess how to manage in concert with other key competing initiatives.
- Determine what communication strategies will be employed.
- Determine program rollout strategies.
- Determine how to assess the impact of the changes.
- Assess the need for changes to supporting technology.
- Communicate with the steering team and key stakeholders as appropriate.

Design Meeting Management Process

- Kick off the design and development phase.
- Plan and implement the first design meeting. Establish the purpose of the design meeting and the meeting discussion topics. Minimally, the purpose of the first meeting should be to:
  ✔ Establish the design criteria.
  ✔ Ensure that all members of the design team understand the design challenge.
  ✔ Communicate the macro schedule; create a detailed project timeline for the design phase.
  ✔ Ensure the commitment and availability of all design team members.
  ✔ Create (ideally) a rough draft of the macro design and objectives for each component of the program.
- Plan and manage subsequent design meetings. The follow-on design meetings should stay focused on macro elements of the project:
  ✔ Ensure the program is on track.
  ✔ Manage interdependencies between projects; manage and resolve key issues.

Program Design

- Develop the design specs:
  ✔ Construct the vision for the end state.
  ✔ Identify the gap between where you are now and the end state.
  ✔ Determine strategies to close the gap.
  ✔ Specify objectives for each component of the program.
  ✔ Create the overall macro design program.
- Reality-check the design as it evolves against the cultural factors, etc., prevalent in the organization in which the intervention is being directed.
- Review existing training and organizational interventions.
- Determine if existing programs can be redefined to fit the requirements of this program.
- Conduct benchmarking as appropriate.
- Design an evaluation plan (determine how the program impact will be assessed).
- Revise preliminary cost estimates associated with each element of the project.
- Decide which aspects of the program will be developed internally and which will be purchased outside.
- Develop a preliminary production schedule.
- Develop an implementation schedule.

- Communicate with the steering team and key stakeholders as appropriate.

Program Development

- Produce the various materials defined by the macro design (e.g., training materials, software or computer-based programs, supplementary audio-visuals, leaders guides, collateral material).

- Consult additional content people as required.

- Test the products/program (pilot/beta) as appropriate.

- Maintain cohesion of effort through effective management and communication.

- Review and update the schedule as appropriate.

8. **Implement the Program**

- Launch the program per the plan.

- Review feedback on the program as it unfolds.

- Review and revise the implementation schedule as appropriate.

- Determine if changes or modifications to the implementation process are required; adjust the program accordingly.

9. **Evaluate the Results**

- Evaluate the results as specified in the evaluation plan.

- Document what's going well, what could be improved.

- Communicate findings to the steering team.

- Adjust the program as appropriate.

- Find a way to share learnings (what worked and what didn't) with other interested parties throughout the organization.

The Opportunity Grid: A Strategic Planning Tool

By Chandler Cox

Audience	Managers
Purpose	—Learn a method for targeting performance improvement resources —Be able to use the opportunity grid to identify key needs/opportunities
Suggested Uses	Tool for strategic planning workshops Tool for individual managers to assist in planning and tracking improvement efforts Executive team tool to determine and track alignment of different perceptions among departments/units with those of senior management

Introduction

The Opportunity Grid is used to examine and critically evaluate current key discriminators (price, service, convenience, quality, etc.) and capabilities against customer priorities. After determining where each of these lie in terms of customer importance and existing satisfaction, specific areas can be targeted for improvement. When using this tool, it is important to remember that tracking is a "snapshot" of status based on current states; changing customer base or product characteristics will change positioning on the grid. Used and tracked on an iterative basis, these data provide critical trend information.

An opportunity grid is a simple tool that enables teams to illustrate customer priorities graphically. The vertical axis represents importance, the horizontal axis represents current performance. Expectations falling in the "opportunity grid," representing high importance but low performance, should generally be the focus of improvement efforts.

It is important to remember when using this tool that the results are no better than the data used to construct the grid. For example, a grid constructed on the basis of what the team believes customer satisfaction and importance to be is not nearly as useful as a grid constructed with information that comes from the customer.

The map can be used in other situations as well. For example, in risk assessment the axes might be likelihood of occurrence and severity. Such a grid could then be used to make protection or risk mitigation decisions.

Exercise: Leader's Notes

Time

Approximately one hour if done individually, and three hours for a group.

Number of Participants

This tool can be used individually or in groups of any number. If using a group format, a facilitated session is recommended.

Facilitator Experience

Group facilitation skills

Materials and Equipment

Individual Format

Customer Satisfaction Analysis (if available)

Product list with quality and availability information

Group Format

Same as above, plus:

Writing tools

Index cards

Small Post-it notes in multiple colors

Handouts

Opportunity Grid Forms - Example

Opportunity Grid Forms - Blank (enough copies for the group)

Procedure

Individual Format

1. Using the customer satisfaction, quality, and availability information, identify key discriminators, such as price, service, convenience, or quality.

2. Determine importance level of key discriminators to customers.

3. Determine customer satisfaction on key discriminators.

4. Plot key discriminators according to importance and satisfaction levels on a blank opportunity grid.

Group Format with Facilitator

1. Brief the group on the concept and types of key discriminators and make sure that everyone understands what these are. Show people the example filled-in opportunity grid and point out how it works. Explain that they will now do their own for their department/unit.

2. Using round robin, solicit key discriminators.

3. Identify existing importance and satisfaction levels. Have each person assign an importance and satisfaction rating to each key discriminator. Assign one Post-it note color to each key discriminator.

4. Plot the key discriminators on the posterboard grid at the front of the room, one discriminator at a time. Write the name of the key discriminator on the grid.

5. Discuss the different plottings and reach a consensus.

6. Repeat steps 3 through 5 for each discriminator.

7. Plot all discriminators on the master grid.

8. When the grid has been constructed, ask the group to offer interpretations of what the results mean. One of the first lines of discussion would be to develop a shared understanding of why the grid turned out as it did. Is it leadership? Materials? Design? Marketing? Quality? What is causing lack of satisfaction in important (to the customer) attributes?

9. Next, have the group suggest some actions that might be taken to "improve" the grid. Some typical suggestions include:

   - Shifting resources from the lower right quadrant to the upper left.

   - Rethinking the items in the lower left quadrant as to why we are devoting any resources to things that are unimportant to the customer.

   - Should the persons responsible for the items in the upper right quadrant be used in the upper left quadrant (redeployment of leadership).

   - How much/many resources should be redeployed from one quadrant to another. The map helps point out where resources should be applied, but does not say how much or how many.

Keep the group from running ahead of their knowledge of the situation. If the grid purports to represent the feelings of the customer, and in fact represents group feelings, then the tool should be used to spur the group into getting real data, and then making decisions.

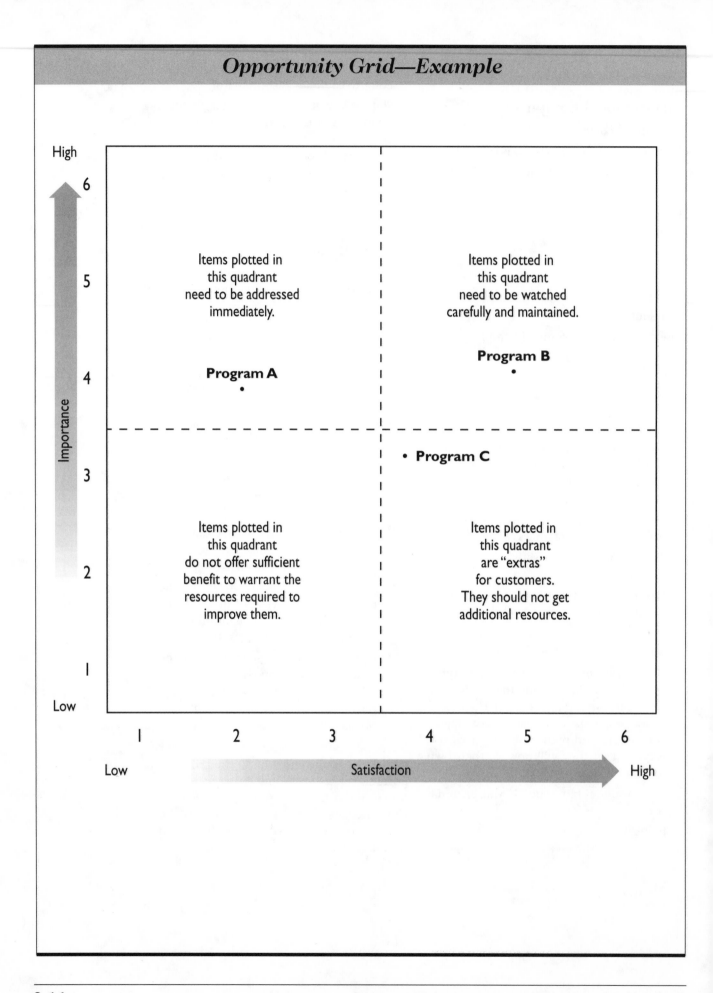

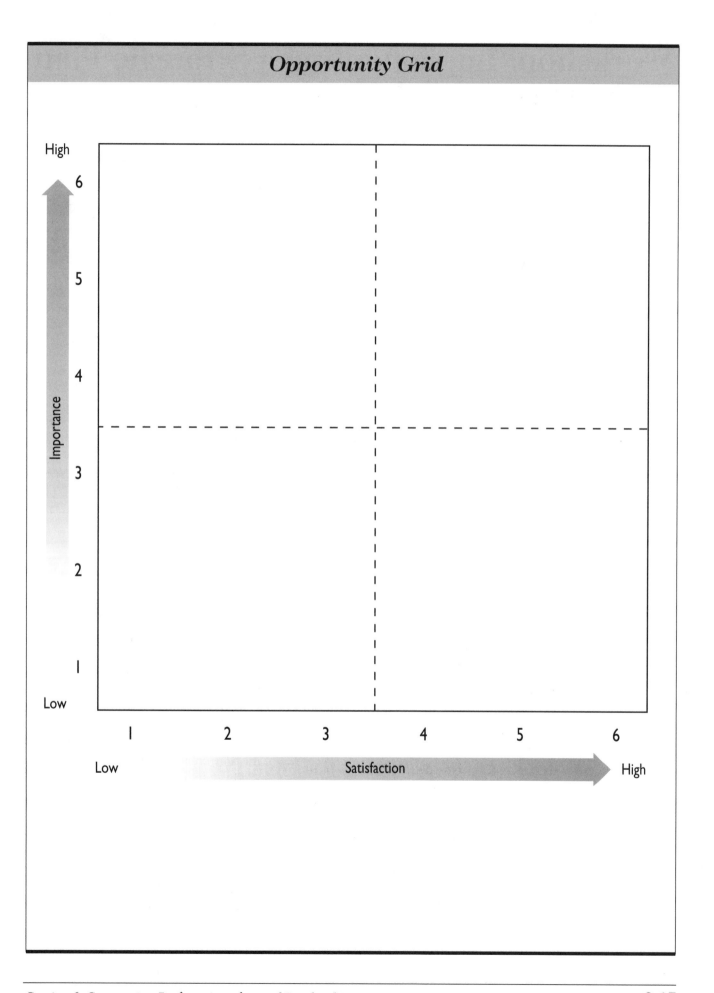

Workshop: Implementing a Strategic Plan at the Operational Level

By Adrian B. Durelli

Audience ➤	Learning Professionals, Department/ Division Management Groups
Purpose ➤	—Use a process and tools to redefine department/division direction, based on organizational strategic goals/plans —Decide how to align their plans and activities to help achieve corporate goals —Determine how their employees can contribute to overall corporate goals
Suggested Uses ➤	Workshop following announced changes in corporate strategic goals; changes in top or department/division leadership; or when current department/division goals have been reached

Introduction

Strategic planning traditionally refers to the top-down perspective of an organization. It reflects the thinking of an organization's CEO and top executives. The strategic plan provides the "road map" to the future, describing the executives' vision for the future and how they intend to move the organization toward that vision.

Coopers & Lybrand defines vision as "a picture of the future, a common goal that sets direction and around which everyone can rally." Setting the direction for an organization remains integral to successful leadership. If setting the overall direction and goals for the organization defines a major function of the organizational leaders, interpreting how departments/divisions and employees will contribute to achieve those goals is an important role of management.

The workshop outline that follows is designed to guide a strategic planning process on a departmental or divisional level that helps managers operationalize corporate goals at their organizational level. Activities include the following:

Day one: understanding the organizational mission; creating the department/division vision statement.

Day two: identifying the skill sets and competencies required to achieve the vision.

Day three: developing goals to achieve the vision; developing strategies and first-year objectives for the goals.

Day four: determining roles, responsibilities, and relationships among supervisors.

Exercises: Leader's Notes

Time

Four to six days, usually divided into two or three two-day sessions (to lessen the impact of consuming this amount of time).

Note: The procedure below is broken out into four days, but actual time frames may differ. The facilitator should make the final decision as to where day breaks are appropriate and how much time is required for each activity depending on the group. After each exercise, the facilitator should poll the group for understanding (using the 5-point scale on page 2-22). If understanding is low, more time should be dedicated to clarifying the group's efforts.

Number of Participants

Works best with groups of no larger than 15 people.

Facilitator Expertise

Group facilitation skills; experience working with management; knowledge/experience leading a planning process, achieving consensus, and project management/planning.

Materials and Equipment

Paper and pens

Flipchart and markers

Post-it notes

Handouts

Presession Worksheet 1

Task Sheet: Vision of a Thriving Organization

Task Sheet: Identify Skill Sets and Competencies

Task Sheet: Developing Goals to Achieve the Vision

Task Sheet: Developing Strategies and First-year Objectives for the Goals

Task Sheet: Role, Responsibilities, and Relationships Among Supervisors/Management Team

Procedure

Day One

Craft the vision. **Note:** Visions are best created in an off-site focus group setting.

1. Prior to the session, send the Presession Worksheet 1 to the participants. Completing this task sheet will get the participants thinking about the departmental/divisional environment and opportunities that may or may not exist. In addition, the completed worksheet can serve as input to other exercises throughout the first session.

2. Explain to the group that the first step of departmental visioning is to confirm the departmental mission. This process ensures that each manager retains a clear understanding of the mission. A mission statement defines a group's purpose. It describes what the group does and whom it serves. In developing the vision for a department/division's future it remains important to align it with both the departmental/divisional mission as well as with the greater organizational mission and vision. This exercise serves as a reality check for the managers.

3. Present copies of the organizational mission and vision and the department/division mission to the manager and supervisors present. Give the group time to review and clarify any questions with the department/division manager. Poll the group on a scale of 1–5 to assess the level of understanding of the missions and vision (where 1= not at all and 5 = completely understand). Use the polling guide on page 2-22.

4. Once the mission has been confirmed, have the same group of supervisors define the vision of the department. Explain that a vision defines the "to be." It relates a picture or story of how the organization will look after a certain amount of time. Currently, most organizational visions define a period of three years from the envisioning. The vision statement contains the goals that will help fulfill the mission and vision of the organization. In the absence of anything else, an effective vision statement would define how an employee does his or her work. For example, if conflicting requirements arose, one should place his or her priority on the action or actions that help achieve an element of the vision. In addition, a vision statement is specific, and the most effective ones are quantifiable. The vision details metrics that can easily be assessed.

5. Hand out the Task Sheet: Vision of a Thriving Organization, which participants will use to begin the visioning process. Read

the directions aloud and have the group follow them.

6. Have the group work collaboratively to craft a unified vision statement. This statement should reflect the common thinking of the group and, if satisfactory, will reflect clearly the department/division's contribution to helping the organization achieve the organizational mission and vision.

7. When the group believes it is done, poll them as to the collective understanding of the department/division vision statement on a scale from 1–5 (see page 2-22). Then take a consensus vote. If there is not consensus among the group, have them refine the vision until all present are satisfied and feel they can commit resources to achieving the vision.

Day Two

Identify the skill sets and competencies required to achieve and sustain the vision.

1. Divide participants into small groups to complete Task Sheet: Identify Skills Sets and Competencies. Read the instructions aloud and answer any questions about the task.

2. Have each small group reach agreement on its list of vital competencies. When all groups are ready, have a representative of each report their group's choices to the full group. Write the choices on a flipchart and post the pages around the room for comparison.

3. Have the large group select the competencies that need action. This may be all or only some of those listed by the small groups. Allow discussion and use decision-making tools if needed to rank the choices.

4. After the group has developed a final list, poll them as to their collective understanding of the choices and their implications (See page 2-22). Then take a consensus vote. If there is not consensus among the group, address areas of difference until all are comfortable with the final list. Note that the next step (outside the workshop process) would be to obtain the needed competencies and knowledge/skills/abilities that are required to achieve the vision.

Day Three

Develop goals to achieve the vision.

1. Divide participants into small groups to complete Task Sheet: Developing Goals to Achieve the Vision. Read the instructions aloud and answer any questions about the task.

2. Have each small group reach agreement on its list of vital goals. When all groups are ready, have a representative of each report their group's choices to the full group. Write the choices on a flipchart and post the pages around the room for comparison.

3. Have the large group select the final goals list. This may be all or only some of those listed by the small groups. Allow discussion and use decision-making tools if needed to rank the choices.

4. After the group has developed a final list, poll them as to their collective understanding of the choices (see page 2-22). Then take a consensus vote. If there is not consensus among the group, address areas of difference until all are comfortable with the final list.

5. Once the overall goals have been set, the participants need to define the strategy and develop a road map for achieving the vision. Have the participants again break out into small groups to complete Task Sheet: Developing Strategies and First-year Objectives for the Goals. Read the instructions aloud and answer any questions about the task.

6. Have each small group reach agreement on its list of vital goals. When all groups are ready, have a representative of each report their group's choices to the full group. Write the choices on a flipchart and post the pages around the room for comparison.

7. Have the large group select the final milestones/objectives list. This may be all or only some of those listed by the small groups. Allow discussion and use decision-making tools if needed to rank the choices.

8. After the group has developed a final list, poll them as to their collective understanding of the choices (see page 2-22). Once

there is understanding, take a consensus vote. If there is not consensus among the group, address areas of difference until all are comfortable with the final list.

Day Four

Define the accountability for the milestones mapped out during the last session.

1. Give all participants Task Sheet: Role, Responsibilities, and Relationships Among Supervisors/Management Team. Read the instructions aloud and answer any questions about the task.

2. If time permits, map the relationships among supervisors/managers. This can be accomplished using several pieces of flipchart paper. First, write every participant's name down on the paper (with adequate space). Then, each participant should draw a line to everyone he or she relies on for some purpose to complete his or her job. If time permits, have participants write the product or service they receive from a colleague on a Post-it note and put those on the correct line on the flipchart paper. For example, if Person A requires procurement approvals from person B, Person A should write:

> From: B to: A
>
> *Procurement*
> *Approvals*

on the Post-it and place it on the line drawn between person A and Person B in the flipchart:

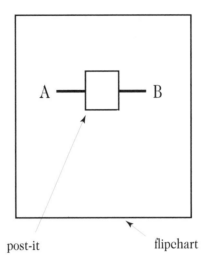

post-it   flipchart

Doing this will provide a visual picture of the interdependencies in the department/division.

3. Have participants complete their forms and any memos of agreement they need to develop.

4. Close the session with the department/division leader, who should explain plans for carrying out the results of the workshop. First, a high review of the plan will be conducted and a date set for a status report meeting. Status meetings should be held on a regular basis (once per month or every two months) as the department/division moves toward its vision. At these status updates, each direct report to the department/division head presents his or her progress with the action items detailed in the strategic plan.

Polling the Group for Agreement and Consensus

After each exercise, it is important to poll the group to ensure understanding, agreement, and/or consensus. Depending on the exercise, one or more pollings may be needed.

If the group does not agree on the scale below that they understand what they have done, spend more time going over results and clarifying outcomes. Once understanding is sufficient, either an agreement or consensus poll should be taken. If the exercise results in a decision that requires participants' commitment of resources and remains integral to the strategic plan, a consensus poll should be used on it as well. The following are the scales used for agreement and consensus. Please note that if all participants rate a 4 or 5, there is sufficient agreement, or in the event of a consensus poll, 4 indicates consensus.

Agreement	Consensus
1 - Completely disagree	1 - No way
2 - Mostly disagree	2 - Significant disagreement
3 - Disagree a little, agree a little	3 - Disagree but nearly there
4 - Mostly agree	4 - Not my preferred choice but can live with, advocate, and implement
5 - Completely agree	5 - Full commitment

Although anonymous polling is recommended, polling can be done in a variety of ways. The facilitator should use the method with which he or she is most familiar and comfortable.

Presession Worksheet 1: Strengths, Weaknesses, Opportunities/Threats, and Constraints Review and Assessment

Purpose: To identify the likely impacts on the department/division and the possible actions the department could take to mitigate or leverage its most significant strengths, weaknesses, opportunities/threats, and constraints.

Instructions:
1. List below only a few strengths, weaknesses, opportunities/threats, and constraints that you think are the most significant for the department/division. You need not have a category (strengths, weaknesses, opportunities/threats, and constraints) represented.
2. For each item you listed, write down what you think the impact will be on the department/division if it does nothing different, and the potential actions that would mitigate or leverage the item.

Definitions:

Strength: A resource, skill, distinctive competence, or other advantage relative to competitors or needs of stakeholders.

Weakness: A limitation or deficiency in resources, skills, and capabilities that seriously impedes performance.

Opportunity/Threat: A situation, event, organization, product, service, or business condition that either will present the department/division with a window to improve its business position (opportunity) or a window in which action must occur or business will be lost (threat).

Constraint: A situation, business condition, policy, etc., that the department/ division has little influence over and must adhere to or cope with.

Strengths, Weaknesses, Opportunities, Threats, Constraints	Impact on the Department/Division	Potential Actions

Task Sheet: Vision of a Thriving Organization

Purpose:

To describe this department/division two to three years from now. Effective visions are specific and describe a changed organization and environment: NOT that we are doing what we have always done, but better. An effective vision provides a focal point and context for selecting strategic goals.

Outcome:

Bullets or statements that provide a vivid picture of the department/division successfully meeting its core purpose (mission) and satisfying its customers' needs and wants.

Instructions:

1. It is three years from now. You have accepted an invitation to visit after an absence of several years. You spend several days on site, receive many briefings, and have the opportunity to inspect operations and talk with some customers.

    You are impressed by and proud of what you have heard and seen, especially since you were part of the team that started this organization on the road to success. Without hesitation you decide you must write about your experience (for publication in the *Wall Street Journal*) so that it may serve as a model for other organizations.

2. Outline the major bullets of this article now. Specifically, describe the operations of the organization and its environment. Consider some of the following:

    Customers, products, and services (the "vital few" customers and why, key products, and services)

    Core business processes (a set of cross-functional business processes that (a) are linked to external customers who are the inherent basis of the organization's mission, and (b) produce the end product/services the customer requires. If improved, they can provide competitive advantage.)

    Culture (the way we do things around here)

    People (number, skills, abilities)

    Technology (computers, communication means, management systems)

    Organizational structure, size, location

Task Sheet: Identify Skill Sets and Competencies

Purpose:

Identify those competencies and skill sets the department/division employees will require to achieve and sustain the vision.

Outcome:

A list of potential competencies and skill sets.

An initial assessment of current employee status vis-á-vis required competencies and skill sets.

Competencies/KSAs to be developed or acquired.

Instructions:

1. Review the vision. Consider yourself an employee two to three years from now. Write down the core competencies you now have or acquired that enabled you to help achieve and sustain the vision. Note the reasons for your decisions.

2. For each core competency you identified, write down the knowledge (K), skills(S), and abilities (A's) required by that competency.

3. Review the list of qualifications of current department/division personnel. On this worksheet mark with a "" the competencies (COMs) and KSAs that are missing.

4. Be prepared to discuss your responses with your small group and develop a group list of the "vital few" competencies and KSAs that must be developed or acquired.

5. Select a spokesperson to debrief the large group.

Competencies to Achieve/ Sustain Vision	Rationale	Knowledge, Skills, Abilities	Missing	
			COMs	KSAs

Task Sheet: Developing Goals to Achieve the Vision

Purpose:

To define and describe the scope of the strategic *Goals* that the Department/Division *must* address to fully implement its mission and realize its vision.

Definition:

1. A *Goal* is a statement (a noun-verb combination) that:

    a. Has an **outcome** (something we want but don't have).

    b. Cuts across internal organizational boundaries.

    c. Could be achieved in between one to three years.

Instructions:

1. Review in your mind the content and results of the activities we have done to this point. Consider the possible actions we have identified and think of some new ones in reference to the vision.

2. In the space below, write down one or more Goal statement(s) that if completed will move department/division toward achieving its vision. For each goal statement you write, list some bullets that describe the scope of activity that pursuing this goal may require.

3. In your small group, review each participant's goal statements and scope for understanding.

4. As a group, add any more the group thinks are needed or not on anyone's list.

5. Choose the "vital few" goals (try to limit them to three or less) from your lists and write them on a flipchart. Write each goal statement on a flipchart page with the scope bullets listed below. Keep track of the reasons for your choices.

6. Select a spokesperson and prepare to debrief the large group.

Task Sheet: Developing Strategies and First-year Objectives for the Goals

Purpose:

To begin to focus more specifically on how to achieve the goals and what it will take to achieve them by outlining a one- to three-year strategy and identifying first-year objectives.

Definitions:

1. A statement of a **Strategy** to achieve the Goal is:

    - Written as a brief, narrative statement or set of "bullet" sentences

    _____

    - Describes a **general approach** to achieving the Goal.

    _____

    - Has a substantive content that could describe such things as **core business processes** that must be improved or reengineered, **barriers** that have to be addressed, and/or **projects or programs** to be achieved.

    _____

    - Highlights the _checkpoints_ that indicate incremental progress along the way to the Goal. These checkpoints are called **milestones.**

      A milestone describes a _state or deliverable_ to be achieved and _the conditions necessary_ to say you achieved it. Completion of all the milestones in a strategy means that you have achieved the Goal.

2. An **Objective** is a _specific result_ that must be achieved during the next fiscal or calendar year to make progress toward a milestone. Objectives are SMART (specific, measurable, achievable, relevant or realistic, and time-bounded) statements of who does what, by when, and with what support of other organizational units.

Instructions:

1. In your small group, brainstorm the strategy, the general approach, to achieving your group's goal.

2. Write a set of milestones that when reached will indicate you are making progress toward the goal, and when all are reached, you will have achieved the goal. (Hint: Try working backwards from the goal, the last milestone.)

3. Look at the milestone or milestones that are within the next 12 to 18 months. For each milestone in that period develop a set of first-year objectives to reach that milestone (usually no more than three).

4. Check each objective against the SMART criteria:

    - **Specific.** Does it describe a result? Sometimes an objective may describe a process. Take a careful look at objectives that describe a process. Try to rewrite them to describe a result.

    - **Measurable.** Is there something you can count that indicates the objective is achieved or that there is a tangible product of the objective? This is more than "checking the box" that a process is completed. If you select something you count, you may need an activity to baseline the measure and install the measurement "system."

    - **Achievable.** Can this objective be accomplished in the time frame specified? Most objectives require three months or longer to be achieved, but generally do not exceed 12 to 18 months to achieve.

    - **Realistic or Relevant.** Describe how the objective contributes to meeting the milestone in relation to the other objectives. Is the measurable result of the objective worth the resources that will be required to achieve it? Do the resources or capabilities required to achieve it exist within the resources of the organization, and will they likely be available during the period the organization will be working toward this objective?

    - **Time-bound.** Is there a completion date specified? How well does it fit with completion dates of the other objectives for that milestone and the overall strategy?

5. Select a spokesperson and prepare to debrief the large group.

Task Sheet: Roles, Responsibilities, and Relationships Among Supervisors/Management Team

Purpose:

To begin to clarify individual and mutual support roles among the managers and supervisors present for achieving the vision. Note: This exercise may not be necessary. The facilitator should work with the department head to determine whether the group would benefit.

Outcomes:

Clarity on what's important to each individual for getting the job done.

Clarity on what's needed by each individual from others in the organization to ensure success.

Instructions:

Fill in the boxes on the attached matrix and be prepared to share your responses with your colleagues.

- Start by writing your name in the space in the first column. Write your colleagues' names in the remaining boxes underneath.

- Go across the page and fill in your answers to questions 1, 2, and 3. If you cannot answer one of the questions, fill in "I don't know." The questions are:

  1. **Main job** (mission). Describe the main job (i.e., mission) in one sentence (use a noun-verb combination) for yourself and each of your colleagues.

  2. **What I need from them.** Leave this box blank for yourself. In each of your colleagues' boxes make a note of what you need from them in terms of products or services to be successful in what you do.

  3. **What I think they need from me.** Leave this box blank for yourself. In each of your colleagues' boxes make a note of what you think they need from you for them to be successful in what they do.

  4. **What they said they need from me.** This is what your colleagues said they needed from you in order for them to be successful.

- Compare notes with everyone else with special attention to answering question 4. Write down the answers you receive to question 4. If there are differences between your answers to question 1 and how your colleagues answered question 1, make a note of the differences.

- Compare the answers you wrote to question 3 and what you were told in question 4. Is there a match (question 5)? Put the appropriate letter in the column.

  If there is not a match, make arrangements to talk further with your colleague to clarify who provides what to whom and when. Put your agreement in a memorandum of agreement for both of you to have.

  If there is a match, make arrangements with your colleague to put this in a memorandum of agreement for both of you to have.

Roles, Responsibilities, and Relationships

1. Manager or Supervisor Main Job (Mission)	2. What I Need From Him/Her	3. What I Think He/She Needs From Me	4. What Manager or Supervisor Said He/She Needs From Me	5. Match Between 3 & 4? (Y/N)

Exercise for Managers: Setting Individual Goals That Support Organizational Strategy

By Sheridan Gates and Jill K. Foley

Audience →	Managers—all levels
Purpose →	—Learn a technique for creating a personal leadership statement —Be able to set long-term goals that support organizational goals —Translate these goals into weekly, actionable tasks
Suggested Uses →	Group exercise for a leadership development workshop Exercise for managers following announcement of new corporate strategic plans or goals Follow-up or add-on to the previous Workshop: Implementing a Strategic Plan at the Operational Level Wrap-up exercise for a strategic planning session among top management

Introduction

Successful leaders must be able to set and achieve individual goals that are in line with the goals and strategy of their organization. They then must be able to translate those goals into actionable plans that will produce solid results that are valued by the organization as well as be personally meaningful to the leader. This exercise will assist managers in creating a personal leadership statement, setting long-term goals, and translating these goals into action. This exercise was inspired by Steven Covey's book, *The Seven Habits of Highly Effective People.*

Exercise: Leader's Guide

Time

Two hours plus pre- and postwork

Number of Participants

Any number—large groups can be divided into smaller ones for discussion

Materials and Equipment

Flipchart, markers, and Post-it notes

Handouts

Prework Exercise

Priority Planning Worksheet

Goal Development Worksheet

Task Sheet

Weekly Planning Tool

Procedure

1. Prior to the training, have participants complete the prework exercise to develop a personal leadership statement, define roles, and set long-term goals.

2. Explain the purpose of the training and answer any questions.

3. Have each participant present his or her leadership statement, role, and goals that they developed as prework and have the others offer critiques and feedback. This is a "sanity check" and a chance to review. Give them the following criteria for evaluating the personal leadership statement (have them written on a flipchart sheet):

- Does it reflect "timeless" principles?
- Is it personally challenging and compelling?
- Is it personally motivating?
- Is it clear?
- Is it dynamic?
- Is it within your control?

Have participants adjust their statements as needed based on group feedback.

4. Prioritize the time dedicated to each role. Instruct participants to review the instructions for the Priority Planning Worksheet. Encourage participants to take time to explore the balance between their roles in order to reach clarity. Refer participants to the attached example.

5. Tell participants that personal leadership statements, planning priorities, and roles and long-term goals should be reviewed as part of weekly planning.

6. Have participants complete the Goal Development Worksheet, considering the sequential items that need to occur in order to achieve their goals.

7. Have participants complete the Task Sheet by identifying the action items that should be completed in the next week for each of their roles and the associated goals.

8. Have participants transpose action items from their personal weekly planning tool. Explain that long-term goals should be put in a "special" place, so that participants can review them as they plan each week.

9. Wrap up the session by asking for participants' reactions to the tasks they just completed. What do they see as the benefits? Do they plan to continue using this approach when new strategic goals come out? Will they pass the tools on to subordinates in coaching or mentoring them?

Reference

Covey, S. *The Seven Habits of Highly Effective People.* New York: Fireside, 1989.

Developing a Personal Leadership Statement

Your personal leadership statement may develop into any size or form. It may be a narrative text, a list of bulletized points, one page long, or a few sentences or short phrases. Your personal leadership statement embodies principles to guide you when making decisions about the most effective use of your time, talents, and energy. It is the key criterion by which everything is directed and evaluated. Whatever format you choose, it should provide a basic direction from which you set your long-term goals.

Your personal leadership statement should answer the following:

> ▶ What do you want to be (behavior characteristics)?
>
> ▶ What do you want to do (contributions/achievements)?
>
> ▶ What are the values upon which the above are based?

It may help you to first think about your responses to the following questions:

> Assume you have only six months to live and during these six months you will remain as a leader in your organization. (You can't quit!) How will you spend your six months? What will you do? What would you like to be remembered for?

No matter the process you choose to develop your personal leadership statement, spend some time in deep introspection, careful analysis, and thoughtful articulation.

_____

_____

_____

_____

_____

_____

_____

_____

_____

_____

_____

_____

_____

Developing Roles and Long-term Goals

At this point, your personal leadership statement may not be finalized. Rarely is it something you can write overnight. It takes deep thought, careful analysis, and many rewrites. Once you are satisfied with it, your personal leadership statement should be fundamentally changeless, requiring minimal modifications.

You can, however, move to the next step of breaking down your personal leadership statement into more specific roles and goals. First, list the specific roles you hold as a leader. Examples might include: project manager, supervisor, committee member, technical expert, and department head. You may even include activities outside of work that require your leadership talents (e.g., parent and home association chairperson). Be as specific as you like. Remember that this must work for you, and no one else.

Second, after you have captured your specific leadership roles, develop long-term goals for each role. Again, this must work for you. Later, you will decide the time frame for when the goals should be realized. (These long-term goals will later be broken down into weekly action items.) Two or three goals for each leadership role will be sufficient. When identifying your long-term goals, review your organization's goals and strategic plan to see how they fit with the organization. In addition, review past performance evaluations to assess those leadership skills that need improvement. For example, you may choose as one of your goals for a supervisor to improve your feedback skills.

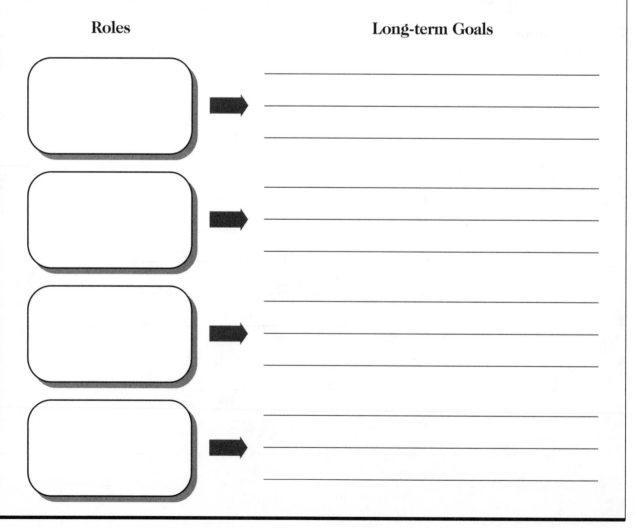

Roles   **Long-term Goals**

Personal Leadership Statement

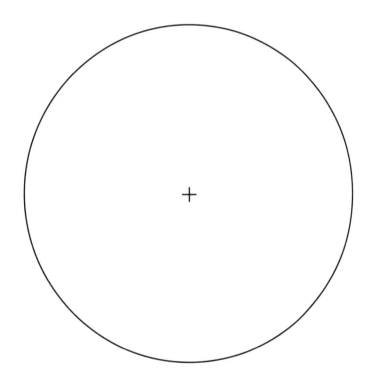

1. Record your personal leadership statement in the box provided at the top of the page.

2. Outside the circle, write each role you play. Record your primary goal directly below each goal.

3. Create a pie chart that divides your time (40 hours, for example) according to each role you play. Each piece of the pie represents the percent of time or number of hours, on average, you would like to dedicate to each role.

4. This is an interactive process. Take time to explore various combinations. There is an underlying goal of setting priorities implicit in this exercise.

Personal Leadership Statement

I am a leader and a change agent. I facilitate our company's shift toward its new vision. I inspire and empower employees to take a meaningful role in our company's business and future. I value risk taking, innovation, honesty, and making a difference. My typical work week is 40 hours:

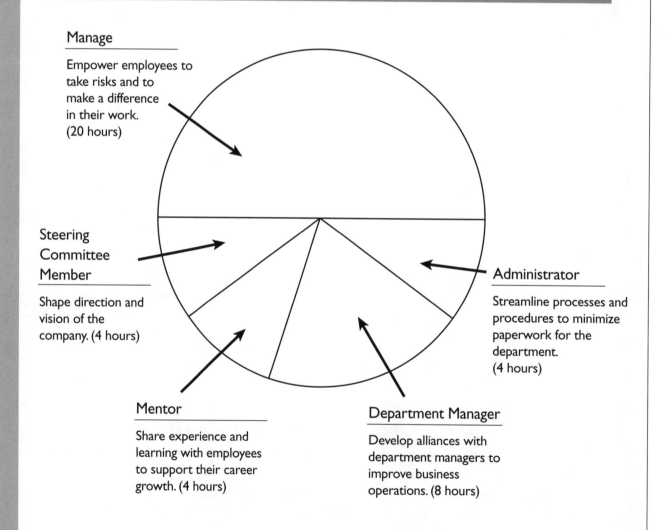

Manage

Empower employees to take risks and to make a difference in their work. (20 hours)

Steering Committee Member

Shape direction and vision of the company. (4 hours)

Mentor

Share experience and learning with employees to support their career growth. (4 hours)

Department Manager

Develop alliances with department managers to improve business operations. (8 hours)

Administrator

Streamline processes and procedures to minimize paperwork for the department. (4 hours)

Goal Development Worksheet

List your three most important goals. Then identify the major steps needed to achieve each goal. You may want to use Post-it notes when brainstorming action steps. Once you have identified key steps, sequence them according to priorities. Then record action steps directly on this worksheet. This will enable you to determine weekly priorities.

▶ 1 _____
_____
_____
_____
_____
_____

1. _____
2. _____
3. _____
4. _____
5. _____
6. _____
7. _____
8. _____
9. _____
10. _____

▶ 2 _____
_____
_____
_____
_____
_____

1. _____
2. _____
3. _____
4. _____
5. _____
6. _____
7. _____
8. _____
9. _____
10 _____

▶ 3 _____
_____
_____
_____
_____
_____

1. _____
2. _____
3. _____
4. _____
5. _____
6. _____
7. _____
8. _____
9. _____
10.. _____

Task Sheet

Roles	Goals	Action Items for the Week

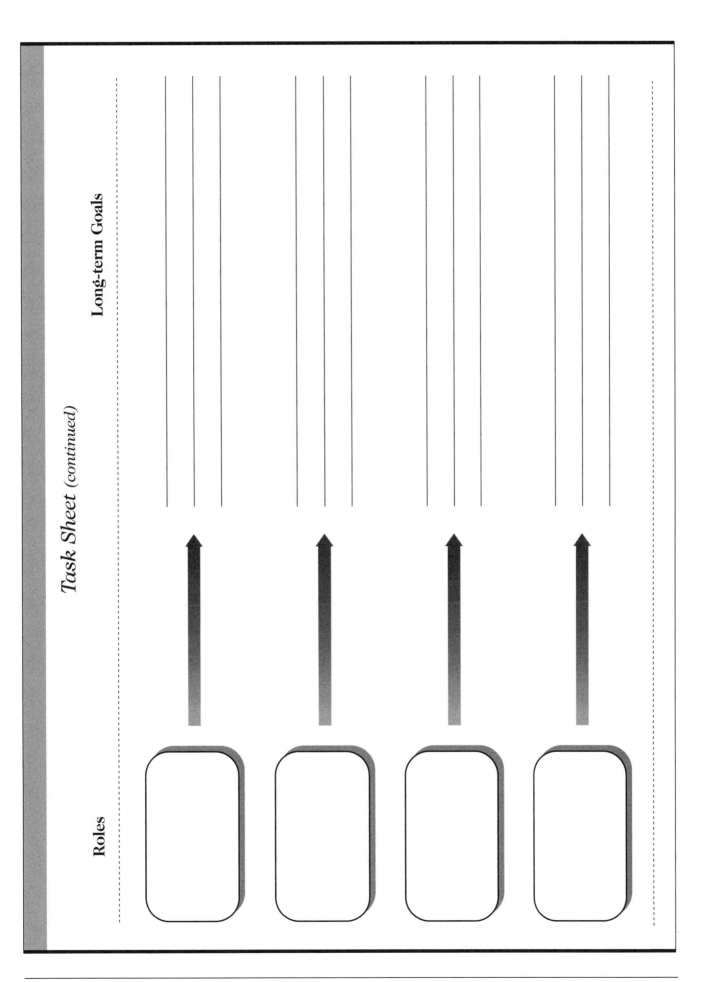

Task Sheet *(continued)*

Roles

Long-term Goals

Weekly Planning Tool

Week of: _____

ROLES	ACTION ITEMS	WEEK'S PRIORITIES	Each Day's Priorities ▲ COMPLE-TION

	SUNDAY	MONDAY	TUESDAY	WEDNESDAY	THURSDAY	FRIDAY	SATURDAY

APPOINTMENTS

	SUNDAY	MONDAY	TUESDAY	WEDNESDAY	THURSDAY	FRIDAY	SATURDAY
7							
8							
9							
10							
11							
12							
1							
2							
3							
4							
5							
6							
7							
8							

SECTION 3: MANAGING CHANGE

Section 3 at a Glance

MATERIAL

	Page	Learning Professionals	Staff and Supervisors	Teams	Management	Self-study/Resource for Training	Group Exercise	Tool
		AUDIENCES				FORMATS		
Enabling the Change to Performance-directed Learning								
From Training Department to Performance and Learning Department: Managing the Change	3-4	●				●		
Creating Organizational Support for Performance-directed Learning	3-8	●				●		●
Supporting Management in Implementing Organizational Change								
Traveling Through Transitions	3-12	●			●	●		●
Making Change Manageable	3-19			●			●	●
Building a Success Team for Managing Change	3-26	●		●	●	●		●
The Missing Piece in Reengineering	3-39	●				●		
Exercise: Promoting Buy-in to Organizational Change	3-49	●	●	●	●		●	
Exercise: Changing Work Behaviors for Higher Performance	3-51	●	●	●	●		●	
Exercise: Overcoming Resistance to Change	3-54	●		●	●		●	

Introduction:
Change Management and the Learning Professional

In high-performance-seeking organizations, change is a constant—because both breakthrough performance improvement and regular, incremental improvement require it. These organizations are adopting change—reliant new management approaches such as business process redesign (reengineering), knowledge management (the learning organization), outsourcing, total quality management (including implementing teamwork, employee empowerment, a sharper customer focus, and regular performance measurement), just-in-time production and cycle time reduction to improve productivity, and new organizational structures that are smaller, flatter, and less rigid. Companies and agencies around the world that get the results they want from these performance improvement efforts have one striking similarity: they use effective strategies and techniques to manage and support the change.

What is organizational change management? Jeanie Daniel Duck compares it to steadying a mobile: When change moves one part of the organizational mobile, change management realigns the other parts to keep the structure in balance. As Figure 1 shows, a variety of factors make up the typical company mobile, and each must be aligned with the new ways of doing business for the change to succeed.

Many of the organizational factors that must change to support performance improvement are related to traditional and evolving learning professional responsibilities. These include:

- *Staff and skills.* Performance-focused and learning professionals are often involved in helping companies determine what knowledge, skills, or abilities employees will need to carry out new functions and/or adopt new values after a change. They also help identify the need for new job groupings, new workload allocations, and new mixes of employee skills.

- *Management and leadership.* Effective leadership for change is vital to a successful change effort, and the ability to assume this role is a fundamental skill today's managers need to survive. Learning professionals can help leadership understand change requirements and develop and implement an appropriate change process and infrastructure.

- *Performance measurement and rewards.* In business it is axiomatic that what is measured and rewarded is what is done. Thus, no element of change management is more important than aligning employee performance criteria with the change and tying rewards and incentives to the new business strategy. This perspective applies as much to performance-focused learning as it does to any other new behavior. For learning to affect performance, its results must be measured and rewarded.

- *Values.* Learning professionals are well suited to help organizations understand new values such as faster production, a greater focus on customer satisfaction, or employee teaming. In addition to bolstering values that support a change, you may need to work on people's values about the change itself. Resistance to any change is inevitable, and helping achieve buy-in is a critical role.

How This Section Can Help

This section has materials that can help with each of the above tasks. The first half of the section focuses on enabling the changes closest to learning professionals—those that are learning-related. Moving from training to performance and learning is itself a major change that is likely to require changes in other parts of the business mobile to succeed. The first two articles, related to "Enab-

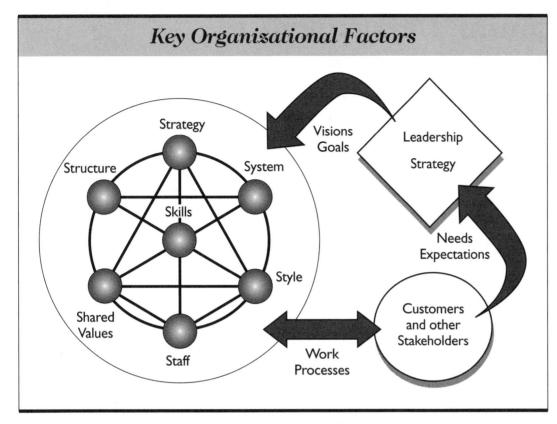

Key Organizational Factors

Figure 1. Key organizational factors.

ling the Change to Performance-directed Learning," have ideas and techniques that can help. In addition, managing learning-related change involves supporting individual employee learners in adopting the perspective of a learning organization. To this end, these articles also contain several exercises and tools designed to promote the application of newly learned knowledge where it counts for performance—back on the job.

Materials in the second half, "Supporting Management in Implementing Organizational Change," provide tools and exercises that bolster the alignment of the organizational factors described above with the goals of the change effort. For example, one article explains how leadership can assess an organization's readiness to change and provides a tool for identifying what organizational supports will be needed for change to succeed. Another offers a schema for developing a change management organizational structure that communicates and supports cohesive change throughout a company, no matter how large. The remaining pieces can help you promote buy-in to a change and address the competency issues it creates.

From Training Department to Performance and Learning Department: Managing the Change

By Jane Green

Audience	Learning Professionals
Purpose	—Learn techniques for working with executives and managers to promote and implement a new performance learning focus —Understand the importance of taking steps to enable acceptance of the change
Suggested Uses	Self-study Resource for training presentation or information-sharing Training prework or handout

Introduction

To develop performance and learning perspective in a high-performance-seeking organization, training departments must view the organization as a system and embrace a systems approach to its architecture and processes. This perspective is fundamental, because the extent to which the system operates as one total entity affects the degree to which both organizational and individual employee performance goals can be maximized. However, adopting this focus represents a major change for many training departments, and success may depend on taking the appropriate steps to introduce, implement, and support the new approach using change management techniques.

This article presents an approach to making and managing changes that help refocus a department from providing training to helping an organization maximize performance and business results. Its sequential techniques support change at each step in the process and are designed to avoid or overcome resistance to change both within the department and throughout the organization.

The Change Approach

1. Align your energy and activities with the organization's mission and vision.

One of the first tasks is to review, understand, and model support for the common mission. Review the company's strategic plan, keeping in mind improvement opportunities. Consider how to align your responsibilities with the strategic plan. Think about how best to become a valuable business partner who makes significant contributions to business practices within the organization.

2. Partner collaboratively with organization leaders.

Meet and offer to work with key leaders to discuss your vision of change and solutions that will improve performance and affect the business positively. Gain trust by offering to work on at least one of their organizational challenges or business concerns and follow through to a successful outcome.

One example of an initial executive partnering might be to take an active role in creating a more open dialogue between the executive and employees. In many traditionally hierarchical, multilayered organizations, communication cascades from top to bottom, often causing employees to hear about organizational change issues from the grapevine long before they get the word formally. This lack of communication can hinder performance.

To improve two-way communication, plan an open communication forum with the executive and employees on a regular basis, ideally, every six months. To the degree possible, schedule the open forum at the individual work sites to encourage information exchange. Lead discussion topics around business issues both from a broad external focus to a more specific internal focus. Encourage employees to ask questions and express concerns openly to receive a response directly from the executive on the spot (or later if research or consultation is required to answer the need).

Using this approach, a CEO can quickly resolve previously unrecognized issues. As success is evident, executive partnering occurs and you begin to gain needed trust and credibility. This is the time to discuss your plans for changing your department's focus and expected positive outcomes to benefit the organization.

There are many other opportunities to partner with leaders. Look for them and be willing to invest in developing long-term performance-oriented relationships and support at the executive level for your new role.

3. Network with key managers.

Managers and supervisors are key contacts in the organization with whom ongoing contact will be mutually beneficial. They will be the primary users of internal performance consulting services due to their roles of supervisor, mentor, developer, and trainer. They offer employee performance reinforcement, competency development, and learning opportunities. In addition to managing employees, these key individuals are held accountable for department processes and productivity. They are potentially able to offer you insights about what they may be dealing with: performance-related issues, current problems, or concerns. Look at business trends and goals of the client with a goal of identifying performance needs rather than training solutions. Listen carefully to their needs and get their feedback on your plans.

During discussions, talk their business language using the manager's terminology. For example, if you are working with the Director of Accounting, know their accounting language. Be willing to learn continually about their business.

4. Model system architecture and desired performance behaviors within your evolving department.

The impact of the new training to performance consulting transition will be increased if you:

• Change the title of your department using language to accentuate performance improvement/organization development/learning rather than human resource development/education/training.

• Revise your department's mission statement as needed so the focus is performance and performance-outcome related.

• Revise your client needs assessments to reflect their goals and needs, rather than arbitrarily scheduling rigidly structured classes.

• Redesign staff roles and responsibilities to reflect performance consulting competencies along with their training knowledge and skills.

• Use competencies to measure staff performance. (ASTD has developed competencies for performance consulting.)

5. Implement a communication strategy.

Keep the organization informed about the "new" department at every opportunity using multiple approaches. For example, publish an article in the corporate newsletter about a positive outcome of your new performance improvement efforts. Send an invitation to participate in a train-the-trainer session for a quality improvement project. It also can be effective to plan a special event to inform people in the organization about changes in the training department and how those changes will affect them. Create interest and explain the WIIFM (what's in it for me) with consideration for their business goals. Opportunities are limitless with regard to your activities, so be certain to "tell your story."

6. Develop best practice or competency models for your department and others in the organization.

Position descriptions need major work in most organizations, and when a manager completes the lengthy document, job qualifications and responsibilities may have already changed. A more effective and practical approach is keeping best practice or competency models updated. These models need to be used prior to hiring employees, during mentoring and performance evaluation, and when new skill sets need to be added. Best practice models document exemplary performance of best performers in order to measure and document the performance of all employees. They are generally position-specific. Competency models document the skill and knowledge together with the best practice. They may cross common positions across departments within an organization. Either model needs objective, quantifiable metrics to document performance results.

7. Review performance discrepancies and identify training implications.

Develop and execute needs assessments that departments or work units can use to identify performance gaps. Focus on causal relationships between desired operational results and what employees must do to accomplish those results. When consulting with managers about performance cause and effect issues, ask business- rather than training-oriented questions. For example, ask them which under- or non-performers' work behavior is costing the organization/department/employee? Other areas to probe include environmental issues, adequate supplies, team work, technological needs, or other issues that may negatively affect employee performance.

To address the findings of the needs assessment, you may need to be prepared to facilitate learning about:

- Leadership development
- Effective communication
- Managing organizational change
- Maximizing employee performance
- Hiring competent employees
- Client relationship-building
- Strategic planning

How to Talk to Managers About Performance

In her book entitled *Performance Consulting: Moving Beyond Training,* Dana Gaines Robinson offers the following guidelines.

When assessing performance needs, it is fairly simple to identify operational issues; but do not stop there. Ask performance-related questions that help to identify any causal relationship between operational objectives and what employees must do to accomplish those results.

1. Begin with questions about the highest level need the client presents.

2. Ask "as is" questions around the need. Discover what employee behaviors are observed currently.

3. Have the client describe the "to be" state, or what behaviors would be modeled by an ideal employee.

4. Then ask the "cause" questions. Consider factors that may be contributing causes of performance gaps.

During the consultation, determine where the client "feels the pain" the most. Is it low morale, loss of revenue, diminished productivity, or increased competition?

- Financial planning
- Business process reengineering
- Technology

With the organization's mission as the foundation, training and development in each of the above areas can give managers further insights to identify performance gaps and develop a plan for improvement

8. Manage resistance to change.

It is best to implement changes over time and pay attention to resistant forces, such as clinging to the belief that traditional training will "fix any employee problem" or lack of understanding about why it is important to link business goals with an employee performance approach. As with any change transition, difficulties will arise. One challenge is changing the paradigm of managers, either within or outside of the training department. Managers or supervisors may still expect the status quo and call for "training to fix an employee performance problem." To address this resistance, remain goal-centered, listen to concerns managers may have about the new training framework, determine desired outcome, and agree on best approach.

9. Evaluate effectiveness through the client's view.

The bottom line for managers is the degree to which your new approach improves their employee and business performance, service, products, or cost-related factors. Quantitative measures are the best way to evaluate your results and make your case.

References

Broad, M., and Newstrom, J. *Transfer of Training.* Reading, MA: Addison-Wesley, 1992.

Covey, S. *Principle-Centered Leadership.* New York, N.Y.: Simon & Shuster, 1991.

Robinson, D., and Robinson, J. *Performance Consulting: Moving Beyond Training,* San Francisco, CA: Berrett-Koehler Publishers, 1995.

Stolovitch, H. and Keats, E. *Handbook of Human Performance Technology: A Comprehensive Guide for Analyzing and Solving Performance Problems in Organizations,* National Society of Performance Improvement, San Francisco, CA: Jossey Bass, 1992.

Creating Organizational Support for Performance-directed Learning

By Edward Jones

Audience ⟶	Learning Professionals
Purpose ⟶	—Understand the importance of providing organizational support for learning and skills application —Learn which factors most enable performance-directed learning —Learn how to use these factors to create a supportive environment for training and to diagnose the reasons for poor results
Suggested Uses ⟶	Self-study Tools for assessing current level of organizational supports and planning interventions to increase positive factors Training prework or handout

Introduction

Organizational factors can either promote or inhibit learning and/or application of new knowledge or skills on the job. These factors can be motivational, behavioral, or value-related, and the perception of learners about the factors can be as important as the reality. This article discusses which factors are most likely to enable or disable performance learning and presents approaches to creating an organizational environment that supports developing and using new knowledge and skills for improved results. Understanding these factors can also help you diagnose why training or other learning experiences achieve or do not achieve the desired result.

Which Organizational Factors Enable Learning and Skills Application?

Enabling factors, based on quantitative research, appear below in descending order of importance. When present, each can enable

your learner to use new skills from training and add value to your organization.

1. The learner perceives that the organization will reward the use of skills learned during training.

Perception, not reality, evokes behavior. Rewarding trained behavior through formal company performance appraisal programs is the most direct method to achieve this perception. A company can also use other less direct methods of reward, including management presence and participation in training events, follow-up of utilization of trained skills, and organizational reporting or tracking of skill use. Ask management to issue invitations to training events, instead of issuing them yourself, to increase the perception of possible organizational reward.

2. The trained employee's supervisor or boss shows interest in the use of skills on the job by the learner, demonstrated by positive action to coach and/or reinforce skill use.

Three "boss-related" behaviors are critical: the boss tells the learner when the skills are not being used; the boss rewards skill use; and the boss encourages skill use. Because the boss represents your organization to most of your employees, encourage boss interest in skill use to achieve the perception that the organization will reward skill use. Positive action means boss behaviors that include coaching and reinforcement as the most effective way to reward, encourage, and enable learned behaviors.

3. The boss shows interest in use of skills on the job by the learner, without coaching or reinforcing.

Virtually any interest your managers show in your training events, or in skill use after training, is a powerful support for learning. Absent coaching and reinforcing, it is the next best thing.

4. Learners perceive that they have the ability to use the skill correctly.

Learner confidence increases the probability that skills will be used at the critical moment. Help the learner develop the perception of ability by creating opportunities for the learner to practice using the skill on the job and receive boss encouragement. Effective learning experiences build skills, and therefore confidence, which translates into confidence on the job.

5. The learner believes that the skill, when used correctly, will have a positive effect on the work or work group.

This factor is as much a function of your company's culture as it is the past experience and resulting beliefs of the learner. You often use training or learning as a change agent, but change is embraced by few cultures. Help your learners to believe that skill use will benefit the organization, the work, or the work group.

6. The learner's values agree with the program values.

What culture is to the organization, values are to the individual. Encourage the boss and others to explore values prior to training, or during training, and to address misunderstandings, enabling alignment of learner and program values.

7. The learner believes that the skills are important to the company.

Ensure that solid communications from management, the boss, and even your department are used to tell about the importance of the training to your company. This can make a significant difference to skill use at the critical moment.

8. The learner believes that the skills will work in the present work environment.

Your work environment is a complex sociotechnical arena full of variables that affect learner behavior. Show your learners that the skills can work and skill use will be improved.

Optimizing the Learning Environment Before, During, and After Training

Research conducted by the author has shown that these eight enabling factors have unequal relative strengths. Knowing this can help you prioritize your efforts to optimize the learning environment before, during, and after training. Look at each enabling factor in Table 1 when planning a training event and decide how to optimize each. Review each in relation to events that occur before, during, and after training. Balance each stage of the training program's development, implementation, and follow-through against each factor to gain valuable insight into how each stage must be tackled. For example, the second factor, "The boss shows interest in the use of skills on the job by the learner, demonstrated by positive action to coach and/or reinforce skill use" urges you to seek ways to ensure positive boss action in the form of coaching and reinforcing. Before training, when you define training program objectives, you might well decide to include boss coaching and reinforcement as an essential objective. This might lead you to develop a method to ensure boss coaching and reinforcement, such as a "Train the Boss Seminar" or a "Boss Coaching and Reinforcement Seminar" as part of program design. During training, you might include the boss as one of the trainers, or include the boss in a "training graduation" event. Finally, after training, you might develop an audit to follow

Table 1. Factors That Enable Application of New Knowledge and Skills

Rank	Enabling Factor	Enabling Strength
1	The learner perceives that the organization will reward the use of skills learned during training	100
2	The boss shows interest in the use of skills on the job by the learner, demonstrated by positive action to coach and/or reinforce skill use	84
3	The boss shows interest in use of skills on the job by the learner, without coaching or reinforcing	65
4	The learner perceives that he or she has the ability to use the skill correctly	55
5	The learner believes that the skill, when used correctly, will have a positive effect on the work or work group	53
6	The learner's values agree with the program values	51
7	The learner believes that the skills are important to the company	47
8	The learner believes that the skills will work in the present work environment	42

up on boss coaching and reinforcement activities, or hold a "class reunion" event for bosses to encourage coaching skill use and problem solving.

Using the Factors to Evaluate Training Program Effectiveness

If you're proactive, you won't wait for management to question the effectiveness of your training event or other learning experience. You'll get in front of the issue by evaluating training effectiveness quickly after training has taken place. You can "fix" transfer of training skills problems before skills learned in training are completely forgotten. Use tools, such as the following matrix (Table 2), to evaluate how well your organization performs on each enabling factor. The matrix can help you identify what needs to change to create a supportive environment. In your plan of action, identify the desired change, who needs to make the change, and how to make the change happen.

Summary

Your training programs must result in skill transfer to achieve value in your organization. Learn how to use organizational factors when developing, implementing, and measuring results, and your training programs will yield better results. Prioritize and focus your energy on intervening variables that have the greatest return for the effort you expend. Use the intervening variables to manage training before, during, and after

Table 2. Creating an Environment That Supports the Application of New Knowledge and Skills

Enabling Factor ▼	Before Training Event		After Training Event	
	Supportive Behavior or Policy?	Adequate Communication of Support to Work Force	Supportive Behavior or Policy?	Adequate Communication of Support to Work Force
1. Organizational Reward				
2. Boss Coaching and Reinforcing				
3. Boss Interest Without Coaching				
4. Learner Confident about Skill Use				
5. Skills Positively Affect Work Group				
6. Learners' Values Agree				
7. Skills Important to the Company				
8. Skills Work in Present Environment				

Plan of Action

Change 1
1. What needs to change:

_____

_____

2. Who needs to make the change:

_____

_____

3. How to make the change happen:

_____

_____

Change 2
1. What needs to change:

_____

_____

2. Who needs to make the change:

_____

_____

3. How to make the change happen:

_____

_____

Change 3
1. What needs to change:

_____

_____

2. Who needs to make the change:

_____

_____

3. How to make the change happen:

_____

_____

Traveling Through Transitions

By Bill Trahant and W. Warner Burke

Audience ➤	Learning Professionals
Purpose ➤	—Understand key change management issues and success factors important to HR departments —Be able to help their organization assess its readiness to change and determine where extra effort is needed
Suggested Uses ➤	Self-study Resource for presentation on this topic The assessment tool "Lay of the Land" could be used with any change effort

What does it mean to "manage" change? It involves gauging an organization's readiness for change, overcoming employees' resistance to change, and measuring the results of change initiatives. As trainers and HR practitioners, many of us are dealing with these issues as our organizations continue to downsize, restructure, reorganize, and reengineer.

Conventional business wisdom holds that implementing organizational change is an inexact science. Change isn't easily measured, tracked, monitored, or assessed by traditional mechanisms. Conventional thinking also holds that many organizational problems stem from personality conflicts among department heads and other organizational factions, not from larger systemic issues. Consequently, many change efforts have been informal, limited to certain departments, and unsupported by management. Other efforts have been announced by senior managers with fanfare, only to be deep-sixed in favor of more pressing concerns.

Still, most people agree nowadays: Change is the one constant in organizations. But few organizations and HR practitioners have found solid approaches for managing this constant.

Change Is Core

The growing pressure on HR professionals to be the managers of change is due to several reasons. One, many reengineering efforts haven't worked because they ignored the human variables. Many downsized and restructured organizations are waking up to the fact that in failing to deal effectively with survivors, they've seen productivity suffer and no rebound in employees' morale and motivation.

Many organizations are also realizing that they must either find or develop standard approaches for managing change on a sustained basis. Evidence shows that change efforts can be maintained successfully over time, if they're carefully orchestrated with other organizational practices such as executive leadership, customer focus, commitment to quality, employee empowerment, and training. Change initiatives should also be linked to efforts to improve overall performance and profitability.

In other words, change must become institutionalized as a core organizational value and systemically reinforced in these areas:

- When customer feedback is used to refine work processes.
- During ongoing communication from company leaders to employees about working smarter and better.
- When employees' quality-improvement accomplishments are acknowledged and then factored in to their performance appraisals.
- When the organization's performance goals and employees' job performance are

linked through reward, recognition, and measurement systems.

To be successful, change must be implemented at two levels: transformational and transactional. Based on the Burke-Litwin model, the transformational level involves an organization's mission, strategy, vision, and culture. The transactional level involves systems that facilitate people's work, including policies, procedures, rewards, and communication. The people charged with spearheading change need ways to identify and deal with the systemic issues that are at the heart of the organization's need for change. They must identify the roadblocks, and they need the appropriate tools.

Taking a Snapshot

First, it's important to take a close look at the organization and its interrelationships. One

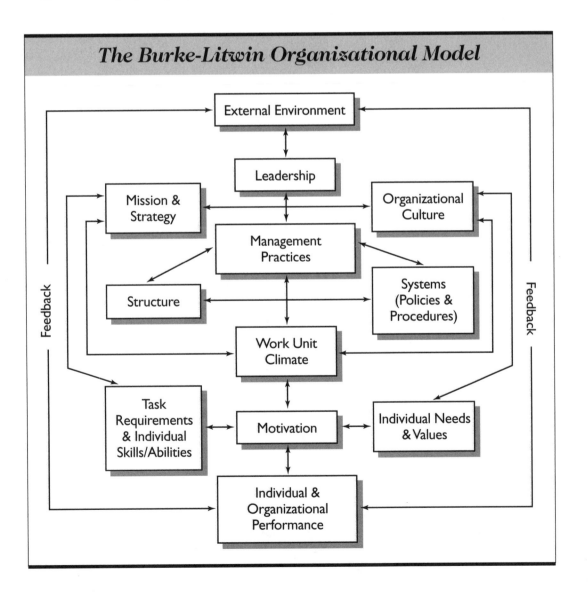

way is to use a change-management assessment instrument to get a snapshot of the organization's characteristics and how it works. Then you can construct a change-management plan. For an example of a survey instrument, see the box, Lay of the Land.

The Lay of the Land survey examines the following areas:

External environment. This includes the marketplaces, world financial conditions, and political factors that could affect an organization's performance currently or in the future.

Management values and practices. The survey should elicit employees' perceptions of executive practices and values with such questions as, "Do senior managers try to stay in touch with staff at all levels?" "Do senior managers motivate employees to work toward common goals?" "Do employees trust the organization's management team?"

It's also important to examine the mission and strategy to ascertain what employees believe about the purpose of the organization and how it intends to achieve it.

Organizational culture. In many organizations, the culture is implicitly understood even when it isn't expressed. The survey probes employee thinking to unearth both the overt and covert rules, values, and principles that guide the organization's behavior and responses to the external business environment.

Organizational structure. The survey examines the organization's structure in order to develop formal and informal profiles of the ways decisions are made and how power is shared, fragmented, or diffused. The survey also examines current management practices. Do managers motivate people to do their jobs, be involved, and commit to the organization? How do managers develop people?

Organizational systems. These include such areas as information management, goals, budget, policies, procedures, and protocols. Do the organization's information systems help people do their jobs? Do the human resource policies ensure effective employee recruitment, selection, and placement?

Work climate. The climate indicates to what extent people perceive teamwork, trust, recognition, and cooperation to be part of the organization's work ethic. The survey asks about the task requirements and skills people need to do their jobs. Do they feel appropriately niched? Do they like their work? Are they motivated? Does their work give them a sense of connection to the organization? When people aren't motivated or don't understand how their roles relate to the organization's larger goals, that signals a "system disconnect" that must be addressed.

Performance. Simply put, to what extent do people think that their organization is performing at maximum effectiveness?

The survey also collects demographic data for categorizing the findings by such variables as age, function, and department.

The survey questionnaires are tallied and scored by computer. Using factor analysis, you can score items in each of the categories to come up with an overall image of the way the organization works. Then a regression analysis can provide a sense of which organizational dynamics are most important. Answers to questions about mission, strategy, leadership, and culture (transformational factors) have more numerical weight in affecting performance than answers to questions about structure, systems, management practices, task requirements, motivation, and individual needs and values (transactional factors). Weighting respondents' answers helps place employees' issues and concerns in order of priority. Then the most critical areas for change can be identified. The numbers draw a sort of map by focusing on the domains most likely to affect organizational performance and effectiveness.

Survey questions can vary, depending on the nature of the organization and its problems. Some organizations do have strong, visionary leadership but out-of-sync systems that don't reward behavior that supports company goals. Or, employees think their managers support change but that the organization's outdated computer technology prevents people from being more effective.

Lay of the Land

Here are some questions for determinining your organization's readiness to implement change.

External Environment
- How does your organization compare with its competition in the marketplace?
- To what extent do you and others inside the organization understand who your customers are?

Mission and Strategy
- How familiar are you with the stated vision and mission of the organization? Are they compelling to you?
- Are you clear about what the organization is trying to achieve and your role in that?
- Do you think the goals are achievable?
- Is the rate of current change in the organization appropriate?
- To what extent do you think the organization is making progress?

Leaders
- To what extent do leaders visibly and consistently support the mission and goals of the organization?
- Do leaders motivate people to work as a team?
- Is leaders' conduct trustworthy and ethical?
- Do leaders communicate clearly and consistently about changes that affect employees and their jobs?
- Are leaders consistent and decisive?
- Do they send mixed messages?

Culture
- To what extent is the organization's culture empowering?
- To what extent is it oppressive?
- Do you spend time taking new approaches to your work?
- Do you spend a lot of time fighting fires and the bureaucracy?

Structure
- To what extent does the organization's structure help you and your coworkers perform your jobs?
- If you're currently in the midst of downsizing or restructuring, do you understand the rationale for the changes?
- To what extent do you think change has been managed effectively?

Management Practices
- How would you characterize the organization's management style?
- Do managers motivate people?

- Are employees involved in making decisions that affect their work?
- Does management encourage open communication?
- Are employees developed informally and formally?
- Do managers encourage innovation?
- Do they act with integrity toward subordinates and peers?

Systems, Policies, and Procedures
- Do the organization's systems, policies, and procedures help or hinder you in performing your job?
- To what extent do the organization's technology in and policies on compensation, benefits, training, and career development help you perform your job?

Work Climate
- How well do people work together in their work groups?
- To what extent does teamwork, trust, recognition, cooperation, and appreciation of diversity exist in your own work group?

Skills and Job Match
- Are you clear about what you need to do to be successful in your daily work?
- Is your work challenging?
- Do your skills match your job?

Motivation
- Do you feel empowered in your job?
- What is the level of employee morale in the organization?
- Are people satisfied with their work?
- Do they feel they're making a significant contribution to the organization's goals?

Individual Needs and Values
- To what extent are you able to achieve a balance between your work and personal life?
- Do you take pride in the organization?
- Do you feel secure about your job?

Performance
- To what extent do you think the organization achieves the highest possible level of performance from you and other employees?
- Is your organization profitable and productive?
- Does it have a good reputation?
- How is it perceived by people outside?

If an organization has problems with transformational issues (for example, it's unclear about future goals or has a disempowering culture) the survey should emphasize transformational issues—such as mission, strategy, leadership, culture, and performance.

If an organization is well under way with change initiatives (for example, it has downsized, restructured, and embraced a new mission but still has problems with productivity and morale), the survey should illuminate transactional issues that might be hindering employees from performing to their potential. Such issues include organizational structure, systems, management practices, work climate, motivation, task requirements, and skills.

A diagnostic survey instrument ensures that recommendations for change are based on a substantive, supportable, and research-based understanding of the crucial issues, not on guesswork or anecdotal data.

Case in Point

Recently, we worked with a major financial-services firm that used the survey as a cornerstone in its change-management efforts. Three years prior, the company was on the verge of financial collapse. But thanks to the leadership of the senior management team, it was able to bounce back, redefine its mission, and reposition itself in the industry.

Still, problems remained. The company had difficulty getting employees out of the mindset of performing transactions with customers and into the role of being business advisors. The firm wanted to overhaul its image, put more emphasis on customer service, and bring management practices and employees' behavior into tighter alignment with new organizational goals.

First, we used the survey to gather data about the degree to which employees had internalized the company's new mission, changed their attitudes, and adopted measurable new behaviors that would affect customers' perceptions of service levels.

Next, the survey helped reinforce new goals by providing a vehicle for conveying (through the use of new terms and concepts) to frontline workers what they should focus on. The survey also proved useful in capturing and recording employees' concerns about the changes and in identifying rough spots. This enabled senior managers to fine-tune their change management approaches.

The survey, conducted twice in two years among departments, served as a benchmark for determining the extent of change during the third year. Both times, the survey measured employees' perceptions of the external environment, how the company compared with the competition (for example, whether senior executives were transforming the company effectively), and the extent to which managers empowered people in serving customers' needs.

Employees were also asked about the technology they used, their compensation and benefits, and whether they thought the company was committed to providing people with the training and career-development opportunities required to ensure high-quality customer service.

Last, employees were asked to comment on the company's overall performance. Were all employees working as a team to build a stronger reputation, boost profits, and maximize people's talents? Did employees think the company would survive?

The Vision Thing

The initial survey generated a wealth of findings. It revealed an organization in transition but with the raw talent, desire, and energy to achieve its goals.

In terms of vision, employees were clear about the changes the company had to make. Most were experimenting with new ways to do their jobs. And top leadership was viewed as committed to change and supportive of employees in making it happen. Employees noted an emerging culture that valued risk-taking and experimentation. Managers were perceived as knowledgeable and entrepreneurial—important traits in bringing about organizational change at the level of people and processes.

In the first survey, some negative indicators also emerged. Employees were frustrated about the company's antiquated computer and information systems, describing them as barriers to rapid and responsive customer service. And there was distrust among departments, though the relationships within work groups and departments were good.

Employees also felt that the old culture was dying, but nothing new had replaced it. They said they often didn't know what the rules were and were uncertain how to handle some customer situations.

The findings showed a close link between employee morale and motivation and the state of the company's culture, structure, and systems. The company revamped its information systems, upgraded its technology, and reduced employees' paperwork. It also took pains to reward, recognize, and reinforce new and innovative employee behaviors. In fact, it went on a hunt for employees who were providing superlative customer service. It videotaped the success stories and distributed the tapes throughout the organization to serve as examples. As a result, customers' satisfaction levels increased.

The second survey a year later showed that the same issues remained. People still reported IS problems, inadequate time for training, and low morale. But there were reasons for optimism. One, employees' frustrations stemmed from an inability to accomplish what they knew needed to be done, and not from confusion or anxiety about what they were supposed to do. People also reported feeling more empowered and confident in doing their jobs. They were clearer than ever about where they and the organization were going. It seemed that leadership's efforts to enact a new vision were paying off.

The second survey also showed significant pockets of improvement to both productivity and profitability. An analysis of the survey results, when integrated with financial-performance measures, showed that changes in management practices accounted for the improved finances. The divisions in which people were allowed greater discretion in servicing customers produced more products and services. In light of that, we recommended that empowering management practices be consistent across the organization. Upgrading existing technology became a major priority.

The second survey also revealed an intriguing and quite directive finding. People communicated strongly that they wanted the company's leaders to continue being on the front lines of change, not shrinking back. So, we urged senior managers to stay close to the people and to keep playing a vital, highly visible role. We recommended that they not delegate change leadership to others or send signals that things had returned to business as usual.

Keys to Success

Clearly, managing change effectively requires a sophisticated appreciation and understanding of the multiple variables at play. The case study highlights a key lesson about organizational change: If an organization is committed to change, it must give such efforts time. And it must put into place the appropriate systems and structures. But even when change is well orchestrated, things can go off key. For example, employee motivation and morale may flag just because people are aware of their destination before they're able to get there.

Many organizations opt for short-term solutions to business problems. But long-lasting and successful change requires a sustained effort and commitment. In our experience, the single most important determinant of success is strong, committed senior leadership in the earliest stages of change—hands down. Why? Because leadership is transformational. It is ground-breaking, ground-clearing work. Senior leaders are the levers of change. In many cases, they're the only people articulating the organization's new vision.

But as change progresses, it becomes more transactional. Other factors become important. The company we surveyed inaugurated its change efforts prior to our arrival. Much of our work focused on reinforcing what the senior leadership team had already instituted. But to ensure long-term success, we also had work to do on the transactional level.

It's important to conduct surveys every 12 to 18 months during the front-end part of a change initiative in order to gauge the effectiveness of the initial effort and to discover any impediments to progress. As change becomes a core organizational value, it's still important to conduct surveys about every two to three years to monitor the organization's growth and vitality and to troubleshoot problems that may arise due to changes in the external environment. For example, new technology may threaten the company's product line.

Harmony and Strategic Intent

More than ever, it's clear that an organization's most critical resource is its human assets. Employees must understand their roles and functions in making change happen. People and processes must be in tight alignment in order to support short-, medium-, and long-term goals. Dartmouth professor Vijay Govindarahan says that such alignment enables an organization to become internally "harmonized" and to develop a higher-order characteristic he calls "strategic intent."

Strategic intent refers to an organization's ability to stretch so it can accommodate customers' changing needs and the marketplace's shifting demands, without necessarily knowing how. Strategic intent also refers to an organization's ability to leverage its core competencies (intellectual assets) in order to gain and retain marketplace advantage, to position itself for entry into new markets, and to potentially compete on an ongoing basis in several product or market arenas.

Nowadays, developing strategic intent is crucial, not just for profitability and productivity but also for long-term viability and vitality. In *The Age of Reason,* Charles Handy says, "Change is not what it used to be. The status quo will no longer be the best way forward. The best way will be less comfortable and less easy but, no doubt, more 'interesting'—a word we often use to signal a mix of danger and uncertainty." And, we would add, "opportunity."

For more information about the case study mentioned in this article, see "Organizational Surveys as Change Interventions," by Warner Burke, Celeste Coruzzi, and Allan Church in *Opinion Surveys in Organizations*.

Making Change Manageable

By Kevin Walker

Audience	Teams
Purpose	—Understand the factors that enable change —Be able to identify aspects of their proposed change that need additional support —Be able to develop a plan for managing their change effectively
Suggested Uses	Group exercise Adapt inventory tool for team use

Introduction

Through research and experience, Coopers & Lybrand has identified twelve enablers of successful organizational change. Teams responsible for organizational change initiatives can use the Making Change Manageable Inventory to assess a project in terms of each key enabler and to identify which areas need additional support. The team can then use the Building an Action Plan worksheets to determine ways to make the change more effectively.

Exercise: Leader's Notes

Time

1–2 hours

Number of Participants

Best used with an intact project team

Handouts

Making Change Manageable (MCM) Inventory

Building an Action Plan worksheets

Procedure

1. Explain the purpose of the Making Change Manageable Inventory and how the team will use it.

2. Distribute the Making Change Manageable Inventory and ask each team member to complete the survey individually.

3. When team members have completed the survey, distribute the Building an Action Plan worksheets and ask team members to tabulate individual scores for each enabler, comparing their scores with the Effectiveness number that represents the minimum level for effectively making the change.

4. After each team member has scored the assessment individually, have the team work together to develop a team score for each enabler. Through this process, the team should identify enablers that the team has well under control and those that will need additional attention.

5. After the team has completed the team scores for each enabler, have the team focus on the enablers that have a team score below the effectiveness score for that enabler. Have the team develop actions to improve effectiveness in those areas.

6. If desired, have the team develop a more formal workplan to deal with these actions, assigning tasks to specific team members and establishing a time frame for completing them.

The Twelve Enablers of Successful Change

Enabler	Description
▶ Accountability	Identifying specific roles, goals, and performance measures for the change
▶ Adaptability	Learning from, and taking action based on, the successful and unsuccessful change actions that are taken
▶ Communication	Influencing those who will sponsor, support, implement, or be affected by the change, including the possible determination of a displacement plan
▶ Focus, Purpose, and Vision	Defining articulate descriptions of the technical and organizational compelling need and vision for the change
▶ Involvement	Ensuring that those affected by the change participate fully in decisions and implementation
▶ Leadership	Taking leadership actions through an infrastructure designed to promote and enable change
▶ Measurement and Results	Determining the measurable improvements to be achieved through the change, and identifying the data to be used to track those improvements
▶ Momentum	Responding to shifts in the pace of the implementation of change actions and acceptance
▶ Readiness	Aligning the change with the existing culture and work climate based on an assessment of the "readiness to change" of those individuals, or groups of individuals, likely to be impacted by the change
▶ Recognition and Reward	Reinforcing individuals and groups achieving results consistent with the change, and determining sanctions for those who are not
▶ Skill Development	Providing training to prepare for and enable effective participation during and after the change at all levels
▶ Team Orientation	Using teams throughout the organization to manage, implement, and take ownership for the change.

Making Change Manageable (MCM) Inventory

INSTRUCTIONS: Respond to the MCM Inventory on the following pages in three steps:

1. Complete the survey individually around the change project your team is undertaking.

2. Score your assessment of the effectiveness of your change project using the scoring key.

3. As a team, develop a team score for each enabler. Identify enablers, or elements of enablers, that your team has well under control and those that will need additional attention.

STATEMENT	INDIVIDUAL				
Accountability	Low				High
▶ Responsibility has been assigned to one person for achieving the goal(s) of the change.	1	2	3	4	5
▶ Demanding standards are set for the change.	1	2	3	4	5
▶ Leaders have avoided spelling out a specific response to the change to those responsible for bringing the change about.	1	2	3	4	5
Adaptability	Low				High
▶ A plan has been developed for responding to problems in the change process.	1	2	3	4	5
▶ Structures and systems are successfully aligned with changed practices.	1	2	3	4	5
▶ Changes that have worked have been sustained.	1	2	3	4	5
▶ Changes that did not work have been discarded.	1	2	3	4	5
Communication	Low				High
▶ Communication about the change is simple, direct, and easy to understand.	1	2	3	4	5
▶ The vision and strategies for the change are communicated simply, directly, and often.	1	2	3	4	5
▶ Crisis information about the status quo has been communicated in terms understandable to everyone impacted by the change.	1	2	3	4	5
▶ Individuals impacted by the change will understand how the change will affect them personally.	1	2	3	4	5
▶ Organizational resources of time, people, and money are publicly committed.	1	2	3	4	5

STATEMENT	INDIVIDUAL

Focus, Purpose, and Vision

Low   High

▶ The change is positioned as being consistent with customer needs and expectations.   1   2   3   4   5

▶ The change was initiated in areas of extreme customer dissatisfaction or processes that cause high employee frustration.   1   2   3   4   5

▶ Individuals impacted by the change understand the new skills, attitudes, and behaviors required to support the change.   1   2   3   4   5

▶ The change is aligned with organizational strategy.   1   2   3   4   5

Involvement

Low   High

▶ Respected, long-service managers and staff have been won over as advocates of the change.   1   2   3   4   5

▶ Change leaders have a strong internal power base. Organizational leaders model desired behaviors.   1   2   3   4   5

▶ Change leaders are convinced that the pain of the status quo is greater than the costs of making the change.   1   2   3   4   5

▶ Change leaders demonstrate consistent support for the change.   1   2   3   4   5

▶ Consequences are imposed on those unwilling to accept, or try to accept, the change.   1   2   3   4   5

Measurement and Results

Low   High

▶ The change is proceeding on the basis of facts, measurements, and evidence.   1   2   3   4   5

▶ Minimum expectations for results are specified at all levels.   1   2   3   4   5

▶ Metrics have been established to track the change progress and its difficulties.   1   2   3   4   5

▶ Teams are chartered to achieve measureable results.   1   2   3   4   5

Momentum

Low   High

▶ Changes are implemented at a pace the organization can assimilate.   1   2   3   4   5

▶ Losses in momentum are responded to by increased activity.   1   2   3   4   5

▶ Quick successes are planned to make new behaviors credible.   1   2   3   4   5

STATEMENT	INDIVIDUAL

Readiness

	Low				High

▶ The change planning is based on realistic expectations of the organization's ability and willingness (readiness) for change.   1   2   3   4   5

▶ The need for change is aligned with existing cultural values.   1   2   3   4   5

▶ There was an assessment of culture and climate before beginning the change.   1   2   3   4   5

Recognition and Reward

Low   High

▶ Successes and initiative are recognized and reinforced publicly.   1   2   3   4   5

▶ Overt constructive resistance receives publicly expressed appreciation.   1   2   3   4   5

▶ People are rewarded for creating value and not just for implementing a process.   1   2   3   4   5

▶ Consequences and rewards have been established at all levels for the change.   1   2   3   4   5

Skill Development

Low   High

▶ The ability of those impacted by the change to enact it was assessed before beginning the change.   1   2   3   4   5

▶ Skills needed to enable the change are provided or developed.   1   2   3   4   5

▶ The change is not dependent on massive training programs.   1   2   3   4   5

▶ Skill development is provided just in time to enable change to occur.   1   2   3   4   5

Team Orientation

Low   High

▶ Teams are chartered in all phases of the change effort.   1   2   3   4   5

▶ Teams are chartered to achieve measurable results.   1   2   3   4   5

▶ A team has established a change vision and strategies for achieving that vision.   1   2   3   4   5

▶ The change requires teams to implement it.   1   2   3   4   5

Making Change Manageable: Building an Action Plan

INSTRUCTIONS: Use this scoring key to tabulate scores for each enabler. For the Individual Score, add up each of your responses and compare them with the Effectiveness number for that enabler. The Effectiveness number represents the minimum level for effectively making the change.

For the Team Score, decide upon an overall team score (from 1 to 5) for each enabler. Multiply that number by the factor provided. This represents the team's effectiveness assessment. Compare the team's effectiveness score with the minimum level necessary to effectively make the change. Identify actions to raise the team's score.

Enabler	Individual Score	Effectiveness	Team Score
▶ *Accountability*	_____	12	___ x 3 = ___
Actions to Improve Effectiveness:			
▶ *Adaptability*	_____	16	___ x 4 = ___
Actions to Improve Effectiveness:			
▶ *Communication*	_____	20	___ x 5 = ___
Actions to Improve Effectiveness:			
▶ *Focus, Purpose, and Vision*	_____	16	___ x 4 = ___
Actions to Improve Effectiveness:			
▶ *Involvement*	_____	20	___ x 5 = ___
Actions to Improve Effectiveness:			

Making Change Manageable: Building an Action Plan (continued)

Driver	Individual Score	Effectiveness	Team Score
▶ *Measurement and Results*	_____	16	____ x 4 = ____

Actions to Improve Effectiveness:

_____

_____

_____

▶ *Momentum*	_____	12	____ x 3 = ____

Actions to Improve Effectiveness:

_____

_____

_____

▶ *Readiness*	_____	12	____ x 3 = ____

Actions to Improve Effectiveness:

_____

_____

_____

▶ *Recognition and Reward*	_____	16	____ x 4 = ____

Actions to Improve Effectiveness:

_____

_____

_____

▶ *Skill Development*	_____	16	____ x 4 = ____

Actions to Improve Effectiveness:

_____

_____

_____

▶ *Team Orientation*	_____	16	____ x 4 = ____

Actions to Improve Effectiveness:

_____

_____

_____

Building a Success Team for Managing Change

By Michele A. Armitage and Bernard P. Willis

Audience ➡️	Learning Professionals, Change Agents, Organizational Leadership and Management, Success Team Facilitators, and Core Members
Purpose ➡️	—Understand the benefits of using a Success Team to manage both change *events* and the change *process* —Learn a process for determining when to use a Success Team —Learn the process for creating and launching a Success Team
Suggested Uses ➡️	Contextual information for change leaders Basis for facilitated workshops with executive team planning major change efforts (e.g., computer systems implementations, significant reengineering or reorganization, learning, organization development) Tools for client team meetings to design or plan to support a Success Team structure

Introduction: The Rationale for a Success Team

Experts in organizational development and change today recognize that "change" is not a finite event with a clear beginning and clear ending. Instead, change is understood as a process of transition from "what was" to "what is." And while it is accepted that most change processes are initiated by an identifiable change event (the "change project"), it is less commonly understood that it is the success of the change process that defines the success of the change event, and not the reverse. Implementing a new computer system "on time and under budget" is mean-ingless if employees begin to duplicate work (by performing tasks "on paper" and "in the system"). Likewise, "successfully" re-designing key business processes is point-less if professionals refuse to let go of their old roles and responsibilities.

William Bridges (*Managing Transitions*) de-scribes the change process as consisting of three stages: ending (letting go of "what was"), neutral zone (navigating the transi-tion), and beginning (embracing "what is"). Thus, while planning the concrete elements of a "change project" may follow a pre-scribed order, managing the "change pro-cess" is typically unpredictable and irregular. Each individual may experience the transition process quite differently: some embracing change and moving quickly, others fearing and outright resisting change, and a large number lying somewhere in between.

In practice, this means that change agents need to help managers and employees to (1) understand both the mechanical and psychological elements of change, (2) build individual understanding, ownership, and willingness to change, (3) build organizational ability to change, and (4) work together to manage the transition. Typical change projects include formal methods for developing client skills in implementing the mechanical or procedural aspects of change (e.g., using the new software, creating the new performance appraisal system, designing the new business process flow, etc.). However, techniques for managing the long-term success of change are not so readily available, and change "plans" generally lack a strategy for managing the human side of transition. **Since all change involves a transition that is both mechanical and procedural as well as behavioral and psychological, clients require a means of planning and managing both successfully.**

Models of successful change follow the same basic tenets:

- Successful change is managed change—managing the human, systems, and strategic factors that impact employees' willingness and capacity to change.

- Successful change is managed over the long term. While project life spans are limited in time, change impacts are not.

- Successful change must be managed with an eye on both the change *project* and the change *process*.

- Managers and employees must own the change.

When these tenets are not heeded, overlooked elements of change can surface as resistance, project conflicts, uninformed decision making, inconsistent and often mutually defeating decision making, heightened manager and/or employee anxiety, and falling morale and motivation. And when, under these circumstances, change does occur, it is "forced" change with little support, buy-in, or capacity for long-term success. Thus, while it may be a "successful" change project (on time and under budget), it will not be a successful change process—the change will not be supported over the long term.

A structure of leadership and communication and the requisite skills for managers and employees to manage transition will provide the mechanism for establishing the tenets of change success. Without such a structure guiding managers and employees in managing change success, "change will manage them" (Decker and Belohlav, *Managing Transitions)*. Trainers and change agents can therefore benefit from forming a "Success Team" of cascading leadership and communication focused on building employee ownership early in the change process. Such a system would involve the community as initiators of change, not merely recipients. It would empower clients with the capability and resources for working together to build a critical mass of support, maintain open and multidirectional communication, spot issues, and perform their own decision making and problem solving. Leading authors in transition Diane Decker and James Belohlav emphasize that, in order to be successful, "change has to be perceived as something happening through them, not to them."

A Success Team deals with both "what" is changing (by managing unanticipated results, impacts, fallouts, and benefits of that change) and "who" is changing (by managing change at "all speeds," monitoring, coaching, guiding, involving, and communicating with the target community throughout the transition). As a system of representative cross-functional, cross-departmental subteams that are charged with the sustained success of the change effort, the Success Team is designed to address the tenets of successful change. With a solid, well-developed Success Team in place, the probability of both short- and long-term success increases exponentially.

Figure 1 presents a model of this Success Team and its four components: Sponsors, Transition Leaders, Advocates, and Target Community.

As those ultimately responsible for the outcomes of change, **Sponsors** are charged with setting direction and understanding the fun-

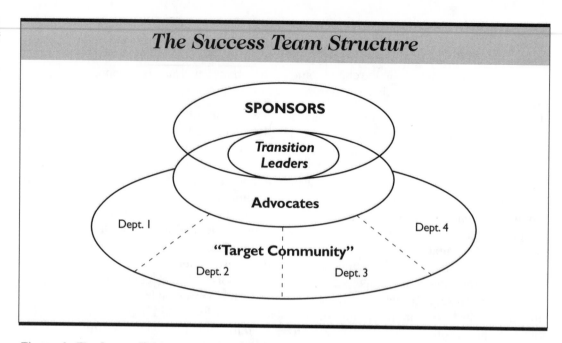

The Success Team Structure

SPONSORS

Transition Leaders

Advocates

Dept. 1

Dept. 4

"Target Community"

Dept. 2

Dept. 3

Figure 1. The Success Team structure has four key levels: Sponsors, Transition Leaders, Advocates, and Target Community (all who are impacted by change).

damental needs for and macro impact of specific changes. They serve as the primary channel for change validation. Additionally, Sponsors are responsible for high-level communications, executive problem solving and decision making, change project visioning, strategic planning and approvals. Their active and visible commitment and support for all aspects of the project are critical; without it, the project will fail over the long term. They need to "walk about" regularly to show support, and ask consistently to be informed. Change Sponsors are usually higher-level executives. **Transition Leaders** and **Advocates** serve as the nucleus of the change effort throughout the life of the change program and beyond.

The worksheets at the end of this piece are designed to guide you through the process of considering and creating a Success Team. They cover key aspects of the process, including:

- Should we create a Success Team?
- Building and implementing the Success Team.
- A sample agenda for a Team session.

- Measuring for success: a sample Team assessment instrument.

Conclusion

A Success Team provides a vehicle for gathering information, maintaining momentum, and making authoritative and informed decisions quickly. As such, it is the nucleus for achieving the long-term success of a change project. It is a system that delivers a vision by monitoring and questioning the process, analyzing options, pushing for smart solutions, taking risks, challenging others, taking the time to listen and to inform, and supporting the overall change. It can enable the organization in aligning its people, policies, and practices with changes in business strategy; establishing cross-functional or departmental communication and strengthening teamwork; increasing the timely dissemination of accurate information; improving the efficiency, effectiveness, or quality of processes or procedures; building employee skill sets; and creating organizational capacity for change, adaptation, and innovation.

References

Bridges, W. *Managing Transitions: Making the Most of Change.* New York: Addison-Wesley Publishing Company, 1991.

Carr, D., Hard, K., and Trahant, W. *Managing the Change Process: A Fieldbook for Change Agents, Consultants, Team Leaders and Reengineering Managers.* Coopers & Lybrand Center for Excellence for Change Management. New York: McGraw-Hill, 1996.

Decker, D., and Belohlav, J. *Managing Transitions.* Quality Progress. April, 1997, pp. 93–97.

Jones, E. *You Developed It, Can Your Training Programs Survive the Reality Test?* Amherst, MA: HRD Press, 1995.

Kotter, J. *Leading Change.* Boston: Harvard Press, 1996.

		Should We Create a Success Team?
Yes	**No**	
		Is the project anticipated to have long-term implications that will need to be managed?
		Is the change project "big" (does it involve a significant investment of time and/or funds and is this investment worth managing)?
		Is the change project "important" (is it high profile or does it have key expected outcomes)?
		Will the project impact more than one staff level of the organization?
		Is it *not* possible for key decision makers to be involved in the change project on a full-time basis?
		Is it *not* possible for all individuals impacted by the change to be actively involved in the day-to-day aspects of the change project?
		Will the change project impact employees reporting to more than one organizational authority (read: individuals capable of enforcing conflicting decisions)?
		Have past change projects been unsuccessful?
		Answering "yes" to many or all of the above questions is a strong indicator that your change project will benefit from the creation of a Success Team.

Building and Implementing the Success Team

▶ Step 1	Understand Core Goals
ASK:	What *must* we do to get from "what was" to "what is?"
Example CORE GOALS	1. INFORM: Collect and actively communicate project-related information. 2. MANAGE PROJECT: Monitor project status; work to keep project on schedule and within budget by eliminating obvious obstacles (e.g., key people not involved in the project). 3. MANAGE CHANGE: Identify and eliminate organizational barriers to project success (e.g., organization lacks key skill sets to support change, current incentive systems discourage change), identify and address the concerns of the impacted community (e.g., Will I lose my job? How is my role changing?), work to avoid or eliminate inconsistent actions and messages.
LOGIC	These core goals should drive not only your session agendas, but also your measures of success.

▶ Step 2	Identify Core Tasks
ASK:	How will we know if we are "on track?"
Example TASKS	1. Solicit peer input; questions, concerns, thoughts, and ideas. 2. Create and administer organizational assessments; review and take action on assessments. 3. Write, approve, copy, and deliver project communications. 4. Create Team session agendas; document Team discussion and agreement. 5. Deliver project status updates in Team sessions. 6. Develop solutions for specific issues; achieve consensus on specific decisions.
LOGIC	These are the day-to-day tasks and activities that will need to happen for the Success Team to accomplish its goals. Identifying the "work" required of the team will be helpful in identifying the specific roles that will need to be filled for the overall Team to be successful.

▶ Step 3	Identify Subgoals and Tasks
ASK:	What would we like to achieve "along the way?"
Example SUBGOALS	1. Increase/improve relevant employee skills. 2. Improve cross-organizational communication. 3. Improve efficiency of related processes. 4. Increase employee creativity. 5. Create increased organizational capacity for change. 6. Become more innovative as an organization.
LOGIC	Maximize the benefit of the organizational investment in Success Team structure without losing focus on core goals.

Building and Implementing the Success Team
(continued)

▶ Step 4	List Team Success Criteria (both short- and long-term)
ASK:	How will we know when we've "arrived?"
Example CRITERIA	1. The computer system "goes live." 2. System users attend training. 3. Users enter data directly into system (and *not* onto paper first). 4. Users make updates directly into the system (without having to print records). 5. Communications are read and understood by users. 6. A certain number of valuable communications are distributed per month (or week or year).
LOGIC	1. People like to know where they are going and to understand how they are going to get there. 2. Identifying specific short-term and long-term success criteria that are *achievable* (but not easy) will give people the "light at the end of the tunnel" they are looking for during the tough times of change. And, better, they'll know when they've "arrived" … they've "won," and it's time to celebrate.
▶ Step 5	Understand and "Staff" Core Roles
Sponsor Role Summary	1. Possess sufficient organizational influence to implement change (read: be capable of supporting both the change event and the change process). 2. Set change direction. 3. Understand fundamental needs (business case) for change. 4. Communicate the need for change in a compelling way. 5. Ask to be informed of project issues, implications, and status. 6. Understand the macro impact of the changes being implemented. 7. Demonstrate active support for the change.
Transition Leader Role Summary	1. As key decision-making managers: represent organization areas expected to be impacted by the change project. 2. Serve as the primary channel for cross-organizational and cross-functional communications at the management level. 3. Learn the details of the proposed change and proactively solve project-related problems. 4. Demonstrate active and visible support for the change project and process. 5. Jointly manage the transition period by sharing experiences and making key decisions relative to the transition. 6. Co-manage and execute formal transition plans. 7. Communicate macro issues, potential solutions, and information to Sponsors. 8. Treat selves as "targets of change" in preparation for management in the changed environment. 9. Serve as advisors and role models for Advocates. 10. Widely communicate the Success Team concept.

Building and Implementing the Success Team
(continued)

Advocate Role Summary	1. As respected and influential peers of the target community, represent their departments/functions. 2. Serve as the primary channel for cross-departmental/functional communications at the target commuity level. 3. Create and execute a formal communications strategy (create ongoing communications that are supported, relevant, and consistent across the project). 4. Actively solicit input (questions, issues, concerns, etc.) from target community. 5. Raise and openly discuss project issues. 6. Communicate relevant information, issues, and potential solutions to Transition Leaders.

▶ Step 6	**Consider Success Team in Context**

1. How many members are ideal versus sufficient? Is the team representative and powerful but not unwieldy in size?

2. What is the scope of the project? Based on "Core Tasks," it may be possible to further refine team roles and responsibilities. Given the example tasks listed above, for example, it may be wise to create the following subroles: *Troubleshooters* (identify and report project concerns and issues); *Author* (drafts formal project communications); *Meeting Manager* (facilitates sessions, prepares session agenda and minutes); *Message Manager* (ensures consistency of action and information across the change project).

3. Which functional areas of the organization will be *directly* impacted by the change project? Which functional areas of the organization will be *indirectly* impacted by the change project? Is the scope of the project such that we should include active representation from each group, or are only key groups required? **Note:** Consider the "domino effect" of change in session and be careful not to overlook organizational groups that are not "obvious" (for example, don't forget that you will need to include technical professionals in Success Team sessions when implementing a new "functional" computer system. They may not "use" the system, but they will support it).

4. Is it anticipated that this change will impact organizational reporting structures? Can we include "future" decision makers?

5. Is the organization "flat" or bureaucratic? Will multiple approvals be required? Are different staff classes accustomed to communicating openly and honestly with their managers/peers/subordinates? **Note:** In relatively flat organizations, it should be possible to "combine" the Transition Leader and Change Advocate groups for many or all of your Success Team sessions. In more bureaucratic organizations, however, it may be necessary to formally "split" the two groups (read: conduct regular but separate sessions for each) at some point in the process. In either scenario, the Success Team concept and operating agreements should be established in early Team (group) sessions.

6. Do groups communicate openly and honestly across functions? Is the organization "integrated" in their view of success, or are certain functional groups "antagonistic" in their view of each other?

Building and Implementing the Success Team
(continued)

7. Where are individuals impacted by the change physically located? Will this facilitate or complicate the communication process? Will this facilitate or complicate conducting team sessions?

8. What is our "target" session schedule—understanding that flexibility will be essential? (For example, Transition Leaders meet twice a month to "staff" the Success Team, discuss anticipated issues, and develop transition plans. The session frequency increases during critical periods, such as when key aspects of the change are "deployed," or when Advocates raise serious time-sensitive issues. Advocates meet weekly at first and during change "deployments" to surface employee concerns and issues and to execute a formal communications strategy. Advocates meet twice monthly during slower periods.) Where will our "target" schedule place excessive demands on member schedules?

9. Who may need to be included for political reasons? How many nay-sayers can you manage (how supportive are the supporters)? Who are the influential personalities you will most need to win over? Are there key members who should be invited but given the option to attend only key meetings (e.g., non-core senior managers, staff with critical and time-sensitive tasks)?

10. Do members "staffed" on the team have the requisite skills for their roles? Do members "fit" their positions?

▶ **Step 7**	**Implement the Success Team**
Phase I Kicking Off the Success Team	The initial phase should involve all Success Team members and facilitators. This will give everyone the opportunity to meet each other and see the team structure "live." This will also help to establish the cross-functional/departmental/organizational nature of the team. Initial agendas should include most or all of the subjects listed on the sample agenda provided below. Sufficient time should be allotted to ensure that all members understand the change, its implications, and their associated roles. All questions should be actively addressed and resources for further inquiries provided. Everyone should commit to their roles and have the capability to maintain them.
Phase I Agent Notes:	The role of the change agent at this point is very active. Tasks include: 1. Facilitate all sessions. 2. Deliver initial presentations. 3. Establish the compelling need for change (project business case). 4. Establish the Success Team vision. 5. Ensure that workable operating agreements are established. 6. Ensure that meaningful and workable goals are established. 7. Schedule sessions—including fixed and regular start and end times (for example, 1:30 p.m. to 3:30 p.m. every other Tuesday). Vacation and holiday schedules should be reviewed to identify and address potential conflicts. Additionally, determine if schedule creates conflicts within the project plan of the change project. 8. Establish back-up members for each Success Team member. 9. Develop and agree to a formal communications strategy.

Building and Implementing the Success Team
(continued)

Phase II Maintaining the Success Team	During this phase, the Success Team will meet regularly to discuss change issues, share information, identify and understand organizational impacts of the change project, and develop creative solutions to problems. Through this phase of the project, the Success Team should be reporting/working off of a somewhat "standardized" agenda based largely on team Core Goals.
Phase II Agent Notes:	The role of the change agent at this point is active (but less and less active over time). Tasks include: 1. Prepare agendas. **Note**: Design each Agenda to ensure that each member's time is optimized. Sessions should have specific goals and desired outcomes. If sessions are not perceived as worthwhile, assess the group to determine cause. If the issue is related to an individual member's lack of commitment to the change project or change process, and that member is not critical, consider excluding that member or modifying team structures. Alternatively, if the feeling is widely held, consider adjusting session content, meeting times, or Success Team facilitation. 2. Design and administer short anonymous feedback forms. These should be administered at the end of each session. Questionnaires should be designed to elicit honest feedback on key issues. Example survey points: I believe that the Success Team is a good investment of my time; I believe the Team is on track in achieving our goals; I believe the Team communicates openly and honestly; I understand the implications of the change we are considering. 3. Identify skills Success Team members will need (e.g., facilitation skills, problem-solving skills) and develop programs to transfer knowledge. 4. Repeat and emphasize Team goals: monitor Team progress toward goals. 5. Stress the long-term importance of the group. 6. Remind the Team of their future ownership role. 7. Ask for personal status updates (testimonials, both good and bad). 8. Identify and assign specific action items for individual members. 9. Encourage and demonstrate a two-way dialogue. 10. Revisit session frequency and team commitment. 11. Acknowledge difficulties and celebrate successes. 12. Remain motivated and 110 percent supportive (this will be difficult at times).

Building and Implementing the Success Team
(continued)

Phase III Launching the Success Team	Although the first two phases involved in building a Success Team are difficult, this third phase is perhaps the most difficult (though it requires the least amount of "work" on the part of the change agent). The role of the change agent during this phase: Do Nothing. This sounds strange at first, but it is only through "doing nothing" (turning over responsibility for session facilitation, agendas, minutes, actions, decisions, etc.) that the change agent is able to determine if the Success Team will succeed or fail. And, while it can be frustrating and discouraging to watch the system "stumble and fall" during this phase, it is more than worth the risk—for superior teams will "pick up" and act to achieve the success of the change project and change process.
Phase III Agent Notes:	The role of the change agent at this point is passive. Tasks should include: 1. Remove yourself from the process. 2. Watch for key behaviors and identify them when they occur. 3. Resist the temptation to facilitate. 4. Ask questions and expect answers. 5. Celebrate Team successes, but emphasize that the process is not over yet.
Phase IV Measuring for Success	Assess the group to see if the Team has reached its goals.
Phase IV Agent Notes:	See the attached example assessment.

| XYZ Project Success Team
Taking Charge of Change | January 1, 2000
1:30 p.m. to 3:30 p.m.
ABC Organization
[Session 1] |

Welcome to this Success Team Session!

Agenda

1.	Icebreaker: Who are we? Can I trust these people?	15 minutes
2.	What the heck is change management?	25 minutes
3.	Why are we changing (business case, compelling need, vision)?	20 minutes
4.	What are we changing (project overview)?	10 minutes
5.	What's my/our role in this change (Success Team concept: This team is <u>very</u> important, roles and responsibilities, commitments) (Core Goals/Tasks/Operating Agreements discussed in later sessions)?	30 minutes
6.	Questions & Answers	20 minutes
7.	Feedback Questionnaire	

My Questions/Action Items

Session Attendees:

	Phone	Fax	Organization
Joe Smith	(123) 456-7890	(123) 456-0987	Change Agent, Inc.
Juan del Pueblo	(321) 654-9822	(321) 654-7890	Changing Co.
Eli Combs	(321) 654-4744	(321) 654-4325	Changing Co.
Eric Deeds	(321) 654-2212	(321) 654-6346	Changing Co.
Kimberly Thomas	(321)654-2553	(321) 654-1324	Changing Co.
Jennifer Alexander	(321) 654-3344	(321) 654-1324	Changing Co.
Steve Gabrys	(321) 654-2222	(321) 654-2633	Changing Co.
Mark Keating	(321) 654-1111	(321) 654-2344	Changing Co.

Measuring for Success

Example: This survey was used to assess Transition Leader "success" (or action items/next steps) in relation to a large computer systems implementation.

Yes	No	Managing a Work Environment in Transition[1]
		Defining Success …
		1. Have I developed my specific "measures of success" for the new system (measures can be strategic, operational, or personal goals)?
		2. Have I detemined exactly what will be required of each of my employees to achieve these measures of success?
		3. Have I communicated my "expectations for success" to my employees (individually and as a team)?
		4. Have I assessed current performance evaluation criteria to verify that they are "in line" with the new expectations I am placing upon my employees?
		Managing Changing Roles …
		5. Have I studied the changing situation carefully to begin to identify how it will change the roles and responsibilities of each of my employees?
		6. Have I identified those employees who will experience "losses" (loss of expertise, loss of "task ownership," etc.) and developed strategies for dealing with those losses?
		7. Have I identified transition (temporary) roles for those employees whose jobs are in the process of being redefined due to this new system?
		8. Have I read my Agency's strategic plan and identified key ways I can use this new system to help my organization meet its strategic objectives?
		9. Have I communicated to each employee the role they will play *during the transition* (whether or not they are using the new system)?
		10. Have I communicated to my employees the role they will play *in the new work environment* (whether or not they are using the new system)?
		11. Have I identified the types of training my employees may need—in addition to formal system training— to succeed in the new work environment ("mentoring" with other employees, training in problem solving or other professional skills, etc.)?
		Managing Changing Behaviors …
		12. Am I keeping a list of behaviors that will need to change for the system to be successful?
		13. Have I explained to my employees that it's okay to make mistakes during the transition?
		14. Have I communicated to my employees the importance of communicating ideas, concerns, and ideas to the Change Advocates?
		15. Have I communicated to my employees the importance of cooperation across different departments of the organization?
		16. Do I have a specific plan for rewarding and recognizing my employees for making the transition to the new system?

---

[1]Adapted from the works of William Bridges, author of "Managing Transitions," 1991.

Measuring for Success (continued)

Yes	No	Leading the Change Process[2]
		17. Have I made arrangements to take control of day-to-day *projectwide* (versus my department-specific) activities and decisions?
		18. Am I watching my own actions carefully to be sure that I am modeling the behaviors and attitudes I am asking others to develop?
		19. Do I understand that behaviors are easiest to shape during times of transition?
		20. Have I made real attempts to understand and fully support the "Success Team" concept?
		21. Have I explained the Success Team structure to my employees and encouraged them to "participate" (for example, by communicating issues and ideas through their Advocates)?
		22. Am I comfortable working with the system for a few months without changing it (even if I have identified areas for improvement)?
		23. Do I view my fellow Transition Leaders as business partners?
		24. Am I comfortable with the fact that I will not have "all the answers, all the time" during the transition?

[2]Adapted from the works of John P. Kotter, author of "Leading Change," 1996.

The Missing Piece in Reengineering

By Nicholas F. Horney and Richard Koonce

Audience	Learning Professionals
Purpose	—Learn a process for aligning competencies with a changed or reengineered work process —Understand the training challenges involved in preparing workers for a new workplace
Suggested Uses	Self-study Model a resource for developing training for learning professionals as part of change management sessions

Is your organization suffering from reorganization fatigue? Have you restructured, downsized, outplaced, and outsourced until all that remains is a skeleton staff of stressed-out employees and senior executives, still waiting for the promised gains in productivity to materialize?

In recent years, hundreds of business books and management articles have been written about downsizing and restructuring: how to do it right, how to do it well, how to use it for sustainable change, and how to squeeze corporate vitality and productivity gains out of reengineered work processes and a slimmed-down workforce. Many of those articles spotlight the stage-setting importance of energetic CEO leadership and "envelope-pushing" missions and visions.

Leadership and organizational goals are important. But something is missing from the literature. Despite the media attention, the verdict on many reengineering efforts today is mixed at best. In fact, a recent business survey by a leading human resources consulting firm suggests that nearly two-thirds of all restructuring efforts are clear failures.

The reasons vary. Many restructuring efforts suffer from poor planning and have paid only scant attention to the importance of clear, consistent, and ongoing communication as part of restructuring initiatives.

Another problem is that workplaces have dealt inadequately with the "people variables" that are always at play in organizations in times of rapid change. Executives and managers need to pay more attention to the stress and anxiety that people feel during transition.

Still another reason for the failure of many restructuring and reengineering efforts is a lack of penetration to the deepest organizational levels. In essence, these initiatives ignore the issue of how people actually do their jobs each day. In other words, they fail to address one of the key ways for people to become engaged and energized as individual agents of change.

What we call competency alignment is a critical underpinning of successful business-process reengineering (BPR) initiatives.

At its best, BPR involves a fundamental rethinking and radical redesign of "core business processes" within an organization. It necessarily implies taking a hard and systematic look not only at the organizational structures, management systems, beliefs, and values that are part of an organization's culture, but also at the jobs that people do on a daily basis and the systems that support and reinforce them.

Reengineering efforts should be targeted toward the specific goal of changing employee behaviors, processes, and systems at the "transactional" level in an organization (the level at which day-to-day business is actually done, according to change-management consultant and theorist, W. Warner Burke).

Unless BPR examines the business at that level, all the CEO exhortations in the world aren't likely to bring about significant, long-term changes—either in organizational effectiveness or in a company's financial performance. Unless BPR pays attention to employees' day-to-day work, people are unlikely to fall enthusiastically into line to support new marketing goals, to work toward achieving the CEO's heartfelt desire to "go global," or to pursue more ambitious customer-service objectives.

Most organizations display an implicit (and sometimes explicit) systemic inertia. Systems and people resist change unless an organization addresses barriers methodically and systematically.

That's why competency alignment is critical. It gets you right down into the heart of an organization. It helps you focus time, energy, and attention on the details of how people work and interact on a day-to-day basis—with each other, with customers, with other stakeholders, with competitors, and with various human-resource processes and information systems in the organization.

By paying attention to how people interact "transactionally" in your company, organization, department, or work group, you put yourself in a powerful position to make changes that can reinforce reengineering goals or dramatic process improvement.

The Competency-Alignment Process

Coopers & Lybrand's competency-alignment process, or CAP, involves the systematic study, analysis, and assessment of job functions, tasks, and skills required by an organization that is reengineering one or more of its work processes. It focuses on analyzing, understanding, and optimally deploying people in the reengineered organization, ensuring the best job fit for everyone.

To do that, it methodically examines employee skill sets in order to determine where and when skill gaps exist and what can be done to remedy deficiencies—either through employee training, skill enhancement, redeployment, outplacement, outsourcing, or other efforts.

CAP provides a baseline methodology for retooling work processes at their most fundamental level—the level of the individual and the small work team. CAP is an ideal mechanism for bringing employees into closer alignment with strategic organizational goals and objectives—a key success factor in creating a high-performing, improvement-driven organization, according to a recent C&L survey. And it provides a means of refining and recalibrating that alignment over time—as job requirements change, as the structure of work within an organization changes, as production or manufacturing processes incorporate new technology, as employee skill sets age, and as external factors come into play.

A systematic and methodical approach can help you implement competency alignment in your own organization as a component of other reengineering efforts you are planning or implementing.

Where does competency alignment fit into the reengineering process? Think of it as a critical subset of larger-scale business-process redesign or reengineering efforts that are in the works or recently completed. It should be a part of any BPR initiative—whether the goal of the reengineering is to redraft your organization's entire mission or to overhaul one key business process, such as research and development, marketing, manufacturing, or product distribution.

For many organizations, competency alignment has been the missing element or link in reengineering efforts. Even if it fell through the cracks in years past, it still may have influenced the outcome of productivity-improvement and change-management initiatives.

Nowadays, organizations can't afford to ignore it. The costs of employee recruitment, training, turnover, retraining, and poor job fit have become so high that they are clearly driving the need for organizations to get the most out of their BPR efforts, at a minimal cost.

Four Stages of CAP

An important outcome of completing competency alignment is the identification of current employees the organization can successfully place in new jobs or on new teams, as part of reengineering a key business process. Doing so takes great care, careful planning, and systematic implementation.

Most organizations should implement CAP in four stages: assess, deploy, learn, and align.

In stage 1, the assessment, it's important to conduct a task analysis of the reengineered process to determine the knowledge, skills, abilities, and competencies people will need in order to be effective contributors. You also will examine the suitability of current job holders to do that work.

A critical outcome of stage 2, deployment, is the identification of people's skill gaps. With this information, you can begin to make decisions about which employees to retain in their current functions and which to slate for outplacement or redeployment elsewhere in the organization.

Stage 3 of any CAP initiative deals with learning. This stage involves the development of skill-acquisition plans (such as training, outsourcing, or recruiting) to fill the skill gaps identified in stage 2.

You might, for example, decide to institute new training programs to help retained employees work more effectively in teams. You might also decide to import at least some new talent from outside the organization through targeted recruitment efforts. Or you might choose to outsource certain tasks that the organization no longer considers essential core functions.

Stage 4 of CAP is alignment. It focuses on

developing and aligning an organization's human resource systems (such as the performance-appraisal system and the compensation system) to sustain the performance of people in the newly reengineered process.

Following this road map can help you ensure successful implementation of competency alignment in your organization. Now, let's take a detailed look at each of the four stages, which are summarized in the box on the next page.

Stage 1: Assessing the Process and the People

This stage is divided into two parts: assessing the competencies that the newly reengineered processes will require and assessing the competency of existing employees to carry out the processes.

Process competency assessment. Let's say that your company or organization has decided to reengineer. You might be planning to reengineer your entire organization as part of a comprehensive change-management initiative (one that involves the systematic reengineering of all business processes, your business strategy, and your information-technology capabilities). Or you might plan to redesign only selected departments or work processes.

In any case, you'll need to get a clear bead on the kinds of tasks that will need to be done. And you'll need to know which skills and competencies people will need if they are to do the work in the future, after reengineering efforts are fully implemented.

In years past, you might have used job and task analysis to get at the heart of productivity problems or to understand better the different elements in a work process. You might have asked job holders to provide the following information:

- The core knowledge, skills, and abilities necessary for doing their jobs

- The amount of time spent each day or week on specific tasks

- Ratings of tasks, in terms of relative importance

That approach to job analysis was valuable in the past. But it becomes difficult to do

The Four Stages of the Competency-Alignment Process

Stage 1: Assess

▶ Assess your process.

▶ Assess your people.

▶ Determine necessary tasks.

▶ Determine necessary skills, abilities, and competencies.

▶ Create a gap-analysis matrix.

Stage 2: Deploy

▶ Develop skill, ability, and competency profiles.

▶ Use the profiles to deploy people into reengineered jobs, to redeploy them elsewhere in the organization, or to outplace them.

Stage 3: Learn

▶ Create training and career-development plans for employees.

▶ Explore the use of different training approaches, formats, and methods.

▶ Outsource non-core functions.

Stage 4: Align

▶ Align HR systems, including reward and recognition, compensation, and performance appraisal.

▶ Conduct pilot tests.

▶ Review, assess, and revise as appropriate.

when you are in the middle of reengineering a core business process—primarily because you don't yet have job holders or "incumbents" in the reengineered process. Instead, you'll need to use subject matter experts (SMEs) within the organization to help identify tasks and to describe the knowledge, skills, and abilities that are likely to be required of job holders once a map of the new process is fully developed.

SMEs can include current job holders, "process owners," key line managers, and others you deem to have broad knowledge of organizational goals as well as of specific processes and work content.

Now let's imagine that you are reengineering your company's order-management process. A key objective in stage 1 of CAP is

to develop a process description, showing how work is performed now and how it will be done in the future. So you'll need to break the process down into individual tasks (for example, planning, order generating, scheduling, and shipping) and ask SMEs to identify the competencies people need for each task.

Initially, what you come up with may resemble a step-by-step view of the order-management process, with lists of specific skills tagged to each of the principal steps or tasks.

Next, work with members of your reengineering team and with the SMEs to map out the way in which work will be done in the future. Ask such questions as these:

• What additional skills and competencies will people need to have?

A New Kind of Tool for Groups

Groupware, or electronic meeting-support, is a kind of software that organizations are using more and more often in brainstorming, data-gathering, and focus group situations.

Groupware technology can help you electronically capture and catalog large amounts of participant input, typically gathered in classroom sessions or through teleconferences. Usually, participants use laptop computers or keypads to input their answers to questions. The technology provides an accurate and quick way to capture data, compile statistics, set priorities for goals and objectives, and build action plans.

When using groupware with focus groups, you may find it helpful to ask participants to review an existing list of tasks, developed ahead of time by the reengineering team. Have focus group members verify that the list is complete and that it accurately reflects all the transactions likely to be required as part of implementing a new work process.

Once participants have signed off on the list, group the tasks and "subtasks" together in clusters. From those clusters, the focus group participants can determine what knowledge, skills, and abilities people will need to have in order to perform future tasks in the organization.

One common groupware feature, rank-order voting, may be especially useful in helping focus groups to determine the relative importance of various tasks, skills, and competencies.

- Will people work together differently than they do now? (For instance, will they spend more time in teams and on collaborative decision making?)

- What new technology will be integrated into the way work is done?

- What new skills will the technology require of workers?

To get answers to those questions and others, try conducting focus group sessions, using groupware technology to catalog and organize people's responses. See the box above, A New Kind of Tool for Groups, for a discussion of groupware as a means for facilitating group sessions and collecting and analyzing data.

What typically emerges from an in-depth focus group process is a detailed list of tasks, skills, and competencies that will be part of employees' work in the future.

A groupware session with subject matter experts will probably yield a sheet of formatted information that looks something like the list shown in the box on page 3-44. This ex-ample was developed as the result of some work with a large financial institution to determine its employees' work tasks, knowledge and skill requirements, and competencies.

What also frequently emerges from such data-gathering sessions are broad themes that suggest how much the nature and structure of work is changing.

For example, nowadays everyone from the boardroom to the loading dock needs hands-on familiarity—and preferably, a high comfort level—with computers. And today's workplace requires many people to have specific experience with such relatively new technology as local area networks, "shareware," the Internet, and Windows applications. Such competencies will be even more essential in the future.

Another competency that people increasingly need in the workplace today is the ability to work effectively in groups. Since more and more work is team-based, you'll want to make sure that subject matter experts in your focus groups fully map the constella-

Job Tasks for Bank Employees, with Related Skills and Competencies

Tasks

▶ Gather closing information

▶ Identify, read, review, and interpret loan documentation

▶ Identify legal issues

▶ Revise and interpret loan histories and amortization schedules

Knowledge and Skill Requirements

▶ Reading comprehension

▶ Knowledge of loan-servicing systems and loan documentation

▶ Knowledge of asset types and loan-classification schedules

▶ Knowledge of loan documentation, ranking and legal issues, terminology, and definitions

Required Competencies

▶ Detail orientation

tion of team skills and competencies that work will require in a newly restructured area of your organization.

By the time you've done all that, you'll have a clear handle on the competencies people will need for doing their jobs in the context of a reengineered work process. And by eliciting comments from process owners, supervisors, and others who are familiar with current processes, you create strong buy-in for the important employee-deployment decisions to come.

At the same time, you may acquire a sense of the work that lies ahead of you in actually implementing competency alignment in your organization, and of the tactics and strategies you'll need to use.

For example, say you oversee training and development programs in a craft environment (such as a tool-and-die manufacturer) where the tradition and emphasis has long been on individual skill. Now, such factors as speed-to-market and concurrent engineering (the simultaneous development of a product and of the process for developing it) have emerged as critical to success.

You may face tough challenges if you intend to introduce team principles or large-scale, technology-assisted design into a manufacturing process in a traditional environment.

Employees may be unfamiliar with (and even hostile to) new technology. They may lack an understanding of teamwork principles; they may have no interest at all in working on teams.

The people-assessment process that makes up the next part of stage 1 addresses such concerns by giving you tools for appropriate selection and retention of employees. It will also help you determine an individual employee's motivation to do new work, so that you can assess his or her suitability for working in an environment of changing norms and expectations.

Employee competency assessment. At this point, you've inventoried the skills and competencies people will need once a work process has been reengineered. So you have a road map with which to assess the suitability of current job holders to perform future jobs in your organization.

Your goal now is to assess the individual skills and backgrounds of current job holders.

Start by developing an assessment tool that looks at their interests and skills in the key areas you identified in the process of competency assessment.

A helpful tool at this stage is a 360-degree

survey that lets supervisors, coworkers, and subordinates provide input on job holders. The responses will form accurate profiles of individual employees and their suitability to fill new jobs in the reengineered workplace.

Many of the questions to ask at this stage are specific to the process being reengineered. Others relate more generally to the work values and work styles of employees and to how well specific people are likely to perform in a reengineered environment. Still others seek to assess people's compatibility with, interest in, and motivation to do tasks in the reengineered job context.

For example, you might ask supervisors, coworkers, and subordinates to rate a person's ability to work with new technology, to think creatively, to deal with new situations, to handle stress, to solve problems, to work as part of a team, and to lead a team.

Some traits tend to predict success in almost any job—especially in organizations that are in states of constant reorganization. See the box, How Do You Spell Success in a Reengineered Workplace? for a rundown.

The outcome of assessing employees' backgrounds and skill levels is a gap-analysis matrix that includes each person who is involved in the work process as it stands before reengineering begins. The matrix covers a spectrum of skill areas that earlier steps have identified as important to the work process in question. For each competency, indicate whether each employee's skill level is weak, moderate, or strong.

Stage 2: Deploying People in a Reengineered Workplace

In essence, the matrix you created at the end of stage 1 enables you to assess the range of people's individual and aggregate abilities across a typical profile of what you need from an employee—both as an individual contributor and as part of a team.

You've now provided people with an overall "rating and ranking"—comparing their strengths and weaknesses with those of their coworkers, and taking into account the skills that are critical to the reengineered jobs. Armed with that information, it's possible to determine each person's suitability for training, for redeployment elsewhere in the organization, or for outplacement.

Determine people's scores on the matrix by taking the responses gathered from their supervisors, coworkers, and subordinates. Subject those responses to computer analysis that gives weighted averages to different

---

How Do You Spell Success in a Reengineered Workplace?

So, you've been charged with leading the effort to assess current employees' suitability for working in a reengineered job context. Surveying those who work with the employees in question can give you a 360-degree view of worker competencies.

Of course, many of the questions you'll ask are specific to the job you have in mind. But several factors tend to predict excellent performance in any job. To be successful in a job today—particularly in organizations that are undergoing incessant internal change and process improvement—a person typically must display the following traits:

▶ The skills and abilities to do the actual work

▶ The inclination or inherent ability to learn and adapt to a changing environment over time

▶ Motivation to do the work

▶ Compatibility with the organization's overall operating and management style

▶ A sense of self-confidence about her or his ability to perform the job over time

---

skills and to the relative skills of one person compared with those of his or her coworkers.

That information will help you make the tough decisions about where and how each employee can best contribute in the reengineered work environment.

Stage 3: Creating the Means for Learning

You've determined the competencies people need for success in performing newly reengineered tasks. And you've profiled current job holders to assess their individual skill levels and their skill gaps.

Now you're in an ideal position to create training and career-development plans for employees, using the information you've collected. You also have the information you need for developing a plan to outsource specific tasks and functions that can now best be done outside the organization—for instance, benefits administration and payroll.

People from human resources, training and development, and various line operations should work in tandem to create training plans for employees. Those plans can be regularly updated and revised as needed. For instance, the introduction of new technology might necessitate additional training. So might the implementation of new work practices, whether they are specific to a single process or common across the organization.

This may also be the time to develop jointly a new learning philosophy for your organization—a philosophy that specifically supports job-redesign and process-reengineering priorities. For instance, you may want to inaugurate just-in-time training, computer-based training, distance learning (if you serve multiple geographic sites), or other training strategies to help support continuous-improvement efforts, whether they are process-specific or people-specific.

BPR presents an excellent time to develop, pilot, and roll out new training initiatives. They are another way to reinforce new work requirements and performance expectations in the reengineered environment.

What kinds of training do employees need to receive?

In addition to process and task-specific train-ing, it's likely that your employees will need to develop better teamwork and communication skills. They may need updated management skills, or training in new technology.

In all likelihood, CAP will by this time have fully delineated the kinds of training you need to offer. Indeed, you may see a "before" and "after" picture emerging—one that gives a clear view of the skills that served employees well in the past, compared with the ones they now need to learn. That picture can point you in the direction you need to go in order to give employees the highest possible skill levels for performing reengineered jobs.

See the box on the next page, Moving People into the New Workplace, for an example of changing skill and knowledge requirements in a reengineered workplace.

Stage 4: Aligning the Support Systems

Clearly, no amount of job reconfiguration is going to work unless you put systems in place to reinforce new behaviors and help support the design of new functions. Key systems include the reward and recognition system, the compensation system, and the performance-appraisal program.

That's why stage 4 of the CAP process must deal with building the right kind of infrastructure to support newly designed jobs.

You'll need to develop new philosophies and policies for performance appraisal, compensation, rewards, and incentives. Your reengineered environment probably includes more collaborative work, so the new systems should use measurements that are more team-based than in the past. You may need to retool your systems to reflect critical success factors such as customer-satisfaction levels, cycle time, quality improvement, and team performance.

But you'll also want to leave room for some measurements that key into individual contributions and effort on the job. For instance, what criteria will you build into your performance-appraisal process to recognize and acknowledge individual initiative?

In the Coopers & Lybrand survey of improvement-driven organizations, respondents from high-performing organizations in both the public and the private sector said their workplaces put a lot of stock in recognizing and rewarding individual as well as team efforts in the workplace.

In those organizations, quality-improvement accomplishments figure prominently in people's annual performance reviews. Job empowerment is a key operating philosophy. You might want to build such objectives into your own performance-appraisal process as well.

To undergird your competency alignment, you'll need to field test the HR systems you are putting in place. Fully test each separate system (such as performance appraisal and measurement, compensation, or recognition) in a trial-period shakedown. Testing can help you ensure that each system is performing to expectations and is helping to reinforce the new work norms.

After you conduct separate tests of the different systems, evaluate the results and make revisions as necessary.

Making It All Come Together

How do you ensure that competency align-

ment becomes a highly effective component of your reengineering efforts?

Success begins with a realization that increasing corporate profitability or organizational effectiveness requires more than cutting costs or shedding staff. Instead, organizations must be purposeful in the ways in which they develop and leverage people as part of reengineering efforts.

Ultimately, the outcome of all this is to increase the bottom line or whatever other measurements your organization uses to gauge profitability or organizational vitality.

It is often easier, in the short term, to increase net income by reducing costs or head count. But true growth and vitality come from sensing new opportunities in the marketplace; building new competencies within the organization; and leveraging the skills, talents, and adaptiveness of employees to achieve organizational aims.

"Any company that is a bystander on the road to the future will watch as its structure, values, and skills become progressively less attuned to industry realities" and to the needs of the marketplace, note Gary Hamel and C.K. Prahalad in their book, *Competing for the Future.*

Moving People into the New Workplace

In the Past, employees ...	Now, they need training in ...
were familiar with mainframe computers and individual PCs	use of local area networks, Windows, Lotus Notes, and other advanced computer technologies
Worked as individual contributors, performing jobs defined by formal written job descriptions	how to work cooperatively on teams to perform project-driven work assignments; conflict-resolution and project-management skills are a must
dealt with very little change in their jobs	how to deal with constant technological and organizational change
did what they were told, each person reporting to one boss who acted as supervisor	serving many different "customers," both inside and outside the organization

---

Pay conscious and purposeful attention to the importance of competency alignment as part of your reengineering efforts. Not only will it boost your organization's sustained vitality and profitability, but it also can enhance the resilience and resourcefulness of your organization and its employees in a climate of constant change.

Exercise: Promoting Buy-in to Organizational Change

By Luan B. Watkins

Audience →	Learning Professionals, Staff and Supervisors, Teams, Management, New Employees
Purpose →	—Develop a common understanding of the organizational change and why it is important to the company —Identify personal benefits of the change —Accept, buy into, and take ownership of the change
Suggested Uses →	Group exercises following introduction or organizational changes or cultural changes Could also be used for new employee orientation

Introduction

In today's environment of empowered employees, leadership's role is to set direction and coach. In order for empowerment to be effective, it is essential that all employees, including all levels of management, understand and buy into the established direction. In addition, buy-in is critical to successful organizational change, and lack of it has derailed implementation in many organizations. While management or a change team begins the process of buy-in during the process of defining and developing the change concept, the most difficult part of the culture change is to get the same level of understanding and buy-in throughout the organization. In order for the concept to become a sustained part of the culture, it is important to roll it out to all employees and get their buy-in. Buy-in is also important for new employees who are entering into a new culture with new values. Helping new employees buy-in to the new organization is often overlooked, due partly to the past lack of a good approach to promoting the buy-in.

Exercise: Leader's Notes

Time

Four to six hours

Number of Participants

Five to 15 is optimal

Facilitator Expertise

Basic process facilitation skills

Materials and Equipment

Flipchart

Marking pens

Tape or pushpins

Hollow plastic golf balls with holes or slots (one for each participant)

Strips of colored copier paper (not construction paper) the size of a fortune in a fortune cookie (5 to 10 different colors)

Scissors

Procedure

1. Identify the Concept

Identify the concept for which you want to establish buy-in and acceptance, such as a company mission statement, values, beliefs, a new goal, or a reengineered organization or department. Typically, the concept has been previously developed by management and written, printed, or stated in some standard format to enhance the common understanding. Present this concept or statement to the participants. For purposes of example, we will use the statement, "We treat each other with trust and respect and operate as a team."

2. Dissect the Key Meaning

While displaying the statement or concept on a flipchart page or in any preprinted form (poster, plaque, etc.), initiate discussion among the participants about the meaning of the statement. Using the example, "We treat each other with trust and respect and operate as a team," the participants might identify *treat, trust, respect, operate,* and *team* as the key words to be defined. Focus the team on the most applicable words for your environment. In this example, it might be *trust, respect,* and *team*.

3. Identify Behaviors

The next step is to identify the behaviors typically associated with each of the key words: trust, respect, team. Taking each word, one at a time, use a round robin brainstorming technique to identify behaviors associated with each word, capturing the ideas on a flipchart. Hang each completed flipchart page on the wall for future reference.

4. What's In It For Me

Referring to the flipchart pages displayed on the wall, ask each participant to identify "what's in it for me" (WIIFM). The participant should identify at least one WIIFM (one way in which they will benefit personally) from each of the key words. They may identify more than one WIIFM if they so choose.

5. Discuss the WIIFMs

Facilitate an open discussion of the benefit each participant believes they will receive from being a part of an organization that believes in and practices these key concepts.

6. Commitment

After the discussion is complete, ask each participant to identify at least one behavior for each key word that they commit to follow. Explain that being a contributing part of the organization is not a one-way street; that in order to receive the benefits, the WIIFM, it is essential that each individual also commit his or her behavior to be in alignment with the new direction or concept. Ask people to write down their commitment.

7. Commitment Discussion

Facilitate an open discussion of the commitments made by each participant.

8. Cutting and Stuffing

The exercise is nearly complete, with participants having identified what's in it for them and made their commitment. This last step provides a reminder to employees of the commitment they have made. Ask each participant to cut two strips of colored paper, the size of a fortune in a fortune cookie, for each key word. In this example, we might have two blue strips for trust, two pink slips for respect, and two green slips for team. (You may also choose to use six different colors, making each strip a separate color.) Next, have the participants write their WIIFM for each of the key words on a different colored strip of paper. In this example, participants should have at least three different colored strips of paper with a different WIIFM on each piece. Next, have them write their commitment on the appropriate colored strip of paper. When the writing is complete, have the participants roll up each strip of paper. Then, for the fun part, toss a golf ball to each participant and ask them to stuff their rolled up WIIFMs and commitments into their golf ball. If they shake the ball, the paper should unroll slightly inside the golf ball. The golf ball is theirs to take back to their work area as a reminder of what's in it for them and their commitment.

Customization

This technique can be used with any concept for which buy-in and acceptance is desired. It does not have to be an established mission statement, values, or any other formal direction statement.

Exercise: Changing Work Behaviors for Higher Performance

By Robert A. Younglove

Audience	Learning Professionals, Staff and Supervisors, Teams, Management
Purpose	—Envision how newly learned skills or behaviors will help them be more successful on the job —Decide to adopt one or more specific new behaviors as a result of new learnings —Make a commitment to the change —Learn how to use self-talk statements to enable and reinforce their behavior change
Suggested Uses	Group exercise to close a training program or other learning experience Coaching or mentoring tool

Introduction

This exercise should be part of every training program whose desire is a behavior change back on the job. Training programs often fail to achieve performance improvement, not because people don't learn, but because humans are creatures of habit and go back to doing things the old familiar way.

The object of this approach is to help people develop new habits, or patterns of behavior, that lead people to be more successful. In current literature, Stephen Covey promotes *The Seven Habits of Highly Effective People*, and Price Prichett reports on the *New Work Habits for a Radically Changing World*.

However, eliminating old habits and replacing them with new ones requires a step-by-step method based on the insights of self-image psychology. These are the same techniques used consistently by athletes to create olympic-quality performance. They

are easy to learn and fun to use, but they require consistent application to make the new habits a lasting change in behavior.

This approach uses self-talk statements that take the intention to change and put it into action by creating a new expectation of our behavior. A self-talk statement is something we say to ourselves about us. They can be positive, such as, "I'm good at remembering names," or they can be negative, such as, "I always lose my temper." We listen to these statements and record them in our subconscious memory as a self-image. This image or picture of how we normally act in a given situation serves to keep us behaving like we imagine we are. A great deal of our behavior is controlled by this subconscious self-image. Learned behavior becomes a habit, just something we automatically do, like driving our car when sometimes our conscious mind is busy thinking about other things. The subconscious mind, which has learned the habit of driving the car through repetition, automatically controls the muscles to stop at red lights and turn at certain intersections to get us to our destination. Consciously we don't even remember going through that intersection, let alone whether we stopped at a red light, but we had to have gone through that intersection to get home.

Self-talk, used repetitiously, will program the subconscious self-image to develop new habits. Over time it reduces the need to force ourselves consciously to behave in the new desired way, and it makes the intended behavior an automatic habit.

Exercise: Leader's Notes

Time

20–30 minutes

Number of Participants

Any number

Handouts

Checklist of new behaviors, habits, skills or attitudes emphasized in the training program

3 x 5 notecards

Procedure

1. At the conclusion of the training program explain the concept and usefulness of self-talk statements and have participants complete one of the following activities:

   • Ask each person to complete the sentence, "I would be more effective in accomplishing my job if I _____." Give some examples of new behaviors taught in the training program, such as, If I were more patient and understanding, more diplomatically assertive, more creative, more self-disciplined, etc.

   • Provide a checklist of new behaviors, habits, skills, or attitudes emphasized in the training program. Ask participants to check all those that would allow them to be more successful in their jobs.

   • In small groups, have participants brainstorm a list of qualities or characteristics that lead to success in their area of work. Start them off with, for example, sense of humor, good listener, attention to detail, etc.

2. Have each participant choose three new habits from those generated by the activities in step one, that they personally want to develop in themselves. Have them write the new desired habits, with one each on top of a 3 x 5 index card.

3. Next, on the same index card, have participants write a statement of intention, starting with, "I choose to ...," or "I am becoming...," or "It is like the new me to ...." Give some examples from your own experience, such as, "I choose to be well organized and know where everything is," "I am becoming an on-time person who gets where I'm going with time to spare," and "It is like the new me to do what needs to be done, when it ought to be done, whether I like it or not."

4. Have participants turn the card over, and on the back side make a list of little things they need to do differently in order to be successful at achieving their good intention. For example, if my intention is to be more organized, then on the back of the 3 x 5 card I might have, (1) use a color-coded system for filing things, (2) make an index of files stored on the computer, (3) put things back where they belong when finished, etc. These are all small behaviors that contribute to the successful development of the new habit.

5. Tell participants to put the 3 x 5 index card in a place where they will see it every day. Suggest places like their day-timer or a desk drawer they open frequently, or perhaps on the visor of their car or the mirror in their bathroom. The object is to read the card at least twice a day, every day, and mentally rehearse through visualization what it would look like to behave in that way. By doing this repeatedly, a new picture or image is created in their memory of how they typically behave in a given situation. For example, "I see myself putting things back where they belong when I'm finished using them."

Tell participants that it may take three to six weeks of using this 3 x 5 self-talk card every day before a new habit is created. The length of time depends on the strength of the old habit. However, this is how new habits can be formed that will lead to greater productivity and success on the job. It is an effective way to help people take what they have learned in the classroom and transfer it to new work habits on the job.

Exercise: Overcoming Resistance to Change

By Kevin Walker

Audience	Learning Professionals, Change Management Teams, Other Teams, Managers, Supervisors, Coaches/Mentors with Responsibilities for Implementing Change
Purpose	—Understand why resistance to change occurs —Learn effective techniques for identifying various types of resistance to change and overcoming them —Practice the techniques
Suggested Uses	Group exercises following introduction of organizational changes or cultural changes Group exercise as part of a broader training on change management Group exercise as part of an executive workshop or meeting that is developing plans for an organizational change Could be included in sessions for Success Team leaders based on the earlier piece, "Building a Success Team for Managing Change"

Introduction

Change is inevitable in today's organizations. Knowing how to predict, or at least recognize, resistance to change and minimize or overcome it is important for learning professionals, managers, and others involved in planning, implementing, and managing change.

Change and Loss

To a large extent, people view change in terms of its effects, and resistance to change stems from perceived loss—loss of the known and tried and loss of personal choice. Examples of employees' fears that create resistance include perception of potential job loss or other adverse outcome; shift in communication patterns; the unknown impact of a new organizational structure; and concerns about their and others' influence, authority, and control under the new plan. Whether the threat is actual or imagined, it should always be treated as real. An effective strategy for reducing resistance is to reduce fear—by removing uncertainties through education and demonstration.

Change and Choice

Another strategy is to involve those affected by the change in planning for it from the outset. People resist the imposition of change that is simply ordered to happen without everyone's prior involvement. In fact, when change is simply imposed, resistance is inevitable. When people are involved in determining how or if a change should happen, their sense of control increases—and they can make constructive contributions to designing and implementing change at the workgroup level.

The degree of ease and success with which an organizational change is introduced is directly proportional to the amount of choice that people feel they have in determining and implementing change. Communication about anticipated changes should incorporate the element of personal choice, highlighting possible options instead of a single, predetermined path.

Value Conflicts

It is also possible that people feel the planned change is ill-fated and will not work or may violate deeply held values and beliefs. This may stem from underlying value differences or intellectual/technical differences in approach and philosophy. The best response is to counter with well-conceived, influential explanations of why the change is needed (the compelling reason for change), incorporating facts, anecdotal evidence, and data wherever possible. Conclusions drawn from inadequate data and weak linkages will invite opposition.

Encouraging Overt Resistance

Encouraging overt resistance is one strategy for identifying and developing responses to individuals experiencing a values conflict. Overtly expressing resistance can help individuals to surface and overcome resentments rooted in loss of control. Indirect resistance is hazardous to the change project and should be transformed into overt resistance whenever recognized. To encourage people to express their concerns, remove fears of retribution associated with the expression of diverse opinions.

Exercise: Leader's Notes

Time

1½–2 hours

Number of Participants

Any number, but larger groups should be divided into groups of no more than 10 for discussion and 4–6 for role play.

Facilitator Expertise

Group facilitation skills

Understanding of change management principles

Materials and Equipment

Flipcharts

Handouts

How to Deal with Resistance

Overcoming Resistance by Source of Resistance

Resistance to Change: Role Play Scenarios

Procedure

1. Ask participants to tell you the first word or reaction that comes into their minds when they hear the word "change." Write the responses on the flipchart.

2. Ask participants to tell the group about an experience they have had in dealing with a workplace-related change—either themselves or in managing employees through a change. What were the responses? What did they do to handle concerns? Were there positive reactions? How did it turn out?

3. Use the introduction to give participants background information about why people resist change and why it is critical to identify and overcome resistance where possible. Answer questions and get reactions to the information.

4. Give participants the handouts How to Deal With Resistance and Overcoming Resistance by Source of Resistance and introduce the process for addressing different motivations for resistance. Get participants to elaborate on and respond to the approaches.

5. Give participants the Role Play Scenarios and assign either pairs (in small groups) or small groups (in larger groups) to talk

through and decide how to handle the resistance. You may want to assign scenarios, or, if the group is small, let each pair pick one or more that are most relevant to them. If time allows, have each group role play the scene before the full group and have the group discuss what was good about the approach and how they might have handled it differently.

The objective of the role plays is to determine how to address the situation constructively. In some of the scenarios management has made early mistakes in handling change that have led to the current problems—a common happening in many companies. Participants may want to point out how problems could have been avoided, but the focus should be on handling what's happening now.

6. Go back to the original flipchart with the word associations. Review them and determine whether participants feel better able to handle responses similar to their own gut reactions. If issues remain unresolved, have the group suggest approaches to overcome resistance based on what they've learned and their experience. Note that handling resistance to change is an art, not a science, and that dealing with it is a skill that will grow with experience and a skill that can only grow more important to managers and teams because of the rapid pace and continuous nature of workplace change today. In addition, some resistance will be impossible to overcome, and the challenge becomes how to proceed constructively in the face of it—another invaluable management skill in today's environment.

How to Deal with Resistance

Peter Block makes these suggestions for dealing with resistance:

▶ Give good faith responses (answer questions fully and honestly, treating them as a serious and genuine inquiry).

▶ Name the form of resistance you believe a person is exhibiting (as simply and directly as you can).

▶ Be quiet and let tension rise.

▶ Give support to underlying concerns.

▶ Return to and review the person's basic wants and your own.

▶ If you have tried everything and there is still resistance, explore the basic wants.

▶ Ask the other person what it would take to reach an agreement.

▶ Determine if it is a "no go" situation.

▶ Decide if you want to:
   —work without that person's support
   —scale down your own goals and position
   —reduce the visibility of your activity
   —abandon the idea altogether
   —provide reassurances.

▶ Some people resist change because they have a low tolerance for change in general. Give them as much reassurance as possible as they move into a world of uncertainty. Time may also reduce anxiety as fears are proven unwarranted.

Overcoming Resistance by Source of Resistance

Source of Resistance	Approach
▶ Low knowledge/technical orientation	Educate and communicate to gain involvement and "buy-in."
▶ Fear of failure	Promote a problem-solving climate through two-way communication.
▶ Power of politics	Involve people in planning and implementation. Provide communication from the sponsor to those concerned.
▶ Difference in goals	Negotiate and agree upon outcomes.
▶ Difference in methods of obtaining goals	Reinforce consensus building and incorporate "best practices" into implementation.
▶ Differences in values	Reinforce how values will be protected. Negotiate methods to maintain both organizational and individual values.

Develop responses to the following situations that would help bring change resistors on board.

1. A company or government agency is developing a new mission statement and strategic plan designed to improve its performance. Some middle and even top managers of technical departments are not cooperating in carrying out their responsibilities in the development process, saying that they are too busy, that they'll get to it when they can, etc.

2. A company or government agency has just announced an organization-wide total quality management initiative that will emphasize teams, reduction of paperwork, and performance measurement. Some workers and even whole departments give lip service to the change but continue doing business as usual.

3. A company or government agency is developing plans to automate functions previously done manually to improve performance. Bad previous experiences with failed technology projects leave many believing that such efforts can never succeed in this organization.

4. News of a major reorganization and office move is leaked before management has finalized the details. Productivity and morale drop, as employees and managers fear being downsized, inability to work in the new location, etc.

5. To improve its competitive performance and profits, a company considers focusing on core competencies and therefore reducing its product/service mix. Some managers believe this compromises everything the company has stood for throughout its existence. Others feel personally threatened because their products/departments would go, but they cast their resistance in terms of facts and figures disputing potential benefits.

6. A merger occurs between two companies with very different organizational histories and cultures. For example, one is proud of its late-hours work ethic and efforts at cost savings in every area. The other emphasizes flexibility in employee work schedules, benefits such as child and elder care programs, and a good environment such as nice offices and a subsidized cafeteria.

7. A company decides to become a learning organization and appoints a Chief Knowledge Officer. Some people assume it's more of a buzzword than a reality and ignore the whole issue. Because the CKO was brought in from outside, the HR/training department feels threatened and doesn't understand its role in the new arrangement. Line managers complain that substantial new training and coaching requirements will inhibit their department's ability to get their "real" jobs done.

SECTION 4: ENHANCING COACHING AND ON-THE-JOB TRAINING

Section 4 at a Glance

MATERIAL

Material	Page	Learning Professionals	Staff and Supervisors	Teams	Management	Self-study/Resource for Training	Group Exercise	Tool
		AUDIENCES				FORMATS		
Coaching for Human Performance	4-3	●	●	●	●	●		●
Mentoring: A Practitioner's Guide	4-10	●	●		●	●		●
Wanted: Chief Executive Coach	4-15	●			●	●		●
How to Use Coaching as a Change Management Intervention	4-20	●	●		●	●		●
Exercise: How to Plan for Effective Coaching and Counseling	4-30		●		●		●	●
How to Give On-the-job Instruction: A Nine-step Approach	4-42	●	●			●		●
Exercise: Giving Effective Feedback	4-46		●		●		●	
Exercise: Positive Reinforcement	4-53		●		●		●	
Exercise: Active Listening	4-55		●	●	●		●	

Introduction:
Coaching and On-the-job Training for Higher Performance

While formal training is an important source of new knowledge and skills, high-performing organizations are relying increasingly on informal, one-to-one learning experiences. A recent study conducted by the Bureau of Labor Statistics found that informal training represents $48.4 billion in wage and salary costs each year. This figure suggests that informal training and information-sharing between supervisors/managers and employees as well as among employees themselves is an important learning vehicle in today's organizations.

In addition, coaching and mentoring is a growing approach used to help employees identify performance learning needs and plan their career path. In ASTD's 1995 Human Resource and Performance Management Survey, for example, 39 percent of respondent companies said they had coaching and mentoring programs. Supervisors also become informal "coaches" when they counsel employees to solve performance-related problems.

To succeed in improving performance, however, these person-to-person approaches require skills for both teachers and learners, mentors and mentored. Many will need to develop new knowledge or sharpen skills to perform their roles effectively.

How This Section Can Help

Materials in this chapter are intended to help performance and learning professionals address key skill needs. The first four articles can help new coaches and mentors understand their roles, and provide tools they can use to improve performance. The next piece provides an exercise to help participants practice planning and carrying out constructive coaching.

On-the-job trainers need to use effective educational approaches, just as formal trainers do. The next article in this section provides a model for developing and providing this kind of learning experience.

The final three inclusions address the "people skills" required to learn from other individuals and to coach. They provide exercises that help participants understand and practice giving and receiving feedback, giving positive reinforcement, and using active listening skills.

References

Bassi, L., and Van Buren, M. Sustaining High Performance in Bad Times. *Training & Development.* June 1997, p. 36.

Benson, G. Research Update. *Training & Development.* May 1997, p. 94.

Vander Linde, K., Horney, N., and Koonce, R. Seven Ways to Make Your Training Department One of the Best. *Training & Development.* August 1997, p. 23.

Coaching for Human Performance

By Kenneth M. Nowack and Scott Wimer

Audience	Anyone who Coaches Managers
Purpose	—Be able to complete an assessment of a manager's competencies —Learn how to structure a coaching intervention for managers
Suggested Uses	Self-study/handout Resource for presentation on topic

You just got a call from the vice president of human resources asking you to work with a senior manager who has been experiencing performance problems. The manager progressed up the ladder after many years on a career track as a technical specialist. He's from the "old school," and typically uses a command-and-control approach to leadership and employee motivation.

But that style is out of step with the new trends in your organization, which emphasize customer service, collaborative teamwork, and participatory approaches to problem solving and decision making. You've been asked to design and implement an individualized coaching process to help the manager understand how he is being perceived, and what impact his leadership and communication styles have on others. It is hoped that the new coaching process will result in an executive development plan that targets the critical competencies required for success in the organization.

You wonder what to do first. You'd like to respond to the request and assist in a way that will benefit the manager, the people reporting to him, and others affected by his management style. It could be a win-win situation, if you can structure and deliver an appropriate intervention, and if the manager

can rise to the challenge and implement the plan successfully.

Four Steps

First, you have to consider how to structure the coaching intervention. When properly designed, individualized coaching can help all levels of managers identify and address their strengths and areas that need development.

Increasingly, organizations are using individualized coaching programs for executive and management development, succession planning, and career counseling. Whatever the context, it presents specific challenges and issues that must be addressed. A structured, systematic approach lends focus and maximizes the chances of success. But it's essential that the coaching be flexible enough to address specific individual and organizational needs that may emerge.

A four-step approach, COACH, can provide a structured approach to management development. Each step is designed to address key issues. The steps are:

1. Contract.
2. Observe and Assess.
3. Constructively challenge.
4. Handle resistance.

Reprinted with permission from *Training & Development*, published by the American Society for Training & Development

To start, the training consultant, the person receiving coaching, and other relevant parties make a contract or set of agreements so that each knows the objectives, who is responsible for doing what, and how success will be evaluated.

Next, the consultant observes and assesses the coaching recipient to identify his or her strengths and areas for improvement, which will form the basis of an action plan.

Then, the consultant challenges the person being coached in a way that is supportive and compelling so that he or she understands the issues and is prepared to address them.

Last, the consultant will have to handle the resistance the coached person may exhibit when confronted with discrepancies between his or her self-evaluation and feedback from others and when asked to make changes in his or her behavior.

Step 1: Contract

The key to a successful coaching intervention starts with step 1 of the COACH process: contracting. A coaching contract is similar to a legal contract; it's a set of clear, workable agreements. A carefully constructed contract can help clarify the coaching goals, approaches, and outcomes. Many coaching interventions fail because of poor or insufficient contracting. A clear contract lets all parties know what they're getting into and helps lessen any anxiety, resistance, and anger.

To begin the contracting process, the training consultant has to identify the client (that isn't as obvious as it may seem), the other relevant parties (such as the client's manager), and everyone's needs and desires, including those of the consultant. After all, he or she has some ideas about the necessary conditions for a good outcome.

Next, it's the consultant's responsibility to ensure that all parties understand and agree on the main terms of the contract. When in doubt, don't assume anything. It's better to risk annoying people by stating and restating the obvious than to hope that they're all in agreement.

In this step, the consultant's job is to help all parties identify the relevant, foreseeable issues and to make sure they discuss and agree

on them. Throughout, it may be necessary to work to maintain the contract. Regardless of its clarity, people can remember points differently or try to change them.

A fuzzy contract, one in which people make vague agreements because they don't want to face difficult issues, can spell trouble. If the consultant thinks the contract isn't workable, it's better to turn down the assignment than to hope the situation will change. Sometimes, political considerations weigh against negotiating forcefully. In such cases, it may be best to recommend an external consultant.

The contract should clarify these areas:

- The client. Is it the person to receive coaching? His or her manager? The HR department? Other key executives?
- The definition, parameters, or scope of the project.
- The purposes and intended outcomes of the coaching intervention, stated and unstated.
- The involvement, if any, of others within the client's system, such as his or her manager.
- Who "owns" the intervention and who is accountable for what activities or outcomes.
- How the need for the coaching intervention will be communicated to the client.
- Who will receive feedback.
- How and in what form the feedback will be delivered.
- How the coaching intervention will be monitored and evaluated.
- What follow-up to use, such as 360 feedback.
- How the results will be translated into an individualized development plan.
- How the data, results, and findings will be used, such as integrating them into planning.

Step 2: Observe and Assess

Once the issues of the contracting step are clarified, the COACH process turns to design and implementation. The goal is to observe the coaching recipient and assess his or her strengths and areas needing development. The training consultant should design a comprehensive approach for observing and assessing the targeted competencies.

In selecting the approach, it's important to tailor it to the specific needs of the client and the organization. It's best to use multiple assessment approaches.

The matrix below describes typical management competencies and several assessment approaches.

The competency areas most commonly evaluated include:

- Communication (listening, meeting management, presentations).
- Interpersonal (negotiation, conflict management).
- Task management (delegation, team development, performance management).
- Problem solving and decision making

An Assessment Plan to Identify Management Competencies

	Personality Inventory	In-basket Simulation	Behavioral Exercises	360 Feedback
▶ Communication Skills				
Oral communication	●		●	●
High-impact presentation			●	●
Listening			●	●
▶ Task-management Skills				
Planning and organizing	●	●		●
Delegating		●		●
Administrative control		●		●
Performance management			●	●
▶ Interpersonal Skills				
Leadership and influence	●	●	●	●
Diversity and sensitivity	●	●	●	●
Team skills	●		●	●
Negotiotiation and conflict management	●		●	●
▶ Problem-analysis Skills				
Strategic-problem analysis	●	●	●	●
Decisiveness	●	●	●	●
Judgment	●	●	●	●
▶ Self-management Skills				
Career orientation	●			
Stress tolerance	●			
Initiative	●	●	●	
Self-insight	●			●

A Case Study

Louise is a manager in a department with more than 100 people. Though she is competent technically, many of her staff find her difficult to deal with on a personal level. When her boss approached her about her management style, Louise contacted the HR department to see whether it could give her some coaching assistance. Sally was assigned to work with her.

▶ Contract

Sally met with Louise to become acquainted and discover her coaching needs. She gave Louise some options to think about and got her OK to talk with Louise's boss about his views. Sally and Louise agreed to meet later to decide how to proceed. At that meeting, Louise said she wanted to use 360 feedback to learn how people in her department view her as a manager. She agreed that she'd share the results with her boss and that she'd work with Sally to address issues that arose in the feedback.

▶ Observe and Assess

Next, Sally used a 360 instrument and conducted semi-structured interviews with Louise's staff. Sally found that they had respect for Louise's technical skills, extensive experience, and analytical abilities. But they resented her arbitrary decision-making style, abrasive and critical manner, and unwillingness to delegate meaningful responsibilities. Many feared her and would just try to get through the day rather than use their abilities and contribute fully.

▶ Constructively Challenge

Sally didn't look forward to presenting the information to Louise, though she knew she had to. The meeting was uncomfortable, but Sally was able to present the feedback clearly and directly without sugarcoating it. She also tried to be gentle and supportive. To clarify some points, Sally used her own observations to help Louise understand why people perceived her the way they did.

▶ Handle Resistance

Despite Sally's care in presenting the assessment, Louise wasn't consistently receptive. At one point, Louise criticized her staff, saying that their perceptions were biased, that they were envious of her position, and that they were upset about organizational problems that had little to do with her. Louise also challenged Sally directly, saying that she was unprofessional because she took the staff's side and was "taken in" by disgruntled people with an ax to grind. Sally handled the resistance by not taking it personally and by realizing that it's a typical response to hearing negative information about oneself. Sally pointed out gently that Louise might be using those rationales to discount information that she found disturbing.

After some discussion, Louise acknowledged that possibility and decided to address her issues head-on. They agreed that she would attend a class on delegating and participative management, and have several coaching sessions with Sally to work on some of the more difficult problems.

Louise did attend class and meet with Sally for coaching. Though she didn't find it easy, Louise was able to make some significant changes in her behavior. She also said that she was proud to be able to handle some difficult management situations differently than she would have in the past. After six months, Sally did a follow-up assessment with Louise's staff. She found that some issues remained, but they reported that Louise's management style had improved considerably. People also said that her department was more productive and less tense.

(strategic and long-range planning, judgment).

- Self-management (stress management, career development).

A job-profile analysis can enhance the organization's strategic training plan to identify the core competencies required for future performance. The analysis can also serve as a review of the necessary knowledge, skills, and abilities to perform successfully in the client's current job.

First, identify the relevant competencies and then select the tools most appropriate for measuring them. A wide variety of assessment instruments are available to measure critical skills and knowledge; personality and style; and interests, values, and career orientation. They include paper-and-pencil instruments, behavioral exercises, role plays, simulations, leaderless group exercises, and an integrated approach that combines those techniques. For example, one way to assess knowledge is by using situational interviews, simulations, and work-sample tests.

The training consultant should avoid the trap of using only techniques with which he or she is familiar and comfortable.

A job-profile analysis can also help the training consultant define the competencies to be targeted. Ideally, the analysis should include the client's departmental strategic plan to identify the major competencies required for future performance and a review of the necessary knowledge, skills, and abilities to perform successfully in the client's current job.

A multirater instrument can provide feedback on the client's personality and style (such as leadership, communication, and interpersonal skills). Many off-the-shelf instruments can provide insight into a person's personality and style. Diverse style measures are often used for team building. Such popular organizational marriage-counseling-type tools can help managers become more aware of how others view their leadership and interpersonal styles and how their styles affect staff, team members, and customers.

Newer-generation, five-factor personality inventories can provide a comprehensive overview of the client and how he or she approaches personal and organizational challenges.

It can be useful to gather information about the client's interests, values, and career orientation by using a structured interview process or career assessment instrument.

Sometimes in management coaching interventions, it's necessary to refer to outside resources (such as therapists, alcohol and substance recovery programs, and family counselors) to help a client with personal or lifestyle issues that are interfering with his or her job performance. It may also be necessary to conduct a computerized health-risk appraisal or medical checkup.

When selecting the assessment approaches, it's important to consider these issues:

- The critical competencies that will be targeted.

- The assessment approaches and tools that will be used to measure the key competencies.

- Who will provide data on the relevant competencies (peers, staff, customers, the client's manager, and so forth).

- The context in which data are collected so that they yield the most accurate results.

- Who will provide the feedback and how it will be delivered.

- To what extent confidentiality will be maintained throughout the feedback process and how that can be assured.

- How results will be assembled and summarized to provide maximum clarity about the client's strengths and areas needing development.

Step 3: Constructively Challenge

The third step in the COACH process involves challenging the client in a constructive, not critical, way with the information collected in the observing and assessing step. The information should be summarized and delivered to the client in a way that helps him or her understand and accept it without becoming defensive. Otherwise, the best contracting efforts and measurement approaches aren't likely to help the client improve the targeted performance behaviors.

In this step, the consultant should deliver the information using oral and written feedback. If using separate computerized feedback reports, it's advisable to prepare a final summary report that focuses on development. The consultant should maintain confidentiality and provide nonevaluative observations and comments about the targeted competencies. It's important not to assign labels or make predictions about the client's future success based on the assessment results.

One important issue is whether the client is realistic about his or her strengths and areas that need development. Some managers have unrealistic views of their skill levels. They either overestimate or underestimate.

Overestimaters tend to rate themselves higher than others rate them, so they become defensive about the feedback. The consultant should listen, focus the feedback on specific behavior, and avoid describing personality traits or attitudes. The idea is to share information using specific examples. That helps the client get a handle on what he or she may be doing that caused the negative feedback.

Underestimaters may lack confidence. Often, underestimaters fear failure, so they tend to be perfectionists and self-critical. The consultant should give them a lot of examples of their successes to help them have a more accurate, positive self-image.

In this step, it's important to address these issues:

- How to present the feedback so that it facilitates the client's acceptance and understanding.
- How to balance confrontation with support.
- How to share feedback with the client's manager and others so that the client retains dignity and an appropriate degree of control.
- How to best balance quantitative and qualitative data.
- What special considerations to give in delivering feedback to people whose self-evaluation is different from the feedback.
- How to give feedback to an overestimater.
- How to give feedback to an underestimater.

- How to pace the feedback so that the client can assimilate all of the issues and still focus on the most important ones.

Step 4: Handle Resistance

In almost all management coaching processes, the client will exhibit some resistance to the process itself or to the feedback. The training consultant should be prepared to deal with the client's anger, frustration, and direct or indirect challenges.

Typically, people who lack insight about the areas in which they need improvement resist the most. The consultant must work hard to understand the client's feelings, especially the fears and anxieties he or she may not feel comfortable acknowledging. That requires a high degree of support, active listening, and probing to uncover the source of the resistance. It's important to recognize that when people are resistant, they're unlikely to accept feedback as valid or commit to changing their behavior.

Handling resistance can be especially challenging. It's natural for the consultant to feel that after his or her hard work in the earlier steps, the client should appreciate that and go along with the recommendations. The consultant may miss subtle signs of resistance. With experience, however, it's possible to learn not to take resistance personally. If a consultant is comfortable with a client expressing resistance, it's easier to help him or her identify and deal with his or her feelings. That paves the way for the client to do the hard work of behavioral change.

The following are critical issues in this step:

- How to spot resistance, whether overt or subtle.
- How to handle the client's defensiveness, denial, and anger.
- How to handle the client's anxiety and low self-esteem.
- How to translate the coaching into a specific action plan that addresses the client's issues rather than going through the motions so that he or she appears to comply.
- How to monitor and evaluate the client's progress with his or her development plan.
- What process to use to follow up.
- What type of resistance the consultant is

most vulnerable to and how to avoid getting hooked.

- How to distinguish between resistance that is just resistance and valid criticism of the coaching or feedback.

In addition to following the steps of the COACH process, it's also important for the consultant to seek and be receptive to feedback about his or her role as coach. In fact, the essence of coaching is helping others deal with feedback. And who are we to assume that feedback applies only to others and not to ourselves?

Mentoring: A Practitioner's Guide

By Adrianne H. Geiger-DuMond and Susan K. Boyle

Audience ➡	Any Mentors or Mentorees; Managers Considering Adopting a Mentoring Program
Purpose ➡	—Understand the appropriate roles for mentors —Recognize the benefits of mentoring high-performing employees —Learn guidelines for mentors and mentorees —Learn how to evaluate a mentoring system
Suggested Uses ➡	Self-study/handout Resource for presentation on topic

Douglas Aircraft Company in Long Beach, California, has a tradition of mentoring that goes well beyond lip service. Two important elements help establish mentoring as an integral part of the corporate culture:

- Senior management's visible, frequent, and continuing support.

- Mentoring as part of the long-term strategic plan published by the CEO of Douglas's parent company, McDonnell Douglas Corporation (based in St. Louis, Missouri).

Mentoring has management support because Douglas's leaders are convinced of its benefits. They believe that mentoring improves the pool of talent for management and technical jobs and helps to shape future leaders. They consider mentoring to be an effective vehicle for moving knowledge through the organization from the people who have the most experience and learning. And they find the mentoring process to be a valuable source of objective feedback for participants.

The mentoring process is part of the company's management development strategies.

The process follows this basic outline:

- Douglas identifies high-performing employees.

- Those people are introduced to the mentoring process as a way to help define development objectives.

- The company matches the high performers with executives who can help them meet their objectives.

- Together, a "mentoree" and mentor determine goals for the mentoring relationship.

Now, let's look at Douglas's mentoring process in more detail.

Choosing Mentors and Mentorees

Management identifies high-performing employees based on criteria established by its parent company. Managers also consider other factors, such as readiness for promotion, when selecting mentorees.

The potential mentors are senior managers

Reprinted with permission from *Training & Development*, published by the American Society for Training & Development.

who volunteer their time. Before they can join the program, they must outline the knowledge and guidance they believe they could contribute to a mentoring relationship.

Mentorees select three potential mentors from the list of volunteers. A steering team made up of line managers, program administrators, and human resource advisors matches the mentorees with their mentors. The team bases those decisions on the mentoree's preferences, the mentor's self-report, and development objectives that the mentoree and his or her supervisor have set.

In addition, the steering team follows certain guidelines when creating the pairings. For example, the team can assign no more than two mentorees to a single mentor. That guideline is necessary because of the busy schedules of most executives: Many mentors have trouble scheduling even as little time as one hour each month to spend with each mentoree.

Another caveat is that a mentor should be outside of his or her mentoree's direct chain of command. Presumably, executives are already mentoring and coaching employees in their own groups, as part of their commitment to developing people. Besides, Douglas learned through experience that being mentored by one's boss's boss can create awkward situations for mentorees and their supervisors.

Douglas's current mentoring process has now been in place for more than four years. It builds on prior mentoring activities at the firm, including informal experiences, several pilot programs, and grass-roots mentoring efforts. Participants and managers seem to think that the current process is an improvement over the old efforts.

"In previous years," says Barbara Clark, general manager of finance for Douglas, "I learned of my employees' involvement in the mentoring program only by accident. Supervisors were excluded from information on the program."

Because supervisors had no involvement in the mentoring process, they had no understanding of it, or of the extent of their employees' participation. To promote understanding, Clark, a member of the mentoring steering team, was sure to invite supervisors to the initial briefing for mentors.

The initial meeting introduces the mentoring process and covers process objectives, mentoring myths, the role of the mentor, and participant expectations and concerns. Attendees receive separate checklists for the mentors, the mentorees, and their supervisors. They also receive behavior guidelines for all participants.

The briefing is conducted by a team consisting of line managers, human resource professionals, and the program administrator.

Initially, program participants are unsure of their roles. What are they expected to do? How will they start the mentoring discussions? What will they talk about? The briefings help to answer those questions. Mentors learn that they may play different roles at different stages in the mentoring relationship—and that they may be more comfortable with some of those roles than with others.

Mentorees attend a separate briefing to enable them to air their concerns and to help them build networks among themselves. Many mentors wonder whether the mentoring process will result in changes in their jobs; the briefing lets them know that promotion is not a by-product of Douglas's mentoring process. The focus of the mentoring is on development goals that enhance performance on the job.

The Mentoring Begins

The mentoring process starts with the mentoree and his or her supervisor. They hold a personal-development discussion that covers the employee's strengths, her or his development interests, specific skills the employee will work to develop for the future, and a development plan.

The supervisor's involvement at this stage, as well as in the briefings, ensures that the boss understands the goals of the process and the roles of the mentor and mentoree. In fact, before mentoring begins, the mentor contacts the supervisor directly to discuss the employee's development objectives.

Those objectives become the starting point for the first few discussions between the mentor and mentoree. The discussions clarify each person's expectations of the mentoring relationship. In many cases, the

Roles for Mentors

Communicator

▶ encourages two-way exchange of information

▶ listens to mentoree's career concerns and responds appropriately

▶ establishes an environment for open interaction

▶ schedules uninterrupted time to meet with mentoree

▶ acts as a sounding board for ideas and concerns.

Counselor

▶ works with mentoree to identify and understand career-related skills, interests, and values

▶ helps mentoree evaluate appropriateness of career options

▶ helps mentoree plan strategies to achieve mutually agreed upon personal goals.

Coach

▶ helps to clarify performance goals and developmental needs

▶ teaches managerial and technical skills (on-the-job training)

▶ reinforces effective on-the-job performance

▶ recommends specific behaviors in which the mentoree needs improvement

▶ clarifies and communicates organizational goals and objectives

▶ serves as a role model to demonstrate successful professional behaviors—leads by example.

Advisor

▶ communicates the informal and formal realities of progression in the organization

▶ recommends training opportunities from which the mentoree could benefit

▶ recommends appropriate strategies for career direction

▶ reviews the mentoree's development plan on a regular basis

▶ helps the mentoree to identify obstacles to career progression and to take appropriate action.

Broker

▶ expands the mentoree's network of professional contacts

▶ helps bring together different mentorees who might mutually benefit by helping each other

▶ helps link mentorees with appropriate educational or employment opportunities

▶ helps the mentoree identify resources required for career progression.

Referral Agent

▶ identifies resources to help the mentoree with specific problems

▶ follows up to ensure that the referred resources were useful.

Advocate

▶ intervenes on the mentoree's behalf, representing the mentoree's concerns to higher-level management for redress on specific issues

▶ arranges for the mentoree to participate in high-visibility activities within or outside the organization.

(Adapted from "Training Managers for their Role in a Career Development System," by Zandy B. Leibowitz and Nancy K. Schlossberg; from Training & Development Journal, *July 1981, volume 35, number 7.*

Guidelines for Mentors and Mentorees

Successful mentoring relationships don't just happen. Even when the company has a workable mentoring system, the relationship will not be a productive one unless the mentor and mentoree both understand their roles. Here are some guidelines that can help.

▶ One of the most important aspects of a good mentoring relationship is to meet on a regular basis—at least once a month. You cannot develop a good relationship if you don't get to know each other, so take the time to meet!

▶ As a mentoree, you need to know where you are going. It is frustrating for the mentor to ask you what you think and hear you say, "I don't know." Be prepared to discuss alternatives you are considering, and ask for input on those alternatives.

▶ Be a good listener.

▶ Do not betray confidences. This is true whether you are the mentor or the mentoree. When the other party tells you something, remember that it is for your ears only, and not for distribution.

▶ Mentors should discuss strengths and developmental needs with mentorees and provide guidance in developing these areas. They should provide feedback on technical and interpersonal competence, as perceived by customers and influential decision makers. And they should help mentorees set appropriate career goals.

▶ Mentors should help mentorees understand how to participate within the organizational structure, and should provide information on available opportunities in the organization.

▶ Mentorees should not be overly sensitive to criticism. If you are the mentoree, remember that criticism is offered to help you grow and understand, so don't be defensive.

▶ Mentorees should not brag about their relationship with their mentor. This can put the mentor on the spot.

▶ Mentorees should not get too personal about themselves. Keep the relationship on a business level. Mentors are there to provide business advice. They may feel uncomfortable mixing personal information into the mentoring relationship.

▶ Both parties should be sensitive to the issues of sexual harassment or discrimination. Be aware of the risks in the business environment; keep behavior within appropriate bounds.

▶ If either the mentor or the mentoree finds that he or she is not able to develop a successful mentoring relationship, that person should contact a member of the steering team that guides the mentoring program.

▶ The most important element of a successful mentoring relationship is trust. Once trust is broken, so is the relationship.

discussions serve as an icebreaker, which is particularly important if the mentor and mentoree don't already know each other.

Together, they develop simple goals for the mentoring relationship, based on the objectives set by the supervisor and the mentoree.

For example, say that a mentoree in the manufacturing group determines, along with the supervisor, that the employee needs exposure to the financial side of the business. The mentoree is matched with an executive from the finance group.

At their initial meeting, the mentor and mentoree might decide that during at least part of their mentoring meetings, they will discuss return on net assets (RONA), so that the mentoree will understand how his or her department's product affects the entire company's RONA.

At midyear, and again at the end of the 12-month mentoring process, the mentor and the supervisor review the employee's progress toward meeting the development objectives. And at year-end, the mentor and mentoree discuss their mentoring relationship and whether it accomplished its goals.

How Is It Working?

To determine how well the mentoring system is accomplishing its goals, Douglas uses an evaluation method that is also a learning tool. The company measures the effects of the mentoring discussions and evaluates the mentoring relationship.

In a recent evaluation, 25 out of 43 participants responded to a written survey.

Feedback from the respondents shows at least an 80 percent overall satisfaction rating with the mentoring process. In follow-up phone calls, many of those who did not respond to the written survey said they'd had too few meetings with their mentors to be able to answer the questionnaire items. In fact, the most frequent concern from mentorees is that time constraints made it difficult to schedule meetings with their mentors.

The current mentoring system at Douglas is not a static one. The steering team has revised and improved the process over the past four years, based in part on the participant evaluations.

Douglas's mentoring program is designed to be one year in duration. At the end of the year, the process begins again: Participants are selected, mentors are solicited, and matches are made. A mentoree may choose to continue with the same mentor for up to two consecutive years.

The dictionary defines a mentor as "a wise and trusted counselor." Businesses pay a lot of lip service to the importance of providing such counsel to less experienced employees. But the actions that an organization must take in order to make mentoring happen are often confusing and unclear.

Mentors and mentorees need clear guidelines that provide them with a road map for getting started and for keeping the mentoring relationship building. And both parties—along with the employees' supervisors—need ongoing instruction, counseling, support, and follow-through.

Wanted: Chief Executive Coach

By Lynda McDermott

Audience	Learning Professionals, Executives
Purpose	—Understand the appropriate roles for mentors —Learn how to motivate them to accept this role —Learn the characteristics of a good executive coach
Suggested Uses	Self-study Resource for presentation/training session on this topic

If you haven't yet placed a help wanted ad or called executive recruiters, you had better hurry: Coaching is a management imperative. The ad might read as follows:

Wanted: chief executive coach. Will ensure that the company develops workers to operate at their full potential. Under this person's direction, employees will abide by the motto, "Learn and change or die," and the company will enjoy competitive success.

Based on years of working with senior executives, I don't think that such an ad, even in the *Wall Street Journal,* would attract a flood of applicants let alone anyone who meets the qualifications. Most senior executives view their primary roles as protecting and enhancing shareholders' value, establishing corporate strategy, and avoiding litigation, bankruptcy, and prosecution.

Coaching peers and associates isn't on their job descriptions. Despite the need for executives to take on the role of coach, I hope that coaching doesn't become the latest management fad because it's too important for that.

Why Executives Won't Coach

Here are some scenarios I've experienced as an HR professional that exemplify executives' "coaching avoidance":

On a Friday afternoon, a senior utility company executive called me and began describing several disappointing incidents that had occurred with one of the people who reports directly to him—scenes that he had either observed directly or that had been brought to his attention. After a lengthy discussion in which we explored the options for dealing with the issue, the executive decided to talk through the incidents with and counsel the employee. But I sensed that he was thinking, "Why should I have to do this?"

In another case, a vice president decided to provide a recently promoted manager with a communications coach to help the new manager improve his public speaking and corporate image, even though the VP knew that the conversation would be uncomfortable.

In both cases, the executives reluctantly stepped up to the coaching plate. I've advised other executives in similar situations, and I have seen a pattern. A staff member—often the same age as the executive or older with tenure—isn't meeting expectations.

Save luck, the situation could be reversed. Because the employee's behavior isn't illegal, immoral, or life-threatening, the executive puts off the confrontation. But the behavior continues, the relationship begins to strain, and the executive asks me, "Can you work with Joe?"

What's Wrong with This Picture?

In a recent survey of consultants and upper-level executives, my company asked, "Do you see evidence that executives resist coaching?" Ninety percent said "yes." The reasons fall into these categories:

- Skills. "I'm uncomfortable with coaching." "I don't know how to coach."
- Role conflict. "I have too many other demands on my time." "Development's not my job."
- Values. "You make your own bed."

If these executives are leaders, why don't they see developing effective followers as their job? In looking for the answer, I reflected on the key characteristics of the best sports coaches. They operate comfortably from the sidelines. They're passionate about the game. They derive deep satisfaction from developing game plans and cultivating players to execute those plans. In effect, they create learning organizations with continuous practice, hands-on simulations, and video-based feedback. They hold players accountable for scoreboard performance, but they also bench players for breaking ranks with team values. They know they may win in the short term with individual superstars but that over time they need a fully functioning team.

Sports coaches focus primarily on their players—motivating, drilling, and strategizing with them. They spend little time on administrative tasks and marketing, except for periodic media appearances. Business CEOs, on the other hand, typically devote less time and attention to their players and more time in meetings with peers, bosses, financial analysts, and key customers.

Why Executives Won't Coach

Based on the results of a survey of consultants and top executives, here are some reasons executives resist coaching:

- fear or discomfort with confrontation
- rate it as a low priority
- requires too much time and patience
- concern that they'll appear weak in having hired or promoted the employee
- don't want to spend time developing employees
- think that the person being coached will be insulted and resistant
- expect others to figure things out for themselves
- don't know how to coach
- are more self-centered than other-directed

- are unaware of the benefits of coaching
- think that coaching shouldn't be necessary at a certain level
- think it's difficult to coach people of same age and pay level
- aren't held accountable for performing a coaching role
- don't see the value
- think it's easier to ignore, circumvent, or terminate problem employees
- think that they'll solve the problems themselves and get credit
- think it's HR's role

For example, an experienced manager took over a plant with old equipment and a new group of young managers. Realizing that he had to pull them together into a strong team, he initiated a series of leadership and team-building sessions. In addition to identifying certain actions for improving the plant, team members said that they wanted the seasoned manager to coach them so that they could learn from his experience. He begged off for six months, saying that the employees "should learn how to run the place by themselves."

So, why won't business leaders coach? Perhaps they don't want to be on the sidelines; they want to be out front. They don't want to nurture and empower; they want to direct and control. Maybe they aren't comfortable in the coaching role. Or, they don't want to participate in the unglamorous process of guiding, praising, and critiquing. But executives who have had positive coaching experiences—either as a coach or a player—report several benefits of coaching:

- Clarifies issues and expectations.

- Creates an environment for solving problems instead of avoiding them.
- Provides personal satisfaction by contributing to others' growth.
- Opens up mutual dialogue to improve work relationships, productivity, quality, and creativity.
- Nurtures others' self-esteem and confidence, eliciting more and better contributions from employees.
- Builds employees' commitment and loyalty.
- Raises the organization's performance bar.
- Encourages employees' continuous personal development.

But even the best coaches can't put points on the scoreboard or make changes happen on their own. Employees must accept ownership of their performance. In turn, coaches can learn from listening to and watching others perform. But to motivate executives to coach, they must see that the time and patience are worthwhile, personally and orga-

Wanted: Chief Executive Coach

The Ideal Coach

Here's how senior-level professionals who responded to a survey describe the ideal coach:

- creates a relationship that isn't forced or contrived
- develops trust and mutual respect
- provides goals and honest information
- takes time to develop relationships by showing a personal interest in employees' development
- shows empathy for personal and professional issues
- provides specific guidance on both personal and business issues
- leads by example; works at improving his or her "needs development" areas

- doesn't force his or her own goals on employees; doesn't push his or her own agenda through employees
- paints the big picture
- talks with employees, not to them
- provides specific performance criteria
- is comfortable and secure; lets people grow
- provides informal feedback, not just a checklist
- helps employees plan for improvement

Section 4: Enhancing Coaching and On-the-job Training

4-17

nizationally. Otherwise, no amount of training or exhortation will get them to embrace the role.

What Makes a Good Coach?

When asked, "What makes a good manager?" Tommy Lasorda, manager of the Los Angeles Dodgers for 20 years, said, "Managing is like holding a dove. Squeeze it too tight, and you kill it. Open your hand too much, and you lose it. My responsibility is to get 25 guys playing for the name on the front of their shirts and not the one on the back."

According to Webster's, a coach is "a person who instructs or trains." We have sports coaches, voice coaches, piano teachers, fitness instructors, and dog trainers—all coaches. Many of them have replaced the word *teacher* with *coach,* perhaps because most of us remember teachers as people who stood in front of a classroom and asked us to take tests. Now, we want instruction and feedback from people who understand how to help us learn.

Two years ago, I decided to learn how to play the piano. As an adult learner, I dreaded the idea of scales and lessons from a big red book. But at the start of every lesson, my piano coach asked, "So, how do you want to fall in love with your piano in the next hour?"—or some other agenda-free phrase. That's a lesson to be learned. As a coach, an executive's role is to help "coachees" express where they are and where they want to be, and then help them get there. It's a mutual process of development.

Recently, we asked some senior-level professionals to identify the characteristics of an ideal coach. They said that a good executive coach is someone who:

- Is highly regarded and successful in the organization.
- Works closely enough with employees to observe their behavior in a variety of situations with diverse individuals and at many organizational levels.
- Respects individuals and is able to work with them in a supportive, nonjudgmental way.
- Has expertise in an area that employees want to improve in their own performance.
- Understands the organization's culture and how employees' behavior is evaluated within that culture.

No one will possess all of these characteristics. But the closer a coach comes to this description, the more effective he or she will be. Such coaches can help others examine their strengths and areas in need of improvement. They can help people identify the changes they must make in order to foster their own growth. And they can help develop the required approaches.

Don Shula, former head coach of the Miami Dolphins, with the only undefeated season in professional football history, was asked what helped him get through tough times with his players. "You need convictions," he said, "and open communication at all times." Shula's mission was to be the best—to win within the rules, with class. Another coach, Phil Jackson of the championship Chicago Bulls, demonstrates that there's no best coaching style. In contrast to the "take no prisoners" approach of Pat Riley, former coach of the L.A. Lakers and N.Y. Knicks, Jackson bases his coaching philosophy on Zen Buddhism to get superstars to see that the power of the team is greater than the sum of its parts. Using such coaching tools as spiritual poetry, he challenges players to drop the brute intimidation and "me first" talk. He even convinced superstar Michael Jordan to share in the coaching role.

Sports coaches often pace the sidelines and yell, seemingly eager to play the game themselves. Many were great players, but they're forbidden to go out onto the field. Unfortunately, executives don't have the same rule. Instead of micromanaging, perhaps they should position themselves as coaches on the sidelines.

Coaxing Executives to Coach

How do we convince executives that coaching is part of their job description? One way would be to tie executive compensation to coaching performance. But we don't want mandated coaching. The best coaching I've seen is when the coach receives some coaching on how to coach. Sun Microsystems CEO Scott McNealy admits to having sought the advice of an external coach to help him coach his staff members.

A coach-the-coach approach can help guide executives toward the coaching role, instead of just adding a new item to their job descriptions. A senior vice president bemoaned to me that he was only a few years from retirement and couldn't visualize any of his managers becoming his successor. So he and I discussed each manager's potential. The VP realized that he wasn't giving the managers opportunities to perform their duties while he coached from the sidelines. We outlined a game plan, and he began creating time in his schedule for heart-to-hearts with each manager. Six months later, the VP said that he liked the new role of coach, though he admitted that it took time to let go of the reins. He even began to see one of the managers blossoming into a potential successor.

Here are some ways to initiate a coach-the-coach effort:

- Suggest that executives use 360-degree feedback in their teams, including the executives themselves. This will give the executives information about their leadership and coaching, as well as create a forum for open dialogue among team members on their interrelationships.

- Suggest that each member of an executive team select a buddy (a peer) to help him or her work on a particular skill area. The top executive can work with a team member (preferably) or with an external coach.

- Provide "training camps" of short, skill-building sessions on such topics as active listening and constructive feedback.

Too often, coaching replicates the parental, military, or bureaucratic models that are hierarchical rather than lateral. The new coaching requires executives to shift from dispensing advice to a "performance partnership" with the goal to improve organizational and individual effectiveness. As teams take on a more important role in organizations, we reject the "I'm in charge" types in favor of executives who behave more like facilitators.

Not all executives can become chief executive coaches. But if they neglect this critical role, they limit their leadership influence. Perhaps they just need a gentle reminder, such as the one on Superbowl champion coach Barry Switzer's desk, inscribed on a clear block of crystal: "There is no limit to what can be done if it doesn't matter who gets the credit."

How to Use Coaching as a Change Management Intervention

By Mary Ashton

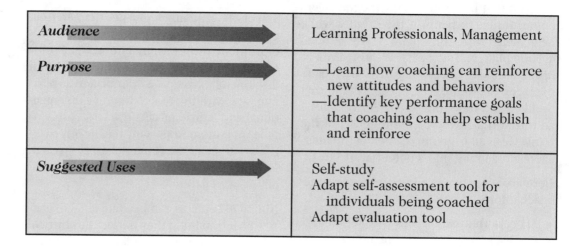

Audience	Learning Professionals, Management
Purpose	—Learn how coaching can reinforce new attitudes and behaviors —Identify key performance goals that coaching can help establish and reinforce
Suggested Uses	Self-study Adapt self-assessment tool for individuals being coached Adapt evaluation tool

Coaching can play an important role in any change management initiative. With the use of a well-developed strategy and approach, organizations can use coaching to:

- Reinforce the norms, values, and behaviors required to achieve business success.

- Rethink and refocus styles of communicating and decision making.

- Support risk-taking and the real-time learning and feedback gained from taking risks.

- Support the development of effective role models.

- Identify organizational behaviors that are problematic (and often reinforced unknowingly by the behaviors of leaders).

- Identify the steps and practices for breaking away from the old norms and mindsets that serve as barriers to positive change.

When linked to a training initiative that supports the concepts and behaviors targeted for coaching, coaching can help individuals, units, and entire organizations grow and change in powerful ways.

Developing a Coaching Approach

In the context of this article, the term "coaching" refers to a process through which a specified coach helps an individual or group of individuals practice new behaviors that are more closely aligned with the business strategy, the performance expectations of the organization, or the goals of a strategic change initiative (your organization can choose how it wants to frame its coaching methodology). Although coaching may be thought of as a one-to-one activity, when implemented as part of a change management or organizational effectiveness initiative, coaching may not only work to realign the behaviors and performance of individuals, but it can also help drive the management competencies required for leading and driving the organization's business success.

Sample Coaching Framework

An effective coaching framework is developed as an extension of an organization's strategic business goals. In developing this framework, an organization's leadership team must answer two questions: The first question helps the team identify the critical performance goals for which coaching may be required; the second question helps the leadership team identify and agree to norms and behaviors that they want to see—and reinforce—in others and themselves. Here are the questions:

1. "What do we need to do to strengthen the effectiveness of our organization through people?"
2. "What are the key behaviors that our people must demonstrate to achieve these performance goals?"

Three to five performance goals might be sufficient to answer the first question for your organization. Examples of performance goals are as follows:

- Strengthen Coordination and Accountability. *(Everyone must understand the role they play in driving the success of the whole business.)*
- Effectively Communicate and Work Together. *(Everyone must understand how we, as an organization, need to communicate and work together to achieve success.)*
- Plan and Use Resources Effectively and Efficiently. *(Everyone must know what we need to do and when we need to do it in order to achieve success.)*
- Use Verifiable and Meaningful Data to Improve Performance. *(Everyone must know how we measure performance to attain and maintain success—you get what you measure!)*

Examples of behaviors that support these goals are listed on the following self-assessment tool. While formal competency studies are often considered the most effective method of identifying behavioral requirements, effective approaches to coaching can often be developed without formal studies. The key is getting the leadership team on the same page when it comes to the strategic behaviors that need to be communicated and reinforced throughout the organization.

Principles of Coaching

In addition to identifying and articulating performance goals and behaviors, a coaching strategy needs to articulate the overarching principles that guide the coaching process. Some proven principles include the following:

1. Target the individuals for coaching who have the greatest impact upon your business strategy and/or change initiative.
2. Design the coaching process around the specific needs and interests of the individuals and groups being coached. To do this:
   - Use a self-assessment instrument to encourage personal reflection and goal setting.
   - Structure coaching around the issues of concern to the individuals and groups involved.
   - Use nonjudgmental behavior and constructive feedback during coaching and training sessions to increase self-esteem and risk-taking.
   - Encourage those being coached to identify their own goals for coaching.
3. Motivate interest and readiness for learning through coaching by:
   - Developing trust between the coach and those being coached.
   - Using experiential exercises that promote reflection and the "un-sticking" of old mind sets.
   - Structuring training and coaching interventions around real work and business issues.
4. Encourage trust and open communication with the individuals being coached by:
   - Respecting confidentially (e.g., the coach should not share information from the completed self-assessments with others).
   - Practicing active listening, feedback, and facilitation techniques.
   - Encouraging individuals and groups to take responsibility and action.
   - Using and encouraging proactive communication.
5. Select coaches wisely. Good coaches don't have to walk on water but they do need to:
   - Be credible and respectable.
   - Know how to give objective feedback.
   - Demonstrate care and concern for people and the organization.

Section 4: Enhancing Coaching and On-the-job Training

- Be familiar with your organization and its coaching strategy and approach.
- Have sufficient time (and be willing to make the time) to observe behavior and listen first.

6. Recognize that results from coaching aren't immediate and that an effective coaching process needs to:

  - Provide sufficient time for individuals to rethink old behaviors and to try out and learn new ones.
  - Involve participants in evaluating the coaching experience (it's part of the learning opportunity).

Lessons Learned from Coaching Initiatives

1. Use a structured self-assessment process to encourage those being coached to reflect on their own behaviors and priorities before the coaching starts.

2. Encourage the supervisors of those being coached to communicate the business context of the coaching process and why learning and development through coaching is important and valued.

3. Use coaching to focus those being coached on understanding and solving real problems within their organization.

4. Use training and coaching as mutually reinforcing interventions.

5. As always, record and celebrate success!

Sample Coaching Tools

Coaching tools help define and shape the coaching process. Use these tools (included) as a guide for structuring your organization's coaching approach.

—Self-assessment Tool

—Sample Coaching and Learning Evaluation

Business Leadership and Operations

Strengthen Coordination and Accountability

	Importance to My Job	How Effectively I Do This		
	Not Important — Very Important	Not Effective — Very Effective	Not Sure	Not Applicable
1. Work with others to set and clarify expectations.	1 2 3 4 5 6 7	1 2 3 4 5 6 7	☐	☐
2. Seek employees' input on upcoming changes that affect their job.	1 2 3 4 5 6 7	1 2 3 4 5 6 7	☐	☐
3. Talk with employees about upcoming changes so that they understand how these changes relate to business success.	1 2 3 4 5 6 7	1 2 3 4 5 6 7	☐	☐
4. Assist employees in working through changes that affect their job.	1 2 3 4 5 6 7	1 2 3 4 5 6 7	☐	☐
5. Show interest in people's ideas related to their job and the business.	1 2 3 4 5 6 7	1 2 3 4 5 6 7	☐	☐
6. Seek out opportunities to communicate and work together on improving performance across the mail stream.	1 2 3 4 5 6 7	1 2 3 4 5 6 7	☐	☐
7. Clarify business roles and responsibilities with my supervisor.	1 2 3 4 5 6 7	1 2 3 4 5 6 7	☐	☐
8. Set my business goals and objectives.	1 2 3 4 5 6 7	1 2 3 4 5 6 7	☐	☐

Developed by Wendy Boiles

	Importance to My Job	How Effectively I Do This		
	Not Important — Very Important	Not Effective — Very Effective	Not Sure	Not Applicable
9. Work with employees to set their business goals and objectives.	1 2 3 4 5 6 7	1 2 3 4 5 6 7	☐	☐
10. Communicate issues and problems that affect the mail stream.	1 2 3 4 5 6 7	1 2 3 4 5 6 7	☐	☐
11. Recognize employees on a regular basis.	1 2 3 4 5 6 7	1 2 3 4 5 6 7	☐	☐
12. Ask for feedback from others.	1 2 3 4 5 6 7	1 2 3 4 5 6 7	☐	☐
13. Give feedback to others.	1 2 3 4 5 6 7	1 2 3 4 5 6 7	☐	☐
14. Use two-way communication to identify and work through performance issues.	1 2 3 4 5 6 7	1 2 3 4 5 6 7	☐	☐

Team Building and Facilitation Skills

Effectively Communicate and Work Together

	Importance to My Job	How Effectively I Do This		
	Not Important — Very Important	Not Effective — Very Effective	Not Sure	Not Applicable
1. Set meeting purpose and agenda.	1 2 3 4 5 6 7	1 2 3 4 5 6 7	☐	☐
2. Help groups define their purpose and goals.	1 2 3 4 5 6 7	1 2 3 4 5 6 7	☐	☐
3. Ask questions for clarification and understanding.	1 2 3 4 5 6 7	1 2 3 4 5 6 7	☐	☐

		Importance to My Job	How Effectively I Do This	Not Sure	Not Applicable

4. Listen in order to understand others' points of view.

Not Important — Very Important: 1 2 3 4 5 6 7
Not Effective — Very Effective: 1 2 3 4 5 6 7
Not Sure ☐ Not Applicable ☐

5. Sumarize what others say to ensure understanding.

Not Important — Very Important: 1 2 3 4 5 6 7
Not Effective — Very Effective: 1 2 3 4 5 6 7
Not Sure ☐ Not Applicable ☐

6. Solicit information and input from others.

Not Important — Very Important: 1 2 3 4 5 6 7
Not Effective — Very Effective: 1 2 3 4 5 6 7
Not Sure ☐ Not Applicable ☐

7. Help others explore ideas and opportunities.

Not Important — Very Important: 1 2 3 4 5 6 7
Not Effective — Very Effective: 1 2 3 4 5 6 7
Not Sure ☐ Not Applicable ☐

8. Encourage the sharing of feedback.

Not Important — Very Important: 1 2 3 4 5 6 7
Not Effective — Very Effective: 1 2 3 4 5 6 7
Not Sure ☐ Not Applicable ☐

Problem Solving and Performance Improvement

Use of Verifiable and Meaningful Data to Improve Performance

1. Bring people together to identify and solve problems.

Not Important — Very Important: 1 2 3 4 5 6 7
Not Effective — Very Effective: 1 2 3 4 5 6 7
Not Sure ☐ Not Applicable ☐

2. Identify meaningful data to assess performance.

Not Important — Very Important: 1 2 3 4 5 6 7
Not Effective — Very Effective: 1 2 3 4 5 6 7
Not Sure ☐ Not Applicable ☐

3. Establish performance measures that are linked to business goals.

Not Important — Very Important: 1 2 3 4 5 6 7
Not Effective — Very Effective: 1 2 3 4 5 6 7
Not Sure ☐ Not Applicable ☐

4. Use and validate data to monitor business problems.

Not Important — Very Important: 1 2 3 4 5 6 7
Not Effective — Very Effective: 1 2 3 4 5 6 7
Not Sure ☐ Not Applicable ☐

5. Seek out underlying causes of problems.

Not Important — Very Important: 1 2 3 4 5 6 7
Not Effective — Very Effective: 1 2 3 4 5 6 7
Not Sure ☐ Not Applicable ☐

Self-assessment Tool *(continued)*

	Importance to My Job	How Effectively I Do This		
	Not Important — Very Important	Not Effective — Very Effective	Not Sure	Not Applicable
6. Use reports on a regular basis to make decisions.	1 2 3 4 5 6 7	1 2 3 4 5 6 7	☐	☐
7. Help others to understand reports and data for decision making.	1 2 3 4 5 6 7	1 2 3 4 5 6 7	☐	☐
8. Base decisions on an assessment and comparison of costs and benefits.	1 2 3 4 5 6 7	1 2 3 4 5 6 7	☐	☐

Use Resources Efficiently and Productively

	Importance to My Job	How Effectively I Do This		
	Not Important — Very Important	Not Effective — Very Effective	Not Sure	Not Applicable
1. Determine performance standards.	1 2 3 4 5 6 7	1 2 3 4 5 6 7	☐	☐
2. Assess how resources are being used compared with specific standards.	1 2 3 4 5 6 7	1 2 3 4 5 6 7	☐	☐
3. Discuss performance with employees.	1 2 3 4 5 6 7	1 2 3 4 5 6 7	☐	☐
4. Develop an action plan that addresses performance problems.	1 2 3 4 5 6 7	1 2 3 4 5 6 7	☐	☐

Sample Coaching and Learning Evaluation

PART I – To help us assess the coaching, training, and teamwork activities conducted over the past few weeks, please indicate which of the activities listed below you have thought about, tried out, and/or actively worked on as a result of these sessions. We would also like to know if you feel these activities are currently supported, or should be more widely supported, by management.

After reviewing each activity, please use the boxes within the five columns to record a check mark as appropriate:

COLUMN A, check if you feel you *have learned something about or have become more interested in this activity.*

COLUMN B, check if you *have personally worked on or been involved in this activity.*

COLUMN C, check if you would *like more information about or training in this activity.*

COLUMN D, check if this activity is *currently being practiced and encouraged by management overall.*

COLUMN E, check if this activity *should be more widely practiced or encouraged by management.*

STRENGTHEN COORDINATION AND ACCOUNTABILITY	A	B	C	D	E
Set and clarify expectations.					
Seek employees' input on changes.					
Talk with employees about changes.					
Assist employees in working through changes.					
Show interest in peoples' ideas related to their job and the business.					
Seek out opportunities to communicate and work together on improving performance across the mail stream.					
Clarify business roles and responsibilities.					
Set my business goals and objectives.					
Work with employees to set their business goals and objectives.					
Communicate issues and problems that affect the mail stream.					
Recognize employees on a regular basis.					
Ask for feedback from others.					
Give feedback to others.					
Use two-way communication to identify and work through performance issues.					

EFFECTIVELY COMMUNICATE AND WORK TOGETHER	A	B	C	D	E
Set meeting purpose and agenda.					
Help groups define their purpose and goals.					
Ask questions for clarification and understanding.					
Listen in order to understand others' point of view.					
Summarize what others say to ensure understanding.					
Solicit information and input from others.					
Encourage the sharing of feedback.					

USE OF VERIFIABLE AND MEANINGFUL DATA TO IMPROVE PERFORMANCE	A	B	C	D	E
Bring people together to identify and solve problems.					
Identify meaningful data to assess performance.					
Establish performance measures that are linked to business goals.					
Use and validate data to monitor business problems.					
Seek out underlying causes of problems.					
Use reports on a regular basis to make decisions.					
Help others to understand reports and data for decision making.					
Base decisions on an assessment and comparison of costs and benefits.					

USE RESOURCES EFFICIENTLY AND PRODUCTIVELY	A	B	C	D	E
Determine performance standards.					
Assess how resources are being used compared with specific standards.					
Discuss performance with employees.					
Develop an action plan that addresses performance problems.					
Analyze and make decisions based upon performance measurements.					
Make resource decisions based upon an understanding of costs, benefits, and budget constraints.					
Investigate the impact of potential decisions and events to prevent additional problems.					

COLUMN A, check if you feel you *have learned something about or have become more interested in this activity.*

COLUMN B, check if you *have personally worked on or been involved in this activity.*

COLUMN C, check if you would *like more information about or training in this activity.*

COLUMN D, check if this activity is *currently being practiced and encouraged by management overall.*

COLUMN E, check if this activity *should be more widely practiced or encouraged by management.*

PART II – Feedback and Suggestions: To assist us in evaluating the value of the coaching and training activities overall, please take a few moments to answer the following questions. Your candid comments will be greatly appreciated.

1. What has been the most valuable aspect of the coaching and training you have received over the past few weeks?

   _____

   _____

   _____

   _____

2. What experiences (opportunities, successes) have you had in using some of the tools and techniques presented through the coaching and training? (In other words, please explain how you have used any of the communication, problem-solving, data analysis, or team-building techniques in performing your job.)

   _____

   _____

   _____

   _____

3. In terms of changes in others' behaviors, actions, or attitudes (individuals or groups), what have you seen or experienced that you feel may have been influenced by the recent coaching, training, and team-building activities?

   _____

   _____

   _____

   _____

4. If you could make recommendations to management regarding what they could do to further support the ideas and techniques presented through coaching and training, what would your recommendations be?

   _____

   _____

   _____

5. How could the coaching, training, and team-building activities be improved to better meet the needs of our organization?

   _____

   _____

   _____

   _____

ONCE AGAIN, THANK YOU FOR TAKING THE TIME TO SHARE YOUR THOUGHTS WITH US.

Exercise: How to Plan for Effective Coaching and Counseling

By Scott Parry

Audience	Supervisors and Managers
Purpose	—Learn a process for planning constructive interpersonal communication —Be able to analyze interpersonal communication to identify aspects that need improvement —Understand the characteristics of constructive counseling —Internalize the value of this information for job performance
Suggested Uses	Group exercise for those who have or will assume coaching and individual performance improvement responsibilities Could be adapted for self-study or one-to-one learning

Introduction

There are three steps to the planning of any interpersonal communication. First, we must assess the situation. Second, we must decide what our objectives are—the desired outcome. Third, we must decide what information we want to give and to get, and in what sequence. That is, we must develop our game plan, or strategy.

Most of us have objectives in mind (step two) when we interact with others. What we tend to do, however, is spend too little time on steps one and three. The following outline should be helpful.

1. Assess the Situation

What do I know about this other person? What information am I likely to need when we talk? Should I talk to anyone else before the session? Have I gotten all sides of the story? What are the other person's objectives likely to be? How is the other person likely to react to our talk? Is it likely to be conducted on a parent-child or an adult-adult basis?

2. Decide on Your Objectives

What are you trying to accomplish? Are you "going for broke," or does this session pave the way for another one? How will you know you've succeeded? What evidence will you look for to tell you that you can conclude the session? What specific action do you want each of you to take as a result of this session? By what date? (That is, what time frame is needed to carry out the desired action?)

3. Develop Your Game Plan

What information do I want to give? What information do I have to get? What is my strategy (sequence) for the giving and getting of information? What analogies, explanations, and examples will I use to make my information understood? Where do I want to be directive and nondirective? Where should I be neutral and avoid influencing the employee (low bias)? What are my opening and closing lines?

In a simple interaction that will last only 5–10 minutes, these three steps can be done mentally in a minute or so. But when the interaction is likely to take longer and be more involved (e.g., a performance appraisal, a problem-solving session, a career discussion), then it's a good idea to spend more time, say 10–20 minutes, planning for the session.

Exercise: Leader's Notes

Time

1½–2 hours

Number of Participants

Any number, but smaller groups are better for the discussion aspects of the exercise.

Facilitator Expertise

Group facilitation skills; hands-on experience in coaching/counseling is a plus.

Materials and Equipment

Flipchart and markers

Answers to Questions About Counseling Session Script 1

Handouts

Coaching and Counseling Planning Sheet (blank, for participant use on the job)

Counseling Session Script 1

Questions About Counseling Session Script 1

Coaching and Counseling Planning Sheet (Sample)

Counseling Session Script 2

Procedure

1. Explain the process for planning coaching and counseling interpersonal communications, based on the introduction to this piece. Have the three steps written on a flipchart and refer to the chart in your discussion.

2. Hand out the blank Counseling and Planning Sheet and go over the questions. Ask participants why they think these questions are important in planning constructive communication. Are these steps things they already use on the job? Do they encounter situations in which this approach would be helpful? Not helpful?

3. Hand out Counseling Session Script 1. Give participants about 10 minutes to read it and make notes on it about what they liked and disliked regarding the way Rudy, the supervisor, handled the interaction.

4. Hand out the Questions About Counseling Session Script 1. Give participants about 15 minutes to answer them.

5. Go over the script paragraph by paragraph and ask participants what they thought was positive about the interaction and what they thought Rudy should have done differently. Why would different approaches positively affect performance? Use Answers to Questions About Counseling Session Script 1 to make additional points, and discuss the questions and answers with participants as relevant.

6. Hand out the filled in version of the Counseling and Planning Sheet and Counseling Session Script 2. Give participants about 15 minutes to read them.

7. Ask participants their reactions to the materials. Are they surprised by any of the recommendations? Do they disagree with any and, if so, why? What do others feel?

8. Ask participants what general principles of constructive communication they derive from these materials. List them on the flipchart.

9. Ask each participant what particular piece of information he or she learned that will be useful on the job. What benefit to performance do they anticipate: theirs, an employee's, their department's, etc.? (You might tell them that you plan to ask them this, and give them a few minutes to think about it first.)

Coaching and Counseling Planning Sheet

1. What is the situation in brief?

_____

_____

2. What are my objectives? What am I trying to accomplish?

_____

_____

3. How will I know if I've succeeded? What evidence will I look for to tell me that I can conclude the session?

_____

_____

4. What are the objectives of the other person likely to be? What does he/she want to accomplish?

_____

_____

5. What specific action do I want each of us to take as a result of this session?

_____

_____

6. What time frame is needed to carry out these actions?

_____

_____

_____

7. What information do I want to give?

_____

_____

_____

8. What information do I have to get?

_____

_____

_____

9. What is my strategy, or game plan, for the giving and getting of information noted in 7 and 8 above? That is, in what sequence do I give and get?

_____

_____

_____

10. (To be completed after the session.) How did it turn out? What did I learn about counseling and coaching that will influence my next session (either with this person or another one)?

_____

_____

_____

_____

Counseling Session Script 1

Directions: In the Notes section that follows the script below, indicate with a few words what you do and do not like about the way Rudy counseled Ted. Every time Rudy speaks (the odd-numbered lines), give your evaluation of the appropriateness of Rudy's comment and/or your suggested wording (what you would like Rudy to have said).

- -

1. *Rudy:* I just had a call from Mr. Sewell. He said that one of his people called you about expediting an order and you refused. What's the story?

2. *Ted:* Mario called me. When I tried to tell him what work I had ahead of the order, he told me that was my problem, and if I didn't want Mr. Sewell on my tail, I'd better push the order through.

3. *Rudy:* What did you tell him?

4. *Ted:* I told him to shove it. He'll get it when he gets it.

5. *Rudy:* You told him to shove it?

6. *Ted:* Yeah, I've got a pile this high (he demonstrates) on my desk, and I can't stop my other work just for them.

7. *Rudy:* Do you think that's the way we should respond to other employees who come to us for help?

8. *Ted:* No, and I don't need a lecture. I know I've been a bad boy. But if you had to put up with Mario's pushy manner, you'd lose your cool, too.

9. *Rudy:* But that's no reason to add fuel to his fire. What you should have done is find out when he has to have it by ... at the latest. Then see if you can get it to him with your normal flow of taking the orders in sequence.

10. *Ted:* He said he needed it immediately; that's what they all say. What we need is a system for stamping the time we receive each order so that we ...

11. *Rudy* (interrupting): What we need is a little courtesy. Now I've got to call Mr. Sewell back and apologize ... or maybe you should, since you caused the mess. No, I'll do it, since it was me he called. What do you want me to tell him?

12. *Ted:* Tell him I'm swamped with orders, but that I'll interrupt everything to dig out his lousy order and send it over.

13. *Rudy:* Good. And next time Mario calls, don't be so childish. Try to count slowly to 10 before you get us both in deep water. Okay?

14. *Ted:* Okay.

- -

NOTES

Questions About Counseling Session Script 1

1. What do you think of the way Rudy began his counseling session with Ted (Line 1)? Would you have started the talk differently?

_____

_____

_____

_____

_____

2. During the first half of his talk with Ted, Rudy asked questions (Lines 1, 3, 5, 7). Was this appropriate?

_____

_____

_____

_____

_____

3. Based on your reading of the script, what do you think Rudy's objectives are in having a counseling session with Ted? Are they appropriate?

_____

_____

_____

_____

_____

4. How well do you think Rudy has achieved his objectives (based on Ted's responses)?

_____

_____

_____

_____

5. Suppose that you have been asked to design a form for use by managers, supervisors, counselors, personnel specialists, etc., in helping them to prepare for a counseling session ... a tool to improve the quality and effectiveness of such sessions. What parts or sections would you have on your form? That is, what question or issues would you list and in what sequence?

_____

_____

_____

_____

6. The comments that Rudy made during his counseling session might be classified as follows:

    Critical...................... (C) .... finding fault, blaming

    Advising................... (A) .... telling someone what to do

    Searching................. (S) .... asking for more information

    Empathetic.......... ..... (E) .... showing understanding

    Reread each of Rudy's comments and label each with one or more of the four letters noted above to indicate Rudy's intent on each comment:

    Comment No.

    1. _____

    3. _____

    5. _____

    7. _____

    9. _____

    11. _____

    13. _____

7. Our interactions with other humans are conducted on either a parent-to-child basis or an adult-to-adult basis. The Critical response (C) is the hallmark of a judgmental parent, while the Advising response (A) is typical of a nurturing parent. Each one treats the other person like a child. Similarly, the Searching and Empathetic responses, (S) and (E), are adult responses that treat the other person as a fellow adult.

    Looking again at Rudy's responses that you labeled above, to what degree was the counseling session conducted on an adult-to-adult basis?

    _____

    _____

    _____

    _____

    _____

8. When should a counseling session be conducted on a parent-to-child basis? When should it be adult-to-adult?

    _____

    _____

    _____

    _____

    _____

Answers to Questions About Counseling Session Script 1

1. Rudy began with a quick, objective, neutral (unbiased) statement of the situation as described by Mario's boss, Mr. Sewell. No problem here. It would be wrong for Rudy to start with small talk or anything that would delay getting to the point. If you feel that Rudy's "and you refused" is a critical comment, this phrase could be dropped. Either way, Rudy's initial comment should get Ted doing the talking. His first step is to find out what happened so that he can assess the situation.

2. Yes. Questions are Rudy's most useful tool for getting the information needed to assess the situation. Rudy is in the fact-finding phase of their talk. However, although his first two questions (lines 1 and 3) are neutral and adult-to-adult, he then asks questions that are biased and parent-to-child (lines 5 and 7). These move the session from fact-finding to fault-finding, putting Ted on the defensive.

3. Although Rudy would probably tell us that his objective was to correct the situation, the script suggests that Rudy also wanted to reprimand Ted. This may get in the way of correcting the situation and reducing the likelihood of a similar recurrence down the road. And these are the objectives that we feel are appropriate.

4. Ted's responses are those of a naughty child, alternately accepting and rejecting blame. "I know I've been a bad boy" and "if you had to put up with ..." and "What we need is a system for ..." Yes, Ted has agreed to process Mario's order, but mainly to get Rudy off his back. And relations between Mario and Ted will probably be worse than ever.

5. The best way to get feedback on how you answered this question is to compare your list of issues and parts of the form with our Coaching and Counseling Planning Sheet. See how many of the questions on the Coaching and Counseling Planning Sheet were asked on your form. See if you identified any issues that would make the Coaching and Counseling Planning Sheet more effective. Then use these issues as guideposts when you prepare for your next counseling session.

   Our purpose in asking this question, of course, is not to test your ability to critique or redesign a form. Rather, we hope the exercise has helped you to come up with a checklist or set of guidelines that you will refer to before you next sit down to coach or counsel an employee.

6. Here's how we have rated Rudy's intent on each comment:

   Comment No.
   1. (S), although you may have seen it as (C)
   3. (S)
   5. (C) or (S), depending on tone of voice and facial expression
   7. (C)
   9. (C) and (A)
   11. (C), ending with (S)
   13. (C)

7. Only at the start (fact-finding stage) was the counseling session conducted on an adult-to-adult basis. However, after the first 4–6 lines, the dialogue lapsed into scolding and blaming, with Rudy blaming Ted and Ted blaming everything else: the workload, Mario's pushy manner, the lack of a system for stamping the time as orders are received.

8. Unlike sessions where the purpose is to discipline or reprimand, a counseling session should be conducted on an adult-to-adult basis. This is not easy, since the person being counseled may find it difficult to accept the fact that there is a problem or that their behavior has not been appropriate. (Mark Twain once noted that there is no such thing as constructive criticism ... the phrase is an oxymoron ... a contradiction in terms!)

   Thus, we believe that all counseling should be conducted on an adult-to-adult basis if it is to be effective. If the person being counseled responds as a parent or child, at least the counselor can remain in the adult state and not let the interaction lapse into an emotional bout whose outcome is a "win-lose" at best and a "lose-lose" at worst.

Coaching and Counseling Planning Sheet (Sample)

1. What is the situation in brief?

   One of our managers, Mr. Sewell, called to report that Ted refused to expedite an order for one of his people, Mario. Ted is a good man, but doesn't always handle orders in the sequence they come in. He's not as well organized as he should be, and therefore may get shaken under pressure.

2. What are my objectives? What am I trying to accomplish?

   A. To get the immediate problem solved—the order sent to Mario.

   B. To address the long-range problem—getting organized and prioritizing the handling of orders.

   C. To accomplish this in a way that is supportive of Ted and that doesn't add fuel to the fire.

3. How will I know if I've succeeded? What evidence will I look for to tell me that I can conclude the session?

   I want Ted to see the need for actions A and B noted above, and to accept them, perhaps even come up with them himself, if I can stay in a nondirective mode and remain adult-adult. Ultimately, I'll know I've succeeded when Ted gets the order to Mario and sets up a system for prioritizing the orders.

4. What are the objectives of the other person likely to be? What does he/she want to accomplish?

   Ted probably knows that he shouldn't have blown up and shouted at Mario. As soon as I bring up the situation, he's likely to be apologetic and defensive and will want me to get off his back. However, my acceptance of his apology won't solve the problem ... at least not over the long term.

5. What specific action do I want each of us to take as a result of this session?

   Ted should get the order to Mario (immediately), and get a system for stamping and prioritizing orders (long range).

   I should call Mr. Sewell to apologize and to tell him the order is on the way. I could also have Ted call him, but (a) that strikes me as punitive ... parent-child, and (b) Mr. Sewell called me and not Ted. I don't want to risk having him bent out of shape.

6. What time frame is needed to carry out these actions?

   Get order to Mario—within the next two hours. New system in place—by the end of next week.

Coaching and Counseling Planning Sheet (Sample)

7. What information do I want to give?

    A. Mr. Sewell called, unhappy.

    B. I know you're quite busy; big backlog.

    C. I want to support you ... help you avoid future problems.

    D.

    E.

    F.

8. What information do I have to get?

    A. Why did you refuse?

    B. What caused the problem?

    C. How can we avoid future occurrences?

    D. What shall I tell Mr. Sewell?

    E.

    F.

    (These questions must be asked in a supportive, nondirective manner ... not as stated here.)

9. What is my strategy, or game plan, for the giving and getting of information noted in 7 and 8 above? That is, in what sequence do I give and get?

    I will listen first and avoid passing judgment. After we've agreed on the problem, I'll get Ted to work out the solution. Here is my sequence for giving and getting the information noted above: 7A - 8A - 8B - 7B - 7C - 8C - 8D.

10. (To be completed after the session.) How did it turn out? What did I learn about counseling and coaching that will influence my next session (either with this person or another one)?

    The session turned out better than expected. Ted was cooperative and is going to work up a system for stamping and prioritizing orders in the future.

    What did I learn? My natural tendency is be very directive: "Do *this,* and *that,* and do it *now.*" Sort of a "shoot first and ask questions later" style. I had to resist the temptation to chew Ted out and tell him what I want done. But I can see from this session that my old style is not as effective as drawing Ted out and getting him to work out the solution. I'm still not comfortable with the new style (it's not natural), but if it works, I'm going to stick with it!

After completing the Coaching and Counseling Planning Sheet, Rudy was prepared to meet with Ted to correct the situation. As you read the script of their meeting, notice the techniques that Rudy is now applying, and how effective they are in getting Ted's cooperation and willingness to correct the situation.

1. *Rudy:* I just had a call from Mr. Sewell. He said that one of his people called you about expediting an order and you refused. What's the story?

2. *Ted:* Mario called me. When I tried to tell him what work I had ahead of the order, and that it meant a lot of extra work for me to dig it out, he told me that that was my problem and if I didn't want Mr. Sewell on my tail, I'd better push the order through.

3. *Rudy:* What did you tell him?

4. *Ted:* I told him to shove it. He'll get it when he gets it.

5. *Rudy:* Now, you say it would mean a lot of extra work for you to dig out the order. I've always felt that you were very effective at finding orders that are buried in the "process" file...

6. *Ted:* Well, it's no big deal to find his order. I just don't like people telling me how to do my job.

7. *Rudy:* I can't blame you for that—no one likes that. What is the status of your current work load?

8. *Ted:* I've got a pile this high (he demonstrates) on my desk, and I can't stop my other work just for them.

9. *Rudy:* Okay. We've found the problem. Mario's request interrupts your regular work, and his manner of asking leaves something to be desired. You already have a heavy backlog of work. As a result, you told him off, which has now led to getting Mr. Sewell and me into the act. Is that a fair description of the situation?

10. *Ted:* Yeah, that's about the size of it.

11. *Rudy:* What are our options at this point?

12. *Ted:* Well, I guess I better go back and find the order and send them the stuff. Otherwise I'll have Mr. Sewell and you on my tail.

13. *Rudy:* When does he need the stuff?

14. *Ted:* He said immediately; they all say that. What we need is a system for stamping the time we receive each order, so we can prioritize special requests based on what the backlog is, and not promise what we can't deliver. Sometimes I ask people what the latest time is that they must have it by. I guess I should have asked him that.

15. *Rudy:* That's a good question to ask.

16. *Ted:* And maybe I'd have had enough time to process his order in the normal flow of taking the orders in sequence.

17. *Rudy:* Good thinking. And I like your idea of stamping the time and date of each order received. I wasn't aware that we weren't doing that already.

18. *Ted:* It's not my idea. We used to do it when Joe was here. But then ... well ... I don't know why we dropped it.

19. *Rudy:* You know, Ted, with your experience around here, I think you're just the one to get it going again. Do you think you could find that old sheet that outlined the procedures, or make up another one if you can't find it? I know you're buried in orders right now, so there's no hurry ... it could be done next week if this week is bad.

20. *Ted:* Yeah, I can do that. And I've got some ideas on how to improve on the old system.

21. *Rudy:* Great. Let me see it when you've got it together, say, by Thursday of next week. Okay?

22. *Ted:* Okay. And I may have it ready sooner.

23. *Rudy:* All the better. Well, I promised Mr. Sewell I'd call him back, so I'll tell him you're pulling his order together now and that Mario will have it within the next two hours. That will please him. Anything else I should tell him?

24. *Ted:* (pause): Yeah, tell him I'm sorry I blew my cool.

NOTES

Lines 1 and 3 are fact-finding in nature. Rudy is simply asking Ted what happened.

Rather than criticizing Ted for his response to Mario, Rudy remains adult. He continues to deal with facts rather than with emotions. Lines 5 and 7 combine the empathetic and the searching (inquiring) responses.

Line 9 lets Ted know that this talk has problem-solving, and not reprimand, as its objective. Although Rudy's "you told him off" acknowledges Ted's inappropriate behavior, there is no blame or scolding in his message. And he returns in lines 11 and 13 to his favorite mode of response: searching (information getting).

Rudy's treatment of Ted as an adult rather than a child brings out the information needed to solve the problem. In line 15, Rudy acknowledges this.

In lines 17 and 19, Rudy treats Ted on an adult-to-adult basis, thereby eliciting responsible adult behavior on Ted's part. This is important to the solution of the problem that Rudy set out to identify and solve.

In lines 21 and 23, Rudy now has an action plan. He knows what each party must do to correct the problem. Notice that in both lines, Rudy is using the searching response (asking questions) to make sure that Ted is committed to and will deliver on his part of the agreement.

How to Give On-the-job Instruction: A Nine-step Approach

By John Sample

Audience →	Learning Professionals, Supervisors, Managers
Purpose →	—Be able to identify factors suggesting the need for on-the-job training —Learn a process for conducting effective on-the-job instruction
Suggested Uses →	Self-study Resource for training presentation or information-sharing Training prework or handout

Introduction: Why Conduct On-the-job Training?

Supervisors are in a unique position to influence the learning and performance of individuals and teams. It is a supervisor who ordinarily conducts periodic job appraisals, and he or she will often write or contribute to the development of job descriptions for their employees. These two factors alone suggest that the supervisor is the one person most likely to provide job-related instruction to his or her employee.

Supervisors who rose from within the ranks will often have technical knowledge and skills, and their job now is to get the work done through the cooperative efforts of others. Unfortunately, most technically trained supervisors will not have had experience in the basics of instructing their employees on how to perform specific tasks. Furthermore, scheduling employees to attend classes run by technically competent instructors who have been through train-the-trainer programs can be expensive, labor intensive, and time consuming.

Learning on the job has great power for the organization. Employees are able to apply directly what they learn from the supervisor. Relationships between supervisors and employees will improve as job expectations become clearer and as feedback increases on job performance. The instruction process becomes a form of positive reinforcement; everybody benefits from this win-win approach to improving performance.

Investigating the Necessity for On-the-job Instruction

Prior to engaging in on-the-job instruction, the supervisor should have received an initiating cue that training may be necessary. These cues can come from several sources, including the following:

- Customer complaints.
- Complaints from coworkers or team members.
- Breakdown with processes and systems attributed to the employee.
- Current tasks not performed to mastery.
- New tasks or responsibilities for the employee.

- Performance appraisal indicating weaknesses.

Next, the supervisor must investigate to determine whether a need for additional instruction is the cause of the problem or whether another factor is responsible for poor performance. Gilbert and Mager and Pipe have long advocated a multiple-factors approach that can lead to performance improvement, including the following:

- Information—adequate understanding of expectations; adequate feedback on performance.

- Resources—adequate equipment, time, support personnel.

- Incentives—contingent on performance; perceived as desirable by employee.

- Capacity—people accurately matched to the job.

- Motivation—desire to perform.

- Knowledge/skill level—ability to do the job.

Prior to engaging in on-the-job instruction, the supervisor should eliminate as many of these factors as possible as causes of poor performance. If lack of knowledge remains as a contributing cause, then conducting on-the-job instruction will be appropriate. Be sure to address all other remaining factors as well, however. Instruction to increase knowledge will be of no consequence to an employee who has inadequate resources or incentives to perform.

Providing On-the-job Instruction: Nine Steps

Providing effective on-the-job instruction involves nine steps, outlined by educational psychologist, Dr. Robert Gagne. They include the following:

1. Gain Attention

Capturing the attention of your learners is an obvious first step to making them receptive to the information about to be delivered. The supervisor can provide a stimulus that focuses the learner's attention. Examples include using verbal signals such as, "We are expected to use a different process in the future," or "It seems like you are having trouble with that task. I should take some time to review it with you." Asking a thought-provoking question or stating a serious problem are other ways to get the learner's attention.

2. Inform the Learner of the Objective

This event is designed to create an expectancy about what is to be learned. Creating a self-expectation consistent with the learning objective will increase the likelihood of commitment to what is to be learned. The supervisor can call attention to the formally stated learning objectives, or discuss the objectives with the learners. Asking the learner to state in his or her own words the essences of the instructional objective will allow the supervisor to determine if the learner understands the objective. In this context, a learning objective is one that states what the learner will be able to perform after the instruction. It important that learners comprehend what they will be able to do or to perform once the instruction has been completed.

3. Stimulate Recall of Prior Learning

Employees will bring to the work setting years of accumulated experiences and learning, some good and some not so good. In a general sense, the supervisor can stimulate recall by asking the learners to think about previous experiences or, in the case of a specific task, to recall what occurred in previous attempts to perform the task. If the instructional objective requires complex operations, then specific recall and review of lower level prerequisite skills may be necessary before on-the-job instruction can proceed.

4. Present the Stimulus

In this context, stimulus means the way the objective of the on-the-job instruction will be achieved. The stimulus for instruction will depend upon what is to be learned. For example:

- If the objective is the *acquisition of information,* then the stimulus could be reading material, a didactic lecture, or a video that depicts the content.

- If the objective requires the demonstration of a *psychomotor skill,* then the stimulus is a demonstration of the task to be performed along with verbal directions.

- If the objective requires the *expression*

of an attitude, then the stimulus is a demonstration of the desired attitude as specified in a policy or model.

5. Provide Learning Guidance

The level of guidance required will depend on several factors, including levels of ability, amount of time to conduct the on-the-job instruction, and complexity of the learning objective. If problem solving is the objective, then guidance that uses a discovery method (as opposed to a highly directive method) may be desirable. In problem solving, the strategy is to expect the learner to solve the problems, and minimal assistance may be provided.

6. Elicit Performance

In this instructional event the "learner" is expected to be a "performer," that is, he or she is expected to perform as instructed. Performance is an inference that learning has taken place. The instructor can expect that performance will not be perfect, and that further improvement will be necessary.

7. Provide Feedback

When performance is being demonstrated, feedback about performance will enable the learner to improve. If a task is being learned that requires an attitude or demonstration of a skill, then feedback from observers (the instructor, other learners) will increase the probability of improvement. Positive reinforcement strategies are important in this step.

8. Assess Performance

It is important that instruction leads to a change in behavior that persists over time. When such change in behavior occurs, we can infer that learning has taken place. We must expect that instruction leads to improved performance, and that such performance is job-related. Performance can be assessed using question and answer and skill demonstrations, and subsequent observations by the supervisor coupled with feedback reinforces the learning.

9. Enhance Retention and Transfer

It is important to give learners strategies for retaining what they have learned, and to be able to transfer their learnings to job-related contexts. Responding to novel circumstances is an example. These efforts at retention and transfer may be discussed in earlier events of the instruction, such as steps 5, 6, and 7. Sometimes, new skills cannot be performed under actual conditions for ethical and legal reasons. Waiting for someone to have a heart attack to practice CPR is an example. Therefore, retention and transfer strategies must be simulated. Role plays and skill practice sessions are examples of instructional strategies useful in this situation.

Conclusion

This approach provides a generalized sequence of activities—or events—that a supervisor might consider when planning an on-the-job learning experience for employees. The worksheet that follows can be used to outline a strategy for using the nine-step model for on-the-job instruction.

References

Broadwell, M. *The Supervisor as an Instructor.* Reading, MA: Addison-Wesley, 1978.

Dean, P. (Ed.). *Performance Engineering at Work.* Batavia, IL: International Board of Standards for Training, 1994.

Driscoll, M. *Psychology of Learning and Instruction.* Boston, MA: Allyn and Bacon, 1994.

Gilbert T. *Human Competence: Engineering Worthy Performance.* New York: McGraw Hill, 1978.

Mager, R., and Pipe, P. *Analyzing Performance Problems.* Belmont, CA: David S. Lake Publishers.

On-the-job Instruction Planning Worksheet

Instructional Event	Instructional Plan
1. Gain Attention	
2. Inform Learner of Objective	
3. Stimulate Recall of Prior Learning	
4. Present the Content	
5. Provide Learning Guidance	
6. Elicit Performance	
7. Provide Feedback	
8. Assess Performance	
9. Enhance Retention and Transfer	

Exercise: Giving Effective Feedback

By Debra Eshelman and Joan Berkson

Audience ➤	Staff and Supervisors, Managers
Purpose ➤	—Understand the rationale behind and components of effective feedback —Be able to determine appropriate uses of feedback —Practice receiving and giving feedback
Suggested Uses ➤	Group exercise for all levels of management

Introduction

Feedback is used to give employees the information they need to perform effectively in the workplace. It reinforces successful behaviors or provides constructive suggestions for improving ineffective behaviors for successful performance of a given job. It may be formal or informal, constructive or reinforcing, and used across all levels of the organization.

Feedback is ongoing communication that fosters continuous improvement. It is based on objective data as well as subjective observations. Specific examples might be a brief comment, such as "terrific presentation," or an in-depth conversation analyzing a difficult encounter. Feedback can be an independent exercise, a dialogue between two people, or a group process. It can be delivered to individuals, teams, and organizations. Much feedback is based on individual perceptions and reactions; however, objective media, such as videotape, audiotape, and assessment tools, are available. The goal of effective feedback is to influence others and either to help give insight for meaningful change or provide positive reinforcement for present performance or behavior.

Providing quality feedback requires great del-

icacy and skill. Effective feedback is timely, specific, accurate, relevant, measurable, and based on business needs. As a result of the feedback, an individual will understand how their behavior or performance affected their workgroup or organization. Additionally, they will know how to modify their behavior or performance to increase the value of their contribution to the organization.

Receiving and processing feedback is also a skill. The person receiving the feedback must understand why the feedback is being offered, have the ability to evaluate and understand the information being offered, and possess the capacity to act upon it in a productive manner.

Exercise: Leader's Notes

Time

Approximately one hour total. Allow 30 minutes for presentation of material, 5 minutes for each role play, and 2 minutes for each debrief.

Number of Participants

15–21 individuals, divided into triads for the exercises

Facilitator Expertise

Group facilitation skills

Experience giving and receiving feedback desirable

Handouts

How to Give Effective Feedback: Tips

Feedback Model and Example

Observer's Feedback Form

Exercise Scenarios

Procedure

1. Review information from introduction and handouts, How to Give Effective Feedback: Tips and Feedback Model and Example.

2. Have participants form groups of three and distribute Exercise Scenarios. Each member will practice role playing in both giving and receiving feedback, and observing a feedback session.

3. Assign roles to be played. Participants in triads determine who will play what role in the first scenario. (Observers take notes on the role plays using the Observer's Feedback Form.)

4. Debrief role-play participants in triads using the Observer's Feedback Form and the observer's notes.

5. Rotate roles and role play a new scenario.

6. Debrief role-play participants in triads using the Observer's Feedback Form and the observer's notes.

7. Rotate roles and role play a new scenario.

8. Debrief role-play participants in triads using the Observer's Feedback Form and the observer's notes.

9. Share debriefs among the large group.

10. Review for lessons learned/next steps.

How to Give Effective Feedback: Tips

▶ Look for good timing and receptiveness. Know when not to intervene or interact and use your judgment about circumstances and emotions.

▶ Provide feedback upon request. If the feedback has not been requested, tell the individual that it will be provided in advance.

▶ Be aware of possible reactions to feedback and consequences. Anticipate reaction and plan/prepare accordingly.

▶ Give positive feedback frequently and generously. "Praise in public."

▶ Provide constructive (critical) feedback thoughtfully, carefully, and privately.

▶ Focus on the value to the receiver, rather than on the "release" for the giver; offer rather than impose feedback.

▶ Focus on the amount of information the receiver can use effectively, not the amount the giver wants to send.

▶ Tie feedback as closely as possible in time to the circumstances.

▶ Focus on sharing ideas rather than giving advice; when possible, allow the listener to decide what to do with that information.

▶ Try to establish a reputation for being accurate, sensitive, constructive, and confidential.

▶ Give feedback that is relevant, consistent, clear, and truthful. It may be prescriptive or nonprescriptive, depending on the circumstances.

▶ Watch emotions.

▶ Own the feedback yourself; state what "I" think or feel rather than speaking in the collective "we."

▶ Offer help when appropriate if you can also influence some of the pertinent circumstances.

▶ Be descriptive rather than evaluative.

▶ Focus on behaviors, not personalities, and focus on the action/behavior rather than the person.

▶ Focus on specific observations rather than inferences; be descriptive and nonjudgmental; stick with *what, when,* and *where* rather than *why*.

▶ Focus on actions during a specific situation as soon as appropriate. Talking about specific occurrences is more valuable than generalities such as *usually, always,* and *never.*

Feedback Model and Example

Model

Your Observations	Description of Behavior	Results of Behavior	Suggested or Continued Behavior
Examples I observed:	Several side conversations during the last meeting.	This disrupted the flow of the conversation and prevented people from paying attention to the speaker.	I would like to suggest that the group observe the ground rules and have only one speaker at a time.

Observer's Feedback Form

Scenario: _____

Feedback Giver: _____

Feedback Receiver: _____

Observer: _____

I. Feedback Giver

1. Characterize, describe, and quantify the nature of the feedback:

_____

_____

Positive feedback:

_____

_____

Constructive (critical) feedback:

_____

_____

2. Feedback Process

Timely	( ) Yes	( ) No
Appropriate	( ) Yes	( ) No
Anticipated reactions	( ) Yes	( ) No
Maintained objectivity	( ) Yes	( ) No

3. Feedback Content

Specific	( ) Yes	( ) No
Objective	( ) Yes	( ) No
Descriptive	( ) Yes	( ) No
Evaluative	( ) Yes	( ) No
Actionable	( ) Yes	( ) No
Relevant	( ) Yes	( ) No

II. Feedback Receiver

1. How did the receiver react or respond (describe behaviors)?

_____

_____

Receptive	( ) Yes	( ) No
Passive/disinterested	( ) Yes	( ) No
Defensive, nonreceptive, or hostile	( ) Yes	( ) No

Other reactions:

_____

_____

_____

III. Evaluation

Was the feedback effective? (give reasons/examples):

_____

_____

_____

Why?

_____

_____

_____

Why not?

_____

_____

_____

IV. Additional observations:

_____

_____

_____

_____

_____

_____

V. Suggestions for making the feedback more effective:

_____

_____

_____

_____

_____

_____

_____

_____

1. One of your employees (role played by the "receiver") has frequently argued with you and has a habit of interrupting others when they speak. This person also snaps chewing gum, eats pungent foods in communal space, reads the paper at his/her desk, and engages in other disruptive and/or unprofessional behaviors. The employee gets the job done, however, and is always on time for work. One day you see the person with his/her feet up on the desk and you stop to provide "feedback."

2. Your boss (role played by the receiver) has just sharply criticized and belittled one of your peers who usually seems to be very proficient at his/her job. You have noticed a tendency in your boss to snap at subordinates and to show a flare of temper on a regular basis. In addition, you have heard fellow employees complaining about this behavior. On the other hand, you have always been treated courteously and fairly with only occasional "flare ups," which you have let pass without responding. You know that your boss seems to look to you as a sounding board and decide to provide him/her with some feedback.

3. One of your peers (role played by the receiver) frequently criticizes your mutual boss behind his/her back but doesn't seem to notice the effect of this behavior on others in the workgroup. Members of the workforce have noticed this disrespectful behavior, but haven't said anything to cause concern. Your peer is an excellent worker, gets the job done, and is courteous to others with whom he/she works. You decide that it's time to provide some feedback.

4. Most of the members of your organization greet each other in a courteous and cheerful way and display a sense of teamwork. One of your friends (role played by the receiver), however, seems detached and nonconversant with others. Your friend is well mannered, efficient at the job, and helps others when asked to do so. While you admire your friend's professional skills, you are concerned that he/she isn't perceived by others as a real part of the team. You believe that some feedback is in order.

Exercise: Positive Reinforcement

By G. Douglas Mayo

Audience →	Supervisors, Managers
Purpose →	—Practice giving positive reinforcement —Have resources for further study of this topic
Suggested Uses →	Self-study of resource list materials

Introduction

Positive reinforcement in its various forms and ramifications has proved to be one of the most potent factors affecting learning and shaping human behavior. Psychologists, including B.F. Skinner and Albert Bandura, have studied the concept extensively with favorable results and have suggested a number of useful applications. Successful trainers, likewise, have utilized positive reinforcement for decades to enhance learning and retention. Simply stated, the positive reinforcement model holds that, when an action taken by a person (such as speaking up in a seminar) is followed by a feeling of satisfaction (such as the positive feeling resulting from instructor or peer approval of what was said), learning and retention are enhanced, and similar actions on the part of the person are likely to continue.

Exercise: Leader's Notes

Time

30 minutes

Number of Participants

3–36

Facilitator Expertise

Some prior knowledge of the positive reinforcement concept, such as may be acquired from reading one or more of the references, is desirable but not essential.

Materials and Equipment

Paper and pencil

Procedure

1. Introduce the activity with information from the introduction above.

2. Ask the participants to form groups of three people each. Ask each group to describe in written outline one or more instances from their experience in which they experienced positive reinforcement. Include:

   - The setting.
   - The action you took.
   - Who provided positive reinforcement.
   - How you felt.
   - Whether or not you persisted with similar actions later.

3. After about five minutes, designate three of the groups to participate in the following activity. The first group presents one of their instances orally. The second group's task is to comment on the report of the first group in such a way as to provide positive reinforcement concerning the report. The third group's task is to comment on the second group's performance in such a way as to provide positive reinforcement for their comments.

   Three more of the groups may be asked to follow a similar procedure, if desired.

4. Summarize the activity by asking:

- Is an instructor in a good position to provide positive reinforcement? If so, why?
- Is the positive reinforcement model applicable to situations outside the classroom? If so, identify several such situations.
- What opportunities do you have to provide positive reinforcement on the job?
- What does the positive reinforcement model have to say about ridicule and criticism in the classroom? In the workplace?
- Would it be correct to say that "success" is a generic name for positive reinforcement?

References

Bandura, A. *Social Learning Theory.* Englewood Cliffs, NJ: Prentice-Hall, 1977.

Bandura, A. *Social Foundations of Thought and Action.* Englewood Cliffs, NJ: Prentice-Hall, 1986.

Bandura, A. Human Agency in Social Cognitive Theory. *American Psychologist,* 44, 1989, pp. 1,175–84.

Peters, T., and Waterman, R. *In Search of Excellence.* New York: Warner Books, 1982.

Skinner, B. *Beyond Freedom and Dignity.* New York: Bantam, 1971.

Skinner, B. *Reflections on Behaviorism and Society.* Englewood Cliffs, NJ: Prentice-Hall, 1978.

Skinner, B. *Recent Issues in the Analysis of Behavior.* Columbus: Merrill, 1989.

Skinner, B., and Epstein, R. *Skinner for the Classroom.* Champaign, IL: Research Press, 1982.

Wood, R., and Bandura, A. Social Cognitive Theory in Organizational Management. *Academy of Management Review,* 14, 1989, pp. 361–84.

Exercise: Active Listening

By Robert C. Bartolo, Jr.

Audience	Staff and Supervisors, Managers
Purpose	—Practice using active listening/ communication skills
Suggested Uses	Group exercise to train coaches and mentors in this skill
	Group exercise to train employees to use this skill in receiving instruction and feedback from superiors
	Could follow a discussion of or training presentation on this topic

Introduction

Active listening is a critical skill for any coach or mentor. It is also essential for the employee receiving coaching or mentoring. This exercise provides instruction and practice in this skill.

Exercise: Leader's Notes

Time

Variable (about 3 minutes per participant, plus 5 minutes for setup and 10 minutes for debriefing/processing)

Number of Participants

Any number

Facilitator Expertise

Group facilitation skills

Materials and Equipment

None

Procedure

1. Introduce the exercise by explaining the objectives and how it will work. You should choose a subject (either by yourself prior to the exercise, or with the group of participants) upon which there would be a variety of opinions (e.g., a current topic in the news, initiatives in the workplace, or a philosophical topic).

2. One person starts the discussion by speaking for two minutes on his or her opinion of the subject.

3. As facilitator, randomly choose the next person to continue the exercise. That second person should summarize what the first speaker said, using appropriate techniques ("It sounded like you said ..." or "What I thought I heard you say was ..."). The first speaker should confirm or reject whether the summary was accurate. If the summary was accurate, the second person should then state his or her own opinion on the subject. If the summary was not accurate, the second person must use active listening/communication skills (asking questions to draw out information, get clarity) to get an accurate understanding of the first person's opinion.

4. Randomly choose the next person, who will repeat the process. (Choose randomly rather than "down the line" to ensure that all participants are forced to listen, and be prepared to answer during the whole exercise.)

5. Continue until every person has had a chance to speak. You should summarize the last person's discussion and state your opinion (optional).

6. Debrief by asking the participants questions about their experiences during the

exercise. ("How easy was that? Difficult? Have you used these techniques before? When are some other good opportunities to use these techniques?") Feed back to the group any observations that you made during the exercise.

SECTION 5: ENABLING TEAMWORK

Section 5 at a Glance

MATERIAL	Page	AUDIENCES				FORMATS		
		Learning Professionals	Staff and Supervisors	Teams	Management	Self-study/Resource for Training	Group Exercise	Tool
Tools and Techniques for Building Diverse Teams	5-4	●		●	●	●		●
Global Work Teams	5-12	●		●		●		
Decision-making Tools for Teams	5-17			●			●	●
Exercise: Parts of a Whole	5-21			●			●	
Performance Assessment: Taking Your Team's Pulse	5-23			●			●	●

Introduction:
Looking to Teams for
Learning and Performance Improvement

With the advent of Total Quality Management and employee empowerment, more and more of the work of an organization is done through teams. Coopers & Lybrand defines a team as a group of people, each affected by the same process or processes, working toward a common goal and using common methods.

They may include executives, managers, supervisors, employees, external customers, vendors, and partner organization representatives. Today's teams have a variety of purposes, including:

- Management teams, which lead quality activities and large improvement efforts or which meet regularly for decision making.

- Change teams, which handle change management activities.

- Issue management teams, which work on key issues of a strategic plan or other special issues.

- Unit work teams, which guide and support departments or other business units.

- Improvement teams, which are chartered to conduct discrete performance improvement projects.

- Self-managed teams, which manage and improve their specific processes.

When asked in a recent study conducted by ASTD what their companies were doing to become more effective, 65 percent of those responding cited the use of teams. This trend is understandable, because teams bring many strengths to an organization. They are a means of maximizing skills and insight, breaking down structural/organizational barriers, bringing out hidden talents in individuals, and operationalizing employee empowerment. Teams also provide training for leadership and give members the opportunity to learn new skills such as group dynamics. In high-performing organizations,

improvement teams will learn quality methods such as statistical process control and process mapping.

For learning professionals in results-driven businesses, teams also are a growing focus of training and learning activities. For example, 83 percent of HR executives in a 1996 ASTD survey said that learning occurs in teams in their organizations, and 1997 respondents to the same annual survey rated teamwork training number two in the top 10 trends.

How This Section Can Help

Learning professionals may be involved in teaching about teams and how to run them effectively, in teaching or consulting on team facilitation skills, or in teaching and facilitating teams themselves. This section addresses each of these needs.

The first two entries provide information for meeting two of today's newer team-related challenges: creating and maximizing the potential of culturally diverse work teams, and multinational teams in a global organization. Special attention to overcoming barriers and fostering trust are key success factors, and these materials can help learning professionals provide advice or training for effective team building in these situations.

The next three pieces provide tools and exercises for helping teams operate efficiently and effectively. They provide a process and exercises for teaching teams different decision-making techniques, including brainstorming options, multivoting to narrow the choices, and team consensus technique for making a decision everyone can support. Other issues addressed include helping team members understand and appreciate their role on the team and how to deal constructively with inevitable team conflict and tension.

In addition, performance assessment is as important an issue for teams as it is for all aspects of high-performing organizations. This chapter closes with an exercise to help teams plan and measure how effective they have been in achieving their goals.

References

Bassi, L., Cheney, S., and Van Buren, M. Training Industry Trends 1997. *Training & Development*, November 1997, p. 53.

Benson, G. Battle of the Buzzwords. *Training & Development*, July 1997, p. 52.

Carr, D., and Littman, I. *Excellence in Government: Total Quality Management in the 1990s.* Coopers & Lybrand: Arlington, VA, 1993.

Tools and Techniques for Building Diverse Teams

By Bruce Hunt

Audience ➡	Facilitators of Diverse Teams, Self-directed Teams (especially diversity councils), Managers, Learning Professionals
Purpose ➡	—Appreciate the benefits of diverse teams —Understand the stages of team life —Be able to help diverse teams overcome barriers at each stage that can hinder team success
Suggested Uses ➡	Resource/tool for team facilitation Resource for presentation on diverse teams

Making Diverse Teams the Most Effective Teams

Because of the dramatically changing demographics of the workforce, today's teams are likely to be composed of diverse individuals, different on variables that are immediately apparent (e.g., race and gender) and on variables that are not so apparent (e.g., beliefs and learning style). This diversity can and should be an asset in team effectiveness rather than a liability. There is a growing body of evidence that diverse teams, if well-managed, can produce higher quality and more innovative results than homogeneous teams.

Teams, like all organisms, go through predictable stages of growth and evolution. The tools and techniques in this piece are organized according to the four stages of group development—Getting Started (Forming), Learning to Disagree (Storming), Getting on Track (Norming), and Achieving Results (Performing). They may be used to guide the progress of temporary teams (those convened to accomplish specific and limited purposes alongside the "regular work" of the individuals who make up the team) as well as full-time teams (teams that regularly deliver the goods and/or services of the organization, such as sales or manufacturing teams).

Discussion of each of these stages of development includes a series of individual questions and team questions. The questions are intended to be the right questions posed at the right time to help individuals ruthlessly confront their immediate experience. The answers to the individual questions will give team members a personal journal of their participation on the team. In addition, the discipline of capturing their unique experience will help individuals to cultivate the skill of introspection, a skill that is essential for working with diverse groups.

The capacity for introspection is one of the essential characteristics of effective leaders. Warren Bennis found that leaders recognize that "true understanding comes from reflecting on your experience." Bennis claims that "reflecting on your experience means having a Socratic dialogue with yourself, asking the right questions at the right time in order to discover the truth of yourself and your life." While this is a useful habit to cultivate in life, it is especially important for members of teams to discover their unique truths.

The team questions serve a similar purpose for the entire team: to enhance performance as well as learning. The investment of time and energy in considering, individually and corporately, answers to these questions will benefit the team not only because "the unexamined life is not worth living" but also because the unexamined life of a team is not possible to live successfully.

Discussion of the individual and team questions, when written down, will furnish a recorded history of the team's common journey, the often neglected *process* of the team's functioning, rather than the *content* of the actual work performed. Presumably there will be another record that will document the agreements and deliberations on the task itself.

What We Know (or Think We Know) About Teams

Three images of a team are commonly used. The **plate of marbles** image suggests that teams are basically a collection of autonomous individuals who bump up against each other and therefore influence one another, but there is no genuine connection among them. The **mechanical image** suggests that a team is a great machine made up of replaceable parts. The **organic image** suggests that a team is an organism, whose continued health and functioning requires the interdependence of its various components. Because the organic image allows for richer analysis and describes more accurately the complexity of team work, that is the image we will use.

Teams perform three primary functions: teams recommend things (e.g., task forces), teams make or do things (production teams, sales teams), and teams run things (e.g., management teams at various levels).

In accomplishing these intended results, teams also provide for the development of individuals who participate on the team. Indeed, many people identify participation on an effective team as a significant contribution to their personal and professional development.

A practical definition of a team is a small number of people with complementary skills who are committed to a common purpose, performance goals, and approach for which they hold themselves mutually accountable. This definition of team distinguishes such "real teams" from work groups, who may or may not hold themselves accountable for common goals and may or may not have a

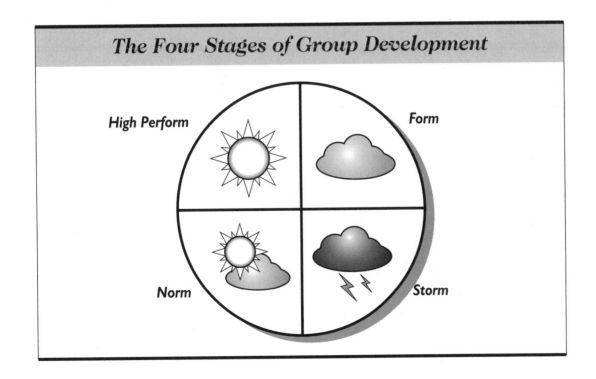

The Four Stages of Group Development

High Perform

Form

Norm

Storm

common approach; it also distinguishes "real teams" from the total organization, which may officially be committed to the values of team work.

Team performance, like individual performance, is a function of four variables:

- **Role Clarity:** Agreement on the charter and mission of the team, what results are expected, and what individual roles and responsibilities will contribute to that achievement.

- **Skills and Abilities:** The extent to which team members are equipped with the appropriate interpersonal and problem-solving skills to achieve the expected results.

- **Organization Realities:** The work of the team does not take place in a vacuum; the norms of the organization may help or hinder team effectiveness.

- **Effort:** Team members' willingness to put in the necessary time and energy to accomplish the expected results. This effort may be seen as a function of the anticipated and realized rewards for participation.

Katzenbach and Smith found that the most powerful influence on creating and maintaining effective teams is the presence of a demanding performance challenge. The purpose for which the team is convened is compelling for its prospective members and continues to hold the team together when obstacles appear on the way. Therefore, it is important for a team's assignment to be both clear and challenging.

Regardless of the team assignment, the team will require a mix of technical, problem-solving, and interpersonal skills. Often teams are formed based on functional representation from various disciplines; while these technical skills provide an important foundation, it is critical that the team be able to address problems and work well together.

Katzenbach and Smith have observed the following: "In our research, we did not meet a single team that had all the needed skills at the outset. We did discover, however, the power of teams as vehicles for personal learning and development. Accordingly, as long as the skill potential exists, the dynamics of a team cause that skill to develop. The challenge is to assure that the available skills

are actually used and that opportunities to develop new skills are sought out."

Where the norms of the organization define a "robust performance ethic," teams are more likely to be utilized and to be effective. However, as Taylor Cox notes, those organizations that have a high-prescription culture are less likely than low-prescription cultures to provide an environment for diverse teams.

Team effort and team commitment emerge from the complex interaction of the task itself, the values of the team members, and the likelihood that the effort will result in the fitting levels of satisfaction on the part of the team members. Where people believe that the team can make a difference in the organization, and that they can make a difference on the team, motivation to contribute is increased. Where the organization recognizes the team's contribution in some appropriate way, commitment is strengthened.

What We Are Learning About Diverse Teams

In some organizations cultural diversity is seen as a problem to be overcome. Others view increasing workforce diversity as a "good deed," helping to reverse the historical impact of discrimination and stereotyping. While these orientations to diversity do drive many of the organizational initiatives presently under way, many organizations are beginning to make a business case for diversity: when properly managed, diverse groups can have performance advantages over homogeneous ones. However, effectively managing diverse teams means overcoming potential barriers to their success inherent in each of the four variables that shape team performance.

Role Clarity: If placing a performance challenge in front of a team is the single most galvanizing ingredient for team performance, the past experience of nonmajority people in being denied opportunities to take on challenging tasks may be a barrier to diverse team effectiveness. All members must thus be encouraged to believe their contribution is needed and valued. In addition, organizations must guard against reducing the expectations they have for diverse teams.

Skills and Abilities: Stereotyping of nonmajority groups may result in assuming that members of these groups lack the skills (functional, problem-solving, or interpersonal) to contribute to the team's work product. Such assumptions must be replaced by objective determination of the team's skill mix.

Organization Realities: Some cultures are easier for diverse teams to thrive in than others. In high-prescription organization cultures, for example, the following can be barriers:

- A narrow view of right and good behavior.

- A prevalence of evaluative, judgmental behavior and people who are quick to express criticism.

- A general intolerance of mistakes and more managerial response to mistakes than recognition of positive contributions.

- Management, especially senior management, that not only defines goals and strategies but also prescribes methodological and tactical details of how work is performed.

By contrast, low-prescription organization cultures are characterized by the following:

- Except for core values like integrity and quality, a wide range of work styles and behaviors are defined as right, good, or appropriate.

- Members refrain from evaluating ideas until they are clearly understood and are able to react to ideas in ways other than by evaluating them as good or bad.

- Taking calculated risks is tolerated and even encouraged. Failure, within limits, is viewed as a learning opportunity and an inevitable cost of innovation.

- Positive deviations from performance norms receive equal or greater management attention than negative deviations.

- Within the constraints of integrity, safety, and ethics, individuals (and teams, we would add) have great latitude to create their own approaches to their work.

Therefore, a low-prescription culture is more conducive to the formation and effectiveness of diverse teams.

Effort: Coopers & Lybrand has found that people who feel themselves to be "outsiders" quickly get discouraged, lose interest, and may even seek revenge on the "insider" group. Individual and team effort in a diverse team depends on the inclusiveness of the team and the legitimacy of the team's contribution to the organization.

The questions that are posed for each stage of the team's growth are intended to help individuals and the total team to identify and confront potential barriers to team effectiveness.

Stage 1: Forming

When teams are first brought together, uncertainty and ambiguity abound. Individuals wonder whether the investment of their time and talent will be worth it. What are we supposed to do? How are we going to do it? How much time will this enterprise take? What are the boundaries of our task? What hidden motives do others bring to this work?

The answers to these questions cannot be provided by a memo from top management; they must be hammered out by the team in dialogue with each other and with those who have commissioned the team's formation.

The initial meetings of a team that is diverse or multicultural are especially critical, because there is so much information to be put on the table. Even seemingly homogeneous teams, by function, by race, or by gender, may have surprising differences among members, but the risk for a multicultural team is that unexamined assumptions will get in the way of the team's formation and productive work.

Teams that want to become *real* teams should pay particular attention to first meetings and actions. This is particularly important for authority figures on the team; people will be watching carefully the words and actions of leaders in order to test the credibility of the assignment and the believability of the ground rules. It is also important to decide what kinds of conversations to hold in the early stages and how long to devote to those conversations. Often it is tempting to dive into the task without regard to all the "touchy-feely" issues that go into group building. In fact, there may be some advantages to plunging in, if it can be done with some tentativeness. Do not expect to have everything nailed down the first time around. Some of

Stage 1 Questions

▶ **Leadership**

1. What are the real reasons this team was formed?
2. What are the real reasons I was selected (or chose) to be a member of this team?
3. What is the unique contribution that I can make to this team?
4. What will make my participation on this team satisfying for me?
5. What can I do to help the team get started?

▶ **Team**

1. Who are we and what resources, including experience, do we bring?
2. What are some of the differences among us? (Differences are valuable.)
3. What are some of the things we have in common? (looking for common ground)
4. What is our charter? For what purpose(s) were we convened?
5. How do we understand the boundaries of our task? What are some things we are not being asked to do?
6. What are the ground rules we want to establish to govern our behavior?
7. What roles do we need to be effective?

   ▶ *Contributors* give the team the valuable technical expertise it needs to solve problems and meet its goals. They provide the data, and they provide it in a manner in which it can easily be used. And they often serve as trainers and mentors of other team members. They help the team set high standards, define priorities, and make efficient use of team meeting time and resources.

   ▶ *Collaborators* play a key role in keeping a team goal-directed and focused on the steps necessary to reach that goal. They serve as models by working outside their prescribed jobs and being willing to spread around the kudos of team success. In a pinch, they will drop everything to help out other team members. They are open to new ideas that may affect the team's efforts and to feedback about their own performances.

   ▶ *Communicators* are process-oriented team members who are effective listeners and facilitate participation, conflict resolution, consensus building, feedback, and the building of an informal, relaxed climate.

   ▶ *Challengers* are team players who openly question the goals, methods, and even the ethics of the team, who are willing to disagree with the team leader, and who encourage the team to take well-considered risks.

8. How will we provide for leadership? What do we expect of the leader(s)?
9. What about time? How often will we meet? For how long? When do we expect to be finished with our task?

the same questions team members come in with will resurface again at later stages of the process.

Stage 2: Storming

Once the early excitement and energy of the start-up process have passed, teams often encounter unexpected bickering and (apparently) trivial arguments. There are struggles for control, efforts to influence the direction of the team, and occasional divisions into subgroups, cliques, or alliances. Motives are suspect, hidden agendas are attributed. Some of the real information may come forward in conversations after meetings; members may be accused overtly or covertly of not "carrying their weight."

It is important in this stage to find ways to surface conflicts so that they do not go underground and intrude on the team's deliberations in indirect and surprising ways.

Active listening skills are essential during this stage, although very hard to practice because of the atmosphere of conflict. Try establishing a rule that you will paraphrase what you have heard from other members before you disagree with them.

Some members may decide that the effort and time is not worth it; attendance at meetings may be less regular, and some individuals may be tempted to abandon the project as fruitless.

While diverse teams should celebrate their diversity and the strength that comes from their differences, it may be useful for the team to search for appropriate "common ground." The team mission and ground rules can help to identify those commonalities.

Unlike the commons in the village, the common ground on which a diverse team intends to stand can be expanded. In fact, that is one of the important strategies for helping the diverse team go through the storming stage of its development. If the team has done an initial job of getting on the table the competing interests that its members have, then an approach that allows the team to work the overlaps, or the common ground, will be useful.

During this period of tumult in the life of the

Stage 2 Questions

▶ **Individual**

1. Some of the reasons we are having difficulty as a team are…

2. I really have difficulty listening when…

3. Some of the ground rules we are violating are…

4. When there are conflicts on the team, I…

5. In order to improve team effectiveness, I will START…, I will STOP…, I will CONTINUE…

6. Is there any evidence of turf problems?

▶ **Team**

1. What are the apparent disagreements on this team?

2. What are some possible explanations for the conflicts?

3. What conflict management modes do we prefer? (avoiding, competing, compromising, accommodating, collaborating)

4. What ground rules (new or old) will help us through this stage?

5. Some things we will STOP, START, and CONTINUE doing are…

6. What are some defensive routines that are operating?

Stage 3 Questions

▶ **Individual**

1. Some of the things I appreciate about being on this team are...

2. Some of the things I dislike about being on this team are...

3. Some things I am doing now that I did not do when the team was formed are...

4. Some things that others are doing now that they did not do when the team was formed are...

5. My ideas and opinions are heard rarely...occasionally...almost always.

6. The team counts on me to...

▶ **Team**

1. How has this team changed since we got started?

2. What ground rules are working well?

3. What ground rules shall we change or add?

4. How shall we include new members of the team?

5. Have team members stand up and arrange themselves around a center that represents the heart of the team. Talk about who stands near whom, and why some people are closer to the center than others. Another alternative is to have individuals place people according to how they have experienced their contribution to the team. Discussion of this exercise should suggest changes in team functioning.

---

team, preoccupation with narrow roles or job responsibilities is not appropriate. It is insufficient to claim, "I did my part," or, "That's not my job." Focusing on the common purpose and the common responsibilities is critical. We are in this together.

Stage 3: Norming

After the upheavals of the previous stage, the team begins to experience a new cohesion and confidence.

Having survived the battles, it is time to settle in on the task once again and to reaffirm the ground rules now based on experience rather than anticipation.

Individual members find themselves playing different or enlarged roles on the team. Quiet members are more willing to speak up and to disagree with louder or more powerful members. Leadership roles will be shared more widely.

The challenge for the team is to maintain high standards of quality, to continue to ask tough questions, to be flexible in moving from divergent to convergent thinking, from looking for alternatives to deciding among alternatives (deciding may still be a challenge for a diverse group).

Suspicion of easy or premature consensus is the primary challenge of this stage.

Stage 4: Performing

A mature and high-performance team really "hums." Members of the team take pleasure in working together; they produce tangible results; they may develop a special language and special rituals to celebrate (and maintain) their high performance. It is tempting at this stage to compromise standards, to avoid tough issues in the name of team cohesion, to get so focused on past accomplishments that more immediate opportunities are missed.

At this stage, some temporary teams outlive

their usefulness and stagnate. Subtle changes in the environment may go unnoticed. The high-performing team will find occasions to celebrate and report on their accomplishment, and if unable to find a new and challenging mission, may disband. It is important that the team decide on its future, whether the ultimate choice is to seek a new challenge or to disband.

Enabling Diverse Teams: The Right Support at the Right Time

All teams, including those that are diverse, will experience these four stages of development. The particular hurdles that diverse teams must overcome will vary, and may be particularly challenging because of unexamined biases, expectations, and stereotypes.

As in so many situations where managing diversity turns out to be not fundamentally different from managing any group of people, the steps and skills identified are useful in building teams in any circumstance. If we were all managing well, we would be managing diversity well.

Teams are expected to report (and perhaps implement) the results of their work. The high-performing team will consider the norms of the organization in determining how to report not only results but also the learnings that come from introspection.

Stage 4 Questions

▶ **Individual**

1. I am proud of the following contributions I made to this team…

2. Some things I have learned by participating on this team are…

3. Some stereotypes and biases I have revised based on this team's performance are…

▶ **Team**

1. In what ways did our differences help and hinder our performance?

2. How can we apply what we have learned to other situations in the organization?

3. How shall we celebrate our accomplishments?

4. What rewards are appropriate for the team's performance?

5. How shall we report our accomplishments in a manner consistent with the values of this team?

References

Bennis, W. *On Becoming a Leader.* Reading, MA: Addison-Wesley Publishing Company, 1994.

Cox, T. *Cultural Diversity in Organizations.* San Francisco: Barrett-Koehler Publishers, 1993.

Katzenbach, J. and Smith, D. *The Wisdom of Teams.* Boston: Harvard Press, 1993.

Parker, G. *Team Players and Teamwork.* San Francisco: Jossey Bass Publishers, 1991.

Global Work Teams

By Sylvia Odenwald

Audience ➤	Learning Professionals, Managers planning to initiate a global work team, any global Team Leaders or Facilitators
Purpose ➤	—Be aware of the trend toward global training/learning strategies —Recognize the cultural challenges in developing effective global teams and providing training for them —Learn the competencies required for global team leaders and members
Suggested Uses ➤	Self-study/handout Resource for developing a presentation on this topic

The concept of teamwork is hardly new. And no one disputes that the business world is now a global work environment. These two realities have created a need for global work teams—and inspired a search for the key competencies of global team members. As yet, there are none set in stone. Still, it's safe to set forth a few generalizations:

- The competencies of global team members must accommodate the team's cultural makeup, mission, geographic distribution, and technological capabilities.

- Team members must have nontechnical as well as technical skills so they can work together smoothly in conditions of rapid change.

- Each team will develop its own dynamics and culture.

Currently, case studies provide a variety of proposed competencies. For example, several years ago Digital Equipment, based in Marlboro, Massachusetts, formed multicultural teams to consolidate operations and sell more products. At the time, teams at Digital's worldwide operations were made up of representatives from three development sites and six manufacturing sites. These cross-functional teams were from such areas as marketing, manufacturing, design engineering, product development, customer support, sales, and distribution.

The teams' goals were to develop recommendations and identify issues. An internal organization-development consultant assisted each team in targeting issues, planning meetings, establishing agendas, and facilitating interventions. The teams received training in team building, foreign languages, and valuing differences.

All team members from countries outside the United States were assigned American partners and invited to spend time with their families. To promote Digital's global emphasis, all manufacturing sites displayed flags from employees' native countries.

"These efforts reduced the time of new-product handoffs from one to three years to only six months," says John Purnell, former manager of organizational effectiveness at Digital and now managing partner at Purnell Associates in Cincinnati, Ohio. He says that communication and teamwork both within teams and between sites increased.

Based on Digital's experience, Purnell suggests the following competencies for global team members:

- Appreciation of people's differences and the value of their time.
- Skills in listening, conflict resolution, project planning, flowcharting, and mapping.
- Knowledge of computers.

Determining the Context

In addition to competencies, there are other important considerations. First, a global work team should determine whether the culture of its members is high context or low context. In a high-context team culture, members tend to build relationships and develop a level of trust before focusing on tasks. In low-context cultures, members tend to view relationship building as a wasted effort that diverts attention from the work at hand.

Team members should also view each other's behavior in the context of cultural variables. For example, Koreans, Thais, and Saudis (people from high-context cultures) often view American business people as insincere due to their direct approach, insistence on data, and need to make decisions quickly. Another consideration is that most team members want to feel that they're part of the team, that they're valued and respected, and that their tasks are important no matter how disparate their backgrounds, skills, and motivation levels. That doesn't mean that team members have to become close friends or even like each other. Some social separation is natural. They don't have to eat lunch together every day as if they're a high school clique. They can even work side by side at times without talking. But the barriers between members shouldn't interfere with the team's work. When they do, the involved parties should be reassigned.

It's important that organizations not expect all global team members to be catalysts or change agents. Sometimes, all that's needed is someone to perform a task repeatedly and well.

For example, the Egyptian government (some of the details have been changed to protect confidentiality) is involved in a 12-year project to build roads, canals, and other facilities. Though it had sufficient money, the government realized that it didn't have enough expertise and labor at its disposal. So, it looked for a global solution, which presented many challenges. Could the project's Egyptian leaders find the required range of expertise from engineering to training? Could they find enough workers willing to relocate? Would they want to bring their families? Where would they live? How would they bridge the language barriers?

The Egyptian government contracted with an Australian construction-management firm to help complete the development plan and to supply expertise and employees for building the facilities and training Egyptian workers. The construction firm also faced many challenges. Where could it find enough people with the necessary skills who would be willing to work on the project? It also sought a global solution.

The construction firm brought together more than 6,000 workers from various countries. It also contracted with a Norwegian company to provide engineers. But how would these resources become effective teams?

How difficult would it be to manage the diverse cultures?

To meet these challenges, the construction firm formed teams at all levels of the organization, including on-site teams at the project locations throughout Egypt. Now, as subprojects are completed, the Norwegian teams train the Egyptian workers to maintain and operate the finished facilities. The process will be repeated every three years until the project ends.

Initially, many differences and potential conflicts arose among team members. Language was a problem. English was chosen as the official language on work sites, but workers used their own languages with coworkers from their own cultures. Another problem was the effect of cultural values on the work schedule. Norwegian workers wanted to work Mondays through Fridays with no overtime; Egyptian workers wouldn't work Thursdays and Fridays because those are religious days. The goals of the construction-management team required that all teams work in tandem. So, how did it merge the workers' opposing philosophies?

First, the management team realized that it couldn't impose a specific structure. It had to let each team find a solution. In one instance, it was overlapping shifts. The unexpected benefits were that the shifts increased contact between the teams and created a productive 10-day work week.

Global work teams should approach every issue with that kind of flexibility.

Transcultural Competence

Team members and team leaders need basically the same competencies, though leaders' competencies should be more generalized.

The team leaders should have a proven track record in the ability to learn and coach others. They should understand the overall project, each work area, and each area's relationship to other areas and team members. They should possess interpersonal skills and understand group processes, the complex interpersonal dynamics that can open or block the doors to productive teamwork.

Leaders must be able to synthesize the diverse cultural needs and perspectives of team members. They must be culturally astute, flexible, and able to deal with ambiguity. They should recognize that cultures have values and beliefs that team members won't and shouldn't violate. Leaders must be able to deal with differences without compromising any team member's integrity.

Team leaders must be aware of members' individual needs, as people and as team contributors. But they should also know when and how to bring the team together. They must help move team members from collision to coexistence to collaboration. In other words, they must direct team members away from fear and hostility toward mutual acceptance and trust and finally toward processing ideas and information.

Leaders must also:

- Assess the skills team members need to do their jobs.
- Handle members' personal agendas individually.
- Diffuse perceived inequities and explain to members what they'd gain or lose.
- Enable diverse groups to understand why projects are done a certain way.
- Assess members' attitudes about such team functions as assignments, reports, deadlines, and conflict resolution.
- Focus members on the desired outcomes in order to gain their willing compliance.

Global team leaders must be able to coordinate across time, distance, and culture. In some cases, they manage teams in which the members speak different languages, use different technologies, and have different beliefs about authority, time, and decision making. In fact, the team members may never have met face-to-face.

"All leaders are or will be global," says vice president Patrick Canavan of Motorola, headquartered in Schaumburg, Illinois. He defines "global" as being anywhere in an organization's web with a geographic scope of responsibility. In other words, global is defined by the work environment, not by time, space, or job title.

As Motorola's director of global leadership and organization development, Canavan understands that all global leaders—whether they are executives, managers, or team leaders—must show transcultural competence through the following behaviors:

- An interest in different cultures and business practices.
- A nonjudgmental initial reaction to cultural differences.
- A conceptual understanding of the power of differences.
- The ability to model product-and-service cultural diversity.
- The ability to learn from traveling and interacting with employees in other areas of the world.

Canavan says that the most essential qualities of a global leader are the following:

- Physical stamina.

- An expanding repertoire of behaviors.
- A sense of humor.
- A personal belief that life is a journey.
- The ethnographic data-collection skills of cultural anthropologists.
- A commitment to the greatness of his or her organization.
- A deep connection to a higher purpose through participation in the organization.

Says Canavan: "Global leadership isn't a state; it's a process. All members of the organization in positions of leadership are in the process. Within the organization, leadership is the evidence of thought, word, and deed that contributes to the system's survival and growth. This requires occasional acts of bravery and risk, which alter the course of the system through influencing and modeling the behavior of others."

C.K. Prahalad, professor of business administration at the University of Michigan, offers his own list of necessary qualities for global team leaders:

- Physical stamina.
- Expertise, perspective, and curiosity.
- Personal excellence and discipline.
- Accountability and trust.
- A tolerance for ambiguity.
- Language and stress-management skills.
- Interpersonal and intercultural competence.
- The ability to learn.
- The ability to forget.
- The ability to work across geographic distances and in multiple teams.
- Loyalty to family, country, beliefs, profession, and organization.

China: A Special Case

"Every competency needed by expatriate workers must be accentuated in China," says Dennis Gerlach, deputy director of education, training, and development for Ford China Operations, based in Saline, Michigan.

"In other countries, training is like running in the sand on a beach. You can't go too fast, and you have to watch out for uneven ground, the cultural differences. But in China, training is like running in four feet of water. The motions are the same, but the progress is slower. Your energy level must be high all of the time."

Gerlach says the upside is that in China, trainers are warmly received and looked up to for their knowledge. Ford provides language-immersion courses for global team members and training in business development, international preparation, and Chinese learning processes. Ford has found that interactive games and survival exercises have been effective in promoting cooperation between the American and Chinese team members. Gerlach cautions us, however, that the Chinese must be prepared to participate in such activities, which are new to them.

The Role of HR

"Tapping into the forces of global organizations and learning organizations has barely begun," say Michael Marquardt and Angus Reynolds in their book, *The Global Learning Organization.* But increasingly, international organizations are developing global human resource strategies and training. HR managers can no longer adapt the past for the future. They will have to break the molds. The changes will affect all activities, including team selection, performance measurement, and training design and delivery.

"Taking a back seat is no longer acceptable," says Rick Swaak, vice president of international human resource services at the National Foreign Trade Council. "You have to get in there and take risks."

Swaak says it's exciting to see current practitioners flock to symposiums on cost containment and business competitiveness— and to see them come up with solutions that reveal a deep understanding of business and the world.

One challenge is finding sufficient time for team members to learn new global skills. John Cone, director of organizational-effectiveness teams at Sequent Computer Systems, says:

> "Competitive organizations need to imbed learning into the course of work and make it transparent, much like the help file in computer software. For example, instead of conducting separate classes on effective

Competencies Within Categories

Here are some competencies, by category, that global team members should have to ensure success:

Leadership
▶ Tolerance for ambiguity
▶ Flexibility
▶ Persuasiveness
▶ Patience
▶ The ability to gain consensus
▶ Coaching skills
▶ An orientation to change

Communication
▶ Listening and interpersonal skills
▶ Presentation and writing skills

Project Management
▶ Skills in delegating, scheduling,

forecasting, interviewing, and strategic planning
▶ A focus on bottom-line goals

Conceptual
▶ Skills in problem solving, decision making, and negotiation
▶ Open-minded
▶ Innovative
▶ Perceptive
▶ Anticipative
▶ Discerning

Technical
▶ Computer skills
▶ Task- and function-oriented

meetings, we teach some employees to become expert observers and coaches. Then, we place them in business meetings to counsel the meeting leaders during breaks on how to implement an activity that might improve the meeting. In other words, we're training in real time."

This quote is from an article by Marcia Atkinson, "Build Learning into Work," in the September 1994 issue of *HR Magazine*. Atkinson says that the fact that many organizations are calling their training organizations "universities" suggests a broad focus, concern for the complete development of all employees, and leading-edge thinking. Educational institutions are also getting into the spirit by offering competency programs, such as the five-week global leadership program at the University of Michigan. Participants visit China and other countries for two weeks to learn how to develop a business plan in an unfamiliar environment.

At the Core

Organizations also need core competencies of a global nature. Gary Hamel and C.K.

Prahalad in their book, *Competing for the Future: Breakthrough Strategies for Seizing Control of Your Industry and Creating the Markets of Tomorrow,* describe core competencies as the bundles of skills and technologies that enable a company to provide a particular benefit to customers. In that context, organizational core competencies are a composite of employees' individual skills.

Hamel and Prahalad propose three conditions for an organization to develop global core competencies:

- It has to train team members constantly in new skills.

- The competencies must be used and reconfigured continuously in order to be sustained and nurtured.

- Work groups must include teams of employees who cut across functions and organizational levels.

A final thought from Gary Hamel: "An organization should never be viewed as just a collection of business units. Rather, it's a collection of competencies that reside between or around existing products."

Decision-making Tools for Teams

By Craig Petrun and Nancy Letsinger

Audience ➤	Any Teams
Purpose ➤	—Learn to use tools for generating and narrowing options and developing consensus —Understand when each tool is appropriate —Practice using the tools on work-related tasks
Suggested Uses ➤	Individual tools introduced to and practiced by teams on a just-in-time basis Material could be the basis of a training for facilitators or team leaders in how to use these tools

Introduction

Team-based decisions are often essential to an organization's success. They are usually required when the resources that must be applied to reach a successful outcome are not solely under the control of one person. This is a principal reason for convening a team in the first place. Therefore, team members have to understand the nature of the task they are being asked to support, and they must have the opportunity to influence and consent to the outcome in order to ensure team success.

Team facilitators and leaders, trainers, and consultants need tools to help teams create ideas and alternatives; to test the emerging decisions; and, when required, to reach agreement. Tools helpful in this process include brainstorming, multivoting, and the team consensus technique. The following are instructions for facilitating each of these processes.

Exercise: Leader's Notes

Time

The time for each of the processes is vari-able, depending on the nature of the problem and how large a team is involved.

Number of Participants

Processes can be used with small or large groups. However, for the team consensus technique, subgroups should develop the decision template. Even for a small group of eight people, it's best to have a smaller group of approximately 2–4 people complete this task.

Facilitator Experience

Group facilitation skills

Materials and Equipment

Flipchart and markers for all three

Overhead transparency markers and yellow stickies (3 x 5) for the Brainstorming Alternative Using Yellow Stickies exercise.

Electronic meeting tools (e.g., Consensus Builder—Wireless Keypads; GroupSystems for Windows—laptops connected via a local area network) and transparencies for breakout groups reporting to a larger group can be useful for the team consensus technique.

Procedure

Brainstorming—Nominal Group Technique

1. Explain that the purpose of brainstorming is to help the team generate ideas.

2. Frame the brainstorming topic for the team.

3. Write the topic on a flipchart so that everyone on the team can see it.

4. Allow members of the team time to write down their ideas silently and collect their thoughts. They should then rank order their ideas.

5. After each team member has had the opportunity to complete the "silent writing," and if the team is large enough, put people into groups of three and have them present their ideas to each other and try to come up with more.

6. On flipchart paper collect each team member's ideas one at a time in round robin style.

7. As each flipchart paper fills up, tape it to the wall in the room (don't forget to number the pages). Discourage team members from judging any idea at this point, but remind them only to suggest ideas that are not redundant.

8. Add new or different ideas if the team comes up with them during the round robin collection.

9. When all ideas are collected, help number them.

10. Have the team review the final list to be sure it represents fairly all the options suggested.

11. Reinforce that during brainstorming, the ideas are not to be judged. The purpose of brainstorming is to create options. Teams that narrow their options too soon reduce their effectiveness. As a facilitator, when you help the team consciously keep these two processes separate, you help them improve their effectiveness. One way to help the team maintain this separation is to set aside one complete team meeting for brainstorming only. Use the next meeting for decision making.

An Alternative: Brainstorming with Yellow Stickies to Create Affinity Diagrams

One problem facilitators may have with groups during brainstorming is keeping the team interested and energized. Yellow stickies are a tool that keeps team members actively involved in this activity. Advantages to this approach are that you get a lot of ideas fast; similar ideas are combined quickly; all team members understand what is written and why things were combined; and team members "own" the process and content. Use this approach when creativity is important and the subject matter is difficult to discuss.

1. Give each member an ample supply of stickies.

2. Have them write down one idea per stickie. (Use an overhead transparency marker and make sure the idea is in a sentence.)

3. When they are done, have all members get up and post their stickies on one of the walls (this is the energy part). The facilitator can quickly categorize these by content to create an affinity diagram.

4. Have members stay at the wall; read all the other stickies; ask clarifying questions about those they don't understand; add new ideas (stickies) as they think of them; and add to ideas posted or combine your idea with another (with permission of the author).

Multivoting

1. Explain that the purpose of multivoting is to pare down a list of issues or ideas to those with the highest priority to the team.

2. Identify the questions that need to be voted on and list them on a flipchart. Establish criteria for voting (e.g., cost, strategic alignment).

3. Give each team member a number of votes equal to approximately half the number of items on the list (e.g., 10 votes for a 20-item list).

4. Explain that each person may give only one vote to a given item (e.g., members vote for their personal top 10).

5. After one round of voting, drop the items with few or no votes from the list.

6. If the top four to six items are not clear at this point, do a second round of voting with fewer votes per person (e.g., five votes if the list now has 10 items). For most problems, a list of more than four to six items for further discussion and prioritization is unwieldy.

The Team Agreement Technique

This technique enables teams to develop a template for or definition of how they want to achieve consensus on the assignment of individual personnel to teams. The decision template consists of the ground rules for discussing issues raised by the group and the actual numerical examples that will define when the team has reached consensus during the team vote.

This approach also allows the team leaders, the individuals in an organization who are most affected by team membership, to participate in the decision process. The technique was originally developed to assist team leaders in reassigning team members to new teams.

1. Introduce the technique.

2. Work with the group to review the proposed team assignments (model) and explain how this will be used as the baseline and how problems with these assignments will be stated as "issues."

3. Allow time for the individuals to brainstorm the issues with the current personnel assignments and to decide which must be addressed (i.e., a decision must be reached) during the meeting (use multivoting if needed).

4. Split the group into subgroups and give out the following assignments:

Subgroup 1: Developing the rules to guide the presentation of the issues. For example:

1. The issues will be presented by the facilitator.

2. The submitter of the issue will be given two minutes to explain his/her suggested change.

3. The other impacted team leader(s) will be given two minutes to respond.

4. The group will then be asked to discuss and comment on the issue. Each group member wishing to comment will be given two minutes.

5. The submitter and other impacted team leader(s) can present rebuttals, limited to two minutes for each.

6. A group vote will then be conducted. The issue will be phrased as a suggestion/motion to change the strawman proposal. A vote *for* the issue (a "10") is a vote for changing the proposal. A vote *against* the issue (a "1") is a vote against changing the issue as stated. Votes can be cast anywhere in between 1 and 10. Several examples should be developed that can be used during the voting process.

Subgroup 2: Collecting and developing the list of the individual issues into a list that can be used during the voting process. These issues focus on those individuals whom the team leaders feel must be moved or placed into a new role other than the original defined in the initial team makeup proposal. This list should be reviewed by the entire group and updated based on this input.

Subgroup 3: Developing the rules for defining consensus. For example (when using a 10-point rating scale):

1. Group consensus to *support* changing the model is achieved when the group vote average is at least a 6, provided there are less than two "1" votes.

2. Group consensus to *oppose* changing the proposed model teams is achieved when the group vote average is less than 6, provided there are less than two "10" votes.

3. Whenever a second vote is taken and the group still cannot achieve consensus, the issue will be placed in a "parking lot" to be revisited by the group at a later time.

4. If consensus is still not reached when the issue is revisited, ask a group leader for a final resolution.

The Consensus Scale

10 = Strongly support changing the proposed model

5 = Can live with the recommended change to the proposed model

1 = Stongly oppose changing the strawman proposal

Example Vote Outcomes

1. Group Average = 7 (with one "1" vote): Consensus has been reached, according to the group definition, to support the suggested change to the proposed model.

2. Group Average = 7 (with two "1" votes): Consensus has not been reached.

3. Group Average = 4 (with no "10" votes): Consensus has been reached to not support the suggested change. The proposed model will remain with no changes on this issue.

Example: How This Process Works

Issue: The proposed team model has Jim working for team leader Susan, but team leader Bill wants Jim to work for him. Bill is responsible for writing up the issue, identifying solutions to consequences of the suggested change, and mapping it to the model.

1. Facilitator presents the issue.

2. Bill explains his suggested personnel placement change as well as his solutions to its consequences.

3. Susan has a chance to give her reply.

4. The group has a chance to provide additional input or comments.

5. Bill has a chance to give a rebuttal, followed by Susan.

6. The suggestion/motion is phrased in a format similar to the model. For example, "The motion is to change the team model such that Jim will work for Bill instead of Susan."

7. A group vote is taken and a decision is made based on the previously developed criteria, or another vote is taken following a timed discussion period. If consensus is still not obtained, the issue is placed on hold.

Exercise: Parts of a Whole

By Kristin Arnold

Audience	Nonmanagement Teams
Purpose	—Appreciate that team members are all playing individual roles as parts of a greater whole —Appreciate that their team is playing a part in a larger, corporate whole
Suggested Uses	Exercise at an early team meeting (after the team's mandate and goals have been established)

Introduction

This simple exercise is an entertaining way to make an important point: Each individual on the team has a valuable role to play, as does each team in the company, as part of a larger whole.

Exercise: Leader's Notes

Time

About 45–60 minutes, depending on the size of the team

Number of Participants

Six or more

Facilitator Expertise

None needed

Materials and Equipment

Flipchart and colored markers

Procedure

1. Explain that this activity is a way to see how we are all parts of a whole. We begin with a picture of our product, and we all add value to that product. Each of us can relate to a part of that product, or as a contributor to the final product. (If you like, give some examples.)

2. Draw a picture on a flipchart of the major product your company produces or contributes to. Some manufacturing examples might be a plane, a train, a bulldozer. For a service industry, draw a picture of the major product your company services or a picture of the location. Keep the picture simple.

3. Ask each team member to come up to the chart and draw the "part" of the whole that they believe the team is addressing. For example, if the major product is a plane and your team's process is assembling engine parts, they might draw an engine. They should then explain to the team (1) what the part is, and (2) why they have identified the team's mission with that part. Note that we have lots of colored markers up here—and don't worry about your artistic ability—you can explain your drawing to us!

The team will struggle with your assignment, but let them struggle because you are looking for them to express creatively their team's contribution to the company or improvement effort.

4. Move the focus to the team members as parts of the team "whole." Have members define their perceived team role and

how they think it will contribute to the effectiveness of the whole. Be sure each person leaves with a basic understanding of his or her role; have the team discuss it if some people are unclear about how they fit into the whole.

Performance Assessment: Taking Your Team's Pulse

By Richard P. Kropp, Jr., and Kristen Ciolkosz

Audience ➤	Any Kind of Team
Purpose ➤	—Define team goals —Define individual goals on the team —Establish measurements for tracking progress and a schedule for regular assessments
Suggested Uses ➤	Exercise for establishing team goals at the outset of team life Exercise for teams that are losing sight of their goals or whose goals have become vague Quarterly measurement exercise for all teams

Introduction

Measuring and monitoring team performance can be a difficult task. Teams establish missions and goals with specific outcomes in mind. To achieve these outcomes, it is critical that teams have some way to monitor their performance constantly and consistently. The assessment that follows is designed to give teams and their individual members a means of monitoring and measuring both the team's and the individual team member's performance as they move toward goal achievement. It is most effective when used on a quarterly or more frequent basis. The more teams are able to work together to stay on track, the greater their chance of being effective, efficient, and productive in meeting their goals.

The assessment is useful for teams at any stage of life. Teams that are newly formed can use this assessment once their mission and goals have been established to help write team and team member expectations and responsibilities. Teams that have moved through the team formation cycle more than once (meaning they are in the performing stage or are reforming) can begin using it at any point. The sooner the team is able to use this assessment to take the team's pulse, the greater their chance of staying on track.

Exercise: Leader's Notes

Time

Varies

Number of Participants

This assessment is intended for use by a team leader and the team. It should be completed when the full team is present, if possible.

Facilitator Expertise

- Ideally, this assessment is facilitated by the team leader.
- If the team should decide to discuss the Individual Team Member Goal Plans, the team may find it helpful to have an outside facilitator present who is skilled in helping teams work through interpersonal as well as team issues.

Materials and Equipment

Copy of the team's mission statement

Flipchart

Handouts

Goal Plan Worksheet

Individual Team Member Goal Plan Worksheet

Procedure

Introducing the Assessment

1. Introduce this assessment by explaining that this is a tool that can be used to help the team track their performance as well as their progress toward goal achievement.

2. Explain that this assessment consists of two elements. The first element is an assessment tool that the team will be creating together. The second piece of the assessment is a tool that each team member can use to monitor their performance as team members. Explain that both parts of the assessment are intended to provide a way for the team and its individual members to check for inconsistencies, missing resources, and/or roadblocks to team goal achievement.

Completing the Team Goal Plan

1. Give each member of the team a copy of the team's mission statement. Explain that as we go through the establishment and creation of our team's performance goals, we should all keep our mission in mind.

2. Give each team member a copy of the Team Goal Plan handout. Explain that this form is a tool that asks that we as a team come to a consensus about what our goal(s) will be, what strategies we believe we will use to accomplish our goal(s), the resources we believe we will need to establish our goal(s), potential roadblocks to successful goal achievement, and how we will know when we have achieved this goal. Explain that for each goal we will be using a separate Team Goal Plan, and we will follow one goal through to completion before discussing our other goals should we have more than one.

3. Ask the team members to take a few minutes to write down individually what the team's goals are on a sheet of paper. Once team members have had a chance to write down what they believe their team goals are, ask each team member (one at a time) to reveal his or her ideas.

Note: Capture the goals on flipchart paper as they are being reported out. Having heard from each team member, start a discussion asking the team members to discuss the findings. Let the discussion continue until a consensus has been reached by the team about what their team goals are. Capture the end goal(s) on the Team Goal Plan and explain that a final version of today's session will be photocopied and sent to each team member for their records.

4. If the team has more than one goal, ask the team to pick one goal that they would like to work through first as a team.

5. Once the team members have agreed upon their goal, ask them to think about what strategies the team might employ to achieve their goal. Let this discussion continue until the team comes to a consensus about the strategies that they will use to achieve their goal.

6. The third step in the Team Goal Plan asks the team members to develop a preliminary list of resources that will be needed to accomplish the goal. Again, this is a process that should continue until a consensus has been reached about what resources will be needed to reach goal achievement.

7. Identify potential roadblocks to the team's success.

8. Explain that in order for the team to be effective and efficient it is necessary to develop a set of criteria that will allow the team to measure its success. These criteria can include time frames, check lists, or percentages. What is important is that these criteria are specific enough that they can be used to measure the degree of the team's success in terms of both quality of the outcome and whether or not the goal was achieved. Continue this discussion until a consensus has been reached.

9. If the team has more than one goal,

begin the process all over again and walk the team through each step one at a time for each goal.

10. Once each of the goals has been discussed, explain that the Team Goal Plan(s) may have to be modified in the future. Therefore, it is the team's responsibility to decide upon the frequency with which the team will revisit the plan. Explain that a suggested minimum for revisiting the plan is quarterly, but the decision is up to the team. A consensus agreement is critical at this point to achieve team member support. Ask the team to establish the criteria for discussing the Team Goal Plan should a problem, issue, or idea arise before the next agreed-upon meeting.

11. The next and last step after reaching consensus for a time frame for revisiting the Team Goal Plan is for the team to set a date to reconvene to discuss the plan.

Completing the Individual Team Member Goal Plan

1. Explain that the Individual Team Member Goal Plan handout is intended to help team members focus attention on how they are working toward helping the team achieve their goal(s) as well as how each member believes the team is working to achieve individual goals.

2. Explain that this assessment is for personal use and development and does not have to be shared with any other member of the team. It is intended to help the individual reflect on the goal achievement process and how the individual believes it is working. Use this form as frequently or as infrequently as you would like, but remember that achievement of team goals requires each team member's effort and reflection.

3. Explain each of the statements beginning with the first statement, which asks the team members to discuss any accomplishments that they personally have made since the team last discussed the Team Goal Plan.

4. The second statement asks the individual to discuss any roadblocks that have gotten in the way of successfully achieving the team's goal(s). Ask the team members to make a note of any actions taken or solutions that they found to overcoming the roadblocks.

5. The third statement asks the individual team member to list any accomplishments that have been made by the team since the team last discussed the Team Goal Plan.

6. The fourth statement asks that the individual team member identify those roadblocks that have been barriers to the team's ability to achieve its goal(s).

7. Finally, team members should identify the links between their individual team member accomplishments and the team's accomplishments.

8. Explain that the findings of the Individual Team Member Goal Plan are for the individual team member's personal use, but if they think that sharing their findings during the meetings about the Team Goal Plan would be helpful, it is a welcome suggestion but not mandatory.

Customization

The team may decide to work on one team goal per meeting rather than working through all of the goals in one meeting.

- The team may decide to form subteams with each subteam taking a goal to work through. If this option is chosen then the team as a whole should discuss and modify each subteam's findings until a consensus has been reached about the Team Goal Plan.

- The team may limit the number of goals used in the Team Goal Plan so that they only work through two or three goals that are seen as having priority.

Team Goal Plan Worksheet

Team Goal:
▶ _____
_____
_____
_____
_____
_____
_____

Strategies for Team Goal Achievement:
▶ _____
_____
_____
_____
_____
_____
_____

Resources Needed:
▶ _____
_____
_____
_____
_____
_____
_____

Potential Roadblocks to Team Goal Achievement:
▶ _____
_____
_____
_____
_____

Criteria for Success:
▶ _____
_____
_____
_____
_____

Individual Team Member Goal Plan Worksheet

List any personal accomplishments since the last Team Goal Plan meeting:

▶ _____
_____
_____
_____
_____

Identify the roadblocks to your success as a team member in working toward achieving the team's goal(s). List any actions taken or solutions found to eliminate the roadblocks.

▶ _____
_____
_____
_____
_____
_____

List any team accomplishments since the last Team Goal Plan meeting.

▶ _____
_____
_____
_____
_____
_____

Identify any roadblocks encountered by the team in working toward the team's goal achievement. List any actions taken or solutions found to overcome these barriers.

▶ _____
_____
_____
_____
_____

Identify the link between your individual accomplishments as a team member and the team's accomplishments.

▶ _____
_____
_____
_____
_____

SECTION 6: PROMOTING INNOVATION AND CREATIVITY

Section 6 at a Glance

MATERIAL

Material	Page	AUDIENCES				FORMATS		
		Learning Professionals	Staff and Supervisors	Teams	Management	Self-study/Resource for Training	Group Exercise	Tool
Survey of Innovation Capability	6-4	●			●			●
Bright Ideas	6-28	●			●	●		
Learning From a Masterpiece	6-30	●				●		
In the Throws of Creativity	6-35	●		●	●		●	
Test of Creativity: Self-assessment Exercises	6-38	●	●	●	●	●	●	
Imagine That	6-51	●	●	●	●		●	
The Wonderful World of "What If?"	6-55	●	●	●	●		●	
Random Thoughts	6-57	●	●	●	●		●	

Introduction:
The Role of Innovation and Creativity in High-performance-seeking Organizations

Coopers & Lybrand defines creativity as the generation of ideas and alternatives and innovation as the transformation of those ideas and alternatives into useful applications that lead to change and performance improvement. Both of these capabilities are critical to developing and maintaining the adaptability that enables organizations to achieve high performance in a changing global environment. To stay competitive, businesses must create new strategies, new products, and new ways of manufacturing, distributing, and selling. The ability to innovate rapidly provides a particularly competitive edge.

Many organizations claim to value innovation. For example, about one in four of the mission statements featured in "The Mission Statement Book" (which lists the mission statements of about 300 companies) included innovation as either a core value or part of the competitive strategy. However, not all companies put this capability into action. According to the Juran Institute, a typical U.S. company implements only 0.16 new ideas a year. The pace is set by industry leaders in innovation, such as the Japanese company, Toyota, which implements 46 new ideas a year.

Coopers & Lybrand's recent survey of improvement-driven organizations suggests several steps organizations can take to improve their performance in innovation and creativity. First, employees at all levels of the organization should be encouraged to develop ideas for new products and services, and management should accept and act upon many ideas. Second, high-performing organizations emphasize learning and innovation to help manage risk and speed time-to-market for new products. This includes valuing creativity in learning initiatives, such as course design, delivery, and evaluation.

Learning professionals have important roles to play in the process of making an organization more creative. They can be involved in consulting with management to create the strategy and infrastructure to support innovation, help develop an environment conducive to creative thinking and innovation, design and present learning experiences that foster creativity, and model innovation by making their own learning products and training programs more creative.

How This Section Can Help

This section contains resources to help organizations address key success factors for becoming more innovative. The first is a survey that allows managers to assess the strengths and weaknesses of their organization or unit. The survey questions also introduce key concepts relating to developing innovation capacity, and the discussion of the results underlines success factors. The next article, "Bright Ideas," has ideas for establishing an environment that allows creativity to flourish—on the job and in training situations. In "Learning From a Masterpiece," learning professionals can pick up strategies for improving their own creativity and use an assessment tool for determining how creative their current learning activities are.

The remainder of the section features exercises to teach, model, and enable creativity. These activities show participants the value of nontraditional approaches and provide techniques for jump-starting creative thinking.

References

Carr, D., and Johansson, H. *Best Practices in Reengineering.* New York: McGraw-Hill, Inc., 1995.

Godfrey, A. Creativity, Innovation, and Quality. Juran Institute Web Site (HYPERLINK http://www.juran http://www.juran.com/juran/articles/article 003.html).

Ostrenga, M., et al. *The Ernst & Young Guide to Total Cost Management,* Vol. 8. New York: John Wiley & Sons, 1992.

Vander Linde, K., Horney, N., and Koonce, R. Seven Ways to Make Your Training Department One of the Best. *Training & Development.* August 1997, p. 25.

Survey of Innovation Capability

By David Francis

Audience ➤	Managers, Learning Professionals
Purpose ➤	—Understand attributes of and success factors for developing innovative organizations —Explore the organizational dimensions of innovation —Assess the innovations, strengths, and weaknesses of their organization —Be able to begin a process for improving the innovation of the organization
Suggested Uses ➤	Process an assessment tool for initiating a creativity enhancement program organization-wide or in a department or unit Use survey over time to monitor progress on innovation promotion efforts.

Introduction

The first step in improving organizational innovation performance is determining what aspects of the organization currently support, enable, discourage, or prevent creative thinking and behavior. The survey that follows allows managers to assess the strengths and weaknesses of their organization or unit. The survey questions also introduce key concepts relating to developing innovation capacity, and the discussion of the results underlines success factors.

This activity also includes a handout that describes the attributes managers need to develop and sustain a creative organization. It concludes with a process for deciding where to focus initial actions to correct problems that block creativity or create new supports for innovation.

Exercise: Leader's Notes

Time

90 minutes

Number of Participants

Unlimited (participants will need to work in small groups during the session)

Facilitator Expertise

To facilitate this session you would benefit from an understanding of organizational aspects of innovation. The following books will help.

O'Hare (1988). *Innovate! How to Gain and Sustain Competitive Advantage*. London: Basil Blackwell.

Utterback, J. M. (1994). *Mastering the Dynamics of Innovation*. Boston: HBS.

Wheatley, M. J. (1994). *Leadership and the New Science*. San Francisco: Berrett-Koehler.

Materials and Equipment

An overhead projector and a flipchart

Overheads

Handouts

Survey of Innovation Capability

Survey of Innovation Capability: Scoring and Ranking

Scoring Sheet

Explanation of Results

20 Attributes of the Innovative Organization

What to Do

Procedure

1. Introduce the session by saying that innovation is a vital aspect of today's organizations and explain that the group will examine the extent to which their own organization supports or blocks innovation. This can be illustrated with examples from your own experience (5 minutes).

2. Distribute the Survey of Innovation Capability and ask everyone to complete it on their own organization or unit (20 minutes).

3. Give a lecturette on the attributes of the innovative organization using the overheads attached. The content from this lecturette may be supplemented with material in the Survey of Innovation Capability: Scoring and Ranking section (15 minutes).

4. Distribute the Survey of Innovation Capability: Scoring and Ranking handout. Emphasize the instructions at the front of this section. Ask participants to break into small groups (25 people). Members of the same unit/team/organization should work together (5 minutes).

5. Ask groups to complete the analysis as directed (35 minutes).

6. Invite each group to share at least one insight that they have gained from the session. These should be recorded on the flipchart (5 minutes).

7. Pass out the handout, 20 Attributes of the Innovative Organization. Note that 20 different aspects of the organization must be managed to create the preconditions for innovation.

8. Pass out the What to Do handout and ask the small groups to fill it out together. Note that innovative organizations do not emerge from the end of a production line like pressed steel components, but rather, if the environment is favorable, they grow like crystals. Organizations have to overcome all barriers to innovation. If these problems are not faced or resolved, they become blockages.

Innovation blockages inhibit the flow of creative and implementation energy. When a blockage is fully cleared, it enables positive energy to flow and, in a way, the cleared blockage becomes a driver. Each organization has to find ways of overcoming blockages and transforming them into drivers. Twenty blocks to innovation can be identified along with each's hazards to innovation effectiveness. However, each of these blockages can also become a driver and a source of innovation energy. Seen in this way, the display of the survey results of your organization gives much information.

Customization

The survey can be used for full organization analysis using a wide sample.

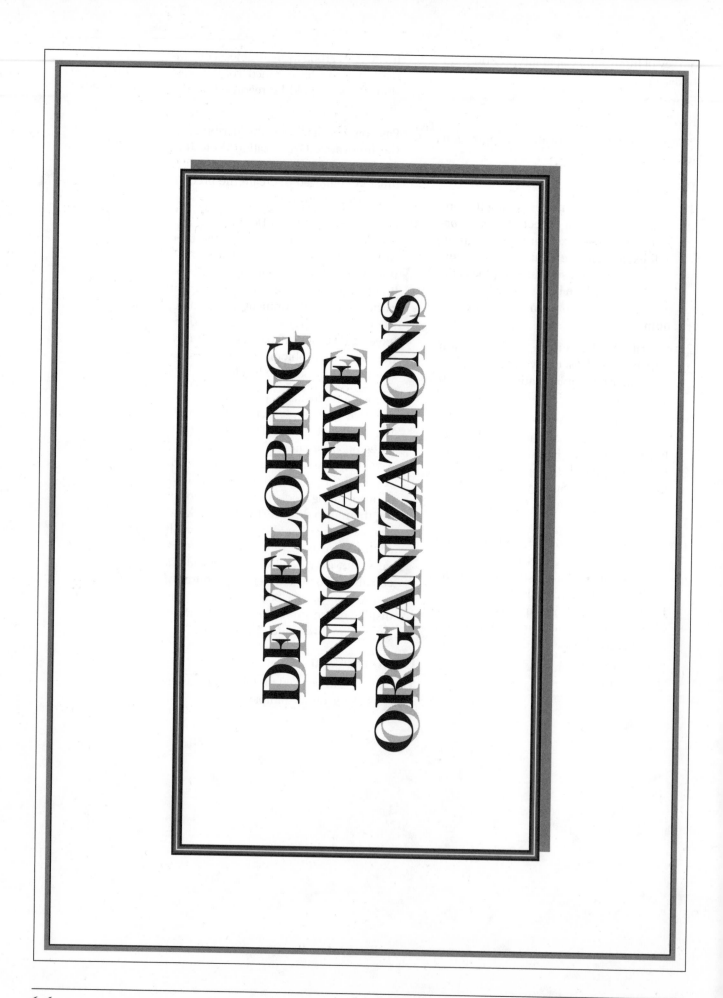

The Big Four "I" Killers

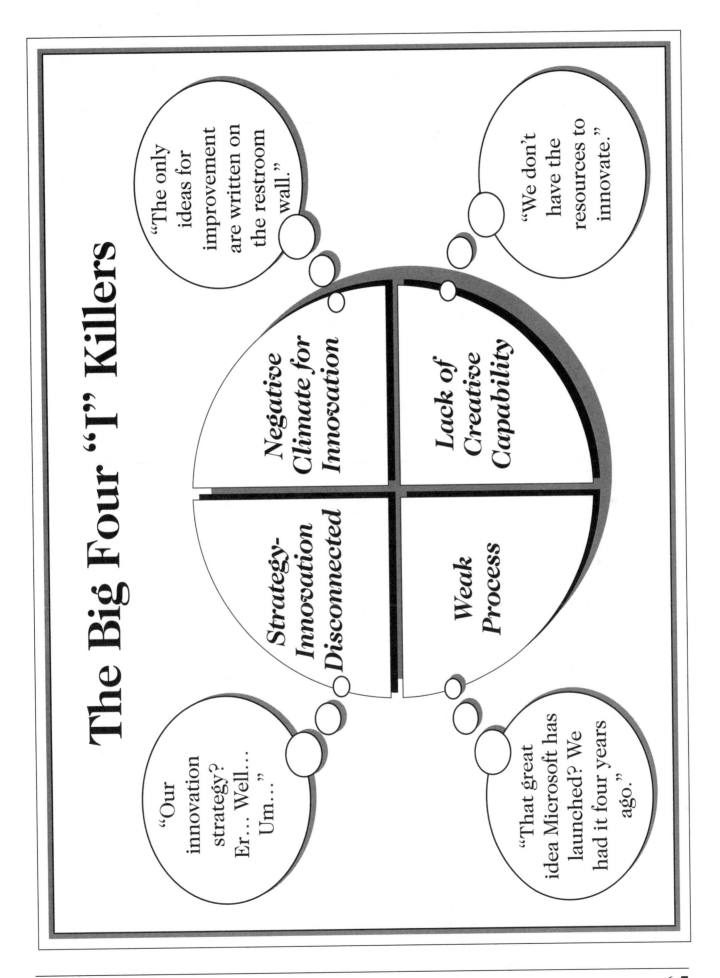

Six Insights from Research

▲ Organizations require different innovation patterns

▲ There are periods of innovation intensity

▲ You will need "organizations within organizations"

▲ You must get a lot of things right

▲ Innovation can be managed but not fully predicted

▲ Innovation is not a substitute for a great strategy or strong organization

20 Innovation Killers

- ▲ Lead for Stability
- ▲ Don't strive for competitive advantage
- ▲ Starve innovators of resources
- ▲ Invent everything yourself
- ▲ Let innovation programs just grow anyhow

And...

"The way to get on around here is to avoid making waves."

▲ **Empower no one or everyone**

▲ **Demand conformity**

▲ **Switch off your staff**

▲ **Ignore the masters**

▲ **Disparage learning**

And...

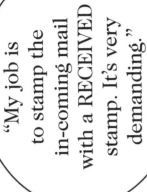

"My job is to stamp the in-coming mail with a RECEIVED stamp. It's very demanding."

▲ Recruit unexceptional individuals

▲ Permit silos

▲ Organize for stability

▲ Lack a theory of what needs to be done

▲ Neglect to build all needed competencies

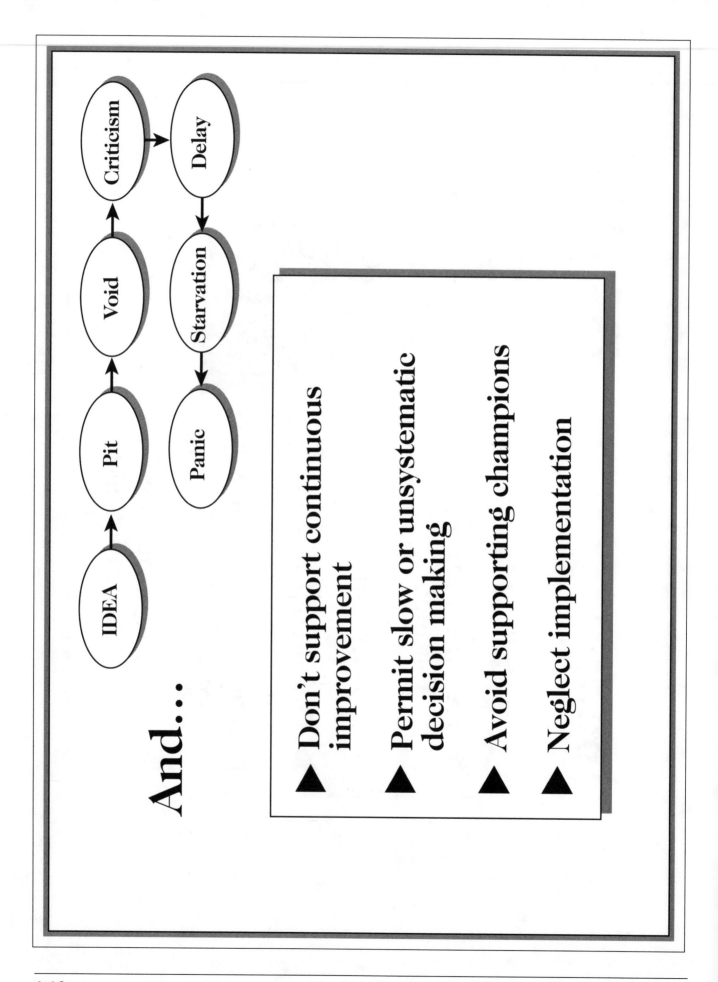

And...

▲ Don't support continuous improvement

▲ Permit slow or unsystematic decision making

▲ Avoid supporting champions

▲ Neglect implementation

A Weak Link in Your Innovation Chain?

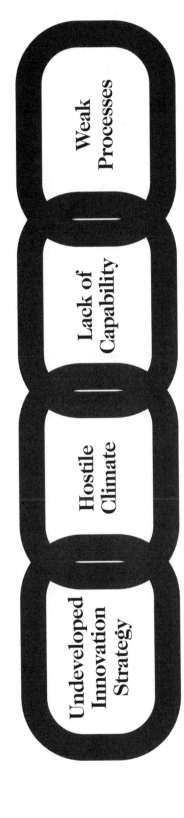

Undeveloped Innovation Strategy

Hostile Climate

Lack of Capability

Weak Processes

What to do?

▲ Define it

▲ Ask "Does it matter?"

▲ Explore it

▲ Unblock it

Survey of Innovation Capability

Innovation is vitally important. This survey will help to provide the information needed to improve innovation in your organization.

Please fill out the questionnaire with care and honesty; the intention is to benefit everyone. Individual results are never identified by name, so remain strictly confidential.

Below you will find a definition of the organization being reviewed by this survey. Keep this in mind throughout. (If the box has not been completed, please define the part of the organization that you are reviewing in the box before you proceed further.)

The organization (or part of the organization) being reviewed is _____ .

Instructions

Below you will find 100 statements. Look at each statement and circle the appropriate number in each case.

In some cases you may feel that you do not have sufficient knowledge to be objective, but please answer each statement even if you give a subjective opinion.

The statements may appear to be repetitive, but there are subtle differences between them—so please consider each item separately.

Look at each statement and circle the appropriate response in each case:

This statement is true:
- *1 To little or no extent*
- *2 To a slight extent*
- *3 To a moderate extent*
- *4 To a great extent*
- *5 To a very great extent*

1. This organization can demonstrate a recent history of adopting radical ideas. 1 2 3 4 5

2. Every employee is 100 percent clear about what "business" we are in. 1 2 3 4 5

3. Top managers ensure that we have sufficient research and development resources to develop new ideas. 1 2 3 4 5

4. Customers' perceptions of our products (or services) are measured frequently. 1 2 3 4 5

5. All parts of the organization pull together to support major initiatives. 1 2 3 4 5

6. Everyone is encouraged to speak up, even when senior people are challenged. 1 2 3 4 5

7. Very high standards of performance are expected from all employees. 1 2 3 4 5

8. Employees welcome new ideas. 1 2 3 4 5

9. Those with technical skills are highly respected. 1 2 3 4 5

10. The organization invests in training to ensure that people learn new skills. 1 2 3 4 5

11. Individuals with exceptional talent are recruited. 1 2 3 4 5

12. Teamwork is highly productive. 1 2 3 4 5

13. There is just the right level of administration systems, not too much, not too little. 1 2 3 4 5

---

14. Managers strive to understand new ideas in great depth before making changes. . . . 1 2 3 4 5

15. The organization has fully analyzed what new technologies will be needed
    in the future. 1 2 3 4 5

16. Ideas for improvement are always being implemented. 1 2 3 4 5

17. Top priority is given to developing new products or services. 1 2 3 4 5

18. Decisions about launching new products (or services) are taken only after
    very careful analysis. 1 2 3 4 5

Look at each statement and circle the appropriate response in each case:

This statement is true:	*1*	*To little or no extent*
	2	*To a slight extent*
	3	*To a moderate extent*
	4	*To a great extent*
	5	*To a very great extent*

19. Individuals promote ideas themselves and get them "to fly." 1 2 3 4 5

20. Projects are managed efficiently and effectively. 1 2 3 4 5

21. Top managers share a well-developed vision of how the organization needs
    to change. 1 2 3 4 5

22. This organization maintains a real edge over its competitors. 1 2 3 4 5

23. There is a high (i.e., larger than competitors) investment in developing
    new ideas (research and development). 1 2 3 4 5

24. Top management has carefully considered how markets will change in the future. . 1 2 3 4 5

25. New ideas are driven through despite setbacks or difficulties. 1 2 3 4 5

26. Employees are empowered to take significant initiatives themselves. 1 2 3 4 5

27. Individuals are held fully accountable for their performance. 1 2 3 4 5

28. Employees understand how their efforts can help the organization to be
    successful in the future. 1 2 3 4 5

29. Technical specialists share their knowledge across the organization. 1 2 3 4 5

30. Staff, at every level, are actively looking for ideas and techniques from the
    best in the world. 1 2 3 4 5

31. Creative individuals are well rewarded. 1 2 3 4 5

32. Departments cooperate to get things done. 1 2 3 4 5

33. The organization's structure encourages new ideas to be developed. 1 2 3 4 5

34. A great deal of time is spent in understanding ideas for improvement—before
    they are implemented. 1 2 3 4 5

35. There are well-developed plans to develop new capabilities that will be needed to be successful in the future. 1 2 3 4 5

36. The organization learns from what goes well or badly in order to operate better next time. 1 2 3 4 5

Look at each statement and circle the appropriate response in each case:

This statement is true: *1 To little or no extent*
                                       2 To a slight extent
                                       3 To a moderate extent
                                       4 To a great extent
                                       5 To a very great extent

37. There is an effective process for developing new products/services. 1 2 3 4 5

38. Senior management will take bold decisions. 1 2 3 4 5

39. People who want to get new things done are given full support. 1 2 3 4 5

40. Ideas are implemented efficiently throughout the organization. 1 2 3 4 5

41. The organization's leader inspires confidence in all employees. 1 2 3 4 5

42. Recently introduced products (or services) are extremely attractive to customers. . 1 2 3 4 5

43. Our research and development effort is being spent in ways that will make us stronger in the market. 1 2 3 4 5

44. We measure (benchmark) exactly how we compare with other firms. 1 2 3 4 5

45. Management insists that only a limited number of initiatives are undertaken at once—to prevent overstretching the organization. 1 2 3 4 5

46. People (at every level) are rewarded for taking initiatives themselves. 1 2 3 4 5

47. Managers and professional staff are given specific objectives to develop new ideas. 1 2 3 4 5

48. Senior managers can rely on getting full support from employees when they want to get something done. 1 2 3 4 5

49. Specialists take their technical training and development very seriously. 1 2 3 4 5

50. Everyone receives detailed feedback on his or her own performance. 1 2 3 4 5

51. Outstanding individuals are valued in this organization. 1 2 3 4 5

52. People who need to work together are highly cooperative. 1 2 3 4 5

53. The way that we are organized stimulates creativity. 1 2 3 4 5

54. Everyone is extensively well briefed before a change is introduced. 1 2 3 4 5

55. This organization is building the right capabilities to be strong in the future. 1 2 3 4 5

Survey of Innovation Capability (continued)

Look at each statement and circle the appropriate response in each case:

This statement is true:
  1 *To little or no extent*
  2 *To a slight extent*
  3 *To a moderate extent*
  4 *To a great extent*
  5 *To a very great extent*

56. Everyone adopts the approach that "everything can always be improved." 1 2 3 4 5

57. The process we use for developing new products is sufficiently flexible for today's competitive world. 1 2 3 4 5

58. When it is necessary, decisions are taken quickly. 1 2 3 4 5

59. Senior managers will support anyone with a good idea. 1 2 3 4 5

60. Initiatives are implemented rapidly. 1 2 3 4 5

61. Top managers have gained universal support for their vision of how the organization should develop. 1 2 3 4 5

62. This organization is striving to be truly world class in every aspect of performance. 1 2 3 4 5

63. Once it is agreed that an idea for a new product (or service) should be developed, all necessary resources will be made available. 1 2 3 4 5

64. We learn through our strong links with industry associations, universities, and consultants. 1 2 3 4 5

65. Top managers take personal responsibility for major initiatives. 1 2 3 4 5

66. People in this organization adopt an "I can do it" attitude. 1 2 3 4 5

67. Those who develop new ideas are rewarded more highly than others. 1 2 3 4 5

68. Everyone who works here is committed to making this organization highly successful. 1 2 3 4 5

69. Professional and technical experts are fully involved in planning new products and services. 1 2 3 4 5

70. All managers and professionals are working on a personal learning and development plan. 1 2 3 4 5

71. Innovative individuals are given full support to develop ideas. 1 2 3 4 5

72. People get together and use a "think tank" approach to solve problems. 1 2 3 4 5

73. Decisions to support or kill an initiative are taken by those managers who really understand the issues. 1 2 3 4 5

Look at each statement and circle the appropriate response in each case:

This statement is true:
1 To little or no extent
2 To a slight extent
3 To a moderate extent
4 To a great extent
5 To a very great extent

74. Those leading a change can fully describe the advantages and disadvantages to anyone affected by it. 1 2 3 4 5

75. The organization is currently building the resources needed to implement senior management's long-term plans. 1 2 3 4 5

76. People actually doing the work suggest a flow of ideas for continuous improvement. 1 2 3 4 5

77. The organization will turn an idea into a product (or service that can be made or delivered) efficiently. 1 2 3 4 5

78. When a decision to develop a new product or process is taken, everyone who is affected is quickly informed. 1 2 3 4 5

79. People who drive through changes are recognized as "heroes." 1 2 3 4 5

80. Those who make our products (or deliver services) are extremely capable. 1 2 3 4 5

81. The leader in the organization ensures that fundamental changes are implemented, even if they are unpopular. 1 2 3 4 5

82. This organization has found ways to reduce costs and, therefore, provide customers with better value than competitors. 1 2 3 4 5

83. We are strong in research and development (when compared with others in the same industry). 1 2 3 4 5

84. The organization has teamed with other organizations when there has been something important to learn. 1 2 3 4 5

85. Senior managers who bring about change are especially valued. 1 2 3 4 5

86. A visitor would say, "This organization buzzes with energy." 1 2 3 4 5

87. Every manager has objectives to develop new ideas. 1 2 3 4 5

88. Everyone helps people who are developing a new idea. 1 2 3 4 5

89. Professional and technical experts are highly valued. 1 2 3 4 5

Look at each statement and circle the appropriate response in each case:

This statement is true:
    1 To little or no extent
    2 To a slight extent
    3 To a moderate extent
    4 To a great extent
    5 To a very great extent

90. A great deal of effort is invested in developing the organization so that problems are solved more effectively. 1 2 3 4 5

91. People with exceptional talent stay for a long time. 1 2 3 4 5

92. Information is freely shared across departmental and functional boundaries. 1 2 3 4 5

93. The organization makes resources readily available to develop new ideas. 1 2 3 4 5

94. Senior managers agree upon what needs to be done to develop the organization. 1 2 3 4 5

95. Effective action is being taken to create the new capabilities that the organization will need in the future. 1 2 3 4 5

96. Everyone's creativity is used to find solutions to problems. 1 2 3 4 5

97. We produce new products (or services) faster than competitors. 1 2 3 4 5

98. Major decisions are extensively reviewed so that we can do better next time. 1 2 3 4 5

99. People with ideas can win resources to develop their proposals. 1 2 3 4 5

100. This organization is good at "getting things done." 1 2 3 4 5

Survey of Organizational Innovation: Scoring and Ranking

Directions

Take your completed survey and copy the scores onto the answer grid on the next page. Add up the scores in each vertical column.

Copy these totals next to the appropriate roman numerals on the chart shown here. The highest scoring category is ranked one, the second highest scoring category is ranked two, and so on.

	INNOVATION STRENGTHS	Ranking
Ia	STRONG INNOVATION LEADERSHIP	
Ib	INNOVATION INCREASES COMPETITIVE ADVANTAGE	
Ic	PRODUCTIVE INNOVATION RESOURCES	
Id	ACTIVE EXTERNAL LINKAGES	
Ie	DIRECTED INITIATIVES	
IIa	SELECTIVE EMPOWERMENT	
IIb	INNOVATION DEMANDING	
IIc	HIGH ENROLLMENT	
IId	RESPECT FOR MASTERY	
IIe	CONTINUOUS LEARNING	
IIIa	EXCEPTIONAL INDIVIDUALS	
IIIb	PRODUCTIVE TEAMWORK	
IIIc	APT ORGANIZATIONAL FORM	
IIId	GUIDING CONCEPTUAL MAPS	
IIIe	COMPLETE COMPETENCIES PORTFOLIO	
IVa	ACTIVE CONTINUOUS IMPROVEMENT	
IVb	HIGH-PERFORMING NP-PD	
IVc	SOUND DECISION-MAKING PROCESSES	
IVd	SUPPORTED CHAMPIONS	
IVe	EFFECTIVE IMPLEMENTATION	

Scoring Sheet

1	2	3	4	5	6	7	8	9	10	11	12	13	14	15	16	17	18	19	20
21	22	23	24	25	26	27	28	29	30	31	32	33	34	35	36	37	38	39	40
41	42	43	44	45	46	47	48	49	50	51	52	53	54	55	56	57	58	59	60
61	62	63	64	65	66	67	68	69	70	71	72	73	74	75	76	77	78	79	80
81	82	83	84	85	86	87	88	89	90	91	92	93	94	95	96	97	98	99	100
Ia	Ib	Ic	Id	Ie	IIa	IIb	IIc	IId	IIe	IIIa	IIIb	IIIc	IIId	IIIe	IVa	IVb	IVc	IVd	IVe
I					II					III					IV				

Ia STRONG INNOVATION LEADERSHIP

The organization is led by people who create a context within which innovation thrives.

The key characteristics of organizations with strong innovation leadership are:

1. Radical thinking at the top.
2. Effective top team.
3. Creation of a proinnovation context.
4. Development of stretching visions.
5. Leader expects innovation.

Ib INNOVATION INCREASES COMPETITIVE ADVANTAGE

The organization has a well-developed strategy that identifies the capabilities, technologies, products, services, and processes that are necessary for continued competitive advantage.

The key characteristics of organizations that innovate for competitive advantage are:

1. There is a clear definition of "the business we are in."
2. The firm has a coherent competitive strategy.
3. Innovations that add value are continuously identified.
4. There is a strategic commitment to innovate faster and further than competitors.
5. Innovations that do not provide competitive advantage are dropped.

Ic PRODUCTIVE INNOVATION RESOURCES

Sufficient investment is made to enable the organization's innovation strategy.

The key characteristics of organizations that have productive innovation resources are:

1. Budgets assign sufficient percent investment for innovation.
2. R&D investment is strategically focused.
3. R&D is fully integrated into the firm.
4. R&D managers influence strategic decisions.
5. ROI on R&D is measured.

Id ACTIVE EXTERNAL LINKAGES

There are strong linkages that bring challenge, insight, ideas, and support.

The key characteristics of organizations that have active external linkages are:

1. Customers are deeply involved in design of new products and services.
2. Managers have a rich-picture understanding of future market development.
3. The firm undertakes systematic benchmarking.
4. There are active links with industry, universities, and consultants.
5. The firm has developmental alliances.

Ie DIRECTED INITIATIVES

Innovation projects are owned by senior managers and driven through.

The key characteristics of organizations that have directed initiatives are:

1. Innovation is expected in every area of the firm.
2. Senior managers "own" important initiatives.
3. Innovative projects are seen through despite obstacles.
4. Only achievable numbers/scale of programs are undertaken.
5. Senior managers are assessed on their innovative prowess.

IIa SELECTIVE EMPOWERMENT

The high-energy culture supports able individuals to take initiatives.

The key characteristics of organizations that have selective empowerment are:

1. High self-confidence.
2. Can-do ethos.
3. Selective empowerment policies (empowering able people).
4. Positive culture.
5. Flow of "Chi" energy.

IIb INNOVATION DEMANDING

Everyone is expected to innovate.

The key characteristics of organizations in which innovation is demanded are:

1. Stretching individual objectives.
2. Accountability for innovating is accepted.
3. Objective-setting system requires innovation.
4. Reward-system reinforces innovation initiatives.
5. Established success criteria for innovative initiatives.

IIc HIGH ENROLLMENT

People support innovation initiatives.

The key characteristics of organizations in which enrollment is high are:

1. Full communication of developmental goals.
2. Willingness to move forward.
3. Support for management initiatives.
4. Generic "buy-in" to the organization's development.
5. Helping ethos.

IId RESPECT FOR MASTERY

Those who have a deep specialist knowledge help guide the organization forward.

The key characteristics of organizations in which there is a respect for mastery are:

1. Respect for technical/professional skills by decision makers.
2. "Masters" act as teachers and mentors.
3. Continuous development of expert capability.
4. High involvement of professional/technical specialists in decision making.
5. Effective processes for integrating experts into mainstream operations.

IIe CONTINUOUS LEARNING

Challenge and learning are natural, continuous processes.

The key characteristics of organizations in which there is continuous learning are:

1. High investment in learning.
2. New paradigms sought and explored.
3. Extensive learning from action.
4. Self-ownership of development.
5. Teams and organizational learning pursued.

IIIa   EXCEPTIONAL INDIVIDUALS

Exceptional individuals are recruited, rewarded, respected, and retained.

The key characteristics of organizations in which exceptional individuals are employed are:

1. Recruitment of exceptional individuals.
2. Reward of exceptional individuals.
3. Exceptional individuals fit into the organization.
4. Retention of exceptional individuals.
5. Motivation of exceptional individuals.

IIIb   PRODUCTIVE TEAMWORK

The organization gains because people work well together.

The key characteristics of organizations that have productive teamwork are:

1. Dynamic teams.
2. Cross-functional networking.
3. Absence of interpersonal blockages.
4. Focused group creativity "think-tanks."
5. Effective meetings/encounters.

IIIc   APT ORGANIZATIONAL FORM

The structure and form of the organization helps (not hinders) the innovation process.

The key characteristics of an apt organizational form are:

1. Absence of excessive "bureaucracy."
2. Organizational structure supports innovation aims.
3. Loose/tight control mechanisms.
4. Innovative organization recognized as being distinctive.
5. Inherent organizational flexibility.

IIId   GUIDING CONCEPTUAL MAPS

Innovations are directed by a developing theory of what needs to change and why.

The key characteristics of organizations that have guiding conceptual maps are:

1. Coherent "action-theory" driving innovation.
2. Critical evaluation of current strengths (helping factors) and weaknesses (hindering factors).
3. "Buy in" to "action-theory" being used.
4. In-depth model of how things could/should be.
5. Consensus on "action-theory" from decision makers/opinion leaders.

IIIe   COMPLETE COMPETENCIES PORTFOLIO

The organization continuously develops capabilities to support a stream of relevant innovation.

The key characteristics of organizations that have a complete competencies portfolio are:

1. Comprehensive skills and technological audit.
2. Developed competency model guiding organizational development.
3. Integrated portfolio of competencies.
4. Capabilities and technologies matching strategic objectives.
5. Program for building tomorrow's competencies.

IVa ACTIVE CONTINUOUS IMPROVEMENT

There is an ethic that says "everything can always be improved."

The key characteristics of organizations that have active continuous improvement are:

1. Continuous product/process improvement program.
2. Strong analytical skills.
3. Widespread acceptance of the "CI Ethic."
4. Acceptance of bottom-up innovation.
5. Widespread facilitation of creativity techniques.

IVb HIGH-PERFORMING NP-PD

There are effective processes for managing new product-process development.

The key characteristics of organizations that have high-performing NP-PD are:

1. NPD is seen as a key activity.
2. NPD processes are managed.
3. NPD activities are focused and targeted.
4. World class solutions are the only acceptable ones.
5. NPD is rapid.

IVc SOUND DECISION-MAKING PROCESSES

Timely and wise decisions are taken about initiatives.

The key characteristics of organizations that have sound decision-making processes are:

1. Potential up sides and down sides fully examined.
2. Alternative options fully examined.
3. Speedy decision making.
4. Clear communication of decisions.
5. Incisive decision review process.

IVd SUPPORTED CHAMPIONS

Those who can make things happen are enabled and supported.

The key characteristics of organizations that support champions are:

1. Entrepreneurship is institutionalized.
2. Champions are supported.
3. Patrons are skilled.
4. Champions are recognized as heroes.
5. Availability of resources to champions.

IVe EFFECTIVE IMPLEMENTATION

Innovative ideas can be quickly and effectively implemented.

The key characteristics of organizations that can effectively implement innovations are:

1. Strong program and project management.
2. Seamless integration between innovators and doers.
3. Intensive standardization process.
4. Effective "production" capability.
5. Rapid application of "the learning effect."

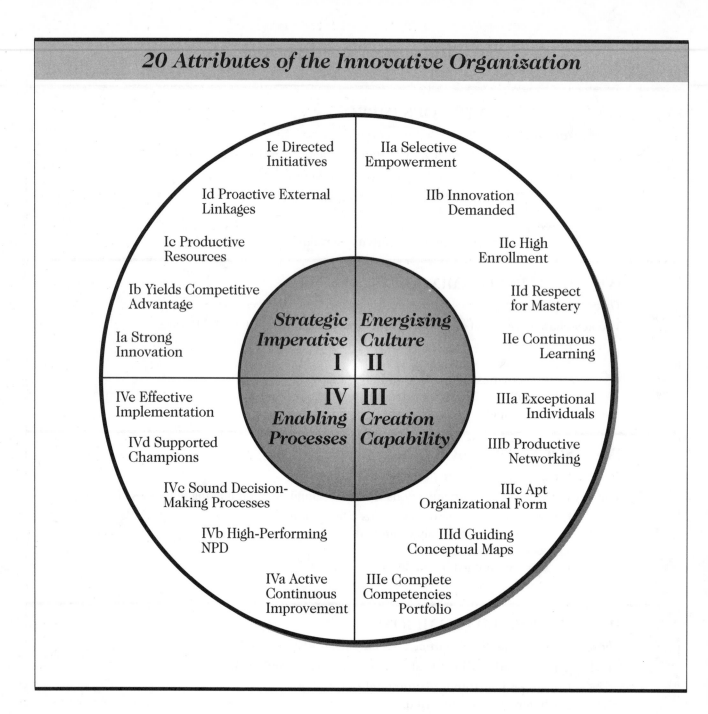

What to Do

List below the three lowest scores for yourself and for the group average.

Lowest Individual Scores   **Block Title**

1. _____

2. _____

3. _____

Group Average

1. _____

2. _____

3. _____

Block Title

The innovation blockages (those with the lowest scores) are probably the major issues your organization has to face. These results need to be verified by discussion and further evaluation.

Select one probable blockage. Look back in the explanation section at the five characteristics of organizations that do not have that blockage and ask the following:

Is this a real blockage for us?

Is it important?

Why does the blockage occur?

What can we do to unblock within the next 90 days?

Section 6: Promoting Innovation and Creativity   **6-27**

Bright Ideas

By Michael Michalko

Audience ➡	Learning Professionals, Managers
Purpose ➡	—Learn ideas for making an organization behave like a creative organization
Suggested Uses ➡	Self-study Resource for meeting or planning session on how to help the organization improve performance in innovation

Is your organization locked into the same old ways of thinking? It doesn't have to be. Human resource specialists can help managers and employees jump-start their creativity.

Fifteen Steps

Here are 15 steps for making the most of employee creativity in your organization.

One-a-day. Ask employees to try to improve one work area or an aspect of one work area each day, focusing on the areas within their control. At the end of each day, employees should ask each other what they did differently and better than the way it was done before.

Positive thinking. People shouldn't waste time thinking of reasons why something can't work or can't be done. Instead, they should think about ways to make something work, and then get it done. Ask people to think of three work-related tasks or changes they think can't be accomplished. Then ask them to figure out ways to accomplish them. Then do the same thing yourself.

Three ways. Refuse to accept negative comments about new ideas. Suggest that people think of at least three ways to implement a new idea before they try to reject it.

Let's do lunch. Encourage weekly lunchtime meetings of three to five employees to engage in creative thinking. Ask meeting participants to read a book on creativity; each person can read a different chapter and share information about it at the meetings. Invite creative people from the community to speak to the group.

Changing places. Have people work part of a day in other departments. Afterwards, department heads can hold informal meetings with the visiting employees to solicit their feedback. The department heads should ask the visitors what they'd do differently if they were full-time workers in those departments.

Creative corner. Provide a special area at work for people to engage in creative thinking. Stock the area with books and videos on creativity, as well as learning games and such toys as beanbags and modeling clay. You may want to decorate the area with pictures of employees as infants, to suggest the idea that we're all born with the potential to be creative. Schedule regular times for creative thinking.

Brainstorming board. Put up a bulletin board in a central area and encourage people to use it to brainstorm ideas. Write a theme or problem on a colored piece of paper or card and place it in the center of the board. Provide pieces of white paper on which people can write their ideas to post on the board.

Trading ideas. Suggest that employees conduct an in-house trade show at which they share "how I did it" stories about recent work accomplishments. The show could consist of modestly fashioned trade booths exhibiting slides, photographs, procedure manuals, and so forth to show how employees' ideas and methods were successful.

People are likely to pick up ideas to use in their own departments, and they may team up with people from other departments to help solve work problems. The show could be a fun event and could even include employees' families.

Creative coaching. Ask someone in the organization to fill the role of creative coach. The role would entail encouraging and supporting creativity in all employees. The "position" of creative coach could be rotated among several or all employees.

Creativity by committee. Establish a "creative idea" committee made up of volunteers from different departments. The goals of the committee should be to elicit, discuss, and implement employees' ideas. The committee can record the number of ideas on a thermometer-type graph. The company should recognize and reward employees according to the quantity and quality of their creative contributions.

Play the numbers. Have a monthly "idea lottery," using a roll of numbered tickets. Each time an employee comes up with a creative idea, he or she receives a ticket. At the end of each month, share the ideas with all employees and then draw a number from a bowl. If the number on anyone's ticket corresponds to the number drawn, he or she gets a prize. If there is no winner, the prize can be doubled for the next month.

The Edison factor. Let people know that they are allowed to fail. As Thomas Edison said, "I failed my way to success." Edison conducted 9,000 experiments before he achieved a working light bulb. When an assistant asked why he persisted "in this folly," Edison replied, "Young man, I haven't failed. I've learned 9,000 things that don't work."

Ask people what they think are the organization's three biggest failures in the past three years. If people say none, then the organization isn't trying anything new.

Breaking through. If it isn't broke, break it. Test all of the assumptions about the organization's current systems, processes, methods, and products to see whether they're really necessary and whether there might be better ones.

Open the portals. Conduct a meeting open to employees at all levels to give them the opportunity to discuss issues and suggest ideas. Announce the meeting's theme, and then invite everyone to identify a related issue for which they're willing to take responsibility. When someone suggests an issue, he or she becomes the sponsor, writes the issue on a large sheet of paper, and posts the sheet on a wall. The process continues until all of the suggested issues have been posted.

Next, have participants take part in an "idea marketplace" in which each person signs one or more of the large sheets to discuss the issues. The sponsors get together with their groups in private to discuss the issues and record ideas.

Icons of creativity. Ask people to display items on their desks that represent their own visions of creativity. For example, a crystal ball might represent a view toward the future, jumper cables might symbolize the act of jump-starting people's creative thinking, a bottle of Heinz catsup might represent 57 new ideas.

Reaching for the Stars

Simply put, the key to increasing creativity in an organization is to make it start acting like a creative organization. Suppose that you wanted to be an artist: You would begin behaving like an artist by painting every day. You may not become another Van Gogh, but you'll be more of an artist than someone who has never tried.

When you reach for the stars, you may not capture one, but you also aren't likely to come up empty handed.

Learning from a Masterpiece

By Steve Cohen and Joan Jurkovic

Audience →	Learning Professionals
Purpose →	—Learn approaches for making learning presentations more creative —Be able to evaluate the creativity of their training programs or style
Suggested Uses →	Self-study Resource for training session for learning professionals

If you are like a lot of us, the idea of learning from a masterpiece takes you straight back to Art History 101. But that's not the kind of learning we're going to talk about here. We're going to look at learning in the workplace for performance improvement, and what masterpieces of fine art can teach us about raising the experience of learning to its highest and most powerful level. In fact, we'd like to make the case that there are masterpieces of learning design and that such programs, through their exceptional creativity and effectiveness, offer extraordinary value and possibilities for growth.

Now, you may be thinking that it's a bit presumptuous to talk about sales training programs and leadership development workshops in the same breath as, say, the ceiling of the Sistine Chapel. Okay, you're right. Fine arts and the art of training design have entirely different aims. Or do they?

When you think about it, many of the works in an art history course aren't just the impassioned products of artistic minds. They were jobs. Take the Sistine Chapel. Michelangelo had a client (Pope Julius), a budget (500 ducats), content (the Old Testament), and a goal (to glorify God, the church, and the pope—not necessarily in that order).

Though we tend to think of learning as a prosaic business activity, it also often affects profound issues and beliefs—our relationships with other people, our ideas about success, and our hopes and fears for the future.

So, perhaps the difference between fine arts and the art of training design isn't as great as it might seem at first. Certainly, it's striking that whether you are talking about painting, music, or literature—or workshops, courses, and other training programs—you find a slew of more or less competently executed examples. And you'll find a few that rise well above the rest.

Masterpieces move us, intrigue us, and remain in our thoughts well beyond the ordinary admiration we have for a good, solid piece of work. In training, masterpieces are the extraordinarily smart, memorable, and successful programs. They connect with learners in deeply personal and universal ways, engaging their minds and emotions with an impact that creates real change. That's why when you are buying a learning system, it's to your great advantage to get a masterpiece rather than an also-ran.

So, what should you look for?

Reprinted with permission from *Training & Development,* published by the American Society for Training & Development.

Good Science, Good Business, and Great Art

When you're judging a training program, it helps to break it down into its critical components, which we'll call science, business, and art.

By *science* we mean the soundness of a program's learning methodology. By business we mean how astutely a program is aligned with an organization's strategy and goals. Both dimensions involve well-known processes and readily accessible ideas. To draw a comparison with painting, all artists have a set of tools and methods, as well as customers to please.

Painters have paints, a palette, a canvas, and brushes. They can absorb the ideas and principles of the practice of painting regarding perspective, composition, color, and so forth. They can study other painters. They hope people will appreciate—and buy—their work.

That takes time and considerable skill. But it doesn't make great art. The same can be said for training. No training can succeed without a solid foundation in both science and business. But that alone isn't enough to make people sit up and take notice, or walk out changed. It's art that does that. Call it inspiration, creativity, or whatever you want to; it's the least tangible and most powerful ingredient in learning. And that brings us to an interesting question: If art in learning design is so important and so hard to pin down, how do you get it?

As developers of custom training programs, we face that question every day as we grapple with the unique challenges of each project. What can we do creatively to give life to this information? There is no magic formula. But we have found that certain principles and techniques from the arts can be used successfully to transform the experience, and outcome, of learning.

To help you begin thinking about how art can make a difference in learning for your organization, let us take look at some of the ingredients of inspiration that guide us: surprise, fun, and drama.

Surprise, Surprise!

When you do things exactly the way they have always been done, the result is comfortable and (yawn) forgettable. That's why artists strive to push limits and confound expectations. They use the element of surprise to make us see, hear, and experience the world anew.

In training, surprise is one of our key strategies for introducing new ideas or initiating attitude changes, before people's familiar defenses and assumptions have time to rally the opposition.

Here are a few tactics.

.face about an do In this approach, people turn around to find out what it's like to be someone in a different position. For example, to help its salespeople improve their customer focus skills, a car manufacturer sent them to dealerships outside of their own regions. Posing as customers, they walked through the entire sales process, recording "moments of truth" that critically affected their attitude as "buyers." It was an eye-opening experience—proving the point that it is one thing to talk about what it's like to walk in someone else's shoes and another thing to actually do it.

Get out of order. The obvious way to plan a project or think through a process is to start at the beginning and work through it logically step by step. But by shaking up the accepted sequence of things, people see processes in a new light and become open to fresh approaches.

For example, as part of its service management training program, a railroad company set out to rethink its process for ticket refunds. Using a method called service mapping, it looked at every step in the refund procedure out of order, then reordered all of the steps in a way that made more sense. The startling result was that it was able to shorten to two days what had been a five-month process.

B reak the rh yth m. In music, poetry, and our daily lives, a regular rhythm propels us along and tells us what to expect next. But if the rhythm goes on too long, it dulls us and we stop paying attention. Consequently, we need to break the rhythm.

In training, that can be as simple as being contrary to a group's expectations. For instance, for a performance management workshop, participants watched a video that showed what they assumed were positive examples of how to evaluate employees. What they saw instead was a series of bloopers that were plausible enough so that they nodded in acknowledgment: "Sure, I do that!" By the time they realized that the examples were don'ts rather than do's, they had been disarmed into recognizing their own mistakes, and they became more open to change than they might have had they just been shown what to do.

Combine applesandoranges. With this approach, ideas and solutions come from seemingly unrelated sources. It is used a lot as a creative thinking exercise, but it also works wonders in less overtly creative applications, such as benchmarking.

As a pre-exercise for a customer service course, food retail employees went out to observe unrelated retail operations such as fashion, electronics, and books. They came back with long lists that could be applied in their own business.

Are We Having Fun Yet?

Fun as an ingredient of inspired art? Somehow, that doesn't seem serious enough—unless you consider the Marx Brothers, Mark Twain, or…well, you get the point. Amidst the self-importance and solemnity that so often surround artistic or business endeavors, it's easy to forget that the best way to "get there" can be to have a good time doing it. Think back to your best teachers. They made learning fun. You still remember what you learned from them. It works the same way with adults.

For every dreary and laborious way to make a point, chances are that there is an easy, fun way to make it better. For example, a food manufacturer's sales group played a combination Pictionary-Trivial Pursuit game to exchange information about their business and industry. In another course designed to help employees integrate personal and professional goals, participants turned the classroom into an art gallery filled with collages they had created from magazine photos to describe their lives and work.

Toy with success. If you are a parent (you were a kid), you probably know that children do their most important learning while playing with toys. What changes when they

become grownups? Nothing, except that they might get funny looks if they keep a Mr. Potato Head or wad of Silly Putty on their desks.

It's no wonder that toys have a liberating effect in training. They are not only fun, and a disarming way to break the ice, but they are also a deceptively powerful way to break down the barriers of rigid adult thinking.

For instance, in a career development workshop, participants chose from a pile of toys— a gardening set, an Etch-a-Sketch, a yo-yo, and so forth—the one that represented their careers best. The typically serious, driven business people erupted in laughter as they took turns standing in front of the group comparing themselves and their work to a lump of Play Doh or a Slinky. The silliness of the exercise, however, allowed them to be more bold, truthful, and perceptive about themselves than they probably would have been with a more traditional approach.

Run with your imagination. In a culture in which imagination is often mistrusted, it's hard to recognize it for what it is: a survival skill. Throughout our lives, imagination enables us to develop empathy for others and understand how we fit in a changing, complex world.

Role plays are a familiar learning tool that can be used imaginatively with considerable impact. In one workshop, a private bank that wanted to teach nonsalespeople about its business created several "you struck it rich" scenarios that were handed to participants with great fanfare as they walked into the training . They spent the rest of the session in character as newly wealthy people, learning firsthand about issues the bank's customers face.

Lighten *UP*. It may sound simpleminded, but we have learned never to underestimate the power of playful devices to deliver difficult, complex information. Take for example a computer-delivered, self-study ISO 9000 qualification course that we designed recently. Because there was so much potentially dry, highly technical information to be covered, we worried that learners would get discouraged or derailed. So, to give them the support they needed, we created Dr. ISO— a cheery know-it-all who could answer their questions any time at the touch of an icon.

The Power of Drama

From masked shamans, to medieval passion plays, to documentary films, drama can deliver a message with unmatched power. In training, we sometimes work with drama, literally, in the form of videos, movie clips, and simulations. We also use the strong emotions associated with many training issues as dramatic learning instruments.

Put on a good show. In these fast-paced, visually sophisticated times, production values count for a lot. In fact, we often think of our programs as theatrical productions—with sets (colorfully decorated classrooms or other settings), props (well-designed training materials and job aids), and plot lines (a carefully orchestrated rhythm and flow of information). They all work together to produce a memorable learning experience.

In a coaching workshop, for instance, instructors wore whistles and jerseys, and the walls were decorated with giant clipboards displaying quotes from successful sports coaches. At the end of the course, participants received their own pocket-sized clipboards with the same quotes, for inspiration and a reference back on the job.

Create shock value. Sometimes, it takes a five-alarm wake-up call to jolt people out of their complacency. To learn to adapt in a company undergoing major changes, employees attended a workshop we had designed, in which the first thing that happened when they walked in the door was that they were "fired." Then, they had to reapply for their own jobs. That forced them to rethink the knowledge and competencies they needed to succeed.

We have also used field trips for their shock value and learning value. For example, a group of executives in a course on organizational ethics saw that topic in a different light after a visit to the Holocaust Museum in Washington, D.C.

Compose a soundtrack. Just like in the movies, in training music can help set the tone and heighten people's experience. When we compose a soundtrack for a program, we consider the effect of a wide range of music on the audience we will be working with. The soundtrack doesn't have to be music. We may use the sound of roaring crowds to cheer people on, laugh tracks to loosen up storytelling sessions, the din of a busy street, or animal noises. The possibilities are endless.

Tell a story. Storytelling is one of the oldest ways to teach and transform. Such devices as parables, personal experiences, and metaphors allow people to think about things that would be difficult to approach any other way. Such devices can clarify complicated decisions, help people deal with painful events, or transmit culture and traditions. Storytelling, for example, can help people envision the future they want and how to achieve it.

In a customer service workshop, each participant imagined that he or she had been voted service provider of the year. Then, each had to give a speech to the group, telling what they did to earn that honor.

The Limits of Artistic License

We hope that we have inspired you to seek training that rises to the level of art and that we have given you some ideas how creatively designed programs can help transform people's performance in your organization.

But a word of caution: The ideas we have talked about require a sensitivity to the specific audience, context, and learning need. Used inappropriately, any creative technique can detract from the learning. For that reason, it's crucial to keep in mind the learning goal, the people who will be using a program, the culture of their organization, and other critical factors. It's also helpful to get the advice of people with a lot of experience teaching similar groups and subject matter.

To help you see how effective art can be in a training program, we have put together a self-assessment tool for you to gauge the A.Q. (art quotient) of your programs and ones you are considering purchasing or developing.

In the end, it's simple: Without a solid science and business foundation, training won't get off the ground. But it's art that makes it soar. As you go forward with learning programs for your organization, always aim for a masterpiece.

How to Evaluate Your A.Q. (Art Quotient)

How do your programs rate in applying the art of training?

Here are scales for evaluating the art dimensions of training that you are using or planning to develop. Mark an X closest to the point on each scale that best describes your program.

▶ **Do An About Face**
To understand others, literally put yourself in their position.

```
|_____|_____|_____|_____|
```
looking in   turning heads
the mirror   around

▶ **Get Out of Order**
Shake up the usual sequence of things to see them in a new light.

```
|_____|_____|_____|_____|
```
ready   fire
aim   aim
fire   ready

▶ **Break the Rhythm**
Use offbeat ways to keep people on their toes.

```
|_____|_____|_____|_____|
```
constant   changing
meter   the beat

▶ **Combine Apples and Oranges**
Get unexpected insight from unrelated sources.

```
|_____|_____|_____|_____|
```
separate   fruit
bins   salad

▶ **Play the Game**
Find a fun way to make the point.

```
|_____|_____|_____|_____|
```
couch   join the
potato   league

▶ **Toy With Success**
For serious results, break out the Slinkies and Play Doh.

```
|_____|_____|_____|_____|
```
no   children
kid stuff   welcome

▶ **Run With Your Imagination**
Playing "let's pretend" creates powerful new realities.

```
|_____|_____|_____|_____|
```
been there   out of
done that   the box

▶ **Lighten Up**
Use simple devices to deliver heavy, complex information.

```
|_____|_____|_____|_____|
```
do it the   keep it
hard way   simple, silly

▶ **Put On a Good Show**
Never underestimate the power of good production values.

```
|_____|_____|_____|_____|
```
tuned   standing
out   ovation

▶ **Create Shock Value**
Know when and how to make a five-alarm wake-up call.

```
|_____|_____|_____|_____|
```
ho-hum   wow!

▶ **Compose a Soundtrack**
Make music heighten and deepen the learning experience.

```
|_____|_____|_____|_____|
```
silence   strike up
                               the band

▶ **Tell a Story**
Use parables, personal experiences, and metaphors to teach and transform.

```
|_____|_____|_____|_____|
```
play-by-play   color
                              commentary

Check out the pattern of your responses. Then, take the next step to make the most of the power of art in your training programs by following these suggestions:

- If most of your Xs are on the far left, try to incorporate more art approaches in your program. Look to the right for ideas.

- If most of your Xs are on the far right, could you be too far out when it comes to the art of training? Make sure you balance art with science and business.

The Learning Design Group 1997.

In the Throws of Creativity

By Marianne Hunt and Sue Walther

Audience ➤	Staff and Supervisors, Teams, Mid-level Managers
Purpose ➤	—Learn basic concepts of creativity deductively —Understand behaviors related to innovation
Suggested Uses ➤	Group exercise to introduce a creativity workshop Group exercise to focus on creativity at a regular staff or departmental meeting Team exercise to kick off creative project

Introduction

This exercise introduces participants to the basic concepts of creativity, including team dynamics and its impact on the creative process.

Exercise: Leader's Notes

Time

This exercise takes about a half an hour, more or less depending on the size of the group.

Number of Participants

Ideally, you would want teams of 6–10 people doing the activity together and one trainer/timekeeper per team. If there are not enough trainers to go around, a volunteer from each team should be asked to keep time.

Facilitator Expertise

No special expertise is needed.

Materials and Equipment

Tennis balls (one for each team)

Stop watch (one for each team)

Flipchart paper

Markers

Kirton Model (for use as overhead or to transfer to a flipchart)

Procedure

1. Form teams of 6–10 participants each. Give each team a tennis ball and give the stopwatch to the timekeeper.

2. Instruct the team that you will toss the ball to one person in their group. That person should toss the ball to another group member and so on until everyone has touched the ball once (and only once). When the first person receives the ball again, the order of throws preceding that catch becomes the pattern that the group will follow from there on out.

3. Explain that there are only three rules that they *must* follow, listing them on a flipchart paper in front of the room.

   • The ball must be thrown in the same pattern.

   • The ball must enter and leave each person's hand once.

   • Only one person can touch the ball at any given time.

4. The object of the exercise is to have the

group follow the process outlined above, keeping in line with the rules, in the least amount of time possible. They will have several opportunities to improve upon the process.

5. Have the group repeat the throwing pattern and this time have the first person to throw the ball yell "start" and "stop" at the beginning and end of the pattern. Have the timekeeper keep track of the time it takes the group to complete the process. The timekeeper should begin to record the instances on the flipchart paper in a line graph format (as shown below).

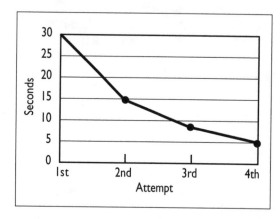

6. Have the groups improve on their processes for about five attempts. They may ask you if they can do a variety of changes within the process. Simply answer by telling them that the only rules are those written on the flipchart paper.

7. Keep close track of the dynamics and dialogue occurring within the groups as the exercise takes place. You will almost always find someone who suggests something innovative only to have another group member shoot down the idea as ridiculous.

8. Once the groups feels comfortable with

their time, tell them that the benchmark for a group of 10 people conducting the activity is .45 seconds. This should get them thinking even more creatively (and it is true!).

9. Allow the groups another three or four attempts at improvement.

10. The groups will want an "answer" at the end of the exercise. Tell them that there is no one correct way to perform the exercise. However, the textbook solution is to have everyone put their hands side by side in a line with palms facing up. The first person is at the top (perhaps on a chair if the group is large) and the last person is sitting on the floor, thus their hands form a slope in which they can roll the ball down in less than a second.

11. Put up the Kirton Model slide. Explain the theory that there is a spectrum of types of people ranging from adapters to innovators. Most of us are somewhere in between. Discuss the characteristics of both types of people (see model).

12. Next, discuss the exercise and the make-up of the groups performing the activity. What were some adaptive or process improvement behaviors? Did you see any innovative behaviors? Discuss any actions that you saw or dialogue that you overheard that exemplified adaptive or innovative behaviors. Explain that both types of people are needed in order to innovate and successfully implement those innovations.

13. Ask the group what happened when you told them the benchmark time? Often what happens is that groups who think they have finished, suddenly have renewed energy for performing the exercise. What implications does this have on our day-to-day group work? What does this say about goal setting and achievement?

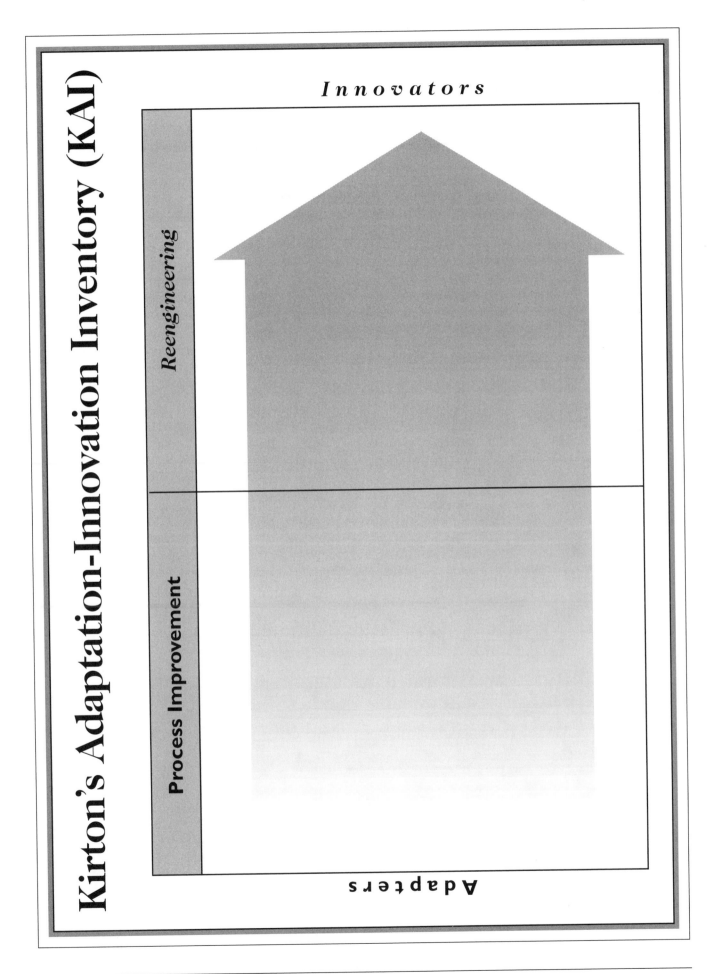

Test of Creativity:
Self-assessment Exercises

By Edward de Bono

Audience	Any Group
Purpose	—Appreciate the value of "out-of-the-box" thinking in improving performance —Assess their ability to think and problem-solve creatively
Suggested Uses	Exercises and resources for a session on innovation and creativity (use one or more tests) Exercise in a team meeting to jump-start creative problem solving Self-assessment in an organization or unit that is focusing on creativity Prework for session on innovation and creativity

Test of Creativity
A Self-assessment Exercise

The left side of your brain handles analytical thinking … logical, rational, linear, numerical, precise. Many aspects of your job call for analytical thinking: planning a project, preparing a budget, learning a procedure, solving a problem, studying alternatives, and making a decision.

The right side of your brain handles creative thinking … expansive, visionary, intuitive, spatial, artistic. Whenever you come up with new ideas or create products, procedures, forms, programs, or plans that are new (or, at least, have never been generated by you before), you are drawing on the right side of your brain.

This self-assessment exercise will help you to get a quick measure of your creativity. There are fifteen questions. Each is timed. We suggest you get a kitchen timer or alarm clock or wristwatch, since you are likely to become absorbed in the exercises and forget to keep track of the time. Alternative: get a friend to be your timekeeper.

On each exercise, read the instructions. Then immediately start the clock.

1. **Five Minutes.** In the space below (and on a separate sheet of paper if you need more space), list all the words you can think of that begin with the letter c. **Start timing now.**

2. The local soft drink bottling company has a fleet of trucks whose drivers make daily deliveries at the same supermarkets, drug stores, and beverage distributors. That is, the drivers visit all outlets on the routes every day.

This July the company noticed a higher than normal absenteeism on Fridays and Mondays. The drivers call in sick. This has meant that the route supervisors have had to drive the routes themselves. Since many drivers have exceeded their allowable sick days, the company is docking the drivers (i.e., not paying them) for absent days. But this has not reduced the absenteeism.

(a) **Three Minutes.** In the space below, list all the reasonable explanations you can think of as to why the drivers are calling in sick on Mondays and Fridays. **Start timing now.**

(b) **Three Minutes.** Assuming the explanations you just listed are valid, use the space below to list all the possible actions the bottling company might take to correct the problem. **Start timing now.**

3. **Three Minutes.** A friend of yours manufactures peanut butter and other peanut products. Peanut shells are a by-product, and your friend has been carting them to the dump for use as landfill … they are, of course, biodegradable.

You're convinced that the shells must have some commercial value if ways can be found to use them and not merely bury them. In the space below, list all the possible uses that you feel should be explored for their practicality. **Start timing now.**

4. **Three Minutes.** Many fruits find their names used in figures of speech. For example, we refer to an unreliable automobile as a "lemon," or the boss or lead performer as the "top banana." In the space below, list all the figures of speech you can think of that have the name of a fruit in them. **Start timing now.**

5. **Three Minutes.** It's scrabble time. Here are your seven letters. In the space below see how many words you can assemble by using some of these letters (and no other letters). A letter may be used only once in each word. **Start timing now.**

N X E Y O T I

Fifteen Minutes. Complete as many of these assignments as you possibly can. Don't spend too much time on any that stump you. Move on to another. You can always return to an item if a new strategy or fresh insight comes to you. **Start timing now.**

6. Describe how you could cut this piece of cheese into eight pieces with only three cuts.

   Answer: _____

   _____

   _____

7. Join the nine dots shown at right by drawing four straight lines without lifting your pencil from the paper.

   Then do the same for the nine dots shown below by drawing three straight lines without lifting your pencil.

8. By drawing one line, convert this odd number into an even number.

   # IX

9. You have a five-minute hourglass and a three-minute hourglass. You want to measure seven minutes. How?

   Answer: _____

   _____

   _____

10. How many squares are there in this figure?

1	5	9	13
2	6	10	14
3	7	11	15
4	8	12	16

   Answer: _____

11. What do the following words have in common?
   canopy, deft, first, laughing, hijack, stupid, calmness, labcoat

   Answer: _____

   _____

   _____

12. Add lines to the two identical figures at the right to convert them into three-letter abbreviations for two world-famous organizations.

   These organizations are: _____

   _____

   _____

13. Nine wolves are in this square enclosure at the zoo. Draw two more square enclosures that will put each wolf in a pen by itself.

14. What is the logic behind this sequence of the numbers one through nine?

   8, 5, 4, 9, 1, 7, 6, 3, 2

   Answer: _____

   _____

   _____

15. Three cans are full and three are empty. By moving only one can, see if you can end up with full and empty cans alternating.

   Answer: _____

The test you just completed covers the major types of mental activity associated with creativity: insight, recognizing relationships that are not easily evident, visualizing, thinking laterally as well as linearly, withholding evaluation (judgment) so as to generate many ideas (brainstorming), using familiar concepts or objects in unfamiliar (novel) ways, and so on.

Creative people tend to have traits that are not shared by most other people. Often they have grown up as "loners," seeking solitude rather than friends and peer group support. They see no reason to conform and meet arbitrary norms. They value their uniqueness and originality. They are not ashamed of having "off-the-wall" thoughts and do not fear the realization that others will see them as bizarre, foolish, or "out-of-touch." They prefer challenge to routine, and value excitement over predictability and fixedness.

Although creativity requires superior intelligence, a high I.Q. is no guarantee of creativity. In fact, only a small fraction of the intellectually gifted are creative. Besides being novel, the fruits of your creativity must also be appropriate or relevant or satisfying to others (for example, aesthetically pleasing in works of art or music). Otherwise, anyone who smears paint on canvas or pounds on piano keys in novel and bizarre ways would have to be deemed creative (and this could include the entire family of man as well as our primate friends … apes, monkeys, and King Kong!).

1. On this first exercise, your mission was to come up with as many words as you can generate in three minutes that begin with the letter c. Did you plunge right in by listing any word that came to mind? Or did you spend a moment planning your creative journey with questions like these:

   (a) Is it better to work through the alphabet so as to avoid later confusion as to whether you've already used a word (e.g., all "ca…" words, followed by "ce…" words, "ch…" words, etc.)?

   (b) Is it better to write only one-syllable words, since you can write more of them in three minutes (e.g., can, cow, cut, chip versus circumference, communications, celebrity)?

   (c) Is it acceptable to use different forms of the same word (e.g., cheat, cheater, cheats, cheating) or would that not be very challenging or original? (Remember—creative people prefer challenge and excitement to routine and fixedness.)

All of these questions are rational, analytical, and draw on the left brain. Creative individuals harness and channel their creativity by planning their approach to a creative assignment with such questions. If you did so, you probably realize that: (a) an alphabetic approach would enable you to generate more words in shorter time, since you are following a system rather than a random process; (b) although one-syllable words can be written more quickly, if you start to pass judgment and edit yourself, your momentum will slow down; (c) if you are highly creative, you're likely to be bored by simply sticking different endings onto a root word. You won't see them as new (original, novel) words, and there won't be much challenge or excitement.

Printed below and on the next page is a list of c words to show how easy it is to follow these (a), (b), (c) guidelines and to generate words as fast as you can write. Writing at a rate of 30 words per minute, you could come up with about 150 words, as shown in the list. (No need for your list to resemble ours, of course.) Take a moment to count the total number of words you generated in five minutes. Divide this number by five.

Enter the resulting number in the box at the right (total divided by five) .... [ ] I

- - - - - - - - - -

CA cab, cache, cad, cadmium, cadet, cadaver, cafe, cage, cake, calf, caliber, cam, came, can, cane, cap, caper, cape, capillary, car, carnage, carpet, care, carry, carrot, carp, case, cast, castle, caste, cat, catch, cater, cattle, cataract, cave, caveat, cavity

- - - - - - - - - -

CE cedar, ceiling, certain, celebrity, celery, cell, celtic, cement, cemetery, censor, census, centennial, century, cent, centimeter

CH chap, char, chat, chant, chair, chablis, chafing, charge, chastise, chapter, charity, chatterbox, cheap, cheat, cheer, chest, check, chef, chip, chicle, chic, chin, chirp, chit, chisel, chimney, chimp, chive, choke, chow, chock, chore, chose, chunk, chute

CI cigar, cilia, cinder, circle, circumference, circumvent, cistern, city, civics, civil

CL clone, claw, clasp, cliff, clique, clump, clip, clown, clutch, clef, clean, clear, cloud, clout

CO cork, con (convent, convex, convert, control ...etc.) corn, cob, cod, coffee, cog, cogitate, coke, cold, color, collate, collide, cop, copper, cope, core, cot, cottage, coddle, cove, covey, cover, cow, cower, coy, coyote, cozy

CR crap, crate, crash, cranberry, crazy, crest, cream, crisp, criterion, croak, crown, crow, croon, crock, crouton, crud, cruller, crust, cruet, cruel

CU cub, cuckoo, cuckold, cud, cuddle, cue, cuff, culinary, culprit, cull, cunning, cup, cur, curt, curdle, curfew, curate, cure, cusp, cuss, custard, cut, cute

CY cymbal, cyst, cynic, cycle, cyclical

2. In this exercise, you generated possible explanations in response to (a), then came up with possible solutions in response to (b). We've listed twelve relevant answers to each. Your responses will differ from ours, of course. See how many plausible responses you came up with.

Enter your total to Parts (a) and (b) in the box at the right .... ☐ **2**

(a) • it's summer and they value their 3-4 day weekends more than the money
  • they really are sick, having exerted themselves excessively over the weekend
  • They have Monday hangovers
  • they are paid so well that the docking doesn't hurt them
  • the Friday deliveries are heavier: more work stocking stores for the weekend
  • the Monday "out-of-stocks" (it's summer) mean more work and second trips
  • the routes are too big ... too many outlets
  • the traffic on Friday and Monday is too much of a hassle
  • weekend sporting events (stadium, arena, coliseum) require much more labor
  • their trucks can't carry enough product for extra heavy Mon.-Fri. deliveries
  • their jobs aren't satisfying; long weekends are providing the balance
  • drivers may be going off in groups for a long weekend (hunting, fishing, drinking).

(b) • provide weekend deliveries for stores that have had "out-of-stock" conditions
  • take advance orders by phone so trucks carry only what they need
  • reduce the number and variety of packages (sizes, cans vs. bottles)
  • hire helpers to work with drivers ... they can run routes if necessary
  • have retirees on reserve to call when regulars don't show up
  • carry more product: use larger trucks or palletized delivery to larger stores
  • increase the penalty for absenteeism
  • reapportion the territory so as to break up larger (out-of-stock) routes
  • set up special weekend "hot line" for dealers to phone for supplemental delivery
  • terminate excessive absentees, replace with drivers with a different work ethic
  • deliver product to sporting events during midweek, not on Friday
  • carry only the best sellers on Monday and Friday (80% of sales come from 20% of product line).

3. Creativity requires superior intelligence. In this exercise, you could channel your thinking into a variety of different fields … agriculture, construction, manufacture, and so on. Your ability to "shift gears" and move your focus from one context to another is important to success on exercises such as this.

    First of all, you should recognize that peanut shells can be used "as is" in some applications. However, by processing them we can greatly expand our list of potential uses, as shown in the list below. We've listed 15 applications … many more than you had time to generate or write in three minutes.

    Enter your total in the box at the right .... ☐ **3**

    Use peanut shells "as is" for:
    • feed for animals (silage)
    • filler in human food (like soy beans)
    • aggregate (additive) in cement for use as stucco … makes it lighter
    • fiber in "scratch coat" (undercoat) prior to fine plaster coat
    • fiber in asphalt as paving
    • pulp to be rolled into special kinds of paper or sheet products
    • insulation (if fireproofing is economical or unnecessary)
    • additive in potting soil … helps it breathe
    • filler in a contained jumping, rolling, bouncing area for children
    • filler (sterilized) in pillows, quilts, blankets (like Kapok)

    Process the shells (shred, grind, pulverize) to use as:
    • mulch and ground cover for planting areas
    • fuel, either alone or as additive
    • packing material (like styrofoam pellets and squiggles)
    • crushable filler in highway and vehicle collision barriers (in bags or plastic canisters)
    • additive to plastic, resins, plaster, cement (fibers add strength)

4. If English is not your native language, you will find an exercise like this to be especially challenging. Let's see how the fruits of your labor compare with ours. Listed below are some candidates for "fruity" figures of speech.

    Enter your total in the box at the right .... ☐ **4**

grapes of wrath	they gave him the raspberry	a blueberry sky
sour grapes	life is a bowl of cherries	that soldier is a cherry
that car is a lemon	turn lemons into lemonade	the apple of her daddy's eye
his new job is a plum	a banana republic	heard it through the grapevine
a peach of a deal	apple polishing is brown nosing	the pineapple failed to detonate
a strawberry blond	he's a real slick apple	the crowd went bananas
a hot tomato	a strawberry mark on her thigh	he painted it lime (orange, plum)

5. Words formed from these letters are listed below. Note the flow, or sequence, in which the mind can be mapped to go from each word to the next. This helps in identifying the full range of possibilities … or as many as three minutes will allow.

    N X E Y O T I

    Enter your total in the box at the right .... ☐ **5**

ONYX	TEX	YET	TONE	ON	EN	ONE	TEN
EXIT	NIX	YIN	NOTE	NO	ET	EON	TOE
OX	NEXT	YON	NOT	TO	IT	TIE	TOY
OXEN	NET	TON	NIT	YO	TI	TIN	TONY

6. Cut the cheese horizontally into two equal cakes. Then cut vertically into four equal 90° wedges.

11. Each of these words contain three successive letters of the alphabet ... nop in canopy, def in deft, rst in first, etc.

7. You must go outside the area of the nine dots to solve each puzzle.

12.

$\angle$/SA

$\angle$/SN

United States of America, or U. S. Army

United States Navy

8. One line will convert a Roman numeral nine into a six.

SIX

13.

9. Start both glasses simultaneously. When the three runs out, two minutes will remain on the five-minute timer. As soon as the two minutes run out, turn the glass over. 2 + 5 = 7.

14. Their names are in alphabetical order:

Eight, Five, Four, Nine, One, Seven, Six, Three, Two

10. 16 individual squares
   4 corner quadrants (e.g., 1, 2, 5, 6)
   1 middle square (6, 7, 10, 11)
   4 arms of a cross (e.g., 2, 3, 6, 7)
   4 corners 3x3 (e.g., 1, 2, 3, 5, 6, 7, 9, 10, 11)
   <u>1</u> biggest square (4x4 squares)
   30

15. Pour the contents of the middle full bucket into the middle empty bucket.

Give yourself two points for each of the ten assignments that you got right. Give one point for half-right answers. The total possible is 20 points.

Enter your total in the box at the right.. ☐ 6-15

HOW DID YOU DO?

Highly creative persons will usually score in the range of 15–20 points in each of the six boxes, for a total of 90–120 points. Moderately creative persons typically score in the range of 10–15 points on each item, for a total of 60–90 points. Add up your scores in the six boxes, and enter this new total in the box at the right .... ☐

What insights have you gained into the nature of creativity and your areas of creative strength and weakness?

Most people are familiar with the exercise shown at the right. Your assignment: connect all nine dots by drawing no more than four straight lines without lifting your marker from the paper. If you've not solved this puzzle before, give it a try right now.

The "nine dots exercise" illustrates one type of creativity ... our ability to break free of artificial constraints and assumptions that conventional thinking has imposed on us. If you assumed that your connecting line could not go beyond the square formed by the eight perimeter dots, then you have limited your ability to solve the puzzle (as Solution A on the next page illustrates).

If you assumed that you were not allowed to fold the paper, then you imposed another artificial constraint, since Solution B shows how you could have drawn one line through the middle column of three dots, then made folds between each of the three columns and through the two flanking columns. By so doing, the two extreme columns become flaps that enable the six outside dots to touch the three middle ones and the line. Have a look at Solution B on the next page.

If you assumed that the word "marker" in our instructions meant a pencil or pen, then you imposed yet another artificial constraint. A paint brush is also a marker, as is a piece of chalk (pastel, charcoal, etc.) used sideways in such a way that one broad line will cover and connect all nine dots. Or did you assume that because you were restricted to "no more than four straight lines" that you were required to use all four? Solution C illustrates the use of a paint brush or marker to make one broad line that covers all nine dots.

The opposite of the "broad line approach," just described, is the "thin line approach." If you assumed that the lines had to pass through the middle of each dot and not go beyond the square, then you can chalk up another self-imposed constraint. The dots are large enough that three thin lines will do the job, as shown in Solution D.

Notice that your failure to see solutions like these is attributable, at least in part, to a number of rather limiting assumptions that you made quite unconsciously ... you weren't even aware of your self-imposed constraints.

Type One: Outside the Dots

And that brings us to one type of creativity, the type we exercise when we attempt to identify and break free from the assumptions and constraints that limit our options. Whether we are planning, designing, envisioning, solving problems, making decisions, or whatever, we should devote time to the "unshackling process" and expand our list of possible options. This is a creative mental activity (right brain, expansive, divergent). Unfortunately, our formal education did not prepare us for it. Most of our teachers have been concerned with conformity ... with rational, logical, analytical thinking (left brain, convergent). They prepared their students for roles in an industrial age that required detailed compliance to repetitive operations, dutiful allegiance to policy & procedures, and, at times, suppression of the creative and innovative human spirit (the playful, experimental, natural child in each of us).

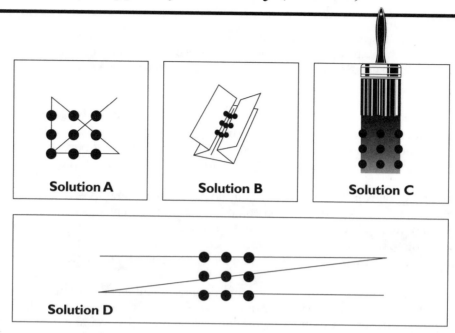

As computers, robotics, and the blessings of an information age have taken over the chores associated with the industrial age, we need to "concentrate more on development of those skills that are done poorly by computers. Development of creativity and holistic thinking ability should have top priority."*

Type Two: Envisioning

This brings us to a second type of creativity: envisioning. Fifty years ago the creators of the comic strip, Dick Tracy, equipped our hero with a two-way wrist radio. Today their dream or vision is a reality. However, when we are asked to take a mental leap into the future, most of us cautiously project forward from today's realities. We attempt to predict what next year will look like, then the year after that, and so on. We believe that past events are the best prediction of the future. Let's call this "forecasting" or "predictive model building" or "planning by extrapolation." It is not creativity.

In today's world of business, envisioning and interpolation are replacing forecasting and extrapolation in strategic planning. Envisioning is creative. It asks, "What do we want life to be like?" without being held captive by "What has life been like?" As Harold Geneen** of ITT puts it, "You read a book from beginning to end. You run a business the opposite way. You start with the end, and then you do everything you must to reach it."

Given today's technology and our ability to visit the moon and achieve numerous incredible goals, it is sad that we have so much discussion and planning of the future based on the past (left brain) and so few visionaries who can articulate visions of tomorrow that excite and galvanize us into action (right brain). On second thought, is the shortfall theirs (we lack visionaries)? Or is it ours (we reject anything that is "way out" or "off the wall" or "untested" or "unsubstantiated by facts and past history")?

  * Thomas R. Blakeslee, *The Right Brain,* New York: Berkley Books, 1983.
** Harold Geneen, *Managing,* New York: Doubleday, 1984.

Type Three: Invention

A third kind of creativity consists of taking what we know about two unrelated events (items, facts, situations, etc.) and juxtaposing them to generate new insights. Let's call this **invention.** Edward de Bono* calls it "lateral thinking."

Thomas Edison and Henry Ford were close friends. Each was creative in the realm of invention. Each was adept at recognizing a need or opportunity in one field and meeting it by drawing on knowledge from another field.

Everyone possesses this type of creativity to some degree: using a coin to pry open a can, using a credit card to open the latch on a door or scrape frost off the car windshield, using a metal coat hanger, shaped into a circle, as the frame for making a Christmas wreath of natural evergreen branches, adding styrofoam pellets to wet cement mix to make light-weight stucco, and so on.

Puns are another example of this type of creativity. The pun has been branded "the lowest form of humor," but it's also clear that people who recognize and who make puns have higher than average "inventive creativity"… the ability to make new, in this case humorous, use out of two separate events (meanings, materials, etc.). The character of "Hawkeye" (Alan Alda) on the long-running M*A*S*H TV series was an inveterate punster, an indication of his creativity as demonstrated by his ability to live simultaneously within and outside Army regulations and conventional surgical practice.

A word on the distinction between invention and discovery. The former is creative and right brain, for the thing that is invented didn't exist previously. The latter is analytical and left brain, since it already existed and was waiting to be discovered, in much the same way that a detective analyzes clues and discovers "who dunnit." Thomas Edison was both … he discovered the best substance to use as a filament for the electric light bulb (after trying hundreds of materials), and he invented the phonograph, moving pictures, office dictation equipment, etc. Edison was "whole brain," an impressive combination of strong left and right brain.

Type Four: Innovative Productivity

A fourth type of creativity is closely related to high output. Mozart wrote 41 symphonies. Bach created hundreds of cantatas. Shakespeare wrote 37 plays and 154 sonnets. Picasso painted hundreds of famous works and thousands of sketches. And, in our own day, Isaac Asimov, the futuristic science writer who over 50 years authored close to 500 published books … ten books per year. Were these men creative or merely prolific? The innovative (qualitative) aspects of their work lead us to say that they were both.

Your ability to generate a lot of ideas in a short period of time is what we are talking about. However, quantity without uniqueness or novelty may not indicate creativity. The fastest craftsman in any field may be productive (facile, prolific, etc.) without being creative.

Thus, we must add a criteria to "high output" if it is to count as our fourth type of creativity. In addition to being prolific, the output must be innovative. Bach, Mozart, Shakespeare, Picasso, and Asimov were not imitators, cranking out at fast pace what their predecessors had done. They were innovators … so much so, in fact, that their late works broke with their successful format of their earlier ones … they outgrew themselves, over and over.

* Edward de Bono, *de Bono's Thinking Course,* New York: Facts on File Publications, 1982.

Summary

We've identified four types of creativity and some advice about putting each to work for you. Here's a brief summary:

1. **GET OUTSIDE THE DOTS.** Identify and discard assumptions and biases that constrain. Draw on your innovative right brain. Your tradition-oriented left brain can evaluate later. Regard statements like "we've never done anything like that before" as an opportunity rather than a squelch.

2. **ENVISION.** Rather than reading the book from front to back, work backwards from an ideal. Envision it in broad, rough form, then fill in details, then see what steps are needed to get there. Don't discard ideas that are "way out" or "off the wall." Remember Dick Tracy's two-way wrist radio and NASA's man on the moon.

3. **INVENTION AND LATERAL THINKING.** Shift your thought from one field or area of knowledge to another. Look for analogies, relationships, parallels. Make pairs out of previously unrelated ideas and phenomena. Shift gears in the middle of trying to solve a tough problem and think of entirely different topics and activities … inventive solutions to your problem may surface.

4. **INNOVATIVE PRODUCTIVITY.** Brainstorming is an example. Go for quantity, not quality … as many ideas as you can generate as quickly as possible. You can always go back later and be selective. Remember that fresh ideas beget other fresh ideas. Go off on tangents, branches, and tributaries, so long as you don't lose sight of the main trunk or purpose. Capture the ideas on paper ("mind mapping" is one technique).

Some Questions

A. Think of something that you and/or your work group did within the last year that was quite creative. Which of the four types of creativity came into play?

B. Think of a personal example to illustrate each of the four types of creativity.

C. Today's technology affords us the opportunity to envision and to realize thousands of innovations that will make our lives easier. Some are already "on line" … fax machines, portable phones and PCs, desk-top publishing. Others are just around the corner:

- A society without paper money … just credit and debit cards.

- National elections where votes are cast via PC networks or debit cards.

- E-mail and/or fax in every home and office, thus eliminating postal systems.

- What additions can you make to the list? (At least two, please)

Imagine That

By Bryan Mattimore

Audience ➤	Any Group
Purpose ➤	—Feel comfortable in dealing with the subject of creativity —Be prepared to take risks and think creatively —Begin to enjoy themselves
Suggested Uses ➤	Quick exercises to open or energize creativity sessions Exercises in team meetings to foster innovative problem-solving approaches

It's 8:30 a.m. on the day of your long-planned, anxiously anticipated creative session. A dozen coworkers sit before you. They have downed their coffee, juice, and danish, and now all eyes rest on you, the presumably fearless leader of this foray into the endeavor called ideation—the creation of ideas.

As you begin talking about the session's goals, expectations, and logistics, you start to have an uneasy feeling in the pit of your stomach. You're sensing that many of the participants don't want to be there. Some seem skeptical, others seem bored, and still others seem just plain afraid of this whole "creativity thing." Worse yet, some participants don't seem to like or trust each other.

How can you shape this disparate group into a creative force capable of shattering mental blocks and leaping psychological limitations? The following exercises can do the trick. For starters, we'll look at what you can do—in 10 minutes or less—to help people feel comfortable, to prepare them to take risks, and to get them laughing, or at least smiling.

Dye Your Hair With Rusty Water

"Those Crazy Inventors" is the name I gave to an icebreaker of my own invention that never seems to fail.

This exercise helps build trust, champion failure, relieve performance anxiety, and get everyone laughing. The vehicle is a short multiple-choice test, and the goal is to select a correct answer from three absurd choices for each question. The box on page 6-52, Those Crazy Inventors: A Multiple-Choice Quiz, gives some sample questions.

This exercise is quick and fun, and the trivia interests most people. More important, though, is that everyone's choices are restricted to the obviously ridiculous. Since participants can't use logic to reach any single correct answer, they must take creative risks. And creative risk-taking is what a successful ideation session is all about. After all, inventors as successful and creative as Henry Ford and George Eastman acted in ways that strike many as absurd, so why can't we?

Reprinted with permission from *Training & Development,* published by the American Society for Training & Development. Parts of this article appear in *99% Inspiration* (Copyright 1994, Bryan W. Mattimore; published by AMACOM).

Those Crazy Inventors: A Multiple-Choice Quiz

For each question, circle the letter of the answer that you think is correct.

1. As part of his grooming regimen, Henry Ford would:
   ▶ a) add particles of sand to his toothpaste to increase its abrasive, tartar-removing qualities.
   ▶ b) dye his hair with rusty water.
   ▶ c) keep the balls of his feet soft by applying a coating of his own saliva to them nightly.

2. George Eastman, inventor of the Kodak camera:
   ▶ a) was a supporter of the 13-month calendar.

   ▶ b) took a photograph of himself every day from age 31 to age 72.
   ▶ c) invented a camera that, when swallowed by cows, took pictures of their four stomachs.

3. Milkman Gail Borden:
   ▶ a) had his tomb built in the shape of a condensed-milk can.
   ▶ b) tried to sell condensed cow's blood as an ingredient in a salad dressing.
   ▶ c) filled a public pool with milk to promote the idea that milk baths were good for the skin.

The correct answers are 1–b; 2–a; and 3–a.

Invariably, after trying this exercise, participants begin to take themselves a little less seriously.

Start at the End

Although ideation sessions are intended as freewheeling creative fests, they benefit from clearly defined goals. Once the stage is set, the best place to start an ideation session is at the end. That means getting each member to articulate his or her goal for the session.

To do this, use an exercise called a "time-track visualization." Ask participants to pretend that the session just ended. Tell them to imagine that the group has just spent the entire day brainstorming, and that the results were nothing short of miraculous. Ask participants to say what excited them about the work and about the ideas that were created.

Invariably one group member will begin, "I'd like to see us create an idea…" Quickly correct his or her phrasing: "What I liked about the ideas we created today…" You want participants to visualize the future by pretending to reflect back on the day that still lies ahead.

This simple exercise personalizes the objectives and gives everyone a stake in the process. Participants tend to say such things as:

- "I like the fact that we created a $100-million, new-product idea that has the potential to revitalize this company."
- "I love the way everyone worked together today to create several ideas that I know will end up saving our department a whole lot of money."
- "I'm excited that we created a name for this new brand that the consumer will both like and easily remember."

In addition to generating ownership, this exercise helps build a powerful group identity. Because all participants express their desires, they can help each other attain their different goals.

This exercise also helps you by outlining the needs, motives, and goals of each participant. Armed with this knowledge, you can direct the session down avenues most likely to lead to desired results.

Finally, the time-track visualization exercise provides both you and the group with a tool for determining the session's ultimate success. You'll find that most groups manage to accomplish all the results they visualized.

Wish Upon a Star

The next exercise helps participants continue to build a shared identity and develop trust in each other, because it requires each person to confide something personal. This exercise also lets you gain quick insights into participants' mindsets, interests, motivations, and unique capabilities.

The exercise, "Fantasy Occupation," asks participants the question: "If you could have any job, what would it be?"

I first created this exercise as a contest for a trade show promotion for a large personnel agency. Among the 596 conference attendees who entered the contest, the number one fantasy job was a secret agent. Other top choices, in order of preference, included actor, U.S. senator, rock star, artist, astronaut, safari guide, comedian, inventor, professional athlete, novelist, and chef.

The interest this promotion garnered among participants and the press confirmed my suspicion that fantasy can be a powerful motivator, as well as a lot of fun. Having your group members imagine a fantasy occupation can free them of limitations associated with their current occupations and usher them into a world of possibilities. Someone who fantasizes about being a professor of philosophy will offer different ideas and insights than someone who would like to manage the women's Olympic basketball team.

The fantasy-occupation exercise allows the group members to get acquainted with new facets about their coworkers' personalities. And it sets the stage for three of the most powerful idea-generation techniques: role playing, excursions, and wishing.

Let's Pretend

Role playing is the grownup version of "let's pretend." When you play a role, you pretend you are someone else. Then you ask this "person" for his or her ideas. When people play roles, they often are amazed to find they can consider issues from wholly different perspectives, or even solve problems "in character" that they could not solve as themselves.

Assign roles by passing each person a card printed with a picture and short biography of a renowned person. (My identity cards include Florence Nightingale, Frank Lloyd Wright, Abraham Lincoln, Benjamin Franklin, Walt Disney, and Dr. Seuss.) Have participants take turns introducing themselves as their characters and offering comments on the problem under discussion. As facilitator, it's your responsibility to make sure that everyone stays in character.

Instead of asking participants to assume other roles, you can have them mentally transport themselves to another time or place. I led one such "excursion" for a group seeking innovative ideas for an interior design firm. We mentally traveled to the Wild West, where we "saw" several horses drinking from the same watering trough. That image—a metaphor for sharing resources—sparked an idea for the firm and a fabric manufacturer jointly to produce and market an interior design video.

I facilitated another excursion during an ideation session for a group seeking a name for a new Frito Lay cheese product. We took an imaginary trip to the South Pacific in a fishing boat, where we hooked the name "Great White Cheddar."

If your group has trouble dreaming up an exciting destination, base the excursion on one of the fantasy jobs mentioned by members. It makes the session even more personal.

The last technique also spins off of the fantasy-occupation exercise. Tell participants to imagine that a genie has granted each of them several wishes. They can wish for things that are totally absurd or impractical or that violate the fundamental laws of nature—indeed, the best wishes often do. By entertaining wishes without limitations, groups then can figure out how to turn a fanciful idea into reality.

I used this wish technique during a creative session I ran for the American Camping Association. The group members sought a new, affordable camp activity that kids would enjoy. Participants wished for Michael Jordan to run a basketball clinic and for Madonna to give a free concert.

Those ideas were new, yes, and would be popular with kids, but they were not exactly affordable. But in discussing how to approximate these wishes, we discovered a wonderful new camp project: Let the kids become their favorite stars! They could make costumes and then give performances or motivational speeches or do whatever else that they imagined their stars would do if they were to visit the camp.

All of these techniques tap participants' dreams and desires to foster mutual trust among the group members and to bring their creative strengths to the forefront. Use these tricks of the creative trade in your next ideation session—and turn brainstorms into breakthroughs.

The Wonderful World of "What If?"

By Marianne Hunt and Sue Walther

Audience ➤	Any Group
Purpose ➤	—Explore ideas that would not have come naturally —Practice thinking creatively —Develop alternative solutions —Break out of typical thought patterns
Suggested Uses ➤	Exercise for teams or other groups to promote creative problem solving

Introduction

This activity can be used when there is a problem or issue on the table that needs to be addressed. The ideas generated by the What-If questions do not necessarily have to solve the problem, but should expand the group's thinking about the subject.

Exercise: Leader's Notes

Time

Depends on the type of problem, how thorough the group wants to be, and how many What-If questions are asked.

Number of Participants

Unlimited, but best in groups of 6–10.

Facilitator Expertise

No particular expertise necessary.

Materials and Equipment

Flipchart paper

Markers

Overhead projector

What-If slide

Procedure

1. Introduce the exercise by reminding participants that asking a dumb question often results in a smart answer, so they shouldn't dismiss any What-Ifs without giving them ample consideration.

2. Ask the participants to consider the current problem or issue that they are trying to solve in the context of the following set of questions. Put the What-If slide on the projector and lead the group through the list, recording their ideas on flipchart paper as they come up.

3. Don't force the group to stick to the questions on the What-If slide. They should also make up their own, perhaps ones that relate directly to the issue they are dealing with.

4. Encourage participants to work backwards with What-If. For example, ask "What if the problem was solved? What would the situation look like then?" Then see what ideas these kinds of questions lead to.

5. Be sure to record all ideas and to solicit input from the quieter participants in the group. Push them to go beyond the obvious and to dig deep into the What-If answers.

Customization

The facilitator may want to develop his or her own list of What-Ifs or choose only one or two of the most applicable questions from the list provided to explore with the team.

What If We ... ?

... Tear it down

... Appeal it to children

... Slow it down

... Simplify it

... Break it

... Freeze it

... Teach it to somebody

... Make it unbreakable

... Make it a law

... Recycle it

... Make it more comfortable

... Make it funny

... Make it sexy

... Set it to music

... Tear it down

... Go backwards

... Do anything ... ??

Section 6: Promoting Innovation and Creativity